THE
ASIAN AMERICAN
ENCYCLOPEDIA

THE
ASIAN AMERICAN
ENCYCLOPEDIA

Volume 2

Chinese in railroad construction – Hmong religion

Editor

FRANKLIN NG

Managing Editor

JOHN D. WILSON

Marshall Cavendish
New York • London • Toronto

Published By
Marshall Cavendish Corporation
2415 Jerusalem Avenue
P.O. Box 587
North Bellmore, New York 11710
United States of America

∞ The paper in these volumes conforms to the American National Standard for Permanence of Paper for Printed Library Materials, Z39.48-1984.

Library of Congress Cataloging-in-Publication Data

The Asian American encyclopedia / editor, Franklin Ng.
    p. cm.
   Includes bibliographical references and index.
   Contents: v. 2. Chinese in railroad construction—Hmong religion.
   1. Asian Americans—Encyclopedias. I. Ng, Franklin, 1947-   .
E184.O6A827 1995
973′.0495′003—dc20   94-33003
ISBN 1-85435-677-1 (set).   CIP
ISBN 1-85435-679-8 (vol. 2).

First Printing

Contents

THE
ASIAN AMERICAN
ENCYCLOPEDIA

Chinese in railroad construction: During the second half of the nineteenth century, as the Far West of the United States underwent its initial developmental surge, thousands of Chinese immigrants worked on the various large and small railroads that knit together cities, regions of economic activity, and eventually the whole nation. Thousands of Chinese workers provided the muscle power for a number of projects including the San Francisco and Marysville Railroad, the Sacramento and Vallejo Railroad, and various lines in the mining regions of Nevada. Until the 1880's, while there was still a shortage of labor in the West, these Chinese immigrants provided essential labor and were accepted and even praised by some for their hard work and skills in laying track.

An Available Labor Supply. Pushed from southern China as a result of many factors that disrupted social and economic patterns there during the first decades of the 1800's, and lured toward the United States with news of the discovery of gold, a stream of Chinese immigrants began to take advantage of improved trans-pacific linkages and to try their luck in the gold mines of California. Having arrived late and incurring the racial hostility of competing Caucasian miners, they found themselves relegated to marginally profitable small-scale operations that increasingly showed diminishing returns. Eventually, by the mid-1860's these early Chinese miners found that they could not sustain themselves in the mine fields and began to seek other work.

At about the same time work on both the transcontinental and other smaller railroad projects began, and in February, 1865, the first group of Chinese were recruited for work on the Central Pacific. Chief Construction Superintendent Charles Crocker and Central Pacific President Leland Stanford saw the Chinese workers as a solution to their need for labor and a way of getting on with the speedy completion of the trans-

Great numbers of immigrant Chinese sailed to the American West during the 1860's to build the transcontinental railroad. (Asian American Studies Library, University of California at Berkeley)

A typical payroll ledger from 1865, recording payouts to Chinese laborers of the Central Pacific Railroad Company. The workers' names appear at the far left. (Asian American Studies Library, University of California at Berkeley)

continental railroad. Both men saw certain advantages in employing the willing and motivated Chinese workers. Stanford saw them as peaceable and hard workers who could and did learn to perform many different skilled tasks. Crocker had some mixed motives in employing the Chinese. He initially thought that the use of Chinese workers at the basic construction tasks might actually promote the available white laborers into higher positions of management and responsibility. Yet over time he came to believe the Chinese workers every bit the equal of white workers with the twin added advantages of being more reliable and less prone to striking.

Use of Chinese construction crews also permitted some savings on the costs of construction. Central Pacific wages for the average Chinese worker were about $30 a month and comparable to what white workers were paid. For cultural reasons, however, including dietary habits, Chinese construction crews

generally organized their own housing and food services, thus alleviating the company from lodging and board expenses for Chinese work crews. For their part the Chinese accepted these arrangements because, even after paying the average $15 to $18 a month for food and housing, it was still possible for them to save some $20 a month, put it toward their immigration costs, or send it home. These small communities were able to retain some of their heritage, even organizing traditional New Year's celebrations and observing other festivals of the Chinese cultural calendar.

The recruitment of Chinese labor was not universally accepted in racially conscious nineteenth century American society, and some white workers were unsettled by the appearance of Chinese in large numbers at the work sites. Demands were raised that the company stop employing them. Crocker responded by claiming that he could not get as many workers as he needed without using Chinese and that if the white workers continued to object then the only solution would be to fire the whites and use Chinese workers exclusively.

Harsh Working Conditions. As the U.S. government compensated the Central Pacific and its competitor, the Union Pacific (which had started in the East and was working westward), on the basis of the miles of track laid by each company, speed became an important factor in the profitability of both ventures. Hence it was decided to have the Chinese construction crews, then in the Sierra Madre mountains, work through the winter of 1866. Living and working in tunnels under the snow, whole work camps and crews were buried in avalanches and snowdrifts sixty feet or more deep. Many of the victims were found the following spring, their bodies frozen while still clutching their picks and shovels.

In the spring of 1867 several thousand Chinese workers went on strike for higher wages and an eight-hour work day. The response was an offer to increase wages by a couple of dollars a month but a rejection of the eight-hour day. Discounting the resentment the Chinese felt or the fact that they might be capable of developing their own thoughts on labor/management issues, the local San Francisco newspaper and many of the managers in the Central Pacific saw the strike as a ploy of the Union Pacific to slow down the progress of the Central Pacific crews. The will of the strikers was quickly broken by Crocker, who isolated the offending construction crews, withheld their provisions, and virtually starved them into submission within a week of the initial strike. After this Crocker had no more

Artist's rendering of white and Chinese laborers nearing completion of the transcontinental railroad in 1869. The sketch was published in the May 29, 1869, edition of Harper's Weekly. (Library of Congress)

trouble with the Chinese crews despite the fact that by 1867, through the use of brokers and arranged importation of even more workers, twelve thousand Chinese were working for the Central Pacific and constituted some 90 percent of the company's labor pool.

The Work Continues. After a meeting of the Central and Union Pacific lines at Promontory Point, Utah, the laid-off Chinese workers either returned to San Francisco to look for work there or fanned out to other railroad projects throughout the West. They worked on the construction of the Central and Southern Pacific's main line in the San Joaquin Valley in 1870 and 1871. In 1876 they manned the crews that connected Los Angeles into the California rail system. In the early 1880's they worked on the Texas Pacific connecting San Diego with El Paso, and they provided the labor for the line connecting Sacramento with Portland, Oregon, in 1887.

Although in the 1880's the anti-Chinese movement gathered momentum and fostered discrimination and even acts of violence against these immigrants, Chinese railroad workers had largely been tolerated dur-ing the railroad boom years as most people realized that they soberly, peacefully, and diligently contributed greatly to the economic development of the Far West.—*P. Scott Corbett*

SUGGESTED READINGS: • Barth, Gunther. *Bitter Strength: A History of the Chinese in the United States, 1850-1870*. Cambridge, Mass.: Harvard University Press, 1964. • Daniels, Roger. *Asian America: The Chinese and Japanese in the United States since 1850*. Seattle: University of Washington Press, 1988. • Takaki, Ronald. *Strangers from a Different Shore: A History of Asian Americans*. Boston: Little, Brown, 1989. • Saxton, Alexander. *The Indispensable Enemy: Labor and the Anti-Chinese Movement in California*. Berkeley: University of California Press, 1971.

Chinese in the Mississippi Delta: During most of the twentieth century, Mississippi had the largest Chinese American population of any Southern state. This was no fluke but came about because Mississippi also had the largest proportion of African Americans, the highest level of white racism, and the greatest persistence

Chinese coolies at work on the Milloudon sugar plantation in Louisiana. (Library of Congress)

of plantation social structure. Therefore the saga of the Chinese in Mississippi not only tells about an interesting and often overlooked group, very different from the Chinese experience in Chinatowns in Northern cities, but also reveals important aspects of Southern social structure.

First Arrival. Chinese men entered the Mississippi Delta, that alluvial flood plain stretching between Memphis and Vicksburg, in 1870, during Reconstruction. White planters brought them in as sharecroppers to threaten the planters' African American laborers, who were voting Republican and in other ways acting "uppity."

Realizing that they could never make money as sharecroppers, the Chinese quickly moved to open tiny groceries, selling mainly to the African American population. Here they found a niche. Most white storekeepers had little interest in catering to black needs from behind a store counter, for although money could be made, status would be lost. African Americans, too, found operating stores difficult, partly because since

they were part of the black community, they could not easily refuse credit to friends and neighbors.

Chinese sojourners prospered and sent for relatives to join them. More than 95 percent remained in grocery stores as recently as 1970. They spread to every large Delta town and most hamlets but did not move to the hills, because plantation social structure was key to their success. White owners demanded that sharecroppers plant only cotton, so African Americans had to buy all their food.

Chinese economic success prepared the way for a social climb. They began with near-black status, competing with African Americans for sharecropping jobs. White officials kept them out of white public schools (as in the 1927 case *GONG LUM V. RICE*), hospitals, playgrounds, Young Men's Christian Associations (YMCAs), and clubs until after World War II in all but the smallest communities. Immigration regulations kept Chinese grocers from bringing their wives into the United States. Some of these men responded by marrying African American women, legally or in common law.

Upward Mobility. During World War II, however, China's position as an American ally prompted the United States to let Chinese women immigrate. Combined with the grocers' new affluence, this made for upward caste mobility. Chinese Americans adopted white lifestyles. They attended Chinese services on Sunday afternoons, in white churches that might not welcome them on Sunday mornings but nevertheless wanted to "do good among the heathen." They founded a cemetery modeled on white examples and a boarding school that hired white teachers. This separated Chinese children from African Americans, both physically and in white minds. They also moved away from their stores, still located in the black part of town.

Around 1945, leaders of the Chinese-American community then assured white community members that they would renounce all sexual relations with African Americans if whites would admit Chinese students into the public schools. This Faustian bargain was struck: Most Chinese advanced to a tenuous acceptance in white schools and other social institutions. Their rise in caste status points to the key difference in their social structural position, compared to that of African Americans. No whites made money off Chinese grocers, except wholesalers, and they profited as the grocers profited. Many whites made money off black sharecroppers, however, and would have lost money if African Americans had received higher wages and status.

Chinese men who loved their black wives and Chinese-African children too much to repudiate them found themselves ostracized by the "pure" Chinese. Although defined as "black," these mixed-race children enjoyed the same positive academic expectations that Asian Americans received elsewhere in the United States. Their school success then led to college and in many cases jobs outside Mississippi.

Conditions Improve. In the 1960's the Civil Rights movement worked wonders for Chinese American social status. The Greenville public schools, for example, would not hire a Chinese Mississippian teacher for their white schools as late as 1965 but found such hiring in their interest by 1968. When their schools were desegregated in 1970, that particular teacher withdrew along with half of the white students to a new "white" (and Chinese) private academy; she later became principal of its elementary division. Even more telling, a Chinese American woman has achieved that pinnacle of success in white Mississippi, homecoming queen at Ole Miss. African Americans resent the grocers' new status, viewing them as surrogate whites who use money made in the black community to buy status among whites and even vandalizing Chinese stores in small race riots.

Ironically the very niche that segregation created for Chinese Americans has been disappearing, now that segregation is over. Chinese Mississippians are rapidly moving out of groceries and out of Mississippi. The population, which peaked at about thirteen hundred in 1967, has now dropped to less than a thousand. Chinese culture is also disappearing among the Chinese Americans of Mississippi. The upward mobility of the Chinese both caused and resulted from acculturation to white Southern society. Among some Chinese Americans, traditional Chinese ethnocentrism bloomed into full-blown white racism. Many second-generation Chinese Americans developed white Southern accents, shunned Chinese language and food, and dated and even married whites. Thus in two ways, the unusual saga of Asian traders among a black underclass is nearing its end.—*James W. Loewen*

SUGGESTED READINGS: • Loewen, James W. *The Mississippi Chinese: Between Black and White.* 2d ed. Prospect Heights, Ill.: Waveland Press, 1988. • *Mississippi Triangle.* Film/Video. Third World Newsreel, 1983. • Quan, R. S. *Lotus Among the Magnolias: The Mississippi Chinese.* Jackson University Press of Mississippi, 1982.

Chinese language: Chinese is one of the oldest living languages in the world. It has been in continuous use, taking into account evolutionary changes, for about four thousand years. The earliest historical evidence of China's written language, known as "oracle bone inscriptions," dates back to about 1700 B.C.E. Even though Chinese is not an international language such as French or English, it is spoken by more people in the world than any other language because of China's tremendously large population. It is also recognized as one of the five official languages by the United Nations. There is no doubt that Chinese is one of the most important languages of the world and of East Asia, given China's size, population, and cultural influence. Even though Japanese and Korean do not belong to the same Sino-Tibetan family of languages as Chinese, Japanese and Korean have adopted and, to some extent, still use the Chinese script.

Grammar. The Chinese language is characterized by a basic simplicity in its grammatical structure. Since Chinese is not an inflected language, there are no declensions for nouns or conjugations for verbs. Tense is also not a feature of the language. The Chinese language is interested more in telling whether or not an action has been completed than with where that action is located on a time line; that is, Chinese is an aspect, rather than a tense, language. The basic Chinese sentence has a subject-verb-object pattern. The functional relationship between the components in a sentence is determined by word order, particles, and prepositions. Yet this does not mean that Chinese does not have a grammar. The universally recognized grammatical categories of number, aspect and voice, subordination and modification, and modality are worked into the language in other ways. There is no evidence to suggest that Chinese is any more ambiguous than other languages.

Tones. Chinese is a tonal language, that is, the tone or pitch pattern of a syllable is a semantically significant part of the phonological unit. A modification in tone changes the meaning of the syllable. In Mandarin, or standard Chinese, there are four tones. The first is a high-level tone indicated by −, the second a rising tone /, the third a dipping tone ∨, and the fourth a falling tone \ .

As an example, take the syllable *ma*. In the first tone, *mā means "mother"; in the second tone, má means* "hemp"; in the third tone, *mǎ* means "horse"; and in the fourth tone, *mà* means "to scold." Tones are also used in English but more to indicate attitudes rather than meanings. For example, "John?" spoken with a slow rising tone implies a question; "John!" spoken with a rapid falling tone implies reprimand. In Mandarin Chinese, the dialect spoken in northern China, there are four distinct tones, but in Cantonese, spoken in southern China, there are nine tones.

Dialects. In the long history of the Chinese language, there evolved seven basic dialect groups. Mandarin, now generally referred to as putonghua (common speech, or standard Chinese), is spoken by two-thirds of the Chinese people, with minor variations, throughout an area beginning in northeast China and sweeping down to the southwest. This standard language is based on the speech of educated Beijing residents.

Along the coast and in the southern part of China,

World War II-era classroom instruction on reading Chinese written characters. (Asian American Studies Library, University of California at Berkeley)

however, great linguistic variety developed. There evolved the following major dialect groups: Wu, spoken in the Shanghai region; Min spoken in Fujian province (Fuzhou in the north, and Amoy or Xiamen in the south); Kejia or Hakka, spoken in Jiangxi; Xiang, spoken in Hunan Province; Gan, spoken in Jiangxi and northern Hunan; Yue or Cantonese, spoken in the Canton region (Cantonese was spoken by the majority of the early immigrants from China); and finally Pekinese, spoken in northern China in the Beijing (Peking) area. These dialects differ from one another primarily in pronunciation and only slightly in grammar. Yet the differences in pronunciation are so great between the north and south that a Cantonese speaker will not be able to understand a Pekinese speaker, much like a Frenchman speaking to an Englishman. In spite of differences in pronunciation, however, Chinese has only one universal written language.

Writing System. The third unique feature of the Chinese language is the writing system, which serves not only as a linguistic tool but also as an embodiment of aesthetic values. Chinese is one of the few language systems that do not use a phonetic alphabet. Instead the Chinese use a pictographic script, composed of what are sometimes called "ideographs" or "logographs" (symbols of words). There are altogether more than forty thousand ideographs or characters in the Chinese language. For basic purposes only about three thousand characters are needed. A standard dictionary contains some five thousand entries of single characters and eighty thousand compound characters made up of two or more single characters.

Chinese characters fall into six general categories. First are the pictographs, in which a small number of characters actually resemble, to some degree, physical objects, such as mountain, water, sun, moon, horse, and rain. Ideographs are characters that indicate ideas such as above, below, big, small, and two. Compound ideographs express more complex relationships, such as crookedness, which is made of a graph for "not" and one for "upright"; east, which is made of a graph for "tree" and one for "sun"; and caught in the middle, which is made of a graph for "above" and one for "below."

The next three categories include words that cannot be pictured readily or indicated graphically. Phonetic loans are borrowings of homophonous words that came from other sources. Phonetic compounds are composites made up of a phonetic and a signific giving the meaning. Derived characters include compounds made of two characters, such as "large-small" for size,

or "long-short" for length.

Putonghua, Romanization, and Script Reform. Standard Chinese, or *putonghua* was adopted as the official national language by the People's Republic of China in 1949. Since the characters themselves do not indicate the proper pronunciation, an official transcription system was devised and adopted by the government in 1958 to aid in the teaching of standard pronunciation. This phonetic system, known as the *pinyin* system, uses the twenty-six letters of the Latin alphabet and is taught in the schools. In most English language publications today, when Chinese names and terms appear, such as "Mao Zedong" rather than "Mao Tse-tung," *pinyin* romanization is used. In recent years, because of the need to achieve greater literacy, the Chinese government has vigorously launched a script-reform program that simplifies a substantial number of complex Chinese characters. So far approximately twenty-five hundred simplified characters have been introduced, thus alleviating to some degree the difficulties of learning the Chinese written language.—*Peter Li*

SUGGESTED READINGS: • Chao, Yuen Ren. *A Grammar of Spoken Chinese.* Berkeley: University of California Press, 1968. • DeFrancis, John. *The Chinese Language: Fact and Fantasy.* Honolulu: University of Hawaii Press, 1984. • Forrest, R. A. D. *The Chinese Language.* 2d rev. ed. London: Faber & Faber, 1965. • Kratochvil, Paul. *The Chinese Language Today.* London: Hutchinson University Library, 1968. • Norman, Jerry. *Chinese.* New York: Cambridge University Press, 1988. • Ramsey, S. Robert. *The Languages of China.* Princeton, N.J.: Princeton University Press, 1987.

Chinese-language schools: Special schools in which children study Chinese language and culture. In the 1870's Chinese merchants who had immigrated to the United States had their children tutored. In 1888 in San Francisco, the Chinese community established the first Chinese-language school. The first school in the East was in New York in 1908.

Until the 1960's only large cities had Chinese-language schools. Then in 1965 the immigration law made it much easier for Chinese families to immigrate. The number of children greatly increased. The overseas Chinese wanted their children to learn Chinese language and culture, so in many cities they established special schools. By 1993 metropolitan Washington, D.C., had more than twenty schools, and California had approximately two hundred.

New York's Chinatown has one of the world's larg-

Classroom instruction in both written and spoken Chinese and in Chinese culture is available in many cities throughout America. (Don Franklin)

est Chinese-language schools. It has more than three thousand students. During the day they go to American public schools. After school each day they go to the Chinese-language school for several hours. This kind of school is unusual. Most Chinese-language schools in the United States meet for two or three hours in public or private school classrooms on a Saturday or Sunday.

Usually students are from three to eighteen years old. The curriculum typically includes Chinese language, culture, history, geography, and customs. Most textbooks are supplied by the Coordination Council for North American Affairs (CCNAA). Teachers also write their own materials or use books published in the United States. More than 95 percent of Chinese-language schools offer only Mandarin Chinese. The others offer Mandarin and Cantonese or southern Fujian.

Many schools also offer such activities as sports, singing, calligraphy, and speech. Sometimes the teenagers participate in the Chinese community's activities. Often parents work very closely with teachers.

Many students in the Chinese-language schools go on to take college-level courses in Chinese because of either personal or professional interests. Global economic development is making Chinese a more important international language, so the Chinese-language schools help preserve the culture and meet many students' future needs.

Chinese laundries: These establishments were a major occupation for Chinese Americans from the mid-nineteenth century to the 1950's and were called an "economic lifeline" of the Chinese community in the United States. When the Chinese first came to America in substantial numbers during the California gold rush of 1849, some of them quickly found out that it was easier for them to make money in the laundry business, which was being conducted mainly by Mexican and American Indian women at the time, as opposed to competing with hostile white miners in the mine fields. Wah Lee is believed to have set up the first Chinese laundry shop in San Francisco in 1851.

High Demand. As California's economy developed and cities expanded, the number of Chinese laundries in that state increased steadily: There were 890 such businesses in 1860, almost 3,000 in 1870, and more than 5,000 by 1880. At the start of the twentieth century, there were about 4,800 Chinese laundrymen in California, constituting 11 percent of the employed Chinese in that state. In other states, however, the percentage of laundrymen in the Chinese population was much higher. In the New York City of the late nineteenth century, for example, at least a third of the Chinese population were laundrymen. In the 1940's, the city had more than 5,000 Chinese laundries. The reason for this difference is that Chinese first came in large numbers to California, where they found more job opportunities. In other states, however, the rise and spread of the Chinese laundries coincided with two developments. First, the rapid expansion of the big Midwestern and Eastern cities such as Chicago, Boston, and New York led to the increasing demand for the services that the Chinese laundries provided. Second,

the anti-Chinese movement, which started in the Western states and culminated in the passage of the CHINESE EXCLUSION ACT IN 1882, forced many Chinese to move eastward and live in the ghettos of the big cities, where they were excluded from most desirable occupations. As a result for many years a large portion of the Chinese in the continental United States relied on the laundry business for a living even though almost none of them had had any experience in laundering before they emigrated to the United States.

Early Years. As immigrants from war-and povertyridden rural areas in Guangdong Province, the Chinese engaged in the laundry business also because opening a hand laundry shop did not require substantial capital or skill, nor did it require a strong grasp of English. In New York City, around the 1880's, to start a small laundry shop required $75 to $200, a sum that a Chinese immigrant could raise. In the nineteenth century, the laundrymen did the washing, ironing, and folding

Inside a Chinese owned and operated commercial laundry. (California State Library)

HONG LEE,
CHINESE LAUNDRY

Soledad St., North of Court House,

SAN ANTONIO, TEXAS.

WILL CALL FOR AND DELIVER WASHING TO ALL PARTS OF THE CITY.

GUARANTEE ALL WORK TO GIVE ENTIRE SATISFACTION.

RAFAEL PEREZ,

BOOT AND  SHOEMAKER,

Houston St., bet. Soledad & Acequia,

SAN ANTONIO, TEXAS.

BOOTS, SHOES, GAITERS, ETC., MADE TO ORDER,

A good fit warranted. Repairing neatly done at reasonable prices.

CHINESE LAUNDRY,

BY SAM CHOISE,

107 Commerce St., few doors from bridge, San Antonio, Texas.

GENTLEMEN'S PRICE LIST.

Shirts 15 cts., two for	25	Handkerchiefs		5
Collars	5	Cuffs, per pair		6
Drawers	10	Vests		25
Undershirts	10	Gent's Clothing, per doz		$1 00
Socks	5	Family Clothing, per doz		1 00

Work taken every day in the week, and returned on the third or fourth day thereafter.
All work guaranteed. When not satisfactory, it will be rewashed without extra charge.
CLOTHING NOT CALLED FOR WITHIN SIXTY DAYS, WILL BE FOR SALE

Advertisements for two Chinese hand laundries operating in downtown San Antonio, Texas, in the early 1880's. (Asian American Studies Library, University of California at Berkeley)

altogether in their own laundry shops. After the 1920's, however, new technology and machines began to transform the industry and the laundrymen no longer had to wash soiled clothes themselves. A typical Chinese hand laundry shop in 1940's-1960's, therefore, received bachelor and family bundles, sent them out to be washed by a wholesale power laundry, and then did the ironing and folding. Before the 1940's the majority of the Chinese laundry shops were small businesses, and few Chinese laundrymen had a normal family life because the Chinese Exclusion Acts banned the U.S. entry of Chinese laborers and their wives, and because prejudice against and legal restrictions on interracial marriages prevented Chinese males from organizing families in the United States. The repeal of the Chinese Exclusion Acts in 1943 and the relaxation of the restriction on Chinese immigration in the 1940's allowed Chinese males to bring their wives to America. Subsequently many hand laundries were operated by families, but the size of a typical hand laundry remained small, though the volume of its business may have increased. Some Chinese merchants established power laundries and laundry supply shops. The conflicts between small hand laundries and power laundries were frequent, mainly over the price for "wet-wash." These quarrels and disputes were in most cases resolved within the Chinese community, but on occasions they were brought to and settled by the court. In cases involving non-Chinese power laundries, Chinese hand laundrymen launched strikes in protest or hired lawyers to defend their interests in court.

Up until the 1960's, the working conditions in the hand laundry shops were usually harsh—the space was small, the air steamy, and the working hours long. Hardworking and frugal as they were, most Chinese laundrymen made little money and survived only on a subsistence level. They lived in the laundry shop and seldom left it. The major entertainment in life for them was going to eat or visit friends in Chinatown on Sundays.

Unionization. Before the 1950's, Chinese laundrymen in many American cities were often singled out for discrimination, especially during economic recession or depression. Their competitors—usually white owners of large power laundries—complained that they charged low rates, worked long hours, and left their job and residential quarters unclean and demanded that municipal authorities pass regulations to restrict Chinese laundries. Between 1873 and 1884, for example, the San Francisco Board of Supervisors passed fourteen ordinances to curb the spread of Chinese laundries. Other cities, such as Los Angeles, New York, and Boston, also passed similar ordinances in the nineteenth and twentieth centuries. To oppose such discriminatory measures as well as to protect their rights and interests, Chinese laundrymen's guilds were organized in San Francisco in the 1870's. Yet these guilds as well as the hand laundry business itself were generally under the control of the Chinese Consolidated Benevolent Association (CCBA) in each city. The largest organization of Chinese laundrymen in the United States that has maintained its independence is the CHINESE HAND LAUNDRY ALLIANCE (CHLA) of New York, founded in 1933.

By the 1950's, the introduction of more efficient modern machines and other equipment into the laundry industry began to provide the urban population with cheaper and more convenient services and lessened the demand for Chinese hand laundries. By the 1970's, as home washing machines began to appear in middle-class households, as self-service laundromats became available in many urban neighborhoods, and as new fabrics that needed no ironing were more often used, the Chinese hand laundry business was in permanent decline and was no longer the economic lifeline of the Chinese community.—*Renqiu Yu*

SUGGESTED READINGS: • Siu, Paul C. P. *The Chinese Laundryman: A Study of Social Isolation. Edited by John K. W. Tchen. New York: New York University Press, 1987.* • Yu, Renqiu. *To Save China, To Save Ourselves: The Chinese Hand Laundry Alliance of New York.* Philadelphia: Temple University Press, 1992.

Chinese martial arts: The term gung-fu, which is most frequently used to describe Chinese martial arts, encompasses historical, religious, cultural, and other elements as well. There are thousands of systems, but Chinese martial arts are generally distinguished by regional origin (South or North) and conceptual emphasis ("hard" or "soft"). The primary difference between the Southern and Northern styles is that the Southern styles emphasize the use of hands, while the Northern styles emphasize leaping kicks. In training the Southern styles stress student interaction (sparring), while the Northern styles stress precomposed movement patterns.

The distinction between "hard" ("external") and "soft" ("internal") styles is much more abstract and is related to the Taoist concept of psychocosmic polarities (yin-yang). The hard schools take a more goal-oriented approach in which an opponent is overcome by a prac-

Lu Chih-Ming demonstrates the use of the tai chi sword. (Asian American Studies Library, University of California at Berkeley)

titioner's superior force (*yang*). The soft schools, by contrast, take a more responsive approach in which the imbalances caused by an opponent's aggressive movements are utilized strategically. These differences affect practice routines: The external styles prepare the body to deliver and resist blows, while the internal styles focus upon control of autonomic functions (respiration and heartbeat), the development of reflexive intuition, and concentration. There is also a striking visual contrast between the linear attacks of the hard traditions and the flexible, unbroken movements of the soft traditions.

While most gung-fu traditions utilize elements from both approaches, the major schools tend to emphasize one or the other. Hence, the systems of tai chi chuan, pakua, and hsing-i all emphasize the spiritual or meditative, while other systems (tong long and wing chun) stress powerful strikes.

Early history. The early history of gung-fu is clouded in legend, but tradition suggests that, like other developments during the first millennium C.E., the development of gung-fu was stimulated by China's increasing contact with other Asian nations via the ancient Central Asian silk routes. Along with trade goods, knowledge and ideas were often exchanged, and Indian Buddhist missionaries influenced Taoist monastic communities. The cultivation of self-defense techniques would have been a natural outgrowth of the nomadic lifestyle of these travelers, who crossed the formidable deserts and mountains of western China. Oral and written sources trace the origin of gung-fu to the Shaolin temple in Henan Province and to the influence of Bodhidharma, a sixth century Indian monk who taught Buddhism to the Shaolin monks. He probably shared ancient Indian yogic traditions, which also emphasize control of autonomic functions but which tend to be more static than their East Asian counterparts. Eventually the Shaolin styles split into Northern and Southern systems within China and were carried to Japan and Korea, where they influenced the development of karate and tae kwon do.

Internal Systems. The internal systems are founded

Gung-fu expert Henry Chung exhibiting the movements of the praying mantis style using the three-section staff—in the hands of the skilled practitioner, a formidable weapon. (Raymond Malace)

on Taoism and emphasize proper breathing to fill the body with *chi*, the intangible, universal energy or life force.

One of the three main forms of the soft school, tai chi chuan, is practiced for daily exercise by millions of Chinese and is also very popular in the United States. Translated tai chi chuan means "supreme ultimate fist" and was documented as early as the Liang period (502-557), although its Taoist origins are probably much earlier. Often referred to as "moving meditation," tai chi practice involves meditation through very gradual changes in posture and breathing exercises to develop *chi*. When practiced as a martial art, tai chi requires the memorization and practice of movement sequences, fighting stances, and "push hands" (sparring with a partner).

The second internal system is pakua, which means "eight trigrams" and is based on the *I Ching*, the ancient *Book of Changes*. Of unknown origins, pakua was probably formulated by a Taoist monk. A trigram consists of a series of horizontal lines, one on top of the other. An unbroken or "strong" line is a *yang* or masculine, line, while a line broken into two equal halves is a "weak" *yin*, or feminine, line. The trigrams are arranged in a circle to represent the eight points of the compass. The basic goal is protection from attack by defending oneself at these points. Circular footwork, intertwining arm movements, and numerous open-palm strikes are used.

Ya Fei, a twelfth century general revered by later generations of Chinese for his heroism and loyalty during the end of the Song Dynasty (960-1279), is credited with developing the internal style of hsing-i, or "body-mind boxing." The traditional five elements (metal, water, wood, fire, and earth) are the basis of the five primary forms of attack. The twelve animals (dragon, tiger, horse, monkey, cock, turtle, hawk, swallow, snake, falcon, eagle, and bear) constitute the twelve sequences of movement.

External or Hard Systems. During the seventeenth century Wong Long, a Shaolin gung-fu master, observed how a praying mantis defeated a grasshopper. Fascinated by the mantis' aggressive, rapid movements, he developed the praying mantis, or tong long style. The main techniques of this Northern style are quick footwork and the "mantis claw."

The most popular hard system is wing chun (beautiful springtime), formulated several hundred years ago by Ng Mui, a Shaolin nun with great gung-fu boxing skills. She then taught her new system to Yim Wing Chun, her disciple and first student, who then passed along to others what had been learned. This Southern style consists of straight-line punches, including *chisau* which involves constant contact with the opponent's hands. The goal is to defend or attack an imaginary centerline along which all the body's vital organs lie. Only two weapons are used: the butterfly knife and the six-and-a-half-point pole. Although wing chun is classified as a "hard" style, velocity and control are more important than force. A modern master of wing chun, Yip Man, taught the legendary Bruce Lee.

Hollywood and Gung-Fu. Lee taught wing chun and later, his new system of jeet kune do ("way of the intercepting fist") in the United States. He played Kato in *The Green Hornet* series (1966-1967), and his *Enter the Dragon* (1973) has become a cult classic. The film biography *Dragon: The Bruce Lee Story* was released in 1993. The popular *Kung Fu* series (1972-1975) starred David Carradine as a Shaolin disciple in the American West. Since the 1960's, martial arts movies, magazines, schools, and books have proliferated throughout the United States.—*Alice Chin-Myers*

Suggested Readings: • Finn, Michael. *Martial Arts: A Complete Illustrated History*. Woodstock, N.Y.: Overlook Press, 1988. • Kauz, Herman. *The Martial Spirit: An Introduction to the Origin, Philosophy, and Psychology of the Martial Arts*. Woodstock, N.Y.: Overlook Press, 1988. • Lewis, Peter. *Martial Arts of the Orient*. New York: Gallery Books, 1985. • Soet, John Steven. *Martial Arts Around the World*. Burbank, Calif.: Unique Publications, 1991. • Wong, Doc-Fai, and Jane Hallander. *Tai Chi Chuan's Internal Secrets*. Burbank, Calif.: Unique Publications, 1991.

Chinese Media Committee community radio programs: Programs introduced in the early 1970's by the Chinese Media Committee of Chinese for Affirmative Action (San Francisco) to give the Chinese American community a voice at a time when Asian Americans were virtually unrepresented in the media.

The first such program, which debuted in 1971, was the *Hon Sing Chinese Community Hour*, a Cantonese program staffed by volunteers from the community. Its programming included news commentaries and discussions of community issues in Cantonese as well as community announcements and Chinese music announced in a bilingual format. In the same year, a Mandarin program, *Chinese Youth Voice* (*Zhongguo Qingnian zhi Sheng*), was started. Produced by volunteers, *Chinese Youth Voice* was one of the first Mandarin-speaking programs in the San Francisco Bay Area. Besides newscasts the hour-long program also introduced the literature and music of the new China.

Shortly after *Chinese Youth Voice* was launched, Asian American activists joined the group and began producing a weekly half-hour English-language broadcast, *Dupont Guy*, which addressed Asian American issues. In 1972 the Chinese Media Committee also initiated Cantonese simulcasts of English-language television news and in 1973 produced and broadcast a program called *Learning Mandarin.*

These programs went off the air one by one during the era of resurgent conservatism and tightened fiscal policies that began in the mid-1970's. *Chinese Youth Voice* was silenced in the mid-1970's; *Dupont Guy* lasted until the early 1980's, and the *Hon Sing Chinese Community Hour* suspended broadcasting in the mid-1980's.

Chinese music and dance: Chinese music and dance has a documented history of at least four thousand years. Contemporary Chinese music and dance is extremely diverse. It includes Han traditional ensemble and solo music, regional opera styles (which incorpo-

rate mime and acrobatics), music literature and ballet influenced by European traditions, international popular music and dance styles, and a host of folk genres that reflect China's ethnic and geographic diversity.

Early Imperial History. Music and dance play a significant role in Chinese legends concerning the earliest emperors, who ruled in the Yellow River Valley in approximately 2,000 B.C.E. Ritual dance songs were used to appeal for good harvests, and standard tunings were adopted to unify the kingdom. During the Zhou Dynasty, which began about a thousand years later, both tuning and instrumental tone color were felt to have cosmological significance reflecting the change of seasons, the eight directions, and the fate of the nation. These beliefs persisted, and the music and gestures associated with ritual ceremonies became known as *ya yueh*, or "elegant music." The word *ya* meant "simplicity and restraint" as well as "elegance," reflecting the Confucian virtues of respect and loyalty. According to accounts from the time, both the music and the ceremonial movements of *ya yueh* were very solemn and dignified. Court musicians were main-

Chinese dancer Chen Guo teaches Chinese dance to New York public school children. The workshop is part of the Asian American Arts Centre's "Arts in Education Program." (Asian American Arts Centre)

tained, and special officials were appointed to collect folk songs as a means of polling public opinion.

Many musical instruments were developed in China during this period, including prototypes of instruments still used throughout East Asia. Court ceremonies required large sets of tuned bronze bells and stone chimes, often ranging over four octaves and capable of playing harmony. Other important instruments included two zithers; the *qin*, said to have been played by Confucius himself; and the *se*, a harplike forerunner of the Japanese *koto*, the Korean *kayageum*, and the Chinese *zheng*. Wind and percussion instruments were used for military processions.

Folk Music and Dance. Folk music and dance grew as an integral part of the lives of the peoples of China. Although agriculture has remained the predominant livelihood in China, shepherding, hunting, and fishing are important in certain areas, and the work songs and dances of various regions reflect these lifestyles. Courtship is another important theme and function in many folk traditions. In addition to folk and court dance traditions, the Chinese have developed very sophisticated systems of movement that combine meditation, exercise, and self-defense, practiced by all age groups. The most popular of these is *tai chi chuan*, sometimes known as "shadow boxing."

Before the mid-twentieth century, most of the population was not given access to written literature but had developed elaborate regional opera genres. These operas use local dialects (supported by mime, music, costumes, and acrobatics) to tell stories from China's long history and to impart cultural values.

International Influences. During the Han Dynasty (206 B.C.E.-220 C.E.) China's geographic boundaries expanded, and increased international trade began via the silk route in central Asia. Central Asian and Indian plucked lutes became popular in China and influenced the development of the *pipa* and *ruanxian*. Gongs were also introduced at this time. During the Sui (581-618) and Tang dynasties (618-907) bands of foreign musicians and dancers were maintained in the royal court in the city of Xi'an, and Buddhist priests introduced narrative songs that influenced the development of regional opera. Bowed lutes were introduced by Mongol invaders in the thirteenth century, and the Chinese versions of these instruments, those of the *huqin* family, eventually became the mainstay of Chinese opera and traditional chamber music ensembles.

In the twentieth century a new form of international influence began as European musical traditions found acceptance in China. In 1927 the Shanghai National Conservatory of Music was established. Popular music and social dancing from Europe and the United States were introduced into urban centers. After the People's Republic of China (PRC) was established in 1949, a period of Russian influence resulted in the study of ballet as well as European classical music. Within the PRC the influence of popular music from abroad was halted at this time, although folk music was promoted by the Communist government.

The Eight Model Revolutionary Operas. During the Cultural Revolution (1966-1969) the only music or dance allowed was that which explicitly glorified the proletarian class struggle. A deliberate synthesis of Chinese traditional opera, European ballet, acrobatics, and European opera was attempted. During this time the resulting eight "revolutionary operas" temporarily displaced the diverse Chinese and European-derived performing arts, and many traditional musicians suffered hardships. After the end of the Cultural Revolution the surviving displaced musicians and dancers returned to their work as performers and teachers.

Popular Styles. After the fall of the Gang of Four the influence of commercial popular music slowly returned to China. Popular music had developed unabated for quite some time in Taiwan and Hong Kong, which had both enjoyed uninterrupted contact with the United States and Western Europe during a period (lasting almost three decades) in which China had remained isolated from most of the non-Socialist world. Eventually popular musicians from within mainland China emerged and began to compete in the growing East Asian market. Despite efforts by the government to participate in popular music culture through broadcasts, sponsorship of talent contests, and so forth, popular identification with global consumer culture represents one of the conflicts that resulted in the Tiananmen Square incident of 1989.

Developments in the United States. Chinese music and dance came to the United States with the first wave of immigrants in the mid-nineteenth century. A familiar American event is the dragon dance, often performed by young community members in public processions. Chinese Americans are also very active as performers and composers in all genres of Western classical music.

In areas with large Chinese populations, frequent concerts of Chinese music and dance are sponsored by Chinese American cultural organizations, and courses of instruction are offered. Several colleges and universities with programs in ethnomusicology also have courses in the performance and study of Chinese traditional arts.—*John Myers*

SUGGESTED READINGS: • DeWoskin, Kenneth J. *A Song for One or Two: Music and the Concept of Art in Early China*. Ann Arbor: University of Michigan, Center for Chinese Studies, 1982. • Liang, Ming-Yueh. *Music of the Billion: An Introduction to Chinese Musical Culture*. New York: Heinrichschofen, 1985. • Mackerras, Colin P. *The Rise of the Peking Opera, 1770-1870*. Oxford, England: Clarendon Press, 1972. • Wang, K'o-fen. *History of Chinese Dance*. Beijing: Foreign Language Press, 1885. • Yung, Bell. *Cantonese Opera: Performance as Creative Process*. Cambridge, England: Cambridge University Press, 1989.

Chinese Nationalist Party. *See* **Guomindang**

Chinese New Year: Among transplanted Chinese traditions, the most widely celebrated event of the year. Like other Chinese holidays, the date of this event is figured according to the lunar calendar. It therefore varies from year to year, falling sometime between January 20 and mid-February on the (Western) Gregorian calendar. Chinese New Year is the most important of all the Chinese festivals because it begins a time when families gather together and anticipate better days ahead. It is also a time when they remember ancestors and give thanks for blessings.

The days prior to the New Year are busy ones with families giving the house a thorough cleaning and purchasing necessary foods for new year's festivities. A member of the family goes to the temple to give thanks for the year's blessings. In larger temples prepared foods may be taken to present to ancestors, although today's procedure may be simplified with less items.

The New Year's eve dinner is an important occasion. Much preparation is involved because this dinner will include special foods such as bird's nest soup,

The Chinese New Year celebration in America anticipates the highly popular dragon dance, with its powerful, exuberant movements. (San Francisco Convention and Visitors Bureau)

Lantern bearers in traditional costumes ride through the streets of downtown San Francisco on a decorated float during the city's Chinese New Year festivities. (San Francisco Convention and Visitors Bureau)

shark's fin soup, pot roast pork, and other special dishes.

For many Chinese, being with family at New Year's is important. Many people will travel to their ancestral homes in all parts of the world for the sake of this gathering. To the Chinese family, unity is an important phase of life, and many Chinese symbols stress this idea.

On New Year's day families eat *jai*, a vegetarian dish that may have as many as eighteen varieties of vegetables, with many being used for symbolic reasons. Bean threads for longevity and ginko nuts for fertility are two examples of this. *Jai* has become very popular with other ethnic groups who enjoy this concoction, of which there are endless combinations according to the cook's whims.

During New Year's day children who greet their elders with "*gung hee fat choy*" (happy new year) may be given *li-see* (lucky money) in return. These gifts were originally wrapped in small pieces of red paper; the modern Chinese may use little red envelopes instead. The tradition of *li-see* encourages and teaches

children to greet their elders.

Following the *jai*, the second evening's meal is also of special entrees. Again it indicates family unity.

On the seventh day, there is usually another meal of special entrees. On this day, everyone becomes a year older.

Chinese customs are many, and on New Year's day one does not cut anything if possible. One does not clean house lest the good luck be swept away, or wash clothes. Above all, families traditionally try to pay all their bills before New Year. This particular practice has become more difficult in modern times.

Certain Chinese New Year traditions have in more modern times been modified. Regardless, at New Year's thoughts of health, wealth, and longevity are on the minds of celebrants everywhere.

Chinese opera: Generally speaking, in the popular American consciousness, Chinese opera is Beijing Opera. The Beijing Opera, which tours the United States with a fair degree of regularity, achieved its current form by the mid-nineteenth century through the gradual amalgamation of features taken from various Chinese regional musical forms. Set in historical periods, domestic themes or military adventures provide the two dominant plot lines.

Performances are usually offered on minimally decorated platform stages, with the orchestra seated in full view of the audience, while highly elaborate stylized costumes and painted faces provide visual interest. The action of the opera is carried through the use of dialogue, song, dance, and an elaborate interplay of highly evolved symbolic gesture and props. For example chairs placed back-to-back become a wall, while chairs with backs to a table form a bridge. An actor employing a particular style of walking while circling the stage signifies a very long journey. Indeed stage gestures have been codified to the point that the actor can choose from an extensive catalog of sleeve movements, seven basic hand movements, twenty pointing gestures, twelve leg movements, various beard movements, and so forth. The formal qualities of production also made the performance of female characters by men seem appropriate, although women began to perform in the early twentieth century. This nineteenth century tendency to have men impersonating women would later be exploited by David Henry HWANG in his play *M. Butterfly* (pr. 1988).

It should be noted, however, that when the Chinese

Chinese actors of the Beijing Opera in full makeup and costume. (Claire Rydell)

opera first came to the United States in 1852 it likely was not the Beijing opera, but the Cantonese opera, that appeared. The latter was one of the many regional types that contributed to the codification of the dominant form so familiar to Americans today.

Chinese popular religion: Chinese popular religion is the religious tradition of China. It developed its modern form in the Ming (1368-1644) and Qing (1644-1911) dynasties, combining BUDDHISM, TAOISM, CON-

The cast of a just-concluded Chinese opera, circa 1930's. (Asian American Studies Library, University of California at Berkeley)

FUCIANISM, and other religious and philosophical systems with local cults. The religion is widely followed even in modern China, and by many Chinese immigrants. Native-born Chinese Americans often maintain at least the outer form of some of the more important and public of its practices.

Historical Background and Major Characteristics. Much of what has become Chinese popular religion developed around the sixth century B.C.E., when Confucius lived and ideas such as Taoism and *yin-yang* developed into coherent schools of thought. Later, between the second and sixth centuries C.E., Buddhism achieved widespread acceptance in China. These various systems of thought and religious beliefs influenced one another but were primarily competitive until the Ming and Qing dynasties, when people began to accept the idea that they were all simply different aspects of the truth. After that, adherents built numerous temples and gradually developed a complex and varied system of religious practice and philosophical outlook.

The resulting religion emphasized fate and morality. Morality centered around the family (all close blood relatives—parents, grandparents, children, siblings,

the children of siblings, uncles and aunts and their children, and even deceased direct ancestors). Younger generations were to show love, honor, and respect to older generations, while older generations were to show benevolence toward the younger. If a family was well ordered, the universe would be in balance and at peace. The seasons would come as they should (bringing adequate rain for crops—hence, enough food), and the country would be well governed and at peace.

To help achieve this, ancestors were worshiped after they had died and were kept informed of all important family affairs. In fact, a primary function of marriage was to produce male children who could continue proper ancestor worship. If a family member shamed the family (such as by disobeying the head of the family or getting in trouble with the law), part of his or her punishment would come during the afterlife, for there was both a series of Buddhist hells and an angry Jade Emperor (ruler of the heavens) with which to contend. In addition succeeding generations of the family might suffer because of the misdeed; but succeeding generations would *benefit* if a family member were virtuous.

As for fate, it could be divined in advance and sometimes even influenced. Fate was thought to operate through the *yin-yang* principle of a balance of opposites, or through the caprice of deities, or simply as a mysterious force on its own. Many temples kept fortune-telling sticks or similar devices so that a person could find out what lay in store and be prepared. Since marriage had far-reaching importance for the family, it was wise to check in advance (using horoscopes and the like) to see if fate would allow the prospective bride and groom a good marriage. Sometimes prayer to a deity could tilt fate in one's favor to ensure the successful conclusion of a business affair, or the birth of a son, or other desirable event.

Temples in the United States. When Chinese began immigrating to the United States, they brought their religion with them. In the 1850's, Chinese built at least five temples in California. (See CHINESE TEMPLES IN CALIFORNIA.) By the late 1880's, there were more than thirty temples and, in addition, at least six in Hawaii, several in Nevada, at least one in Montana and Wyoming, and a few in the Eastern United States. The greatest period for temple building was the 1880's and 1890's. After the 1920's the religion and the temples declined, but even in the 1980's, partly because of the new wave of Chinese immigration, a few new ones were dedicated and a number of the old ones continued in use.

Confucius Church in Salinas, California. (McCrea Adams)

Storefront Buddhist temple in New York City Chinatown. (Frances M. Roberts)

A temple usually houses a number of deities. The three most popular have been Guanyin, Guangong (Guandi), and Tianhou. Guanyin, a *bodhisattva*, is known for her compassion toward all and for protecting women. Guangong, sometimes called the god of war, is known for his fighting prowess and even his love of learning, but especially for his loyalty. He derives from a historical figure, a Chinese general of the third century C.E. Tianhou was also once a historical figure. She came from a fishing family in south China. She became a deity for having miraculously saved one of her brothers from death in a typhoon while he was at sea. She is known for protecting travelers, especially those who travel by water.

In addition to these three deities, many Chinese temples in the United States contain representations of the Buddha and contain symbols associated with *yin-yang*. Some temples are dedicated to the god of the locale (god of the soil), or the god of the north, or the god of water and flood control. (All the above are sometimes interpreted as one deity.) The god of medicine is another favorite.

Regular worship is normally done by the individual, with no set ceremony or time for worship. It usually includes prayers to the preferred deity or deities and the casting of one's fortune. In addition the temples formerly held public "birthday" celebrations in honor of their chief deity, complete with parade, firecrackers, the shooting off of hempen rings ("bombs") by a cannon, and feasts. This was still practiced as late as the 1990's by at least one temple in California. (See BOK KAI TEMPLE.)

Religious Practice Outside the Temple. Religious practice in the home and other places outside the temple has been even more important than worship in the temple. Rites for the worship of ancestors ordinarily took place in the home. In addition a "kitchen god" watched over the family members in the home to be sure everyone behaved properly. *Yin-yang* symbols and pictures of other deities such as Guangong, Guanyin, and the god of wealth might be placed on the walls of the home or business to bring special protection.

Death and burial were rather public affairs. Interment involved a parade to the graveyard, preferably with orchestras, ceremonially dressed mourners, and the like. The newly deceased was to be provided with a house for the afterlife (usually made of paper and burned at the gravesite). In the nineteenth and early twentieth centuries, usually the bones of the deceased were later reinterred in China. Once a year, everyone was supposed to go to the cemetery to "visit" with deceased relatives, bringing them food, special "spirit money," and other necessities.

Finally, many festivals continue to have religious connotations. The dragon of the Chinese New Year's dragon parade is a water deity, for example, who ensures that there will be enough rain to grow crops. Lion dances, often seen in the streets around Chinese New Year, scare away evil spirits. The "birthday" celebrations to the temple deities bring general good fortune. As part of certain festivals, special foods are eaten partly because traditionally they were thought to have magical properties.—*L. Eve Armentrout Ma*

SUGGESTED READINGS: • Chace, Paul G. "Interpretive Restraint and Ritual Tradition: Marysville's Festival of Bok Kai." *Journal of Contemporary Ethnography* 21 (July, 1992): 226-254. • Ma, L. Eve Armentrout. "Chinese Traditional Religion in North America and Hawaii." In *Chinese America: History and Perspectives*. San Francisco: Chinese Historical Society of America, 1987. • Wells, Marianne Kaye. *Chinese Temples in California*. San Francisco: R and E Research Associates, 1971.

Chinese Reform News (*Zhongguo Weixin Bao*): Chinese-language news organ of the Chinese Empire Reform Association and its successor organization, the Chinese Constitutionalist Party, founded in New York City in 1904. After the formation of the Republic of China in 1912 the newspaper supported the Peking government and was critical of Sun Yat-sen and the Chinese Nationalist Party, who were in opposition to the regime.

The paper began as a semiweekly, then became successively a triweekly and a weekly. In 1928, Constitutionalist Party adherents allied with CHEE KUNG TONG leaders founded *The Justice Daily News* (*Kong Wo Yat Po, Gonghe Ribao*) as a successor to *Chinese Reform News*. However, the paper's business declined and it became first a semiweekly and then a weekly before stopping publication altogether around 1933.

Chinese restaurants and cuisine: In the People's Republic of China the preparation and eating of food have traditionally been accorded great interest and respect. During ancient times, for example, food preparation and service were a significant part of rituals performed at the royal court. New Chinese emperors placed great emphasis on the appointing of a royal chef. These chefs tried very hard to outdistance all previous appointees in the quality and desirability of their cooking.

In the West, however, Chinese cooking did not find widespread popularity until after World War II. Before that time Chinese restaurants in the United States and elsewhere had been confined mostly to Chinatowns and other Chinese quarters and offered almost uniformly a Cantonese-style cuisine. Non-Chinese patrons began referring to such establishments as "chop suey houses," a phrase that supposedly came into use after a nineteenth century envoy told his cook to fashion a meal for some unexpected guests by chopping up leftovers. In the United States, at least, the chop suey house ranked with the Chinese laundry as the two most recognizable Chinese cultural landmarks of the urban city. In the postwar era the laundries have slowly disappeared but the restaurants have grown in number, variety, and public appreciation.

The Major Regional Cooking Styles. While often retaining the appearance, aroma, and sound of its historically typical Chinatown setting, the Chinese restaurant has moved into the suburbs. Whatever the ambience or setting, the food served will belong to one style or several styles of Chinese cooking. Some awareness of these traditions will make visiting these restaurants more enjoyable.

Regional cuisines do not coincide with styles of cooking in China, and robust confusion persists as to what constitutes a regional cuisine. Distinctive styles of cooking far outnumber the regional groupings to which they belong. It is sensible, however, to discern Chinese food in terms of four major regional stylings (some would insist on a fifth), corresponding to the four directions.

Northern School. Northern Chinese food, often associated with Beijing (although Beijing really has no culinary tradition of its own and is dominated by Shandong cooking) is marked by the use of garlic, scallion, and soy bean paste (*jiang*) in a variety of cooking methods ranging from barbecuing to quick high-fire stirring. When the mutton (from northwest regions) and other meats are boiled in plain cooking, they are consumed with a rich variety of condiments mixed in to give zest and taste. The staple consists of innumerable fashionings of wheat products from noodles to breads and buns. Rice in recent years is frequently seen at the banquet table.

In ancient China the preparation and consumption of food was a subject of universal interest. Among Chinese Americans today, it is no different. (International Daily News)

Eastern School. Eastern Chinese food is dominated by various cooking styles made famous within the provinces of Jiangsu and Zhejiang, referred to often in Chinese lore as the "land of fish and rice." Here natural flavor is preferred over the zestiness of the north and the spiciness of the west. The food is more often braised and simmered with a blended use of sugar, vinegar, and soy sauce. The Shaoxing wine of Zhejiang has given rise to such dishes as Drunken Chicken and Drunken Crabs. Freshwater products of every description are prized along with rice as the major staple. One may also include the Fujian (with the subregion of Fuzhou) in this Eastern tradition. The talent for creating exquisite broths and soups here is unequalled elsewhere in China.

Southern School. Southern Chinese cooking is called "Cantonese," even though in addition to the metropolitan area of Canton there are the two other culinary styles of Hakka (or East River) and Chaozhou in the same province of Guangdong. South China insists in freshness of food, and the cooking methods are as numerous as they are distinctive. Its roasts and

barbecues are different from the north, and its steaming and parboiling of seafoods are a regional art with international renown. Ginger and scallion are employed in mysterious ways to complement seafood and meat flavor. The cuisine is also noted for certain long- and slow-simmered dishes in earthenware pots, even though its main character of cooking is the high-fire quick stir-fry.

Western School. Western Chinese cooking is characterized mainly by the food of Sichuan, sometimes linked with that of Hunan through their mutual characteristic of peppery spiciness. The Sichuanese, like the Cantonese, are sybarites who have given much thought to food and pleasures of the palate. It is no wonder that they are the only two culinary traditions that have achieved state-banquet stature. With this region's inland position, much of its food is in preserved form: salting, drying, spicing, pickling, and smoking. Preference is given to the more pungent of the vegetables, such as garlic, onions, scallions, ginger, pepper, and chilies. Sichuan cooking has more distinctive tastes than other regions. In addition to the usual five

In America, Chinese restaurants have multiplied in number, variety, and public appreciation. Here kitchen staff of Tony's Chop Suey, Madison, Wisconsin, prepare an order of food. (Mary Langenfeld)

Chinese food is distinctive especially for its great variety.

of sweet, sour, bitter, salty, and peppery, the Sichuan palate (but not the Hunan) discerns a sixth. It is collectively known as *mala*—a combination of the aromatic and the roasted nutty. Sichuan cuisine ranges from the everyday "Pock-marked Granny Doufu" (*mapo doufu*) to the "Duck Smoked in Camphor Wood and Tea Leaves" (*zhang-cha ya*). It bears noting that Sichuan food is not always spicy and peppery; in fact its banquet courses are often interspersed with tiny dishes of sweet and sweet/sour savories.

In the United States. All these major traditions of Chinese food can be found in the United States, although the Eastern variety is perhaps the least known of the four, with Southern Chinese still the most prevalent. It bears pointing out that, with all of its influence on the Western palate, the Chinese sweet foods have not made their deserved impact yet. Fanciers of the Cantonese *dim sum* (literally "heart-dotting") lunch have, however, often discovered the variety as well as exquisiteness of the sweet offerings. Then again, sojourners in Sichuan will surely attest that region's desserts, and habitués of the Shanghai region must have come across such delights as the "eight-treasures pud-

ding" or the succulent glutinous rice dumplings filled with ground black sesame seed paste. The Cantonese have outdone the Shanghainese by cooking these dumplings in ginger soup or adding them to a walnut puree.

Important aspects of Chinese cuisine are available in restaurants, in books, and on television. To appreciate the whole range of Chinese food offerings, however, one must appreciate taste. Elements that go into the arbitration of taste are color, aroma, flavor, and texture. The Chinese culinary tradition has always insisted, with tantalizing interpretations, on a felicitous blending of all four.—*D. W. Y. Kwok*

SUGGESTED READINGS: • Anderson, Eugene. *The Food of China.* New Haven, Conn.: Yale University Press, 1988. • Chang, K. C., ed. *Food in Chinese Culture: Anthropological and Historical Perspectives.* New Haven, Conn.: Yale University Press, 1977. • Claiborne, Craig, and Virginia Lee. *The Chinese Cookbook.* Philadelphia: J. B. Lippincott, 1972. • Lo, Kenneth. *Chinese Regional Cooking.* New York: Pantheon Books, 1979. • Kowk, D. W. Y. "The Pleasures of the Chinese Palate." *Free China Review* 41 (September, 1991): 46-51. • Wang, Dee. *Chinese Cooking the Easy Way*. New York: Elsevier/Nelson Books, 1979.

Chinese Revolution of 1911: Political movement that overthrew the Qing Dynasty, abolished the monarchy, and inaugurated the Republic of China. The ostensible leader of the revolution was SUN YAT-SEN, but its immediate beneficiary was Yuan Shikai.

The Revolution of 1911 had its roots in China's humiliating defeat by Japan in 1895. The defeat exposed the inability of the incumbent Qing Dynasty to defend China's national interests from the rapacious foreign powers and led directly to the first effort by Sun to overthrow the regime. The Qing Dynasty was led by the Manchus, a small ethnic minority originally from Manchuria, who, in 1644, had overrun China and imposed themselves over the majority Han Chinese population. Sun called for the ouster of the Manchus and the restoration of Han rule over China as well as the establishment of a republic in place of China's ancient monarchy. In 1905, he and his supporters in Tokyo founded the Chinese United League (TONGMENGHUI), which in succeeding years launched a series of unsuccessful uprisings in China against the Qing Dynasty.

Sun Yat-sen's, however, was not the only group of Chinese exiles to call for radical change. Another group, led by KANG YOUWEI and LIANG QICHAO, opposed Sun's idea of a republic and favored instead the transformation of the Qing Dynasty into a Japanese-style constitutional monarchy. Meanwhile, within China, the ruling Manchus had belatedly initiated a wide-ranging program of reform, which included the formation of a New Army and the election of provincial assemblies. The Qing, however, was not reforming fast enough to suit many members of the newly politicized elite in China. When revolt sponsored by the Chinese United League unexpectedly broke out in Wuchang, in central China, on October 10, 1911, the local New Army unit and the provincial assembly both refused to back the Qing and supported the rebels instead. The revolution quickly spread to other parts of China. The revolutionaries eventually declared a republic and elected Sun as president. By then, the desperate Qing Dynasty had turned for help to Yuan Shikai, a powerful New Army commander. Yuan, however, on February 12, 1912, forced the Qing emperor to abdicate; in return, Sun, by prior arrangement, yielded the presidency of the new republic to Yuan Shikai.

The overseas Chinese, including those in the United States as well as Canada and Mexico, played a significant role in the movement leading up to the Revolution of 1911. In particular, they were a source of funding for the groups of both Sun and Kang. Both established branches of their respective organization in all the major Chinatowns, which Sun, Kang, and Liang visited as they repeatedly crisscrossed the United States. Thus it was that Sun was in Denver, Colorado, when he learned of the Wuchang uprising that would end his fifteen-year quest to oust the Manchus and establish a republic.

Chinese romanization: Writing or representation of Chinese characters in the Latin alphabet. In English-language publications, the two most widely used forms of Chinese romanization are the Wade-Giles and the *Hanyu pinyin* systems. Names, words, and phrases denoting Chinese characters are likely to be rendered in one of these two systems. Much less frequently used are the *Gwoyeu Romatzyh* and Yale systems, which are restricted in their usage by geography and educational purpose.

Until recently, the dominance of the Wade-Giles system was undisputed throughout the English-speaking world. Developed by Sir Thomas Francis Wade in 1859 and revised by Herbert A. Giles in 1892, the system was the standard for usage in texts dealing with the Chinese language. An exception was the citation of common Chinese place names, which were usually transliterated according to the Chinese Post Office system introduced in 1906.

With the establishment of the People's Republic of China in 1949, an official romanization system known as *Hanyu pinyin* or PINYIN received increased exposure. Especially after the United States and China restored diplomatic ties in 1979, the *pinyin* system began to be used very widely by scholars, linguists, publications, and organizations. The United Nations has adopted the *pinyin* system as the international standard for Chinese romanization.

The *Gwoyeu Romatzyh* system, developed in China

Romanization of Chinese Place Names		
Pinyin	Wade-Giles	Post Office
Beijing	Pei-ching	Peking
Guangzhou	Kuang-chou	Canton
Shanghai	Shang-hai	Shanghai
Sichuan	Ssu-ch'uan	Szechwan
Xianggang	Hsiang-kang	Hong Kong

in the 1920's, is now largely restricted to Taiwan, and even there its use is limited. The Yale system, devised by linguists at Yale University during World War II, was popular in the 1960's among instructors who were teaching the Chinese language at the college and university level. These teachers were supported by a series of textbooks issued by Yale's Institute of Far Eastern Languages. With increased contact with the People's Republic of China and adoption of the Chinese-language materials published there, however, the *pinyin* system became the preferred romanization system for university instruction.

The *pinyin*, Wade-Giles, *Gwoyeu Romatzyh*, and Yale systems all center on the pronunciation of the official dialect of Chinese known as *putonghua* in mainland China and *kuo-yu* in Taiwan. Because many of the Chinese in the United States are Cantonese speakers or of Cantonese descent—this was overwhelmingly the case in the period before the post-1965 immigration—a question has arisen as to the proper way to transliterate Chinese words, terms, and names in the context of Chinese American history. Some authorities prefer to use the *pinyin* system, for the sake of standardization, while others employ the Yale system for Cantonese romanization, because it more closely reflects the usage of the people whose history is being told.

Chinese Six Companies. *See* **Chinese Consolidated Benevolent Associations**

Chinese Student Protection Act of 1992: Legislation permitting Chinese students and scholars to remain in the United States and apply for permanent residency in the wake of the 1989 TIANANMEN SQUARE INCIDENT.

Following the Chinese government's suppression of the prodemocracy movement in 1989, both houses of the U.S. Congress passed a bill that would have allowed Chinese students and scholars to remain in the United States after the completion of their studies rather than returning to their homeland for at least two years, as required by current immigration law. President George Bush vetoed the bill but, in April, 1990, issued an executive order, to expire at the end of 1993, containing many of the bill's provisions.

While this executive order provided a stopgap, it did not satisfy the students and their advocates. In 1992 a similar bill, sponsored by Senator Slade Gordon, a Republican from the state of Washington, again was passed by both houses. Chinese students and scholars, coordinating their efforts via E-mail, lobbied success-fully for President Bush to sign the bill the second time around.

The result was the Chinese Student Protection Act of 1992. The act allowed Chinese students and scholars who had resided continuously in the United States since April 11, 1990, to apply for permanent residency. About 40,000 students and scholars were potentially eligible for visa adjustment under the bill. Moreover, in its final form the act was broadened considerably to include other categories of legal Chinese immigrants, not just students and scholars.

Chinese students: Chinese have purposefully come to study in the United States since the late 1840's. The United States has been seen as a place where specialized knowledge can be acquired, facilitating personal and national interests. International circumstances, national conditions, local exigencies, and personal motivations have influenced these students' experiences in the United States, their decision whether to return home or not, and their efficacy if they do return home.

Early Experiences: Chinese Students in the Nineteenth Century. During the nineteenth century a small number of students from China sojourned to America for education. As was the case for other Chinese who came to the United States, conditions in China created the impetus for their departure. Unlike the Chinese laborers, who faced animus and violence, the students were warmly received, in part because their numbers were small and in part because they were perceived as desirous of "learning" from the United States. Their experiences differed dramatically from those of most Chinese in the United States in the nineteenth century.

By the 1860's imperialism in China had eaten at the nation to such an extent that some Chinese began to question the value of Chinese traditions. In 1860 the Ziqiang, or Self-Strengthening, movement (SSM) was launched by certain key government officials. The purpose of the SSM was to make China strong enough to counter foreign intrusion effectively and to restore

Chinese Immigration to the U.S., 1981-1991	
China	304,000
Taiwan	131,000*
Hong Kong	73,000

Source: Susan B. Gall and Timothy L. Gall, eds., *Statistical Record of Asian Americans.* Detroit: Gale Research, 1993.

* Excluding 1981 (included in China's count).

what officials believed to be the universal efficacy of Chinese culture and civilization.

Two of the officials most active in promoting the SSM were Li Hongzhang and Zeng Guofan. As a result of their efforts, the Chinese Educational Mission was sent to the United States between 1872 and 1881. Chinese officials hoped that students who were part of the mission would return to China with the necessary skills to strengthen China against imperialism.

Yung Wing, one of the commissioners who accompanied these students, had already studied in the United States. Arriving in Massachusetts in 1847, he entered the Monson Academy, a preparatory school. From 1850 to 1854 he attended Yale College, becoming the first Chinese to receive an American college degree. Yung Wing was very successful at Yale. He won two English composition competitions, secured a stewardship of a boarding club, and became the librarian

for one of the college's debating societies. Eventually he married Louise Kellogue, and while he returned to China to work for change, he eventually returned to the United States to live. He became a large shareholder in the Gatling Gun Factory in Connecticut.

The 120 students who eventually arrived in the United States as part of the Chinese Educational Mission came into such intense contact with American values and habits that their experiences quickly transcended routine education. While they quickly became proficient in English, the students also learned to play the piano, dance, paint with oils, and draw. They played sports and according to contemporary reports became quite good at baseball, football, hockey, and ice skating. According to one contemporary observer, the students did very well socially, mixing easily with their American peers. Similar impressions were part of a report by Li Kwei, one of the Chinese representatives

U.S. colleges and universities have proved to be popular destinations for overseas Chinese eager to get a high quality education in the West. (James L. Shaffer)

to the International Exhibition honoring the centennial birthday of the United States. Li noted how eager the students were to learn and that their English, although they had been in the United States only one year, seemed fluent. He commented that they dressed like Westerners and that they were very confident and comfortable around people of different nationalities. In conclusion, he questioned how much benefit these students would be to China when they returned.

The educational successes of the students were less noteworthy than their social transformation. They progressed slowly through school, and when the mission was recalled in 1882, only two or three had advanced to college. The experiences outside the classroom detracted from time spent studying. Even their Chinese studies suffered, and one observer recorded that they had forgotten their Chinese dialects and had given up their Chinese culture for Christianity. This combination of slow progress and what appeared to be the abandonment of their conservative mission and their heritage helped convince the Chinese government that the mission needed to be recalled.

Fueling the Chinese government's increasing temptation to recall the mission was the harsh treatment of Chinese laborers and the emerging anti-Chinese legislation in the United States. While the students continued to be treated with admiration, respect, and even friendship, violence was endemic toward Chinese laborers. This treatment of Chinese was not lost on Chinese officials in the country, and when Congress passed a bill excluding Chinese from the United States, the Chinese government recalled the mission.

Americans protested the recall. The treatment of Chinese in America, the acculturation that was taking place, and increased concern on the part of the Chinese government about the effects of imperialism in China muffled their voices. After the recall China did not officially send students to the United States until 1909.

The Hiatus, 1881-1909. During this period Western nations and Japan contested with one another for influence, territory, and commerce in China. Globally this was a period of heightened colonialism, and in East and Southeast Asia the French, British, and Japanese contended with one another. Cognizant of this, conservative Chinese officials continued to promote the SSM. They remained wary of sending students to the United States and in fact looked more to Japan as a source of inspiration. Going through its own program of transformation, Japan seemed a more likely place to send students for education. As imperialist powers continued to eat away at China's integrity, many students sailed to Japan. By 1907 approximately ten thousand Chinese students had gone there.

China's humiliating defeat in the Sino-Japanese War of 1894-1895 caused a deeper introspection. This rising tide of concern, combined with an eventual decline in a desire to go to Japan to study, gradually led to a reassessment of study in the United States. Perhaps the main developments affecting the Chinese government's consideration of whether to resume an education exchange were the events following the BOXER REBELLION of 1900. Between 1899-1900 the United States issued what have become known as the Open Door notes. These notes were issued by the United States at a time when foreign powers seemed to be carving up China into "spheres of influence."

While the notes were fundamentally designed to serve the interests of the United States, Chinese saw them as an example of how different the United States was from the other imperialist powers. As this perception emerged, the Boxer Rebellion took place in 1900. In its aftermath treaties were signed with foreign powers. The treaties included an enormous indemnity to be paid by China over a specified period of time.

In 1908 the Congress of the United States decided to remit to China the American portion of the indemnity—a sum in excess of $27 million—on the condition that the money be used to facilitate cultural and educational exchanges between the United States and China. This remittance convinced the Chinese government that the United States was different from the other nations, and beginning the next year, students were to return again to the United States for education. (See BOXER INDEMNITY FELLOWSHIP.)

Chinese Students in America, 1909-1949. Between 1909 and 1950 more than twenty thousand Chinese students came from China to the United States to study. This flow of students resulted in an unprecedented cultural exchange. The lives of most of these students when in the United States was comfortable and their experiences transformative. While they attended colleges and universities throughout the country, they were concentrated on the East and West coasts.

The Chinese students in the United States during these years had their lives profoundly affected. They found the country to be exhilarating and beautiful. Chinese students warmed to their life in the country; they also tended to take their mission seriously. These students often found intellectual life stimulating, and they admired many of their professors. Their faculty members were often described as profound, instilling in students a pride in critical thinking and intellectual

Dental school graduate Faith Sai So Leong, 1905. (Asian American Studies Library, University of California at Berkeley)

Chinese students in New York City, circa 1909-1913. (Library of Congress)

honesty. Most of the Chinese students in the United States at this time maintained the same confidence in their ability as did their predecessors. They believed that it was their responsibility to change China and to build a bridge across the ocean.

Most of the students who visited the United States for education came as self-supporting students, government-sponsored students, BOXER INDEMNITY-sponsored students, or Christian mission-sponsored students. As conditions changed in China, so did the conditions of funding and support, from both the Chinese and the American governments. At times students wishing to travel abroad found new regulations affecting them; these varied depending on their individual status. The outbreak of war in Europe caused students to transfer their study from Europe to the United States and prospective students to cancel their plans or shift their emphasis to America. After the United States entered the war, the Chinese government eased regulations and there was a significant increase in the number of students studying in America.

Life in the United States was a respite from the exigencies and battles that gripped China prior to its liberation in 1949. The experiences of Chinese students in the United States were cushioned culturally by the Chinese Students' Alliance of America. This national organization was founded by students in

Berkeley, Oakland, and San Francisco and initially was designed to pass along news and employment tips. Eventually the organization broke up into regional groups but later reconstituted itself as a national organization. In each instance these organizations helped integrate Chinese into the life of the larger community. They sponsored meetings, cultural events, sporting contests, intellectual presentations, and lectures. Chinese students were often asked to give presentations on events in China and were also in demand to discuss China's cultural history.

While Chinese students obviously enjoyed life in the United States, they also worried about China. Their activities often masked this deep concern and made them vulnerable to criticism. At times critics charged that they were too easily accepting of American customs and habits. Some critics believed that students who visited the United States between 1930 and 1949 were more frivolous than earlier students.

While there was significant disagreement among students in the United States about how to change China, all seemed to agree that individuals had the power to direct the future. Most of these students also believed that education was the key to transforming China and therefore liberating the country from foreign domination. Most of them also argued that Chinese needed a new attitude toward the past, a process by which Western-style democracy could be grafted onto China, and a method that would bring rapid industrialization to the nation.

The U.S.-educated students often returned to China filled with expectations that they would change the nation and direct its destiny. Indeed most of them did return to excellent jobs and came to dominate the education system of China. Yet they also returned to conditions that had frequently worsened during their absence. Additionally, as 1949 neared, civil war gripped the nation and most of these students found themselves at odds at least with the philosophies of both the Nationalist Party headed by CHIANG KAI-SHEK and the Communist Party headed by MAO ZE-DONG. As a result many students' experiences in the United States contributed to their alienation from the political forces driving China into civil war and eventually to the victory of the Chinese Communist Party in 1949. Subsequently many returned to America, where they took up permanent residence and eventually became citizens.

Liberation and Chinese Students After 1949. From 1949 to 1978 Chinese students who arrived in the United States for education came from Taiwan and Hong Kong. International events, Chinese determination to avoid what it perceived to be American global designs, and the growing anticommunism in the United States made it impossible for Chinese from the People's Republic of China (PRC) to come to the United States for education.

The formation of the PRC in 1949 occurred at a time when Chinese student enrollment in American universities and colleges had peaked. Since many of these students were not part of the revolution, they became "stranded" students. Not wishing to return to China and often alienated from the Nationalist government under Chiang Kai-shek, they tended to stay in the United States. The U.S. government provided the legal means, ultimately granting those who wished to stay the right of permanent residence.

Chinese Students from Taiwan and Hong Kong. Since the end of the civil war in China, Chinese students from Taiwan have accounted for the largest percentage of Chinese studying in the United States. Initially, students from Hong Kong and Taiwan came to the United States because the educational infrastructures in their homelands were not well developed. These students believed that their livelihood and success depended on obtaining an education. For some from Taiwan, the idea of helping Taiwan develop as a prelude to recapturing the Chinese mainland served as additional inspiration.

Students from Hong Kong believe that the key to the acquisition of success and wealth requires an advanced degree. While many of them go to Europe to study, North America is an especially attractive place. As the colony of Hong Kong developed economically, so did its education system. Yet despite this development, its universities have been unable to service demand, and thus students have flowed overseas for higher education. Economic success has reinforced the emphasis placed on education by families in Hong Kong.

Students from Hong Kong have tended to be relatively at ease in the United States, in part because of their familiarity with Western culture. Many of them have reasonably well-developed language skills prior to arriving in the United States and are at least familiar with the basics of Western culture. Yet most of them tend to rely on mutual support networks, informal and formal. As a group these students from Hong Kong have tended to be wealthier than students from Taiwan and the PRC.

While the students from Hong Kong tend to be adaptable, they have historically returned to Hong Kong to work and live. Until approximately 1990 Hong Kong had not experienced a "brain drain," in part because its two major universities produce very qualified graduates and because students studying abroad return.

Chinese students from Taiwan, by contrast, have tended to remain in the United States. For at least thirty years this "brain drain" was a source of concern for the Taiwanese government. Subsequently economic success and a successful education system in Taiwan have reduced the tendency of students to remain in the United States after completing their education.

Students from Taiwan have tended to emphasize the professional and technical fields—including engineering, natural sciences, medicine, and business. They have also, to a much lesser degree, studied social sciences, humanities, and fine arts. As with the students from Hong Kong, many of these students have at least a rudimentary knowledge of Western culture and thought. While living in the United States, they mix well with Americans and have some trouble mixing with their counterparts from Hong Kong. Many of these Taiwan Chinese students do not speak the dialect spoken by many from Hong Kong and this affects communication between the two groups. Additionally the historical antagonism between the southern and northern Chinese inhibits communication between the two groups.

Students from Taiwan and Hong Kong have been affected by internal and international demands. Internally, both Hong Kong and Taiwan have looked to these students as the source of development and the future. The students from Taiwan have tended to remain in the United States, but since the development of Taiwan's economy has become so successful, many return home. Students from Hong Kong, however, had returned to a life that they found exhilarating. The anticipated reunification of Hong Kong and the Chinese mainland in 1997, however, has brought a greater desire to leave the colony and take up permanent residence in the United States.

The Change in Policy: PRC Students Return for Education. Following the death of Mao Zedong in 1976 and a power struggle among two factions, China's leadership was in the hands of people who prized economic development and modernization. Foremost among these leaders has been Deng Xiaoping who has stressed the need for China to undergo Four Modernizations. The modernizations include agriculture, industry, defense, and science and technology, and emphasis has been placed on quickly transforming China into a developed country.

Fundamental to the ability to fulfill the goals of the Four Modernizations was a core of highly educated people. China's higher education system was recovering from the ravages of the Great Proletarian Cultural Revolution (1966-1976) and therefore had fallen behind in the latest state of knowledge, pedagogy, and technology. If these institutions were to play the central role in the new drive, they had to be modernized. To do this the government established "key" universities and targeted them for special funding. Additionally, the government came to the conclusion by 1978 that to attain this goal it was necessary to send scholars and students overseas for education.

In the fall of 1978 the government announced its intention of sending approximately ten thousand students overseas over the next two years. The govern-

Scores of Chinese students have immigrated to the United States to receive professional and technical training in such fields as computer science. (James L. Shaffer)

Chinese Students in the U.S., 1991-1992

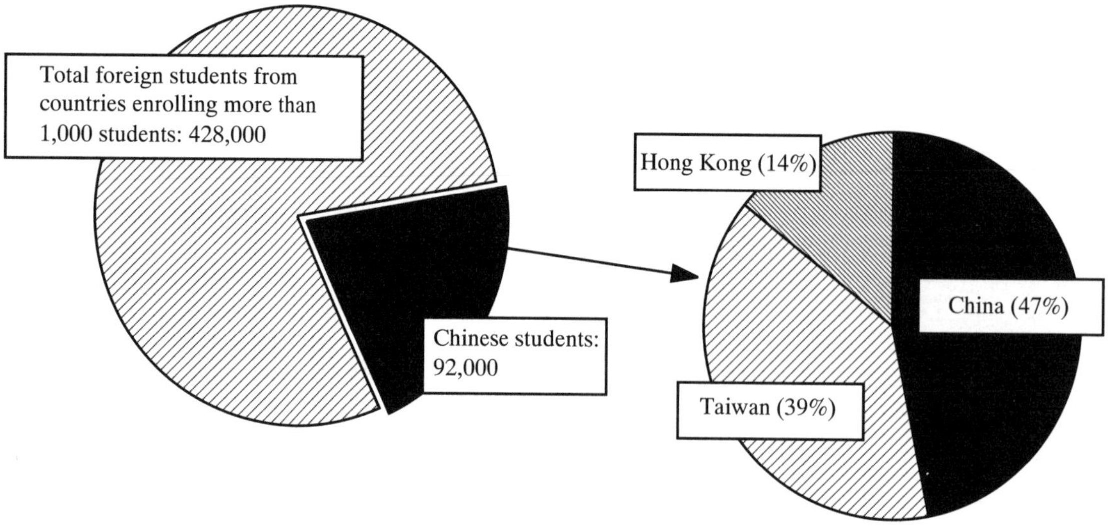

Total foreign students from countries enrolling more than 1,000 students: 428,000

Chinese students: 92,000

Hong Kong (14%)

China (47%)

Taiwan (39%)

Source: *Chronicle of Higher Education Almanac Issue,* August 25, 1993.

ment labeled this a "New Long March," attaching great significance to the process by equating it with the heroic march of the Chinese Communist Party in the mid-1930's. Therefore, with government approval, the president of Beijing University negotiated an agreement with the National Science Foundation to send as many as seven hundred students to the United States.

In exchange for Chinese coming to the United States, select scholars, picked by the Committee on Scholarly Communication with the PRC, would be allowed to go to China to conduct research and study language. The agreement also stipulated that countries sending the students would pay their costs and that both nations would encourage direct contact between universities and individuals in their respective countries. As the agreement was being formalized, the University of California, Berkeley, and Stanford University had worked out agreements with the Chinese. Also, some scholars/students arrived in the United States through private arrangements.

The Chinese who came under the auspices of the Chinese government worked in the technical fields that most closely related to modernization of science and technology. These people tended to be older than Chinese students from Hong Kong and Taiwan, and their presence was overshadowed by the other groups, who in 1979 had well in excess of ten thousand students in the United States. Taiwan students tended to disapprove of their PRC counterparts.

Exchange agreements proliferated, and the number of students in the United States grew rapidly. In the 1980's their ranks included traditional undergraduate and graduate students, those who came to study specific disciplines such as English, and large numbers of scholars doing research or receiving specialized training. The vast majority were in the medical and life sciences, engineering, mathematics, and physical sciences. Many of these students were supported by the Chinese government, and most of the rest were supported either by their host institutions in the United States or by private sources.

As the number of Chinese from the PRC studying in U.S. schools increased, so did the difficulties. The most pressing was the question of a "brain drain." Chinese who came to the United States to study or gain specialized expertise ostensibly did so to help China modernize. As the exchange process matured and more Chinese came to study as self-supporting students, however, a majority decided against returning to China. They did so for a number of reasons, including high-paying jobs in the United States and a fear of returning after the TIANANMEN SQUARE INCIDENT in June, 1989. (See CHINESE STUDENT PROTECTION ACT OF 1992.) The Chinese government expressed concern about this loss of expertise and has made some changes in the regulations affecting overseas education. At the same time the government has allowed for continued study abroad, and the outflow of students has remained relatively stable. While over time the United States has remained the preferred place to study, the percentage of Chinese studying there has declined. Yet this trend reflects government-sponsored students only and does not take into account that the regulations are enforced with varying degrees of strictness.

While the question of the brain drain has concerned the Chinese government, there have been problems for PRC students and scholars in the United States. At times there have been problems in acquiring expertise, especially if that expertise is determined by U.S. government agencies to be "sensitive." There has also been some concern that some universities and colleges promise more than they can deliver because their facilities and faculty may not be sophisticated enough for accomplished scholars or for students in the applied fields. Additionally, Chinese students and scholars have experienced discrimination in the communities where they live. There have been reports of break-ins into their residences, wanton destruction of property, and racist epithets scribbled on doors and walls.

Students from the PRC are often unfamiliar with Western culture and specifically that of the United States. Their English-language skills at times may be problematic. Also they often have much less money than their Taiwan and Hong Kong counterparts.

Conclusion. For most Chinese studying in the United States since 1949, the experience has been productive and has allowed them to acquire an education not easily available in Hong Kong, Taiwan, or the PRC. Their reasons for coming have differed, as has the rate of their return home. The general pattern has been one of success and of receptivity by their American counterparts. While they have had to face much of the discrimination that is often faced by people of color in the United States, their education, hard work, and diligence have made it less virulent. They have made immeasurable contributions to American life and have contributed to a furthering of understanding between Chinese and Americans. As this interaction continues, it should benefit U.S.-China relations and enable Americans to gain a deeper understanding of the people of Taiwan, Hong Kong, and the People's Republic of China.—*Edwin Clausen*

SUGGESTED READINGS:

• Clausen, Edwin. "The Eagle's Shadow: Chinese Nationalism and American Educational Influence, 1900-1927" and "Nationalism and Political Challenge: Chinese Students, American Education and the End of an Era." In "China and the West: Studies in Education, Nationalism, Diplomacy." Special issue of *Asian Profile* (October, 1988): 413-440. These two chapters analyze why Chinese came to the United States and discusses the effect of their experiences on their life and thought.

• Clausen, Edwin. "With Open Arms: Chinese Students and Life in Nineteenth Century American Society." In *Early Chinese Immigrant Societies: Case Studies from North America and British Southeast Asia*, edited by Lee Lai To. Singapore: Heinemann, 1988. This chapter presents an interpretative overview of the life and experiences of Chinese students in the United States during the nineteenth century. The author has written extensively on the subject.

• Kung, S. W. *Chinese in American Life: Some Aspects of Their History, Status, Problems, and Contributions*. Westport, Conn.: Greenwood Press, 1962. Solid analysis of the complexity of the Chinese experience in the United States. The book contains excellent sections on Chinese contributions to the United States.

• Lee, Rose Hum. *The Chinese in the United States of America*. Hong Kong: Hong Kong University Press, 1960. Basic study of the Chinese in America, full of useful data.

• Leung, Edwin Pak-wah. "The Making of the Chinese Yankees: School Life of the Chinese Educational Mission Students in New England." "China and the West: Studies in Education, Nationalism, and Diplomacy." Special issue of *Asian Profile* 16 (October, 1988): 401-412. Excellent article discussing the experiences of the students who were part of the Chinese Educational Mission in the nineteenth century.

• Orleans, Leo. *Chinese Students in America: Policies, Issues, and Numbers*. Washington, D.C.: National Academy Press, 1988. An essential study for any attempt to understand the Chinese students from the PRC and the issues involved. The author is a noted specialist in the field.

• Pepper, Suzanne. *China's Education Reform in the 1980s: Policies, Issues, and History*. Berkeley: Center for Chinese Studies, 1990. Seminal study for understanding the return of Chinese students from the PRC to the United States for education. The volume is written by one of the field's most respected scholars.

• Wang, Y. C. *Chinese Intellectuals and the West, 1872-1949*. Chapel Hill: University of North Carolina Press, 1966. The one volume presenting an excellent study of the effect of the West upon Chinese intellectuals, including students who traveled overseas for education. Packed with information and data, it is also a highly interpretive study.

Chinese Students Monthly (*Zhongguo Liu-Mei Xue-sheng Yuebao*): English-language monthly magazine founded in 1905 as a mimeographed publication, *Chinese Students' Bulletin*, serving as the organ for the Chinese Students' Alliance of Eastern States, U.S.A. V. K. Wellington Koo, later to be a diplomat in China but then a student attending Columbia University, was the editor. As the publication grew in popularity and usefulness as a medium for promoting fellowship among Chinese students, it changed to magazine format in 1906. In 1907 the name was changed to *Chinese Students' Monthly*. In 1911 it became the official publication of the enlarged student organization, the Chinese Students' Alliance in the United States of America. In its two and a half decades of existence, the publication went from a few typewritten pages to one hundred or more typeset pages. From a publication devoted almost entirely to activities of the student world it developed into one that included in its discussions all the important developments and movements in China. Contributors included not only students but also distinguished Chinese and Americans. Between 1927 and 1931, the left-right conflict in the Guomindang in China became reflected in a sustained struggle for control of the Chinese Students' Alliance and the *Chinese Students' Monthly* carried on by supporters of the two factions among the students. Although the more conservative students prevailed in the end, the struggle so demoralized the organization that the *Chinese Students' Monthly* suspended publication in 1931.

Chinese temples in California: Religious places of worship established in California as early as the 1850's as an integral part of society for the first wave of Chinese sojourners and subsequent emigrants to the West Coast.

Following news in China of the California gold rush in 1849, the number of Chinese travelers to the West Coast soared dramatically (more than twenty thousand in 1852). As a result closeknit communities with strong ties to family, tradition, and religion were formed. The first temples were founded from the 1850's to 1880's in major settlements throughout California including San Francisco, Weaverville, Oroville, and Marysville. Historical evidence shows that temples were also built in the towns of Coloma, Monterey, Mendocino, San Jose, Hanford, Newscastle, Grass Valley, and Sacramento as well as further south in Bakersfield and Los Angeles.

For the most part the temple was a room or cluster of rooms within an established association hall. This was typical of urban settings such as San Francisco or San Jose, where the temple was built above a meeting hall, sometimes as high as three stories above the ground, economizing on available space and providing both spiritual sanctity and protection from harassment. In more rural settings such as Marysville, Oroville, and Weaverville, the temple was built as a freestanding one or two-story building that expanded horizontally and thus more closely mimicked the traditional Chinese model of architectural style used for palaces, temples, and homes. The extended compound was greatly abbreviated in California, however, often without an interior open space or courtyard.

Temples were built with community contributions and could take care of all the needs of the community, although where there was a choice, different clans might have supported one place of worship over another.

Within the community, temples functioned much like small businesses, returning to local merchants a significant portion of what was collected for their services. According to the BOK KAI TEMPLE records in Marysville dating to the 1880's, temple expenses and activities fell into several categories: the cost of deity statues and interior furnishings, priestly functions, festival gifts, food and firecrackers, and ceremonial dragons and costumes. Other expenses included temple construction and repair, loans to local merchants, labor fees (temple construction and parade participants), taxes, insurance, and charitable donations. Income was generated by the sale of firecrackers, by leasing the post of temple keeper, and by the sale of religious books.

The temples with the longest continuous records of worship are located in San Francisco, the dominant center of Chinese activity since the gold rush. The Tin Hou (c. 1852) and Kong Chow (c. 1853) temples, both rebuilt after the 1906 earthquake, still operate today with strong followings and honor the deities Tin Hou (*pinyin* Tianhou, empress of heaven) and Guangong (god of war), respectively, two of the best known deities in Chinese folk religion. Tianhou, protectress of the seas, is widely worshiped by seafaring communities in China and was probably favored by the Chinese in California because of the dangerous sea passage to the United States. Guangong, the patron god of soldiers and literature, was believed to grant riches to the fortune hunter, which undoubtedly had a special appeal to the Chinese miners.

Most California temples were of the "general type," where, in addition to the host deity, the worshiper finds a cluster of secondary deities and spirits that oversee all aspects of daily life. There were gods of marriage and fertility, deities of justice, moral authorities, patrons of crafts and trades, guardians of health, and ghost quellers. The kinds of divinities reflected those worshiped in Guangdong Province, from which most emigrants came. A striking omission was the absence of the cult of Confucius. Indeed few members of the scholar-official class, the primary constituency of Confucian temples, came to California to seek their fortunes, and nothing in the early social climate of California fostered the development of an indigenous gentry class. Instead traditional hero cults were left to dominate popular religious culture. (See CHINESE POPULAR RELIGION.)

Though faced with limited resources and time and a shortage of traditional artisans, early Chinese sojourners managed to furnish temples that preserved intact the religious and symbolic imagery of their homeland. Temples were filled with sophisticated examples of religious art—not only statues of gods but also tapestries, altar tables, wall plaques, and elaborate trelliswork panels and gilded paintings, most of which were imported from workshops in China. The ornamental embellishment decorating the pieces conveyed symbolically auspicious wishes for longevity and prosperity,

the triumph of good over evil, and the time-honored values of loyalty and virtue.

Such religious furnishings and paintings can be viewed in extant temples in northern California such as the Wom-Lim Miao (1874) in Weaverville, Bok Kai (1880) in Marysville, and Liet Sheng Kong (1863) in Oroville as well as the Tin Hou and Kong Chow temples in San Francisco. No new temples have been built in the style of the earlier rural constructions, but traditional religious and festival practices still dominate contemporary Chinese communities, with occasional new Buddhist and Daoist shrines (as seen in San Francisco) receiving steady local economic and spiritual support.

Chinese Times: Chinese-language daily newspaper first published in 1924, in San Francisco, California. Serving initially as the official publication of the CHINESE AMERICAN CITIZENS ALLIANCE (CACA), the paper exposed anti-Chinese practices, encouraged Chinese Americans to exercise their right to vote, and covered community news that mainstream newspapers had neglected. Dominated for many years by Walter U. Lum, the paper was a significant voice in the Chinese

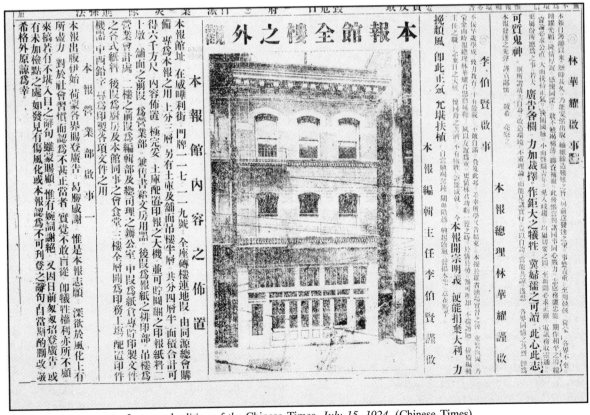

Inaugural edition of the Chinese Times, *July 15, 1924.* (Chinese Times)

American community. In the 1980's, however, its inability to compete with the well-financed *Sing Tao Jih Pao* and *World Journal*, headquartered in Hong Kong and Taiwan, respectively, coupled with escalating costs, led to declining circulation and profits. The paper was sold in 1988, and is no longer affiliated with the CACA.

Chinese United League. *See* **Tongmenghui**

Chinese vegetable farms: These establishments preceded the development of the California agricultural industry and arose in mining counties and developing urban centers. The farms assisted in supplying the needs of the state's growing population in the nineteenth century. Chinese farmers grew asparagus, cabbages, lettuce, onions, potatoes, sugar beets, and other fresh vegetables.

Chinese Workers' Mutual Aid Association: Political organization established in 1937 to promote labor unionism and to attack the feudalistic working conditions in San Francisco's Chinatown. Inspired by the teachings of Karl Marx, the association offered lectures on the labor movement, held regular meetings to address workers' concerns, and was the first to print the essays of Mao Zedong in the United States. The association dissolved in 1956.

Chinese World: Chinese newspaper based in San Francisco, beginning publication as *Mon Hing Bo* in 1891. At the turn of the century, it became an organ of Kang Youwei's Chinese Empire Reform Association (later the Constitutionalist Party; see BAOHUANGHUI), changing its name to *Chinese World* around 1907. After a period of decline, the paper was revived in 1945 when it was purchased by C. Q. Yee Hop (born CHUN QUON), a wealthy entrepreneur. During most of the postwar era, the paper was dominated by editor Dai Ming Lee, who boosted circulation in the immediate postwar years with sharp right-wing criticism of the GUOMINDANG (GMD), at times in the face of GMD threats. The paper added an English section in 1949. In 1969, after a long period during which the Hop family had subsidized the paper to make up continued losses, the *Chinese World* ceased publication.

Chinese Youth Magazine (*Huaqiao Qingnian*): Bilingual magazine founded in 1938 by the Chinese Youth Club (Niuyue Huaqiao Qingnian Jiuguo Tuan, Overseas Chinese Youth National Salvation League of New York City). The club, a progressive organization linked with the CHINESE HAND LAUNDRY ALLIANCE and the *CHINA DAILY NEWS,* had just been established in March of the same year. The magazine was part of its effort to reach the public, especially the youth, with the primary objectives being backing for China's resistance against Japanese aggression and improving the quality of life for Chinese American youth. Besides articles exhorting support for China's struggle, the publication included reports on youth activities in the United States and Canada, discussions of youth problems, and poems and short stories by young Chinese American writers. The magazine was an annual publication. It appears to have ceased as a separate publication after three issues, in 1941, when the *China Daily News* gave the club a full page for publication of a monthly *Chinese Youth Monthly* (*Huaqiao Qingnian Yuekan*).

Chinese zodiac: A series of twelve animal signs represented in the Chinese lunar calendar. (See CHINESE CALENDAR.) The Chinese calendar year consists of approximately twelve full lunar cycles, or about twelve months. Months are often popularly referred to according to a series of twelve animal names that since antiquity have been associated with years and even hours of the day. The Chinese animal cycle begins with the rat, followed by the ox, tiger, hare, dragon, serpent, horse, ram, monkey, rooster, dog, and pig.

Many stories have arisen to explain how the cycle originated. One tale, for example, explains why there are only twelve animals and why the rat was included but not the cat. One day the Jade Emperor invited all the animals to attend a birthday celebration in his honor. On the way to the party the rat saw the cat, apparently headed to the same place and running very fast. This worried the rat, who was afraid of being late. So it told the cat the wrong arrival time for the emperor's celebration. Subsequently the rat arrived first, followed by the ox, the tiger, and so forth. By the time the party began, only twelve animals had arrived. The emperor was so happy that he named a year after each one of these animals. The cat, however, got there late and so did not receive this honor. In its anger the cat vowed to kill all rats; even today its descendants continue that promise to kill rats generation after generation.

Associated with folklore and practice, the twelve signs were incorporated into the Chinese horoscope. A person's personality and fate, it was said, could be determined according to which sign he or she was born under. One born in the Year of the Dragon, for example, is supposed to be generous, determined, and decisive. This individual is sensitive and will be a good leader; he or she should marry someone born in the Year of the Rat, Serpent, Monkey, or Rooster but should avoid anyone born in the Year of the Ox, Hare, or Dog. Charts and books are published that illustrate the full range of these horoscopes and the corresponding personality traits associated with each animal. Such items can usually be found in Chinatowns. Whether or not one believes in the Chinese zodiac, the fun of predicting one's personality and future has remained in the heart of Chinese culture.

Ching, Hung Wai: Civic leader. A successful real estate broker after World War II, Ching is remembered for his staunch support of the Japanese in Hawaii in the face of wartime hysteria.

Of Chinese ancestry, Ching was raised in a poor section of Oahu, Hawaii, and graduated with the Class of 1924 of McKinley High School, a public school known for its prominent graduates. After graduating from the University of Hawaii, Ching went to Yale. He returned to work for the Young Men's Christian Association (YMCA), serving as executive secretary of the University of Hawaii YMCA branch from 1938 to 1941.

Soon after Pearl Harbor was attacked by Japan, Ching and two others were asked to head the Morale Section of the Office of the Military Governor. A task of the unit was to maintain peaceful relations among the various ethnic groups. As trusted advisor to the Federal Bureau of Investigation (FBI) and the Military Governor, Ching unwaveringly stood up for the loyalty of the Japanese Americans.

In January, 1942, all those of Japanese ancestry were discharged from the Hawaii Territorial Guard. Many were university students Ching knew. He suggested that these individuals take positive action. With his encouragement the young men petitioned the Military Governor to accept them for noncombat labor. The result was the formation of the VARSITY VICTORY VOLUNTEERS (VVV). When Assistant Secretary of War John J. McCloy visited Hawaii and saw the VVV at work, Ching took the opportunity to impress on the secretary that the Japanese Americans could be trusted even in the Army. Eventually Japanese Americans were accepted for combat duty.

In May, 1943, Ching met with President and Mrs. Franklin D. Roosevelt and reiterated his support of the Japanese in Hawaii. Ching also went to CAMP SHELBY, Mississippi, to try to mollify the antipathy of the local people toward the 442ND REGIMENTAL COMBAT TEAM sent there for training. Back in Hawaii, Ching spoke to many civic groups, asking them to treat the Japanese American soldiers like American citizens when they returned from the war.

Chinh, Kieu (b. late 1930's): Actor. Chinh, a Vietnamese American, became better known to American audiences following her strong supporting role in *The Joy Luck Club*, one of the most critically acclaimed and commercially successful films of 1993. Before immigrating to the United States, she had spent much of her life in her native Hanoi, in northern Vietnam. She was forced to flee south to Saigon following the country's partition into North and South Vietnam in 1954. During the escape, she managed to get aboard a departing flight, but her father and brother remained behind. She was never to see them again.

In Saigon Chinh lived with a family, attended a Catholic school, and married. At age seventeen she was asked to audition for a role in an American film but turned it down. Subsequently, however, she was cast in one of the first Vietnamese films ever made. As her popularity grew, major roles in many more pictures followed, including the Hollywood productions *A Yank in Vietnam* (1964) and *Operation C.I.A.* (1965). She hosted a television talk show and continued to appear in films on locations all across Asia. By the late 1960's Chinh had become the most famous female film star in Southeast Asia. At the Asian Film Festival of 1972, she was voted the most popular actress in all of Asia.

Chinh fled Saigon following the Communist takeover of the city in April of 1975. Settling in Southern California, she worked as a translator for the Catholic Relief Services and took bit parts in various productions, hoping to revive her acting career. Sometime in 1987 she quit her job to devote herself fully to acting. In 1989 Chinh was cast in *Welcome Home* and *Vietnam, Texas*, two feature films with Vietnamese themes. For a time she was also attached to the popular ABC television series *China Beach*.

Chinmok-hoe (Friendship Society): First Korean social organization in the United States, formed in San Francisco in 1903. The group was established by political activist Ahn Chang-ho as a means of promoting and protecting the interests of Koreans in America.

Chinn, Thomas Wayne (b. July 28, 1909, Marshfield, Oreg.): Businessperson, publisher, and editor. He

Thomas Chinn founded the Chinese Digest—*the first English-language weekly newspaper in the continental United States for and by second-generation Chinese Americans.* (Asian Week)

moved to San Francisco, California, in 1919 and later served as president of his own firm, Gollan Typography, until his retirement in 1980. He was the founder/editor/publisher of *Chinese News* and CHINESE DIGEST, the first English-language weekly newspaper for Chinese Americans. He was also the primary founder, and later president, of the CHINESE HISTORICAL SOCIETY OF AMERICA (CHSA). In 1989 he published his first book, *Bridging the Pacific: San Francisco Chinatown and Its People.*

Cho, Henry (b. 1962, Knoxville, Tenn.): Comedian and actor. A Korean American, he has been doing stand-up comedy since 1986. Much of his material comes from his childhood experiences as an Asian American in the South. As an actor he has been cast in film and television roles.

Chock, Eric (b. 1950): Poet. A cofounder of BAMBOO RIDGE: THE HAWAII WRITERS' QUARTERLY, Chock has con-

tributed to the growing recognition of the distinctive "local literature" of Hawaii. Educated at the University of Pennsylvania (B.A.) and the University of Hawaii (M.A.), he is the program coordinator for the Hawaii Poets in the Schools program in Honolulu. His first book of poems, *Last Days Here*, was published in 1990.

Chonan: Oldest son in a Japanese family. Japanese families are patrilineal; that is, inheritance is passed from father to oldest son.

Chondogyo. *See* **Tonghak movement**

Chop suey: Chinese-style dish made up of various foods such as bean sprouts, bamboo shoots, onions, mushrooms, water chestnuts, and other vegetables. Meat, such as chicken or pork, or fish is added to the whole mixture, which is then served with rice and soy sauce. The name "chop suey" is of Cantonese origin, *shap sui* (*tsa sui* in Mandarin), which may be translated loosely as "miscellaneous bits" or "odds and ends."

Chop suey has long been a staple item of Chinese American restaurants. The majority of the first Chinese immigrants to America came from Guangdong and Fujian provinces of China. They brought with them many of their native traditions, including those pertaining to food; among the latter was the popular meal chop suey. Among these early settlers there were very few women, and the men, with little cooking experience, were forced to fend for themselves if they wanted Chinese food. Moreover the long hours spent working left these laborers no time to prepare elaborate dishes. It was therefore more convenient and relatively easy for them to depend on chop suey, with its variety of vegetables.

Before chop suey became a restaurant item, it was regarded as a dish made up principally of leftovers—people at home simply threw into the pot whatever vegetables and meats were available. Yet however it is modified nowadays, chop suey continues to be popular among the Chinese. Generally speaking, it is a menu item only in those Chinese restaurants in the vicinity of a Chinese community; it is mostly Chinese patrons who order that dish. Also, since it consists chiefly of vegetables (meat is usually preferred over fish, perhaps because of all the bones), it is inexpensive.

Choson: Korea under Japanese colonial rule, from 1910 to 1945. On August 22, 1910, the signing of the

Treaty of Annexation between Japan and Choson Korea terminated the Yi dynasty's rule (1392-1910) and inaugurated Japanese rule. ("Chosen" is the Japanese pronunciation for "Choson.") Korea became a colony of Japan, administered by a military governor-general in Seoul from October 5, 1910, to August 15, 1945. The governor-general had full authority over Korea, issuing ordinances and mobilizing the Japanese troops.

Life Under the Military Regime. Japan's major aim during the period of colonial rule was to secure the economic and strategic interests of the empire, and it did not hesitate to employ oppressive measures to obtain its objective. Korea suffered from Japan's political suppression, social discrimination, and economic exploitation.

At the beginning Japan encountered strong protests and armed resistance by the Korean people, including royalists, unemployed soldiers, and intellectuals. The active leaders who rejected Japan's rule included An Ch'ang-ho and Syngman RHEE. General Terauchi Masatake, the first governor-general, suppressed the Korean resistors by employing the tyrannical system of *Kempei* (military police) and by enforcing oppressive laws and ordinances. The Koreans were completely deprived of their freedom of assembly, speech, and the press. The Koreans were discriminated against by the Japanese in the government and industries. For example the Japanese monopolized the upper bureaucracy of the government, while the Koreans were given low clerical positions. The Koreans were excluded from managerial positions and were paid lower wages than those received by their Japanese counterparts.

In order to exploit Korea and meet the economic demands of the empire, Japan developed transportation, telecommunications, hydroelectric power, and mines. Mines provided the Japanese industries with raw materials. Japan also developed chemical and machine manufacturing plants, taking advantage of available cheap labor. In order to compensate for Japan's food shortage, Japan increased its rice production in Korea. Korean farmers were forced to turn their dry fields into rice paddies. By the 1930's about 50 percent of the rice crop was shipped to Japan, leaving not enough rice for the Koreans. As a result many Koreans suffered from starvation and malnutrition. Furthermore Japan forced thousands of Korean landowners to sell their farmlands at nominal prices and allowed Japanese families to resettle on the lands. In desperation many Korean farmers emigrated to Manchuria, Siberia, or Japan in search of new jobs.

Kyongbokkung Palace in Seoul was built in 1395 by King Taejo, founder of the Choson Kingdom. It comprises large and impressive buildings, several charming pavilions, and elegantly landscaped grounds.

In an attempt to annihilate Korean national consciousness, Japan banned the teaching of Korean history. In order to train government servants, Japan established "ordinary schools," the equivalent of elementary schools in the United States.

Push for Independence. Korean resentment of Japan's exploitation and oppressive rule culminated in the nationwide independence movement known as the March First movement. Korean leaders organized a rally in Seoul on March 1, 1919, to proclaim a "Declaration of Independence." Thousands of Koreans throughout the country took part in the street demonstrations, shouting their demands for independence. They were, however, brutally suppressed by the *Kempei*. Some seventy-five hundred Koreans were killed, sixteen thousand were wounded, and more than two thousand were imprisoned. The March First movement failed, but the push for independence continued outside Korea. In April, 1919, the exiled Korean leaders established, in Shanghai, a provisional government with Rhee as its first president. The leaders of the provisional government split into several factions, and as a result the provisional government became inactive until 1940.

Following the Japanese invasion of Manchuria (1931) and the outbreak of both the Sino-Japanese War (1937-1945) and World War II (1939-1945), Japan transformed Korea into an important economic and military base to carry out its own continental expansion program. Japan expanded its heavy industries, especially its armaments production in Korea. At the same time Japan accelerated its Japanization programs and intensified its oppressive measures in Korea. In 1937 Japan suppressed freedom of religion, forcing the Koreans to worship Japanese Shinto deities at Shinto shrines. Korean-language programs were banned from the high school curricula in 1938 and from elementary school curricula in 1943. The Koreans were forced to adopt Japanese names.

In 1939 the Koreans were conscripted to work in mines, factories, and military bases. As of August, 1945, about four million workers would be assigned to work in Korea and more than one million to work in Japan. During World War II thousands of Korean youths were drafted into the Japanese military.

Declaration of War. In 1940 the Korean provisional government was reactivated in Chungking, China, with Kim Ku as its chairman. In February, 1945, the provisional government declared war on Japan, and about five thousand of its troops joined the Allied forces to fight the Japanese in China. In the United States a number of Korean Americans volunteered to join the U.S. armed forces to fight Japan in the Pacific. On August 15, 1945, when Japan surrendered, Korea was liberated from Japan by the Allies. The country was, however, divided along the 38th parallel and was occupied by Soviet troops in the north and U.S. troops in the south. In 1948 two independent states were created in the divided country: the Democratic People's Republic of Korea in the north (North Korea) and the Republic of Korea in the south (South Korea).—*Won Z. Yoon.*

SUGGESTED READINGS: • Conroy, Hilary. *The Japanese Seizure of Korea, 1868-1910: A Study of Realism and Idealism in International Relations.* Philadelphia: University of Pennsylvania Press, 1960. • Kwon, Ik Whan. "Japanese Agricultural Policy on Korea; 1910-1945." *Koreana Quarterly* 7 (Autumn, 1965): 96-112. • Kwon, Ik Whan. "Japanese Industrialization in Korea, 1930-1945: Idealism or Realism?" *Koreana Quarterly* 8 (Summer, 1966): 80-95. • Lee, Chong-sik. *The Politics of Korean Nationalism.* Berkeley: University of California Press, 1963. • McKenzie, Frederick A. *Korea's Fight for Freedom.* New York: Fleming H. Revell, 1920. • Nahm, Andrew C., ed. *Korea Under Japanese Colonial Rule: Studies of the Policy and Techniques of Japanese Colonialism.* Kalamazoo: Center for Korean Studies, Western Michigan University, 1973. • Oliver, Robert T. *Korea: Forgotten Nation.* Washington: Public Affairs Press, 1944.

Chou, Wen-chung (b. June 28, 1923, Chefu, China): Composer. Chou came to the United States in 1946 and was naturalized in 1958. From 1946 until 1949 he attended the New England Conservatory of Music, receiving an M.A. degree from Columbia University in 1954. A variety of teaching posts followed and he began teaching music at Columbia in 1964; he was named Fritz Reiner Professor of Music Composition in 1984. His many works have been performed in major cities across the United States, and he has been honored by the Rockefeller Foundation, the National Institute of Arts and Letters, and the National Endowment for the Arts (NEA), among others.

Choy, Christine (b. Sept. 17, 1953, Shanghai, People's Republic of China): Filmmaker. Choy was born to a Mongolian mother and a Korean father. She lived in Korea until she was sixteen, when she immigrated to the United States. She was graduated from Princeton University with a degree in architecture and went on to earn a master's degree in urban planning from

Christine Choy. Her documentary Who Killed Vincent Chin?, *made with Renee Tajima, received an Academy Award nomination.* (Christine Choy)

Columbia University. In the early 1970's, she developed her filmmaking skills as a member of Newsreel, a group of socially conscious filmmakers based in New York.

Choy has made more than thirty films and videos. While she has dealt specifically with Asian themes, her works have addressed a diverse range of topics, and many of them focus on the experiences of women and racial and ethnic communities in the United States. She has often worked in collaboration with other filmmakers.

Choy's documentary productions include *From Spikes Spindles* (1976), about New York's Chinatown; *Inside Women Inside* (1978), about the prison system; *People's Firehouse* (1979), about the Polish American community in Brooklyn; *To Love, Honor, and Obey* (1980), about domestic violence; and *Mississippi Triangle* (1983), an examination of the relationship between the African American and Chinese American communities of the Mississippi Delta. In addition, Choy has made the dramatic films *Fei Ten, Goddess in Flight* (1983) and *Money King Looks West* (1985), about the Chinese opera.

One of her better-known works is *Who Killed Vincent Chin?* (1988), a complex documentary about the murder of a Chinese American man by two Detroit auto workers. Made with Renee TAJIMA, the film was widely praised and received an Academy Award nomination. In 1991, Choy paired up with J. T. Takagi to produce *Homes Apart: The Two Koreas*, which explores the division of the country into North and South and its significance for the Korean American community.

In addition to film production, Choy has been active in the formation of Asian American media, helping to establish Third World Newsreel, ASIAN CINEVISION, and the NATIONAL ASIAN AMERICAN TELECOMMUNICATIONS ASSOCIATION. She is an associate professor of film and television at New York University.

Choy, Curtis (b. 1951, San Francisco, Calif.): Producer. Educated at San Francisco State University and Westminster College (Missouri), in 1973 he founded Chonk Moonhunter, a production company specializing in Asian American images. In addition to producing films, he has worked in film as a sound-effects specialist in *Year of the Dragon* (1985) and as a production mixer in *Dim Sum* (1984), *Chan Is Missing* (1982), and *The Joy Luck Club* (1993).

Choy, Herbert Young Cho (b. Jan. 6, 1916, Hakaweli, Territory of Hawaii): Judge. Son of a Korean father who had emigrated to Hawaii as a laborer, Choy grew up in Honolulu. He attended the University of Hawaii and graduated with a B.A. degree in 1938. Upon graduation, Choy was accepted as a student at Harvard Law School, where he received his J.D. degree in 1941. He returned to Hawaii and passed the bar examination in 1941. During World War II, Choy joined the U.S. Army and served from 1942 to 1946. Once the war ended, he returned to Honolulu and went into private practice as a lawyer. He was appointed to serve as attorney general for the Territory from 1957 to 1958, when he returned to private practice. In 1971, President Richard M. Nixon appointed Choy to serve as a federal judge on the Ninth Circuit of the U.S. Court of Appeals in Honolulu. With this appointment, Choy became the first Asian American to serve as a U.S. federal court judge.

Philip Choy. (Asian Week)

Choy, Philip (b. Dec. 17, 1926, San Francisco, Calif.): Architect. One of the first Chinese Americans to teach Chinese American history in the United States, he served two terms as president of the Chinese Historical Society of America (CHSA) and participated in the restoration of the ANGEL ISLAND IMMIGRATION STATION in San Francisco Bay. He coauthored, with H. Mark LAI, *Outlines: History of the Chinese in America* (1973), and was assistant editor of *A History of the Chinese in California* (1969).

Christian Society for the Realization of Justice: Founded by Kim Sang-don and the Reverend Kim Chaichoon in Los Angeles in January, 1976, for overseas Korean Christians. It advocates human rights, opposes totalitarian rule, and works toward the betterment of the Korean community in the United States.

Chu, Judy M. (b. July 7, 1953, Los Angeles, Calif.): Politician. City council member and former mayor of

Judy Chu. (Asian Week)

Monterey Park, California, she helped bridge the gap among the city's different ethnic groups during the "English Only" movement in the late 1980's. She started a city-sponsored after-school child care program and the Asian Youth Center; served on the board of the Garvey (California) School District; and coauthored *Linking Our Lives: Chinese American Women of Los Angeles* (1984).

Chu, Louis H. (Oct. 1, 1915, Toishan, China—Feb. 27, 1970, Queens, N.Y. Novelist and social worker. His *Eat a Bowl of Tea* (1961) was the first Chinese American novel accurately to portray the Chinatown "bachelor societies," the pre-World War II communities of immigrant men forced by the United States' laws to leave their wives and children in China.

Chu immigrated to Newark, New Jersey, in 1924. He received a B.A. in English from Upsala College in 1937, an M.A. in sociology from New York University in 1940, and postgraduate training at the New School for Social Research from 1950-1952. In 1940, he married Kang Wong, with whom he later had four children. He served in the U.S. Army Signal Corps during World War II.

Chu was a well-known figure in New York's Chinatown, where he acted as director of the Golden Age Club, a day center for the elderly funded by New York City's Department of Social Welfare. He hosted a radio program entitled "Chinese Festival," which aired four nights per week on WHOM radio between 1951 and 1961. He also served as the executive secretary of the Soo Yuen Benevolent Association.

Eat a Bowl of Tea, which takes place in New York's Chinatown during the 1940's, depicts the evolution of Chinese American culture from the bachelor society of the early immigrants to the family-centered society that evolved after World War II. Chu's other known work of fiction is the posthumously published short story "Bewildered," the tale of a recent arrival's experiences with the U.S. immigration services, which appeared in the Asian American journal *East Wind* (1982).

When it first appeared in 1961, *Eat a Bowl of Tea* was attacked in the general press as weak in its structure and character development and vulgar in its language. The first edition had still not sold out when Chu died in 1970. Since its republication in 1979 with an introduction by Jeffery CHAN, literary scholars have come to appreciate the novel's honest, realistic, yet compassionate portrayal of Chinatown's bachelor society and the author's lively and accurate translation of colloquial Cantonese speech.

Chu, Paul Ching-Wu (b. Dec. 2, 1941, Hunan, China): Physicist and educator. After completing his undergraduate degree at Cheng-Kung University in Taiwan, Chu emigrated to the United States in 1963 to begin a master's degree program at Fordham University in New York. He completed that degree in 1965 and went on to earn his Ph.D. degree at the University of California, San Diego, in 1968. Upon graduation, Chu joined the technical staff at Bell Laboratories in New Jersey. He left Bell Labs in 1970 to accept a teaching post in the physics department at Cleveland State University. In 1973, he became a naturalized citizen. The University of Houston offered Chu a teaching post in 1979, and he went on to become director of the school's magnetic information research lab in 1984. Building on materials science research pioneered by Nobel Prize-winning scientists at International Business Machines (IBM), Chu developed a ceramic compound based on an yttrium-barium-copper oxide molecule ($YBa_2Cu_3O_7$) that was capable of conducting electricity with no resistance at a higher temperature than ever before achieved. His new superconductor operated under cryogenic conditions that could be produced using liquid nitrogen, an inexpensive, safe, and readily available coolant. Within months of his discovery, Chu became a scientific celebrity who was showered with numerous honorary degrees and awards and was elected to the prestigious National Academy of Sciences as well as the American Academy of Arts and Sciences. Efforts by corporate research facilities and prestigious universities to lure Chu to work for them failed, largely because Chu felt compelled to obey his traditional Chinese sense of loyalty by honoring his professional commitments to the university that had generously supported his research. In recognition of his achievements, the University of Houston established the Texas Center for Superconductivity, a multimillion-dollar research complex headed by Chu that was designed to support greater experimental research and expand the commercial applications of superconducting materials.

Chuck, Maurice H. (b. Oct. 5, 1931, Guangdong Province, China): Publisher. President/chief executive officer of the Chinese Journal Corporation in San Francisco, California, he was the founder/publisher/editor-in-chief of the *San Francisco Journal*, a bilingual weekly community newspaper that started in 1972 and became a daily in 1983. Staffed with volunteer writers, it was the first community paper openly to support normalization between the People's Republic

Maurice Chuck in the pressroom of his printing company. (San Francisco Chronicle)

of China and the United States. Competition with other Chinese-language newspapers forced the paper to cease publication in 1986.

Chun Doo Hwan (b. Jan. 18, 1931, Naechonri, Korea): South Korean president. After Park Chung Hee's assassination in 1979, he seized the presidency from the prime minister through a military coup. Immediately lifting martial law, he instituted a law prohibiting future presidents from seeking a second term beyond the seven-year presidency period. Under this constitution he was elected president of the Fifth Republic of Korea in 1981. During his single term South Korea hosted the 1988 Olympics. Continued absence of reforms for direct democratic elections resulted in mass demonstrations in 1987.

Chun Quon (C. Q. Yee Hop; Sept. 16, 1867, Gangbei Guangdong Province, China—Aug. 11, 1953, Hono-

lulu, Territory of Hawaii): Businessman. Chun was the oldest son in a peasant family. After four years at the village school, he left to help in his father's firewood shop. In 1885 he left for Hawaii. Since at that time there was no direct passage between Hong Kong and Hawaii, he landed in San Francisco. With only ninety cents in Hong Kong money in his pocket, he worked for three weeks at fellow clansman Chun Tim's fruit farm at Suisun while awaiting passage to Honolulu.

After landing in Honolulu, Chun worked at a meat market. In 1887 he struck out for himself, founding Yee Hop meat market in Chinatown. Lum Hop joined him as partner in 1888, and the two worked at the business for twelve years until the 1900 Chinatown fire forced a temporary closure.

In 1902, Chun, Lum, and six others invested $8,000 to expand the enterprise. To avoid confusion with another store of the same name, Chun's initials were added to change the name to C. Q. Yee Hop. In 1912 eight more partners added another $8,000 capital. In 1920 the partnership was incorporated. By the 1940's its assets, most of it in real estate, totaled more than $1 million.

Chun engaged in numerous enterprises. In 1907 he began managing King Market and made it profitable. He purchased twenty-five thousand acres at Kona, Hawaii, for a ranch to supply meat to C. Q. Yee Hop, but it could supply only a small part of the company's needs. He also found a profitable market for objects made from *koa* and *ohia* trees on the property. C. Q. Yee Hop added a *koa* department in 1920 that became Hawaiian Hardwood Company in 1939. In 1933 C. Q. Yee Hop & Company and Chun founded American Brewing Company. In 1943 he founded Yee Hop Realty Company to expand into real estate and insurance.

In 1900 Chun joined the Chinese Empire Reform Association and supported it through its successive changes into the Chinese Constitutionalist and Chinese Democratic Constitutionalist parties. In 1910 he was founder of Mun Lun School. For many years he financed operations at Honolulu's *New China Press*, San Francisco's *Chinese World*, and Hong Kong's *Humanities Weekly*. In 1946 he was a delegate to the First National Chinese Assembly meeting in Nanjing.

Chung, Connie [Constance Yu-Hwa] (b. Aug. 20, 1946, Washington, D.C.): Broadcast journalist. Chung has become one of the United States' most popular and successful newscasters.

After five of their nine children had died in China, William Ling and Margaret (Ma) Chung and their four surviving daughters moved from Shanghai to Washington, D.C., in 1944. In 1946 their tenth child, Connie, was born. In 1965 she enrolled as a biology major at the University of Maryland. She wrote speeches and press releases during a 1968 summer internship with Seymour Halpern, a New York congressman. As a result she became a journalism major and a copy-clerk with Metromedia television station WTTG in Washington, D.C. Chung graduated from college in 1969 with a B.S. degree in journalism. From 1969 to 1971 she worked for WTTG as a newswriter, assignment editor, and on-air reporter.

In 1971, as the Federal Communications Commission was pressuring television stations to take affirmative action seriously, Chung was hired as a correspondent with CBS News in Washington, D.C. She covered George McGovern's presidential campaign, accompanied U.S. president Richard M. Nixon on trips to the Middle East and the Soviet Union in 1972, covered the

Award-winning television journalist Connie Chung. (AP/ Wide World Photos)

Watergate scandal hearings from 1973 to 1974, and covered the vice presidency of Nelson A. Rockefeller in 1974.

In 1976 Chung moved to Los Angeles to anchor the news at station KNXT-TV (a CBS affiliate). She hosted *Terra: Our World*, an award-winning documentary in 1980. By 1983 she had become the highest-paid local news anchor in the United States.

Chung returned to national news coverage in 1984, when she signed a contract with NBC in New York to anchor several news programs and to cover the Democratic and Republican political party conventions. In 1984 she married Maury Povich, then a television anchorman at WTTG. She visited China with an NBC News team in 1987 and interviewed relatives. She returned to work for CBS News in 1989.

Chung has received numerous awards, including national Emmy Awards in 1978, 1980, and 1987.

Chung, Henry (Chung Han Kyung): Political delegate and supporter of Korean independence. At a special conference sponsored by the Korean National Association (KNA) in support of the cause of Korean independence, Henry Chung, Syngman Rhee, and Min Chan-ho were elected as a three-man delegation to represent Korean interests at the 1919 Paris conference. In January of 1919, the delegates applied for visas from the U.S. government but were refused on the grounds that they were Korean nationals under the jurisdiction of the Japanese government. After failing to obtain visas from the British or Canadian embassies in Washington, D.C., Syngman Rhee made a proposal to President Woodrow Wilson that Korea be given trusteeship status in preparation for eventual self-government and placed under the supervision of the League of Nations until an independent government could be established. Despite the delegates' efforts, as well as petitions made by Korean nationalists exiled in China, the Paris peace conference ignored the issue of Korean independence because the Allied Powers supported Japan's assertion that the issue was a private domestic problem. In the wake of the March First independence uprising (1919), Syngman Rhee was elected president of the Korean provisional government. Among his first activities, Rhee issued an executive order in September of 1919 to establish the Korean Commission. As one of the three commissioners, Henry Chung was responsible for conducting diplomatic activities, raising funds, and promoting propaganda that generated support for the provisional government. Encouraged by a congressional resolution expressing sympathy for Korean national independence, Chung produced a book, *The Case of Korea* (1921), that helped make more Americans aware of the plight of Korea under Japanese occupation.

Chung, Myung-Whun (b. Jan. 22, 1953, Seoul, Republic of Korea): Concert pianist and conductor. One of several talented musicians in his family, Chung made his debut with the Seoul Philharmonic Orchestra when he was seven years old. After emigrating with his family to Seattle, Washington, in late 1961, Chung continued his education and completed his high school degree. At the age of eighteen, he moved to New York City to attend the Mannes School of Music. In 1974, he traveled to the Tchaikovsky Competition in Moscow, where he placed second in the prestigious piano competition. Soon after, Chung gave his first solo piano recital at New York City's Carnegie Hall and enrolled at the Juilliard School of Music for further musical training to become a conductor. Chung was

Myung-Whun Chung. (Korea Times)

chosen to serve as assistant conductor with the Los Angeles Philharmonic Orchestra in 1978 and eventually rose to become associate conductor. During the 1980's, he pursued his conducting career in Europe, appearing with several orchestras and opera companies in Italy and serving as music director for the Opera de la Bastille's 1989 gala celebration of the bicentennial of the French Revolution.

Chung Kun Ai (Nov. 26, 1865, Guangdong Province, China—Sept. 30, 1961, Honolulu, Hawaii): Businessman, community leader, and philanthropist. An immigrant to Hawaii and a classmate of SUN YAT-SEN, Chung gained prominence as a result of his business success and charitable undertakings.

Chung was raised in a small village near Macao. He was taken to the Hawaiian Islands at age fourteen by his father, who already had engaged in business there. After reaching Honolulu in 1879, Chung enrolled at Iolani College, a small Anglican boarding school established in 1872. On registering, his name was entered as "Chung K. Ai." He continued to use "Ai" as a family name in Hawaii although his children retained the "Chung" surname, except for the youngest son. Locally Ai became known as "C. K. Ai."

During his two years at Iolani, Ai was a close friend of Sun Yat-sen, who had enrolled there at the same time. Both were strongly attracted to Christianity, and their Christian beliefs soon became an issue in their respective families. After Ai withdrew from school in 1881 the two met on a number of occasions in Hawaii as well as in China and Japan over the next several decades. Ai was an early member of Sun's first revolutionary society, the Xingzhonghui (Revive China Society) and attended its inaugural meeting held in Honolulu on November 24, 1894. In 1911 he also helped found the Wah Mun School (Chinese People's School), a local Chinese-language school connected with Sun's revolutionary movement.

Ai had a long and varied business career. With the help of his father in 1883 he briefly held a partnership in a Chinatown tailor shop. Subsequently he was employed for more than eleven years by an English merchant in Honolulu under an arrangement that allowed Ai to undertake local business ventures on his own. In 1899 Ai founded the City Mill Company and was active in that flourishing building-supply firm for the rest of his life. As manager he invested in other commercial undertakings in Hawaii and in various projects in China.

Ai was active in community affairs. Between 1901 and 1906 he served as president of the United Chinese Society (formed in 1882 to protect Chinese interests in Hawaii) and later was a member of the Chinese and Honolulu chambers of commerce. He also raised funds for the Wai Wah Chinese Hospital and the Chinese Palolo Home for aged and indigent laborers, which he helped to found in 1917. After his baptism in 1896 Ai served on Young Men's Christian Association (YMCA) and mission boards and was a trustee of the Fort Street Chinese Church and its successor, built outside Chinatown.

Ai contributed as well to many relief and rehabilitation efforts in China, including the rebuilding of the Chung ancestral hall and school in his native village. In 1953 he established a foundation to carry on charitable work worldwide. Ai's life and endeavors are portrayed in his autobiography, *My Seventy Nine Years in Hawaii* (1960).

Chung Lau Drama Club: Community-based performing arts organization in San Francisco, California, formed in 1958. It was established to bring classical and modern Chinese plays to the Chinese American community, where there previously had been none. The club has performed more than forty plays, mostly in Cantonese. It has since expanded to include Chinese classical and folk dance.

Church of World Messianity (also Religion for the Salvation of the World): One of Japan's new religions, founded by Okada Mokichi in 1935. (See SHIN SHUKYO.) In Japan this particular cult is called Sekai Kyusei Kyo or Sekai Meshiya Kyo. It emphasizes the fast-approaching day of final judgment and the earthly paradise that will follow it. This sect, which claimed about 800,000 followers in 1977, has spread to the United States.

Chusok: Korean autumn festival feting the thanksgiving harvest moon. Celebrated by Koreans everywhere on the fifteenth day of the eighth lunar month (usually September or October by the solar calendar), it is a day to give thanks to spirits for the abundant harvest of the year and to pay homage to ancestors. Traditional activities include visiting and leaving food at tombs, preparing for the upcoming season, and eating traditional "moon cakes" made on the eve of the holiday.

Chy Lung v. Freeman (1876): U.S. Supreme Court case that declared unconstitutional a California law that discriminated against Chinese. Chy Lung, a Chinese woman sailing from China to California, was seized with twenty other women by a California commissioner of immigration upon arrival in San Francisco. The commissioner demanded that the ship's captain pay a five-hundred-dollar bond in gold for each woman, based on an 1873 California law. That law gave the commissioner of immigration broad discretion, without trial of any kind, to block whole groups of immigrants, arbitrarily characterized as "lewd and debauched women," from entering California. With almost ten times as many Chinese men as women in California at this period, Californians believed that prostitution was the likely purpose for Chinese female immigrants, who therefore became the main targets of· the law. While Chinese prostitution undoubtedly existed, there is no evidence to suggest that it was more prevalent among Chinese immigrants than among those of other ethnic groups.

The court's unanimous opinion described at length how immigration officials could board any ship, single out potential immigrants, and declare them "excluded" persons. They could then require the ship's master to pay one sum for the examination of each immigrant and an additional much-higher fee for preparing a bond document for each immigrant, which had to be signed by two California citizens who had to post the five-hundred-dollar bond in gold. If the ship's master did not do this, he could not land his passengers without a heavy penalty. The commissioner, however, could commute any procedure for any sum he chose to take in cash, from which he could withhold 20 percent for himself before remanding the rest to the California treasury. The U.S. Supreme Court called this 1873 law a "systematic extortion of the grossest kind and in *Chy Lung v. Freeman* declared that it violated the equal protection clause of the Fourteenth Amendment and the Burlingame Treaty (1868) with China. Altogether, twenty-three California statutes were abrogated as being unreasonably discriminatory to Chinese in the late 1800's, but eventually the Court upheld U.S. congressional exclusion of Chinese in 1893.

Cigar Makers Union of California: Protective trade association formed in the nineteenth century. Composed of white proprietors and white journeymen, its main mission was to campaign against the employment of Chinese cigar makers, many of whom were considered "enslaved labor" retarding the advancement of civilization.

Circular-i-Azadi (circular of freedom): Urdu periodical founded by Ram Nath Puri in 1907. Based in both Vancouver and Astoria, with branches in San Francisco, it was published from 1907 until 1908 by the Hindustan Association. The periodical voiced the concerns of the Asian Indian population in North America and supported India's movement for independence.

Citizens Committee to Repeal Chinese Exclusion: Committee founded on May 25, 1943, by a group of American citizens. It was formed to campaign for revoking the Chinese Exclusion Acts in effect since 1882 and to provide the Chinese with a quota basis and naturalization rights. About 250 Americans joined the committee, with Richard J. Walsh, a publisher, as its president.

The committee was formed at a time when China, an American ally during World War II (1939-1945), was entering its sixth year of war against Japanese aggression and when a repeal bill had been introduced in the U.S. House of Representatives amid growing popular pro-China sentiments. To an increasing number of Americans, the existence of the racially discriminatory immigration laws constituted the ultimate insult to their war ally and fellow human beings and served the interests of Tokyo's propaganda machine.

The committee's strategy was to mobilize public support for repeal and present the issue to the U.S. Congress as the demand of the American public. The group launched a vigorous campaign of education to make the public more aware of China's war contributions and the moral and practical reasons for repeal. The issue of repeal was presented not only as a moral obligation to the principle of human equality but also as an urgent wartime necessity to help bolster the morale of an ill-equipped ally in its protracted war against a powerful common enemy. Meanwhile, the committee contacted various organizations throughout the United States, with the West Coast as its area of concentration. Its goal was either to win support or to neutralize the forces of opposition by stimulating dissent. It won support from organizations such as the Congress of Industrial Unions, the Federal Council of Churches, the boards of supervisors of San Francisco and Los Angeles, and national executive dissension within some traditionally proexclusion groups, such as the American Federation of Labor (AFL) and the Veterans of Foreign Wars (VFW).

The committee also approached Republican and Democratic party leaders and secured bipartisan support. It mailed copies of representative prorepeal editorials and articles to all members of Congress to remind them of the strong popular sentiments against Chinese exclusion. At the same time, it urged private citizens to voice their support for repeal to members of Congress.

Over time this mass repealment effort encompassed many other groups and thousands of individuals across the nation. Public opinion in favor of repeal was further expressed at "Salute to China" mass rallies, in pamphlets and articles bearing such titles as "Justice for a Noble Ally" and "End Exclusion Now," and in radio broadcasts of town hall meetings from various U.S. cities. Chinese Americans participated in the movement as well. The Chinese Women's Association of New York, for example, wrote to First Lady Eleanor Roosevelt asking for her support, and Chinese communities in Hawaii made unsolicited contributions to the committee.

The committee concluded its operation after the Senate passed a repeal bill on November 26, 1943, which became the IMMIGRATION ACT OF 1943 (also known as the Magnuson Act or the Chinese Repealer). Though small in size, the committee made an important contribution to the success of the nationwide movement to repeal the Chinese Exclusion acts.

City of Tokio: Ship that brought the first group of more than nine hundred Japanese government contract workers to Hawaii on February 8, 1885. Robert Irwin, Hawaii's consul general, negotiated the labor agreement that subsequently brought about twenty-nine thousand Japanese government contract laborers to Hawaii between 1885 and 1894.

Civil Liberties Act of 1988: Legislation enacted to rectify the injustices committed by the U.S. government toward Japanese Americans and the Aleuts during World War II (1939-1945). Also known as the "redress bill," the act was signed into law by President Ronald Reagan on August 10, 1988. It called for a formal written apology from the president and $20,000 in compensation to each Japanese American survivor of the concentration camps. The $1.25 billion bill also provided up to $12,000 for each surviving Aleut Indian who was forcibly removed by the U.S. government from the Aleutian and Pribilof islands during the war. The bill was based on recommendations made by the government-appointed COMMISSION ON WARTIME RELOCATION AND INTERNMENT OF CIVILIANS (CWRIC).

Payment to the former internees of the camps began in October, 1990. Between that time and the end of 1993, 79,000 Japanese Americans received $20,000 each in compensation.

Civil Rights Act of 1870: U.S. Reconstruction-era legislation that extended civil liberties to Chinese as well as to African Americans. Its provisions included the right to enforce contracts, to sue, to give evidence in a court of law, and to enjoy all benefits of the law for protection.

Civilian Exclusion Orders: Series of orders issued by U.S. Army general John L. DeWitt of the Western Defense Command authorizing the forcible removal of persons of Japanese ancestry away from certain designated military zones on the American West Coast. This plan for removal and eventual relocation of the Japanese went into effect soon after President Franklin D. Roosevelt signed Executive Order 9066 (1942). The exclusion was officially based on a U.S. government policy of "military necessity." In all, five civilian exclusion orders were issued in the first half of 1942.

Coboy-coboy: Wife abduction that occurred among Filipino plantation workers in Hawaii, particularly during the 1920's and 1930's. The term itself is not a Filipino word but appears to have been derived from the term "cowboy," one explanation being that cowboy films of that period showed scenes in which the heroine is abducted by the villain. Abductions of women resulted from the substantially greater number of Filipino men compared to that of women in Hawaii, which made Filipino women, even if married, highly desired by their young male counterparts.

Coboy-coboy occurred when a man or a group of men kidnapped a woman, or when a man paid someone to do the abducting. Despite great fear among both wives and husbands of such occurrences, these incidents were not frequent, at least according to plantation records. Perhaps only two or three cases per year occurred on a given plantation prior to 1940, and only isolated incidents were reported thereafter.

Widespread apprehension and rumor of abductions (in addition to low plantation wages), however, were sufficient to deter many Filipinos from bringing their wives to Hawaii; often, Filipinos sent their wives back to the Philippines. Thus, the fear of *coboy-coboy* also contributed to its underlying cause. In 1920, the ratio was four Filipino males for every female; it increased in 1930 to five men for every woman and declined in 1940 to about 3.5 males per female. Filipino women thus were the object of great attention, receiving gifts and flattery from suitors.

The kidnappings had negative consequences for the Filipino community in Hawaii prior to World War II.

Cockfighting is a popular—and legal—diversion in the Philippines. (Filipino American National Historical Society)

They contributed to a prevalent derogatory stereotype of Filipino men, who were seen as posing a "sex danger" and as being violent and "hot tempered" because of the fights, including murders, that occurred among them over women. Insofar as fear of *coboy-coboy* resulted in fewer Filipino women either going to or remaining in Hawaii, it contributed to the slower development of families and in turn slowed the growth of the second generation of Filipino Americans, with the prospect of greater socioeconomic mobility.

Cockfighting: Gambling contest originating in the Philippines, involving fighting roosters that have a sharp blade attached to their legs. The contest ends when either cock runs away or is maimed into submission, with the victorious bird formalizing the victory by pecking twice at the defeated bird. The sport is known as *sabong* in the Philippines, where it is legal; it is illegal in the United States but is widely practiced nonetheless.

Cockrill v. People of State of California (1925): U.S. Supreme Court ruling that affirmed the constitutionality of California's ALIEN LAND LAW OF 1913 and its 1920 amendment. Cockrill, a lawyer, had agreed to purchase land in Sonoma County owned by another party. The first payment for the sale was made, however, by Ikada, a Japanese citizen. The owners later admitted knowing that Cockrill had signed the contract on Ikada's behalf. Subsequently, Cockrill and Ikada were convicted of conspiring to violate the Alien Land Law, under which aliens ineligible for U.S. citizenship were barred from owning or leasing land.

On appeal, the Supreme Court upheld the conviction, finding that the Alien Land Law did not violate the due process and equal protection clauses of the Constitution, as contended by the plaintiffs.

Cold Tofu: Performance arts group formed in 1981. Cold Tofu is a multiracial improvisational comedy troupe based in Los Angeles, California. Founded by Asian American actors, the group has addressed issues of racial identity and discrimination in its works and has performed in nightclubs and toured colleges and community centers around the United States.

Collins, Wayne Mortimer (1899 or 1900, Sacramento, Calif.—July 16, 1974, on an airplane between San Francisco and Honolulu): Attorney. Collins is best remembered for his defense of two famous clients: Fred T. KOREMATSU, the World War II exclusion order violator, and Iva Toguri (TOKYO ROSE), the alleged wartime traitor. To many Japanese Americans, however, Collins is also remembered as an ardent fighter for civil rights who accepted cases that were considered not only unwinnable but also unpopular.

Much of Collins' work on behalf of Japanese Americans was not widely publicized but was probably among his most personally satisfying. In 1944 he investigated the plight of the so-called troublemakers at the TULE LAKE camp and discovered that many were detained in a stockade without just cause. Collins intervened on their behalf and was instrumental in permanently closing the facility.

In 1945, despite the objections of the American Civil Liberties Union (ACLU), Collins attempted to prevent the deportation of the Japanese Americans who renounced their U.S. citizenship in camp. In defense of these renunciants he successfully argued that the government, through its inhumane treatment of detaining innocent citizens, was primarily responsible for their actions. Collins fought for fourteen years to have citizenship rights restored to almost five thousand Nisei.

Collins also intervened on behalf of three hundred and sixty-five Japanese Peruvians who were scheduled to be deported to Japan after the war. These Peruvian citizens were essentially stateless people. During the war they were extradited by Peru to the U.S. Immigration and Naturalization Service (INS) internment camps and were denied reentry into their own country. Yet since they were not American citizens, they were also not allowed to stay in the United States. Because of Collins, three hundred Japanese Peruvians were allowed to stay, and many of them later became naturalized through the MCCARRAN-WALTER ACT OF 1952. Peru allowed their reentry in the mid-1950's, but fewer than one hundred decided to come back.

To the very end, Collins never gave up fighting for what he believed in. He won many battles but did not live to see the final victories of two of his most famous clients, Korematsu and Toguri.

Coloma: Productive nineteenth century farming town that provided produce for the mining regions where many Chinese and Japanese immigrants resided. It is also the site of Sutter's Mill, where the discovery of gold on January 24, 1848, triggered the California gold rush of 1848. Coloma is located along the American River in El Dorado County.

Colombo: Administrative capital of SRI LANKA (formerly Ceylon), located along the southwestern coast.

In addition to being the country's economic and political center, the city is its primary western seaport to the Indian Ocean, boasting one of the world's largest artificial harbors. Colombo's population was about 615,000 in 1990. SINHALESE constitute about 78 percent, and Tamils about 18 percent, of the city's population, resulting in a government controlled by Sinhalese. Since 1958 the country has been torn by ethnic violence, a reaction to this imbalance of power. The nation's legislative capital remains Sri Jayewardenepura, in Kotte, a suburb of Colombo.

Colombo is also the name for a district of Sri Lanka, with a population of more than 1.9 million people in 1990.

Combined Asian-American Resources Project: Association established by concerned Asian American writers in San Francisco in 1969. The group has in-

cluded such influential writers as Lawson Fusao INADA, Jeffery Paul CHAN, Frank CHIN, and Shawn WONG. Its goals were to conduct oral history projects on topics of interest to Asian Americans, to educate teachers of ASIAN AMERICAN STUDIES, and to publish books of significant value to the Asian American community. The project arranged the publication of new editions of Carlos BULOSAN's *America Is In the Heart* (1946), Louis CHU's *Eat a Bowl of Tea* (1961), John OKADA's *No-No Boy* (1957), and Monica SONE's *Nisei Daughter* (1953).

Commission on Asian American Affairs (CAAA): Agency created in 1972 by the Washington state legislature to serve as a liaison between Asian Pacific American communities and state government. It attempts to ensure full articulation and understanding of community needs by the state. It also seeks to ensure

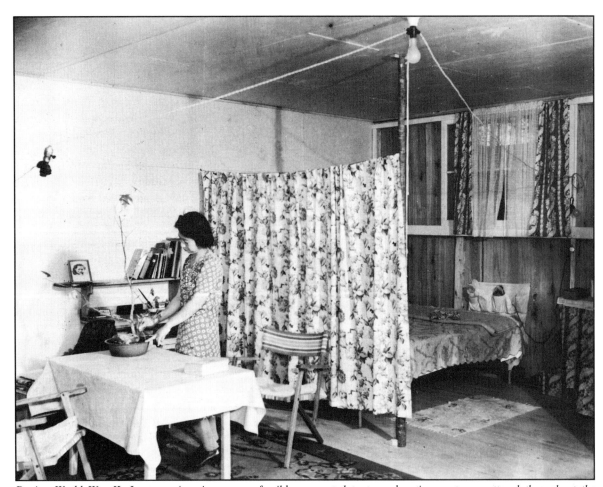

During World War II, Japanese Americans were forcibly evacuated to ten relocation centers scattered throughout the western United States. The interior shown here, from the Jerome relocation compound in Arkansas, is typical of a barracks at the camp. (National Archives)

that the state addresses the needs effectively and to promote cooperation between the community and other groups. The Asian Pacific American community in Washington comprises more than twenty-six ethnic groups, each with its own language and cultural traditions.

The commission became a state agency in 1974, with the governor appointing the director and its board members. Out of its two offices in Olympia and Seattle—center of the state's largest Asian Pacific American community—the group lobbies around federal and state legislative issues, works with state agencies and community-based groups, and produces several publications, including a demographic analysis, affirmative action report, resource directory, informational brochures in different Asian languages, and a newsletter.

State laws on which the commission lobbied include the Court Interpreters Act, requiring testing and certification of court interpreters; English Plus, establishing the state's policy to encourage the presence of diverse cultures and use of diverse languages in business, government, and private affairs; and the Immigration Family Documents bill, allowing courts to accept immigration documents as proof of familial status.

In the federal arena the commission has worked with other groups on passage of redress and reparations for Japanese Americans interned during World War II, the 1991 Civil Rights Act, citizenship for Filipino war veterans, and the Federal Hate Crime Statistics Act.

Beyond the field of legislation, the commission interacts closely with many state agencies, task forces, and committees to ensure that the actions and regulations of the latter address the needs and issues facing the Asian Pacific American communities. Among other activities, it has worked with the Department of Social and Health Services to implement the Immigration and Reform Act, the Minority Justice Task Force to identify and address racial bias in state courts, and the Office of Financial Management to establish a uniform system for collecting and reporting data about Asian Pacific American ethnic groups.

Commission on Wartime Relocation and Internment of Civilians (CWRIC): Special panel formed by an act of Congress in 1980 to study the World War II incarceration of Japanese Americans and to recommend appropriate remedies. The idea for the CWRIC came at a February, 1979, redress strategy meeting between the JAPANESE AMERICAN CITIZENS LEAGUE (JACL) and NIKKEI congressional Democrats. After a

year of lobbying for the commission bill, the CWRIC was established in July, 1980, when President Jimmy Carter signed Public Law 96-317. Members of the commission included Chair and legal authority Joan Bernstein, Vice Chairman and U.S. Representative Daniel Lungren, former U.S. senator Edward Brooke, civil rights activist and former U.S. representative Father Robert Drinan, Chair of the U.S. Commission on Civil Rights Arthur Flemming, former Supreme Court justice Arthur J. Goldberg, Father Ishmael Gromoff, Judge William Marutani, and U.S. senator Hugh Mitchell.

A Rocky Start. In the Japanese American community, the proposal for a government commission was met with suspicion. Many redress activists viewed the action as another JACL attempt to sabotage the reparations part of the proposal in favor of a politically acceptable commission bill and a public apology. The NATIONAL COUNCIL FOR JAPANESE AMERICAN REDRESS (NCJAR), for example, formed because the JACL refused to commit to seeking monetary compensation after mandating at the 1978 JACL convention that it would seek $25,000 for each concentration camp survivor and a public apology. The NCJAR introduced its own redress bill in 1979 with the support of Representative Mike Lowry of Washington and later filed a $24-billion class-action lawsuit against the U.S. government.

Another group that was upset with the commission proposal was the NATIONAL COALITION FOR REDRESS/REPARATIONS (NCRR). It too viewed the CWRIC as a JACL compromise that would prevent the Japanese American community from obtaining true justice. Rather than oppose the CWRIC, however, the NCRR decided that the best strategy was to work with the commission to ensure that Japanese Americans had the opportunity to participate fully in the process.

Gathering Momentum. In 1981 the CWRIC held hearings across the country to gather data for its recommendations. Hearings were set in Washington, D.C., Los Angeles, San Francisco, Seattle, Anchorage, the Aleutian and Pribilof islands, and Chicago. Because of the enormous reaction the CWRIC received from the Japanese American community, additional hearings were arranged for New York and Boston. In Los Angeles so many people wanted to participate in the hearings that extra sessions had to be arranged along with adjoining rooms equipped with speakers to accommodate the overflow crowds. In general, in every city the hearings generated interest from Japanese Americans, the media, and mainstream America.

During the Japanese American internment of World War II, internees were evacuated first to assembly centers before being incarcerated permanently at relocation camps. Here an attendant registers arrivals at the Santa Anita assembly center in Southern California in April, 1942. (National Archives)

The Los Angeles hearings, on a theatrical level, were probably the most exciting of all the proceedings for several reasons. Not only did they feature the largest Japanese American population in the continental United States, but Los Angeles was also the site of the first hearings to be held outside of Washington, D.C., and therefore the first in which the camp survivors themselves had a chance to testify in front of the government commission. For many survivors it was the first time since their internment in the concentration camps that they publicly spoke about their experiences. For the younger Japanese Americans who were born after the camps, it was time to learn what had really happened to their parents and grandparents during World War II. In general it was a time both for healing and for revealing memories of injustice and suffering that had been suppressed for almost forty years.

The Los Angeles hearings were exciting for other reasons as well. S. I. HAYAKAWA, the former Japanese American senator from California, testified against redress by arguing that the so-called "relocation camps" were the result of war hysteria and were for the protection of those interned. Hayakawa, who had not been interned in a camp, was jeered by the audience after his testimony.

The rest of the testimonies at Los Angeles and across the country essentially told a story contrary to Hayakawa's version. Taken together, they created a moving picture of hardship, loss of life and liberty, betrayal, bitterness, and survival. Moreover, Japanese Americans in a very clear and direct way demanded that the government pay for its actions against them to ensure that an episode like the camps would never again be experienced by future generations of American citizens.

Results. In 1983, after conducting extensive research and reviewing testimonies from former camp

Dillon S. Myer was director of the War Relocation Authority, which administered the ten relocation camps to which Japanese Americans were forcibly evacuated during World War II. (AP/Wide World Photos)

In San Pedro, California, Japanese American evacuees prepare to board a train en route to the Manzanar relocation center, central California, in April, 1942. (National Japanese American Historical Society)

internees, World War II government officials, historians, sociologists, and other experts in various fields, the CWRIC released its report, *Personal Justice Denied*. Although the report made no recommendations, it was clear that the commission was emotionally captivated by the personal testimonies. The report concluded that the concentration camps were the result of "race prejudice, war hysteria and a failure of political leadership."

Later in the year, on June 16, the CWRIC issued its recommendations to Congress. First, it urged Congress and the president to pass a resolution to apologize to Japanese Americans for the injustice done to them during the war. Second, the CWRIC urged the president to pardon those convicted of violating the curfew and exclusion orders during the war. Third, it recommended that Japanese Americans be allowed to apply for restitution of positions, status, or entitlements lost because of their incarceration. Most important, the CWRIC recommended that $20,000 be paid to each surviving internee of the camps and that an educational fund be established to demonstrate officially to the nation that a great injustice was inflicted on Japanese American citizens and resident immigrants. In addition the CWRIC also recommended similar remedies for the Aleuts who were forcibly removed from the Aleutian and Pribilof islands. These recommendations were the basis for the CIVIL LIBERTIES ACT OF 1988, signed into law by President Ronald Reagan on August 10, 1988.—*Glen Kitayama*

SUGGESTED READINGS: • U.S. Commission on Wartime Relocation and Internment of Civilians. *Personal Justice Denied*. Washington, D.C.: Government Printing Office, 1983. • Hohri, William. *Repairing America*. Pullman: Washington State University Press, 1988. • Kitayama, Glen. *Japanese Americans and the Movement for Redress: A Case Study of Grassroots Activism in the Los Angeles Chapter of the National Coalition for Redress/Reparations*. Master's thesis. University of California, Los Angeles, 1993. • Scott, Esther, and Calvin Naito. *Against All Odds: The Japanese Americans' Campaign for Redress*. Case Program, Kennedy School of Government, Harvard University, 1990.

Committee Against Nihonmachi Evictions (CANE): Grassroots organization based in San Francisco that organized in early 1973 around the issue of redevelopment in the area's Nihonmachi (Japantown).

In the 1960's and early 1970's, urban redevelopment was viewed by city planners as a way to bring revenues back to the central city. Many areas, including Nihonmachi in San Francisco, had the potential to be tourist attractions but were run-down. Master plans were drawn up for the areas to meet everybody's interests: Residents would benefit from new low-income housing structures, and local small businesses would see increased revenues which in turn would benefit the city. Everything did not, however, work according to plan.

In San Francisco's Nihonmachi, priority was given to the Kintetsu Enterprises Company of America (a conglomerate based in Japan) and its plan to build a $2.25 million tourist hotel on the corner of Sutter and Buchanan streets. The company already owned nearly one-fourth of the property in Nihonmachi, including the Miyako Hotel for tourists, and now wanted to develop more real estate. To the members of CANE, this was unacceptable. While Kintetsu Enterprises was given permission to expand, local small businesses were being pushed out. To make the situation worse, low-income housing was frozen and many long-time residents were being evicted from their homes. For these residents, redevelopment was a nightmare. The area was becoming a revenue-raising tourist attraction at their expense.

The members of CANE, including young Sansei activists, Nihonmachi residents, and local small-businesspeople, fought back with the few resources they had. They wrote editorials in the local Japanese American press and passed out leaflets in the streets to bring attention to the redevelopment issue. CANE also held strategy meetings, networked with other groups fighting redevelopment in other cities such as the Little Tokyo Anti-Eviction Task Force in Los Angeles, and held various demonstrations. Some of their methods, such as chaining themselves together at the San Francisco Redevelopment Agency office, were controversial. Their actions, however, brought public attention to the callousness of big business and city government. Some members of CANE remained active in Japanese American community issues and later became involved in the redress movement.

Committee of Safety: Group formed in Honolulu in 1893 in order to depose the Hawaiian government of QUEEN LILIUOKALANI and install a new one. Composed primarily of former members of the ANNEXATION CLUB, the organization included such influential island leaders as Lorrin Thurston, Henry E. Cooper, and William O. Smith. After the queen in early 1893 declared her intention to impose an authoritarian new state constitution, the committee overthrew her and founded a provisional government. On July 4, 1894, the Republic of Hawaii was established with Sanford B. Dole as president. U.S. president Grover Cleveland later extended official diplomatic recognition to the new administration; formal annexation of the Hawaiian Islands followed in August, 1898.

Comrade Society. *See* **Tongji-hoe**

Concentration camps: Camps in which Japanese Americans were interned during World War II (1939-1945). Beginning in 1942, about 120,000 persons of Japanese ancestry, two-thirds of them American citizens, were evacuated from their homes on the West Coast and incarcerated in camps at widely distant sites.

The term "concentration camps" is preferred by many Japanese Americans and others who believe that the official government designations for the camps do not reflect the true nature of the incarceration. (See JAPANESE AMERICAN INTERNMENT; INTERNMENT CAMPS; and RELOCATION CENTERS.)

Confession Program: Program initiated by right-wing anti-Communist Chinese organizations, particularly the NATIONAL CHINESE WELFARE COUNCIL, which struck a deal with U.S. immigration officials whereby Chinese residents of the United States with irregular immigration or naturalization documents would come forward and confess their guilt for their irregular or fraudulent immigration and naturalization papers, emphasize their anti-Communist political views, and be "forgiven" for these irregularities.

During the 1950's the Eisenhower Administration, reacting to the Communist Party takeover of mainland China in 1949 and the hostilities in Korea in the early 1950's, threatened to initiate a mass deportation of Chinese who had entered the United States fraudulently or who simply had irregularities in their immigration or naturalization papers. Based on fears of Chinese Communist infiltration of the United States, American officials alleged that the People's Republic of China had used fraudulent American passports as a means of sending spies and other leftist agents into the United States. This charge resulted in federal authori-

An image of Confucius. (Library of Congress)

ties investigating thousands of Chinese residents who had irregularities in their naturalization papers or birth certificates, particularly if these were used to obtain U.S. passports.

Apparently seeking to avoid the problems faced by the Japanese during the World War II internment, anti-Communist Chinese organizations sought to take extraordinary measures to establish their loyalty to the United States. The situation was complicated by the fact that many Chinese had apparently entered the United States using false or irregular immigration documents for a variety of reasons during the many years when Chinese immigration was severely limited. While there were irregularities in their immigration documents, these individuals were nevertheless anti-Communist and sought to establish that fact. The authorities in turn were more concerned about subversive Communist activities than they were about mere irregularities in immigration documents, and they accepted a deal proposed by an offshoot of these Chinese organizations, the National Chinese Welfare Council. Under the agreement, if the authorities were convinced that no subversive activities were involved, the immigrants were given legal status. The program allowed the U.S. government to locate and deport a small number of left-wing and Communist sympathizers during this period. The vast majority, perhaps 99 percent of the Chinese with improper papers, were allowed to stay in the United States. The Immigration and Naturalization Service in San Francisco alone processed and accepted more than ten-thousand such confessions.

Confucianism: One of the three main schools of philosophy and religion in China. Together with BUD-DHISM and TAOISM, Confucianism forms the core of traditional Chinese thought. Of the three it has been the most influential. Confucianism is a philosophy based on the teachings of Confucius (551-479 B.C.E.), and later supplemented by Mencius (c. 371-c. 289 B.C.E.) and Xun Zu (fl. c. 298-c. 230 B.C.E.), but it is also more than a philosophy: It is a traditional outlook or way of life that has profoundly shaped Chinese culture.

The traditional Chinese social order was based on Confucian principles: the importance of a patriarchal family structure, respect for elders, the value of education, and obedience to authority. A basic principle of Confucianism is that wisdom and good government begin at home. The emphasis on the family as the basic unit of society has been one of the most enduring

features of the Confucian tradition. Balance, a sense of moderation in all things, and service to the community are also central to Confucianism.

Scholars disagree about the legacy of the Confucian tradition. Some see the dramatic economic development in East Asia in the late twentieth century as attributable in part at least to the pervasive influence of Confucianism. Others, pointing to the Confucian-based educational system that prevailed in China for many centuries, growing increasingly rigid and resistant to new ideas, see Confucianism as a hindrance to development and argue that the reasons for the East Asian surge must lie elsewhere.

The same debate is carried on among Chinese American scholars and writers. Some see the Confucian tradition as a vital part of their heritage, while others reject it (feminists, for example, have criticized its patriarchal assumptions) or regard it as simply irrelevant.

Confucius Plaza Project (New York, N.Y.): Federally funded housing project. A cooperative with 764 units, a school, and a daycare center, it was built for middle-income Chinese residents of New York City's Chinatown. The project prompted community protests in 1974 when the area's Chinese residents realized that there were no Chinese or other Asian Americans employed in its construction.

When the construction company ignored a petition with more than eight thousand signatures asking that the project include Asian American workers, an organization called Asian Americans for Equal Employment (later ASIAN AMERICANS FOR EQUALITY) organized a series of community protests. The effort was ultimately successful, resulting in more than twenty jobs for Chinese workers; in addition, all charges against the protesters were dropped.

The Confucius Plaza campaign reflected the development of Asian American activism in the 1970's. Particularly significant was the fact that the protests, which were generally supported by the Chinese American community and by a coalition of non-Asian activist groups, were opposed by New York City's Chinese Consolidated Benevolent Association (CCBA). In microcosm this episode reflected the declining influence of CCBAs nationwide. (See CHINESE CONSOLIDATED BENEVOLENT ASSOCIATIONS.)

Conroy, E. Francis Hilary (b. Dec. 31, 1919, Normal, Ill.): Scholar. He was one of the first historians to examine early Japanese immigration to Hawaii. He coauthored *East Across the Pacific* (1972) with T. Scott MIYAKAWA and was a professor of history at the University of Pennsylvania until his retirement in 1990.

Constitutionalist Party. *See* **Baohuanghui**

Continuous voyage (1908): Canadian immigration law proviso. It prohibited entry into Canada for immigrants who had not come on a continuous voyage directly from their native country (that is, with no stopovers en route). This legislation had a specific purpose—to cut off the flow of immigration from India to Canada that had been increasing steadily since 1900.

At that time, there were no ships sailing directly from Calcutta to the Pacific Coast. Therefore, Asian Indian immigrants coming from Calcutta had to change ships in Hong Kong or Shanghai. Under the continuous-voyage clause, they could be barred from entering Canada.

One reason for using this roundabout way to keep out Indian immigrants was to guard against charges of discrimination against British subjects. The order itself was carefully worded, but the Canadian government made no bones about its desire to keep Canada "for whites only." The Canadian public, too, was openly hostile, and there were frequent riots against Indian immigrants (mainly Sikhs) who worked in the railroad and lumber towns of British Columbia and Washington.

The continuous-voyage order was thus used to stop undesirable immigration. Even Indians who came nonstop directly from the Fiji Islands were arrested and detained because they had not come straight from their native land. Immigration from India was reduced to a trickle and soon stopped completely.

Because of the restrictions of such immigration laws, immigration from India dropped from 2,623 in 1907-1908 to 6 in 1908-1909. Having achieved their purpose, the Canadian authorities promptly passed a new order allowing non-Asians to enter Canada from countries other than their native country. The door was now open for Europeans who wanted to enter Canada from the United States. (See KOMAGATA MARU INCIDENT.)

Cook, James (Oct. 27, 1728, Marton, Yorkshire, England—Feb. 14, 1779, Kealakekua Bay, Hawaii): Explorer. Cook's wide range of abilities enabled him to become the foremost European explorer and cartographer of the Pacific Ocean. His three voyages delineated the most important geographic features of the Pacific Ocean and established a British claim to Australia and New Zealand.

From the age of eighteen Cook served on a variety of vessels plying British and Baltic waters. Little is known of his early life except that he spent extraordinary amounts of time in study when not at sea. At the age of twenty-seven he was offered command of a merchant ship but chose instead to join the Royal Navy. Cook served with distinction during the Seven Years' War (1756-1763), gaining special notice for charting the St. Lawrence River and the coast of Newfoundland.

Because of his unique combination of skills, in 1768 Cook was chosen to head what was ostensibly a British Royal Society expedition to observe the transit of Venus. Secretly, however, his first voyage (1768-1771) was a mission to forestall the French in discovering the great southern continent, which many Europeans believed to stretch in temperate zones across much of the southern Pacific and Indian oceans. After observing the transit in Tahiti, he circumnavigated New Zealand, proving it to be two islands unconnected to a southern continent, claimed the eastern coast of Australia for Britain, and charted the southern coastal regions of the East Indies before returning to Britain in 1771.

On his second voyage (1772-1775), Cook explored a number of Pacific island groups and pushed three times beyond the Antarctic Circle, proving that a temperate southern continent could not exist. Cook's third voyage (1776-1779), was an attempt to discover a sea passage from northwestern North America to the Atlantic. After becoming the first European to discover the Hawaiian Islands, he sailed north along the Pacific coastline from Washington to Alaska, passed through the Bering Strait, then returned to Hawaii, where he was killed by native Hawaiians, who had previously revered him.

Coolidge, Mary Roberts (Oct. 28, 1860, Kingsbury, Ind.—Apr. 13, 1945, Berkeley, Calif.): Historian. Roberts was educated at Cornell (Ph.B., 1880) and Stanford University (Ph.D., 1896). She taught at Wellesley College from 1886 to 1890 and at Stanford from 1896 to 1903; at Mills College, she was a professor of sociology from 1918 to 1927. One of the first comprehensive analyses of the Chinese in America was her *Chinese Immigration* (1909).

Coolie trade: Following the abolition of slavery in the British and Spanish empires in the early nineteenth century, the need for labor in some New World countries was met for a while by the immigration of Chi-

English sea captain James Cook was the first European to discover the Hawaiian Islands. This painting of him hangs in the National Portrait Gallery, Washington, D.C. (AP/Wide World Photos)

nese laborers arranged by labor contractors engaged in the trans-Pacific traffic in human cargo known as the coolie trade. The word "coolie" is probably the anglicized form of the Chinese word *ku-li* (literally, "bitter strength"), meaning a person doing manual labor. The coolie trade ended in the mid-1870's because of actions taken by the Chinese government in response to the popular outcry at the blatant exploitation of the coolies and other unsavory aspects of the coolie trade.

The Coolie Market. By the mid-nineteenth century, the pace of economic development was quickened in Cuba, Peru, Hawaii, Australia, and the western United States. To build the railroads, exploit the mines, and work the tropical plantations, these countries needed large numbers of men who were willing to toil for low wages and submit to the regimentation of work. The only country that could meet the demand for this type of labor was China.

For generations, people from the congested coastal provinces of Guangdong and Fujian had been traveling overseas to work. Many emigrated because of difficulties making a living at home. The mounting population pressures in China by the mid-nineteenth century led to intensification of social conflict and the outbreak of large-scale civil wars. With personal safety at stake and the economy ruined, large numbers of people found in emigration the only means of physical survival. They were willing to brave the perils of long voyages and accept shocking working conditions.

Structure of the Coolie Trade. The operators of the coolie trade were primarily Britons but could also be Frenchmen, Spaniards, Portuguese, Cubans, and Peruvians. They were, of course, assisted by Chinese collaborators. The first base of operations was Amoy. With their coolie ships anchored offshore, they would send their local agents to round up all potential recruits. Vehement opposition from local people drove them away. Then the operation moved to Swatow and finally to Hong Kong and Macao. Benefiting from the fact that the latter ports were technically foreign soil and thus beyond the control of the Chinese government, the traders built up their physical infrastructure for year-round operations, including depots (known as barracoons) where coolies could be held pending shipment overseas. Then their local agents, known as "crimps," would fan out into the countryside signing up all prospective recruits. While coolies technically were indentured laborers whose conditions of service were spelled out in a contract, in reality since most coolies were illiterate and therefore dependent upon the crimps for explaining to them the terms of the

contract many were undoubtedly misled and cheated out of their rights. When some crimps were hard-pressed to fill their quota of recruits, they would have recourse to kidnapping. Then the coolie ships, with a full load of human cargo, would set sail for a New World destination. Upon arriving, their cargo would be auctioned off to the highest bidder.

As an expression of predatory capitalism, the coolie trade materialized in response to market forces outside the framework of governmental regulations. The government of China at first took no effective steps to stop the activity because historically it assumed no responsibility to protect its overseas citizens; there was in fact an official ban against emigration (not lifted until 1860. Even if it had wanted to, its hands were tied. For much of the 1850's and 1860's, the attention of the government was preoccupied with far graver issues, for example, the Taiping Rebellion and other causes of social upheaval. For about a year in the course of the Second Opium War, the office of the Canton Viceroy, with jurisdiction over the province of Guangdong and Guangxi, was in fact answerable to the Anglo-French joint command rather than to Beijing.

Horrors of the Coolie Trade. The hardship started as soon as the coolies were corralled into the barracoons. Dehumanized, they became simply "commodities." To maximize profit of each trans-Pacific run, coolie trade operators tried to pack as many coolies as possible into their ships with no regard for the coolies' comfort or health. The length of time it took for the voyage varied greatly; the ships often ran out of food or water. Overcrowding, poor sanitation, malnutrition, and despair took a heavy toll on the passengers. Mortality rates of 20 or 30 percent or more were common.

Using brute force to maintain discipline, ship captains often confined coolies to the hold of the ship with the entrance locked or closely guarded. Sometimes the ship caught fire, and all the coolies either drowned or burned to death because the crew forgot to unlock the exits of the hold. On at least one occasion, the coolies were so outraged by the brutal ways of the ship captain and crew that they took revenge by setting fire to the ship, bringing down everybody aboard with them.

Upon arrival at their destination, the fate of survivors depended on the luck of the draw. Some ended up with an employer/master who tried to abide by the terms of the coolie contract and treated them reasonably well. Yet the vast majority were not that lucky. Shamelessly exploited, they were provided with poor housing and inadequate food and were set to work by harsh taskmasters who did not hesitate to whip, maim,

Massive numbers of Chinese coolies were imported to America to build the railroads, exploit the gold mines, and work the plantations. Here a gang of coolies travels by handcar to its gold claims. (Asian American Studies Library, University of California at Berkeley)

or even kill them to maintain control. Unable to speak the local language and ignorant of the law and their own rights, the coolies could not bring their plight to the attention of the public. Often their only way out was to commit suicide or run away. To discourage running away, some employers/masters went so far as to brand their coolies with hot irons as if they were cattle. To retain those coolies who had completed their term of obligatory service as stipulated by their contract, unscrupulous employers would inflate the price of substandard housing and the food the coolies consumed, thereby pushing them hopelessly into debt and making it impossible for them to move away.

End of the Coolie Trade. The trial of a coolie ship captain for murder in 1872 provided a forum for publicizing the evils of the trade. The resultant international indignation strengthened the hand of the Chinese imperial government, which by the 1870's had become rejuvenated with most of the internal troubles resolved. In August of 1873, all coolie ships were ordered away from Chinese waters. When Portugal closed the port of Macao to the coolie ships on March 27, 1874, this infamous episode in East-West relations finally came to an end.—*Jonathan B. Lo*

Suggested Readings: • Campbell, P. C. *Chinese Coolie Emigration to Countries Within the British Empire.* Taipei: Ch'eng Wen Publishing, 1970. • Conwell, R. H. *Why and How: Why the Chinese Emigrate and the Means They Adopt for the Purpose of Reaching America.* Boston: Lee and Shepard, 1871. • MacNair, H. F. *The Chinese Abroad, Their Position and Protection: A Study in International Law and Relations.* Taipei: Ch'eng Wen Publishing, 1971. • Yen, Ching-Hwang. *Coolies and Mandarins: China's Protection of Overseas Chinese During the Late Ch'ing Period (1851-1911).* Singapore: Singapore University Press, 1985.

Coomaraswamy, Ananda Kentish (Aug. 22, 1877, Colombo, Ceylon—Sept. 9, 1947, Needham, Mass.): Scholar. His father Ceylonese, his mother British, Coomaraswamy was educated at Wycliffe College and the University of London. Obtaining a doctorate in geology, he was appointed director of mineral surveys for Ceylon in 1903. Soon shifting his interests to the arts, in 1910-1911 he was in charge of the arts section of the United Provinces Exhibition in Allahabad, India. In 1917 he was appointed as a research fellow in Indian, Persian, and Muslim art at the Museum of Fine Arts, Boston, Massachusetts. He remained there until his death.

Coomaraswamy was a devoted advocate both of the Philosophia Perennis and of Indian art and culture. He was centrally involved both in the cosmopolitan pursuit of truth, goodness, and beauty and in the Asian Renaissance (1908-1947). His work focused on the obtaining of glimpses of wisdom, especially those glimpses afforded via Oriental culture. He argued not for cultural relativism but for a pluralism that recognizes traditions to be precious paths to universal wisdom.

A critic of commercialism, modernism, and egalitarianism, Coomaraswamy was subject to accusations of being an aristocratic reactionary, a feudalist, and a hierarchist. He maintained that, rather than being the aristocratic master, he was merely the obedient servant, faithfully transmitting the wisdom of the ages. Rather than being a feudalist, he was offering a perennial alternative to the chaos and disharmony of modernism. Rather than arguing for an arbitrary hierarchy, he offered an ancient and compelling case for justifiable preference.

Consistent with the substance of the Philosophia Perennis, Coomaraswamy maintained that both biographies and bibliographies are trivial at best, egotistical at worst. His task was to express neither himself nor merely his culture. Rather, his role was one of stewardship of, and piety toward, truth, goodness, and beauty. Nevertheless, copious accounts concerning his life and his work are available.

His bibliography includes several classics in Indian music, theology, philosophy, and art. Those classics include *Mediaeval Sinhalese Art* (1908), *Catalogue of the Indian Collections in the Museum of Fine Arts, Boston* (1923-1930), *History of Indian and Indonesian Art* (1927), *The Transformation of Nature in Art* (1934), and *Why Exhibit Works of Art* (1943), reprinted as *Christian and Oriental Philosophy of Art* (1956).

Coordination Council for North American Affairs (CCNAA): The de facto embassy of Taiwan (officially the Republic of China, or ROC) in the United States. After the United States ended formal diplomatic relations with the ROC and established them with the People's Republic of China on January 1, 1979, the ROC created the nongovernmental CCNAA in order to maintain unofficial relations with the United States.

On the American side, Congress signed the Taiwan Relations Act into law on April 10, 1979. The act authorized the "continuation of commercial, cultural, and other relations between the people of the United

States and the people on Taiwan." It also provided that Taiwan and the United States would establish offices that would be given diplomatic privileges and immunities so that substantive, yet informal, relations between the two countries could continue. (See AMERICAN INSTITUTE ON TAIWAN.) On February 15, 1979, the CCNAA was established. The United States granted the officers of the CCNAA the equivalent of full diplomatic immunity and privileges.

CCNAA offices have been established throughout the United States in twelve major cities (Washington, D.C., New York City, Boston, Atlanta, Miami, Chicago, Kansas City, Houston, Seattle, San Francisco, Los Angeles, Honolulu) and a U.S. territory (Guam). These offices provide economic, trade, cultural, and tourist information about Taiwan. The CCNAA also functions as a consulate and issues visas to people traveling to Taiwan for business or tourism.

Coram nobis: In legal proceedings, a writ addressed to a court that calls attention to errors of fact that call into question a judgment already handed down. This Latin phrase means "before us." In the Japanese American community, *coram nobis* has come to refer to the 1980's legal petitions filed on behalf of Fred Toyosaburo KOREMATSU, Gordon Kiyoshi HIRABAYASHI, and Minoru YASUI, each of whom challenged the U.S. exclusion and curfew policies imposed on Japanese Americans during World War II.

In 1981, while examining archival documents on the above three resisters and on Mitsuye ENDO, law historian Peter Irons discovered complaints from government lawyers that evidence had been suppressed by their superiors in the cases of Korematsu, Hirabayashi, and Yasui. With this newfound evidence Irons was convinced that their convictions could be vacated using the obscure writ of error *coram nobis*. Irons contacted them and all three enthusiastically agreed to take up the fight. Irons proceeded to contact Sansei San Francisco attorney Dale MINAMI to head up Korematsu's legal team in the Bay Area. Peggy Nagae of Portland and Katherine Bannai of Seattle were chosen to represent Yasui and Hirabayashi, respectively. (See PEGGY NAGAE LUM.)

In January of 1983, *coram nobis* petitions on behalf of the three appellants were filed in the U.S. district courts. With phase one completed, the lawyers awaited the government's response.

Korematsu's case was the first to be heard, on October 4, 1983. The government asked Judge Marilyn Patel to vacate Korematsu's conviction and to dismiss the petition, arguing that it was inappropriate to judge the conviction forty years later. Patel denied the government's motion and in her opinion labeled the government response as "tantamount to a confession of error." The judge reminded listeners that she could not reverse the opinions of the Supreme Court and could not correct any errors of law made by the justices. With that in mind in April, 1984, she granted the petition for *coram nobis*, thus effectively vacating Korematsu's conviction.

Yasui's case was heard on January 16, 1984. Once again the government asked the court to vacate Yasui's conviction and dismiss the petition. Yasui's attorneys reminded the judge of the injustice of the internment and argued that the petition should be granted. On January 26, 1984, the judge accepted the government's motion. Because of the amount of time elapsed, the judge found it inappropriate to pass judgment on the previous ruling. Yasui appealed, but he died before a decision could be made on his case.

Hirabayashi received his hearing on May 18, 1984, one month after Judge Patel had issued her opinion on the Korematsu case. The government was growing increasingly concerned about the redress legislation in Congress and over the NATIONAL COUNCIL FOR JAPANESE AMERICAN REDRESS (NCJAR) class-action lawsuit that had been filed. It believed that it could not afford to suffer another setback and therefore viewed victory in the Hirabayashi case as a priority. It used delay tactics and introduced its star witness, who testified to the credibility of cables which allegedly proved the existence of espionage activity in the Japanese American community. The Hirabayashi legal team, however, was prepared and produced its own expert witnesses to discredit the government's case. After many delays, Hirabayashi finally received justice on January 12, 1988.

Cordova, Dorothy Laigo (b. Feb. 6, 1932, Seattle, Wash.): Historian. A second-generation Filipina American, she was director of the nationwide research project "The Forgotten Asian Americans: Filipinos and Koreans," which received funds from the National Endowment for the Humanities (NEH). In 1971, she helped organize the first national Filipino American youth convention, held in Seattle. In 1957, she and her husband, Fred CORDOVA, were among the cofounders of Filipino Youth Activities (FYA) of Seattle. Thousands of Filipino youths have participated in this program, which seeks to prevent juvenile delinquency. A sociology major at Seattle University (1949-1953), she earned a B.A. degree in community development from Western Washington University in 1976. Since 1976, Cordova has been the executive director of the DEMONSTRATION PROJECT FOR ASIAN AMERICANS. In 1982, she and her husband founded the FILIPINO AMERICAN NATIONAL HISTORICAL SOCIETY, which she also serves as executive director. A regent of Seattle University from 1980 to 1991, she was a lecturer in Asian American Studies at the University of Washington in 1988-1989.

Cordova, Fred (b. June 3, 1931, Selma, Calif.): Author. A longtime community advocate, Cordova fought for fair housing and education for minorities long before the Civil Rights movement began in the 1960's.

Cordova earned a B.A. degree in sociology from Seattle University in 1952. In 1957, he and his wife, Dorothy Laigo CORDOVA, were among the founders of Filipino Youth Activities (FYA) of Seattle. In 1959 he established that group's award-winning Princesa Drill Team, Cumbanchero Percussioneers and Mandayan Marchers, which he led for twenty years. By profession a journalist, he has been manager of Information Services at the University of Washington since 1974.

Author of *Filipinos: Forgotten Asian Americans* (1983), he also serves as archivist for the Seattle-based FILIPINO AMERICAN NATIONAL HISTORICAL SOCIETY, which he founded with his wife in 1982 and which he served as president. In 1985 he was a visiting faculty scholar at the Smithsonian Institution and has been a lecturer in Asian American Studies at the University of Washington.

Cortez Colony: Christian Japanese agricultural settlement founded in 1919 by Abiko Kyutaro in the San Joaquin Valley. During the height of anti-Japanese and anti-Asian sentiment, it provided a way for farming families to survive the difficult economic and social climate of the times. As a cooperative, farmers could pool their resources to buy supplies and machines and jointly market their produce.

Credit-ticket system: System that allowed Chinese immigrants to borrow passage money at the port of departure in lieu of repayment after arriving in North America. During the second half of the nineteenth century, thousands of Chinese emigrated to Southeast Asia, islands in the Pacific and Indian oceans, the West Indies, Latin America, and North America. Some emigrated under the infamous coolie system, which often involved kidnapping and years of brutal contracted

servitude in countries such as Peru and Cuba. (See COOLIE TRADE.) Those emigrating under the credit-ticket system came voluntarily and without restrictions on their freedom of movement after arrival. (See CHINESE CONTRACT LABOR.)

Most of those emigrating to North America came from the Chinese provinces of Guangdong and Fujian. They were usually young men, who often had wives and children in China. They were driven by the economic hardship caused from years of drought, famine, and rebellions in their home districts and lured by the tales of gold and good wages in California and the western United States and Canada.

They usually traveled from their home village to Hong Kong, where they booked passage for San Francisco. Some were able to pay for their own passage, but most were forced to rely on the credit-ticket system. Under the credit-ticket system, an immigrant would borrow passage money and perhaps an advance of three or four months' wages (for their family needs) from a broker in the departing port. After arriving in the United States, the immigrant would then repay his debt (usually in installments) to a connecting agent. Debt repayment was usually cleared each year, and before an immigrant could return to China.

Creole. *See* **Pidgin**

Crib papers (also, coaching papers): Extremely detailed lists of answers to questions asked of would-be Chinese immigrants to the United States. Such lists were used by Chinese to memorize events about family life to establish their relationship with a Chinese parent (usually the father) who was already a citizen in the United States. Such papers were a virtual necessity in the face of the extraordinary efforts made by U.S. immigration officials to block suspected fraudulent "paper" sons and/or daughters trying to immigrate. (See PAPER SONS.) Officials asked detailed, probing, often extremely personal questions to discover any discrepancy on which to deny the application for immigration.

The officials believed many Chinese immigrants were fraudulently evading the Chinese Exclusion acts, which severely limited Chinese immigration to the United States. One exemption that allowed Chinese entry was a provision that permitted all American citizens to bring their foreign-born children into the country. Although few Chinese had become naturalized U.S. citizens before the passage of laws barring Chinese naturalization, immigration officials were so opposed to Chinese immigration that they wished to block even this handful of individuals. U.S. officials believed many American citizens of Chinese ancestry were fraudulently creating paper sons and daughters by returning to China and claiming to father children in new or previous marriages. These so-called parents would return to the United States and register their purported children, who could later immigrate. Immigration officials were deeply suspicious if such births were twin sons since this produced two immigrants. Further, the fraud was thought to extend to Chinese American citizens registering nonexistent births, which would create "slots" that could then be sold to totally unrelated Chinese immigrants.

To block this alleged fraud, the officials used extremely rigorous questions to find any discrepancies in the stories told by the immigrants and their fathers in separate interrogations. Such questions included: "How many letters did you receive from your Chinese American father?" "How many steps were there to the front door of your Chinese home?" "Where was the family rice bin located?" Or, "What kind of floor covering was there in the bedroom?"

To ensure the Chinese applicant would be as well prepared as possible, these crib papers provided detailed answers to nearly every question officials might ask. Crib papers were necessary even for valid children of American citizens of Chinese ancestry because the questions were so complex that even a valid claimant might accidentally be denied entry.

Crocker, Charles (Sept. 16, 1822, Troy, N.Y.—Aug. 14, 1888, Monterey, Calif.): Railroad magnate and financier. Enterprising and ambitious, he left school at age twelve and borrowed the money needed to buy the agency for a New York newspaper. He sold the business in 1836, turning a profit of a hundred dollars. In 1849 he went to California to mine for gold. A few years later he was a successful Sacramento merchant. Crocker was one of a handful of men who founded the Central Pacific Railroad in the early 1860's for the purpose of building lines throughout the American West. As superintendent he hired large numbers of Chinese immigrants to work on the transcontinental railroad, which was finally completed in 1869. Crocker preferred Chinese laborers to other laborers, believing that the former were more dependable and productive; they were also cheaper.

CrossCurrent Media: Provides nonbroadcast distribution services for the San Francisco-based NATIONAL ASIAN AMERICAN TELECOMMUNICATIONS ASSOCIATION (NAATA), a nonprofit, tax-exempt group committed to advancing the ideals of cultural pluralism in the United States. through media arts.

Since it began in 1986, CrossCurrent Media has sold and rented films, videos, and audio cassettes by and about Asian Pacific Americans to many consumers throughout the country, with most sales—about two-thirds of its business—going to universities and colleges, followed by secondary schools and libraries. Most of its rentals go to corporations, governmental groups, and community-based groups. It does not market pieces to television, radio, or cable stations but rather focuses its work on academic and other institutions.

A nonprofit entity, its collection of media productions represents a broad spectrum of the Asian Pacific American community. With a solid base of works about the history and experiences of older immigrants, such as Chinese and Japanese Americans, the group's catalog includes a growing selection of pieces by and about other segments of the community, such as Southeast Asians, South Asians, Filipinos, Pacific Islanders, and gays and lesbians. Similarly, beginning with an emphasis on documentaries, its expanded genres include videos and other shorter works, which tend to be more experimental in nature.

Among its most popular titles are *A Personal Matter: Gordon Hirabayashi v. the United States* (1992), a story of one of the Japanese American men who refused to obey the U.S. government's internment orders; *Slaying the Dragon* (1988), which looks at the images of Asian American women in media; *Troubled Paradise* (1991), a look at the impact of progress on the survival of Hawaii's indigenous populations; and *Sa-I-Gu: From Korean Women's Perspectives* (1993), in which Korean immigrant women shopkeepers talk about their life and dreams in the United States.

It has served as the primary source of media materials since the establishment of Asian Pacific American Heritage month, which usually takes place annually in May. Its catalog, designed to be user-friendly, is organized thematically according to ethnicity and issues and also puts together several pieces in special collections to help groups start their own film festivals and to make better selections to fit the needs and levels of knowledge of their audiences.

Crystal City: World War II facility in Crystal City, Texas, used to imprison German, Italian, and Japanese enemy aliens and their families. Crystal City included grounds for farming, living quarters, playgrounds (featuring a reservoir converted into a swimming pool), and utilities. It was one of four internment camps on the American mainland administered by the Immigration and Naturalization Service (INS) of the U.S. Justice Department. Internees were sent to the camps after having been declared national security risks during formal hearings and were subject to deportation at the insistence of the American government. Nondisruptive Japanese evacuees were allowed to live with their families in one of ten relocation centers administered by the U.S. War Relocation Authority (WRA).

Cubic Air Ordinance (1870): One of a number of statutes enacted by the San Francisco Board of Supervisors for the purpose of harassing the Chinese while halting further Chinese immigration. The Cubic Air Ordinance required that each tenement contain at least five hundred cubic feet of air per inhabitant. The law was enforced only in Chinatown, and, where violations occurred, authorities arrested not the white landlords but the Chinese tenants. Violators were both fined and imprisoned. The ordinance was annulled in 1873.

CWIRC. *See* **Commission on Wartime Relocation and Internment of Civilians**

D

Dacca: Capital of BANGLADESH (formerly East Pakistan), located in the center of the country. Combined with the access provided by the river port of Narayanganj, an industrial suburb of Dacca, the city now boasts the largest industrial concentration in all of Bangladesh. Dacca's population was more than 6.1 million in 1991. Dacca is also the name of a division of Bangladesh, with a population of almost 32.3 million people in 1991.

Daihyo Sha Kai: Japanese internee organization formed in October, 1943, at the TULE LAKE segregation center. The Daihyo Sha Kai (representative body) was composed of camp leaders demanding that living conditions there be improved. One representative from each of the center's sixty-four residential blocks was elected to the group, with seven of those individuals forming the negotiating committee.

Tule Lake authorities refused to negotiate seriously with the organization, however, resulting in much internal unrest among the evacuees. The failure of officials to take a more sympathetic approach to the issues being raised provoked a condition of mutual hostility that lasted until the center's closure in 1946. In November, 1943, after violence broke out between camp administrators and some of the evacuees toward the end of a forced negotiating session, U.S. troops were called in to restore order, and martial law was imposed. A curfew was issued and a stockade built in which hundreds of internees were detained without benefit of hearings or trials. Not until January, 1944, was martial law lifted.

Daimyo: Territorial lord in Japan. From around the tenth century, *daimyo* controlled land, levied taxes, and had vassals who served them. By 1867, however, the *daimyo* were mere figureheads, although they remained in power until the feudal period ended with the Meiji Restoration (1868-1912), when, in 1869, the new Meiji regime forced them to return their land to the emperor.

Daniels, Roger (b. 1927, New York, N.Y.): Historian. Daniels is a veteran of World War II and the Korean War. He attended the University of Houston and the University of California, Los Angeles (UCLA), where in 1961 he earned his Ph.D. degree. Professor of history at the University of Cincinnati, he has spent much of his career studying the history of Asian Americans, becoming a leading scholar in the field. Among his many books are *The Politics of Prejudice: The Anti-Japanese Movement in California and the Struggle for Japanese Exclusion* (1962), *American Racism: Exploration of the Nature of Prejudice* (1970; coauthored with Harry H. L. Kitano), *Asian America: Chinese and Japanese in the United States Since 1850* (1988), and *Coming to America: A History of Immigration and Ethnicity in American Life* (1990). He is the editor of an interdisciplinary series, The Asian American Experience, published by the University of Illinois Press. Daniels has also had a hand in the making of such historical films as *Refugee Road* (1982), *Nisei Soldier* (1984), and *Unfinished Business* (1986). During the early 1980's he was a consultant to the U.S. COMMISSION ON WARTIME RELOCATION AND INTERNMENT OF CIVILIANS (CWRIC).

D'Aquino, Iva Toguri. *See* **Tokyo Rose**

Daruma: Japanese doll named after Bodhidharma (or Daruma, in Japanese), the monk who brought Zen Buddhism from India to China in the sixth century. First appearing in Japan during the seventeenth century as protection against smallpox, the doll is still used by some Japanese Americans for luck in business ventures.

Das, Tarak Nath (June 15, 1884, near Calcutta, West Bengal, India—Dec. 22, 1958, New York City, N.Y.?): Student activist, author, lecturer, and political revolutionary. Das campaigned vigorously in the United States on two issues of great importance to expatriate Asian Indians in the early decades of the twentieth century: Canadian and American immigration exclusion laws, and Indian independence from repressive British rule.

As a college student in West Bengal, Das got involved in antipartition politics and fled to Japan to escape arrest by the British Indian government. From Japan, he made his way to the United States, arriving alone and penniless in Seattle, Washington, in 1906. He studied at several campuses in the United States, including the University of California, Berkeley; Norwich University in Northfield, Vermont; and the University of Washington, where he obtained his master's degree in 1911. In 1924, he received his doctorate degree from Georgetown University.

In 1907, while working as a translator for the U.S. immigration service in Vancouver, he published the first issue of *Free Hindustan*, a radical monthly in which he called on all Indians to fight exclusion laws, bring their families to Canada, and contribute to the cause of Indian independence. Das applied repeatedly for American citizenship at a time when anti-Asian sentiment was rampant in the United States. After a long and persistent struggle with the U.S. naturalization service, he became a naturalized citizen in 1914 in San Francisco but continued to clash with authorities because of his radical anti-British activities. (See GHADR MOVEMENT.) Kept under constant political surveillance, he was indicted for "anti-American" plots during World War I (1914-1918) and sentenced to imprisonment in Leavenworth Federal Prison, Kansas. In prison, he was threatened with deportation, but with the help of Friends for the Freedom of India, an organization that he formed in 1921, he prepared his own defense and managed to avoid deportation on the basis of his American citizenship.

Even after he was released from prison, the government kept up its efforts to revoke his citizenship. His American wife, Mary K. Das, was denied a passport in 1926 on the grounds that her husband was Indian. Das vigorously opposed the denaturalization drive until 1927, when all pending cases for denaturalization were finally canceled.

Day of Remembrance: Yearly memorial observed in major American cities having large numbers of Japanese Americans to recall the signing of EXECUTIVE ORDER 9066 (1942). This ceremony typically occurs around February 19, and, into the 1990's, has helped the community to remain mindful of the incarceration of Japanese Americans during World War II. The first such observance occurred during Thanksgiving in Seattle in 1978 and involved a reenactment of the forced relocation of evacuees to the Puyallup assembly center.

A woman places flowers atop a gravestone at the former site of the Manzanar relocation center in central California. (Mike Yamashita)

Dayal, Har (Oct. 14, 1884, Delhi, India—Mar. 4, 1939, Philadelphia, Pa.): Political activist and writer. Noted for his contribution to the extremist phase of the Asian Indian nationalist movement (1905-1919), Dayal played a leading role in the formation of the Ghadr Party in San Francisco in 1913 and in mobilizing Indians residing in the United States and Canada into a team of revolutionaries pledged to overthrow British rule in India.

Born into a well-connected Punjabi Hindu family, Dayal received his B.A. degree from Saint Stephen's College, Delhi (1903) and his M.A. degree from Government College, Lahore (1904). In 1905, he went to England on a Government of India scholarship to study at the University of Oxford. There, his association with V. D. Savarkar, a militant Hindu nationalist, brought him into revolutionary politics. Dayal resigned his scholarship in 1907 and returned to India in 1908 to preach the ideology of revolution.

Dayal arrived in California in 1911. In 1912, while serving on the faculty of Stanford University, he founded the Radical Club in San Francisco and kept up an active propaganda of his revolutionary ideas. In 1913, he established the Hindu Association of the Pacific Coast, with its radical newspaper, *Ghadr*, both headquartered in San Francisco. On November 1, 1913, he changed the association's name to the Ghadr Party, which later launched the GHADR MOVEMENT to free India from British domination. In March, 1914, he was arrested by U.S. immigration authorities as an undesirable alien. Released on bail, he fled to Switzerland and from there to Germany, where he stayed during World War I (1914-1918), organizing support for India's struggle for freedom.

After the war, Dayal became a pacifist and a supporter of the Indian Home Rule movement. In 1927, he was allowed to return to England, where he completed his Ph.D. degree at the University of London in 1930.

A man of encyclopedic knowledge, Dayal lectured widely in the United States and Europe and published numerous articles. He also authored the following books: *Forty-four Months in Germany and Turkey: February 1915 to October 1918* (1920), *Our Educational Problem* (1922), *The Bodhisattva Doctrine in Buddhist Sanskrit Literature* (1932), *Hints for Self-Culture* (1934), and *Twelve Religions and Modern Life* (1938).

Declaration of the All-Korean Convention (1941): Agreement announced by representatives from nine social and political organizations determined to overcome internal factionalism within the Korean community in the United States and to work together against Japanese colonial rule in Korea. The fourteen representatives met in Honolulu, Hawaii on April 20, 1941. The organizations maintained their original structure and purpose but pledged their intention to uphold the authority of the newly formed committee, giving it exclusive control over diplomatic activities and financial contributions in support of Korean independence.

Deepawali. *See* **Diwali**

Dekaseginin: Japanese term designating people who leave home to earn wages. The term is often applied to early Japanese immigrants to the United States. These sojourners were extending a native tradition.

In times of rural depression in late-nineteenth century Japan, many villagers found it necessary to leave their home for limited-term employment in towns and cities. In the early days of Japanese industrialization, management was slow to develop a stable, skilled workforce, and most industrial workers were seasonal or part-time workers. When the harvest was in, the normal seasonal cottage industries having been undermined by cheap manufactured imports, the excess agrarian labor force migrated to urban industrial centers. Wages were low for temporary workers, yet meager wages were welcome in rural households, many of which existed on a bare subsistence level. When the term of employment was concluded, the *dekasegi* worker would return to the home village and resume farming. The number of temporary workers also fluctuated with the demands of the business cycle. In boom times many men and women would leave the farm villages for the urban industrial centers; in slack times temporary workers would return to the agricultural villages. *Dekasegi* were most often employed in coal mining, construction, fishing canneries, and sake brewing industries.

The low wages paid to *dekasegi* allowed management to pay higher wages to full-time employees. As management began to realize the disadvantages of an unstable temporary worker labor force, it began to develop a skilled, elite blue-collar labor force. Not until the 1920's, however, did a majority of heavy industries employ a corps of trained, permanent workers.

Women *dekasegi* workers were employed in spinning mills throughout Japan. Lured by promises of high wages and better living conditions, thousands of young daughters of tenant farmers were "leased" by their parents as temporary workers in textile plants. These women worked long hours and were subject to the ravages of lung diseases and the paternalistic, rigid discipline of the mill operators. Most of the women were virtual slaves until their term of employment expired.

Many, though by no means all, of the early Japanese immigrants came to Hawaii and later to the United States as *dekasegi* workers or sojourners. Most of the early immigrants to Hawaii came as contract laborers who hoped to save money and return home. Gradually, however, and despite the considerable prejudice and discrimination which they encountered, the orientation of many of the Japanese immigrants began to shift toward permanent settlement.

Delano grape strike. *See* **Agricultural Workers Organizing Committee**

Demonstration Project for Asian Americans: Community-based research agency in Seattle, Washington, founded in 1971. Under the leadership of founder Dorothy Laigo CORDOVA, the group has conducted numerous studies and advocacy programs within various Asian American ethnic groups, including Chinese, Japanese, Koreans, Pacific Islanders, and especially Filipinos.

Aware of the dearth of materials about Filipino Americans, Cordova and the agency determined to collect and record stories about the immigrant experience and about settlement in the United States. The organization taught community residents how to conduct interviews and encouraged them to write their own oral histories in order to preserve the story of Filipinos in America.

Some of the tapes, pictures, and other research materials, collected as a part of a National Endowment for the Humanities (NEH) project grant, formed the basis of the pictorial essay *Filipinos: Forgotten Asian Americans, A Pictorial Essay, 1763-Circa 1963*. Written by Fred CORDOVA and published by the agency in 1983, the book became one of the first reference works about Filipino Americans. It contains historical information, family photos, and personal stories about immigration to, and survival in, the United States.

The agency also collected oral histories and photos that Dorothy Cordova organized into a 1985 traveling photo exhibit, "Filipino Women in America, 1860-1985." The organization has focused resources on development of a color poster series on Asian Pacific American role models.

The agency houses the FILIPINO AMERICAN NATIONAL HISTORICAL SOCIETY's National Pinoy Archives, which is designed to preserve materials on Filipino American history and culture and to make them available for education and research purposes.

Denationalization Act of 1944: U.S. law that amended the Nationality Act of 1940 and allowed American citizens living in the United States to renounce their citizenship during wartime. The act (Public Law 405) was signed by President Franklin D. Roosevelt on July 1, 1944.

While the act applied to all American citizens, it was drafted with Japanese Americans in mind. The act had a dual origin. On the one hand, it grew out of the actions of the militantly pro-Japanese faction of internees, the HOKUKU SEINEN-DAN (Young Men's Organization to Serve the Mother Country), at the TULE LAKE relocation center in Northern California. After internees deemed "disloyal" (see LOYALTY OATH) had been segregated at Tule Lake in September and October of 1943, Hokuku members persuaded and coerced many to request expatriation to Japan. Given their treatment at the hands of the U.S. government, many internees understandably believed that there was no future for them in the United States. In all, 7,222 persons—more than a third of Tule Lake's population of 18,000—requested expatriation to Japan.

This was one source of the 1944 act. The other was the U.S. government's fear—always greatly exaggerated—of "subversive elements" among Japanese Americans, and a desire to root them out. The 1944 act, drafted in response to the requests for expatriation, served that purpose. The result was a law that created great confusion and distress among the internees, some of whom renounced their citizenship because they had been told that the government was planning to break up families, deporting the Issei, who were not citizens. Ultimately more than 5,000 Japanese Americans formally renounced their citizenship under the terms of the 1944 act; in addition, a significant number of Issei requested repatriation to Japan.

After the war, President Harry S Truman signed an executive order initiating the removal of the renunciants and the noncitizens requesting repatriation. More than 4,500 were sent to Japan, including about 1,000 adult Nisei, 1,659 noncitizens, and about 2,000 others, mostly children.

The process was stopped by the intervention of attorney Wayne COLLINS, who argued that the renunciations had been made under duress. A 1948 ruling in-

President Franklin D. Roosevelt. (Franklin Delano Roosevelt Library)

validated the renunciations, but that blanket judgment was modified by a 1950 court decision requiring that each renunciation be certified individually as having been coerced, except in the cases of approximately 1,000 children, for whom the blanket ruling still held. In the long run, most of the renunciants applied to have their citizenship restored and chose to return to the United States. As a result of the 1950 decision, however, the last case was not cleared until 1968.

Henry Der.

Der, Henry (b. Dec. 30, 1946, San Francisco, Calif.): Community advocate. He became executive director of CHINESE FOR AFFIRMATIVE ACTION in 1974, and is regarded as a leading spokesperson in the Asian American community. He has fought for the passage of the bilingual election amendments to the 1965 Voting Rights Act, persuaded the Census Bureau to retain the nine Asian American groups in the race question of the 1990 census, and opposed discriminatory university admission quotas.

Deshler, David W.: Labor recruiter and businessman. Stepson of a powerful Ohio politician, Deshler traveled to Korea in 1896 in search of business opportuni-

ties. After his arrival, Deshler established a mining operation in Korea and other enterprises in Japan. Meanwhile, his stepfather used his political connections with the McKinley Administration to secure Horace N. Allen's appointment as ambassador to Korea in 1897. In 1902, Allen was contacted by representatives of the HAWAIIAN SUGAR PLANTERS' ASSOCIATION (HSPA), who wanted his help in developing a plan for sending Korean laborers to work on sugar plantations in Hawaii. Famine in Korea and the royal government's interest in improving its international status by assisting the United States helped Allen gain the Korean emperor's approval of the immigration plan. Allen seized upon a plan to repay his political debt to Deshler's stepfather by asking Deshler to set up the necessary arrangements to facilitate the recruitment of Korean immigrant workers. Deshler posted announcements to recruit workers, hired interpreters to explain the terms of emigration, opened a bank in order to lend money from the HSPA to Korean immigrants to pay for their passage, and used his own ships to transport many of the laborers. Between December of 1902 and May of 1905, approximately seven thousand Koreans emigrated to Hawaii to work on the sugar plantations. In 1905, the Korean government halted emigration as a result of reports of mistreatment and abuse suffered by Korean workers in Mexico and because the Japanese government exerted pressure on Korea to bar Hawaii plantation owners from using Korean immigrants to replace striking Japanese laborers. Deshler secured a substantial fortune from the emigration franchise, profiting handsomely from the $54 subsidy he received from Hawaii plantation owners for each male adult worker who was transported to Hawaii.

DeWitt, John Lesesne (Jan. 9, 1880, Fort Sidney, Nebr.—June 20, 1962, Washington, D.C.): U.S. Army officer. DeWitt was commander of the Fourth Army on the West Coast during World War II (1939-1945). Although DeWitt is remembered as the primary proponent of excluding Japanese Americans from the West Coast during the war, it is clear that he was only one of a number of individuals who took that position. As the only government bureaucrat involved in the debate who did not possess a law degree, he often played the role of middleman while government lawyers argued about the legality of the Japanese American internment.

DeWitt was a career military man. He grew up on Army posts. Following a brief stint at Princeton University, he enrolled in the Army to fight in the Spanish-American War in 1898. Ironically this was the only combat he was to experience. His talent for bureaucracy was his calling.

In the days following the bombing of Pearl Harbor, DeWitt suggested a mass purging of Japanese, German, and Italian nationals from the West Coast for security reasons. Unlike Army Provost Marshall General Allen W. Gullion, who favored the removal of all Japanese Americans, DeWitt stopped short of recommending the imprisonment of American-born Japanese. "An American citizen, after all," he told Gullion, "is an American citizen."

DeWitt's restraint, however, was short-lived. He received intense pressure from the press and West Coast politicians as well as from the War Department and Karl Bendetson, who had been hired by Gullion to organize the internment. Within weeks DeWitt joined his colleagues and became one of the strongest supporters of the Japanese American incarceration. At a congressional hearing on the internment of Japanese Americans, he stated: "A Jap's a Jap. . . . There is no way to determine their loyalty. . . . It makes no difference whether he is an American citizen; theoretically he is still a Japanese and you can't change him."

On February 13, 1942, DeWitt issued his *Final Recommendation*, which had been ghostwritten by Bendetson. In the document DeWitt stated that "military necessity" required the exclusion of all Japanese from military areas to be designated by the Army. This was to be the basis for EXECUTIVE ORDER 9066, signed by President Franklin D. Roosevelt on February 19, 1942. In 1943 DeWitt reiterated and expanded his arguments in *Final Report: Japanese Evacuation from the West Coast* to justify the internment. An altered version of *Final Report* was used in the government briefs against Gordon K. HIRABAYASHI, Minoru YASUI, and Fred T. KOREMATSU.

In September of 1943 DeWitt became commandant of the Army and Navy Staff College in Washington. In 1954 he was appointed to the grade of full general through an act of Congress.

Dharma: Single most important concept in Indian culture, with a wide range of meanings. The term *dharma* originated from the Sanskrit root *dhr*, meaning to "sustain." Its common translation as "duty" misses the term's diversity of meaning and comprehensive role in an individual's life.

Dharma is the foundation of something or things in general, thus signifying "truth." This sense of the word is quite prominent in the *Mahabharata*, where Yudhishthira, a central protagonist, is often referred to as Dharmaraja, since he never tells a lie and is the embodiment of truth. *Dharma* also means that which is established, customary, and proper and thus means "traditional" or "ceremonial."

In the *Mahabharata* again, Yudhishthira (a Pandava) crosses over to the Kaurava camp just before the final battle to pay respects to Bhishma, the family patriarch, and seek his blessing. Bhishma readily offers his blessing. The actions of both characters preserve the integrity of tradition and ceremony.

In addition, *dharma* means one's duty, responsibility, or imperative and thereby one's "moral obligation." This common meaning of the word is quite apparent in Rama's decision, in the *Ramayana*, to honor his father's commitments and go into voluntary exile, renouncing his claim to the throne. *Dharma* is that which is right, virtuous, meritorious, and accordingly ethical. An additional meaning is that it is something required or permitted through religious authority and thus "legal."

Dharma thus represents "correctness"—both in a descriptive sense (the way things are) and in a prescriptive one (the way things should be). It is closely related to the Vedic notion of *rta*, the universal harmony in which all things have a proper place and function. *Dharma* determines the personal actions of the individual that engender or maintain cosmic order. Hence, when people willfully follow the path of *adharma* (the opposite of *dharma*), then the results are nothing less than catastrophic: cosmic disorder.

Dharma has come to mean the sum total of one's obligations by which one "fits in" with the natural and, especially, the social world. As a result, a person's duties are determined by one's social class and stage of life (*asrama*). A Brahmin has his own *dharma*, as does the Vaisya. The obligations of individuals (depending on the caste) include mutually supporting one another, and an imperfect performance of one's responsibilities harms society as well as the world.

Diaoyutai movement. *See* **China politics in the Chinese American community**

Dien Bien Phu, Battle of (1954): Decisive battle between Viet Minh and French forces in North Vietnam. The disastrous French defeat paved the way for the Geneva accords of 1954, which ended not only the First Indochina War (1946-1954) but also more than eighty years of French rule in Vietnam.

In the wake of World War II (1939-1945), the Viet Minh achieved prominence in the Indochina theater because of the end of the Japanese occupation and the weakened French army. Supported by China and the Soviet Union, the Viet Minh forces used guerrilla tactics to tie down French troops and gradually control most of the country. In late 1953, French general Henri Navarre ordered the occupation of a valley near Dien Bien Phu, a small Vietnamese town near the Laotian border, in hope of luring the Viet Minh into battle. French commanders dismissed the enemy as logistically inferior and firmly believed that French artillery and airpower would overwhelm any attempt to storm the garrison from the heights. France, furthermore, was at the time heavily aided by the United States. General Vo Nguyen Giap, the Viet Minh commander,

French troops interrogate a soldier suspected of belonging to the Viet Minh army after routing him from the jungle. (National Archives)

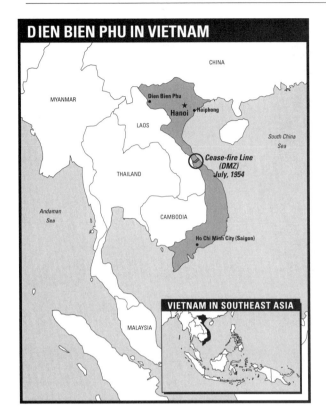

DIEN BIEN PHU IN VIETNAM

CHINA

MYANMAR

Dien Bien Phu

Hanoi ★ •Haiphong

LAOS

South China
Sea

THAILAND

Cease-fire Line
(DMZ)
July, 1954

Andaman
Sea

CAMBODIA

Ho Chi Minh City (Saigon)

VIETNAM IN SOUTHEAST ASIA

MALAYSIA

however, surrounded the base within the first few weeks with more than forty thousand fighters. More impressively, this army was supplied by a constant flow of weapons and food carried across the mountains by tens of thousands of Viet Minh.

Major fighting began on March 13, 1954, with the Viet Minh employing heavy artillery and human wave assaults against the base. Béatrice, one of the base's strongpoints, fell the very next day. The Vietnamese continued this strategy, capturing French strongholds in rapid succession before besieging the few remaining positions. French resistance finally ended when a cease fire was called on May 7, 1954, and the base's commander, General Christian de Castries, was captured by the Vietnamese. Approximately five thousand French troops died, with ten thousand more taken as prisoners; the Vietnamese suffered an estimated twenty-three thousand casualties.

The battle of Dien Bien Phu sent shockwaves throughout the world. Never until then had a Western power incurred a defeat of this magnitude from forces of a Third World nation. Although the Viet Minh victory brought independence from France, it nevertheless hastened an even bloodier conflict: the Second Indochina War (1954-1975).

Dillingham Commission: Hawaii state government panel created in 1907 and charged with persuading Congress that Chinese laborers were crucial to the state's economy. In 1900, when the Organic Act transformed the Hawaiian Islands into the Territory of Hawaii, U.S. constitutional guarantees superseded provisions of the constitution of the Republic of Hawaii. As this meant that legal peonage was now ended, strikes broke out on every plantation. Since the principal strikers were contract laborers from Japan, plantation owners responded by seeking strikebreakers from other countries. An influx of Koreans, Okinawans, and Puerto Ricans began, but the plantation owners were still dissatisfied, recalling that Chinese laborers were the best plantation workers of all. Since the Chinese Exclusion Act (1882) and subsequent legislation excluding Chinese laborers applied to Hawaii from 1900, the territorial government sought a waiver from the federal government. To make this case, the territorial governor, Charles McCarthy, established a commission to undertake a study and report for presentation to Congress. As the chair of the commission was Walter Dillingham, the body became known as the Dillingham Commission. The commission went to Congress in 1907.

When Congress questioned the authors of the report, which claimed that a "labor emergency" existed in Hawaii, one of the questions was why the sugarcane owners sought only nonwhite workers. The memorable answer was that "God did not intend the white man to go out in the cane break." To California congressional delegates there were too many Chinese in the Golden State, so the idea of a ban on all "Orientals" seemed appealing. Anticipating the worst, the Japanese government responded to the furor by agreeing to the so-called GENTLEMEN'S AGREEMENT (1907) with U.S. President Theodore Roosevelt. Under its terms the Japanese government promised to grant no more exit visas to Japanese male laborers. With sources of labor from Northeast Asia no longer available, the plantation owners then began to import large numbers of agricultural workers from the Philippine Islands. From 1907 to 1932 some 119,000 Filipinos filled the need for more workers as the Japanese left the plantations. The Dillingham Commission, which sought more Chinese laborers in Hawaii, was thus a total failure.

Ding, Loni (b. June 8, 1931, San Francisco, Calif.): Filmmaker. The first Asian American to regularly produce programs on Asian American affairs for the general public, she was cofounder of the NATIONAL ASIAN

Pioneering Asian American filmmaker Loni Ding. (San Francisco Chronicle)

AMERICAN TELECOMMUNICATIONS ASSOCIATION (NAATA) and president of Vox Productions, an independent media consultation and publication company. She has taught at major universities, including Cornell University and University of California, Berkeley, and won many awards, including Northern California Emmys for *Nisei Soldier* (1984), and *Bean Sprouts* (1982).

Displaced Persons Act of 1948: U.S. legislation that allowed 3,465 Chinese in the United States to adjust their immigration status. The act was primarily intended to help resettle thousands of Europeans, notably Austrians, Italians, Germans, Polish, and Russians, displaced by World War II (1939-1945). 400,000 slots were authorized by law, and these were to be charged against future immigration quotas of the respective countries.

Fifteen thousand of the numbers allocated were to provide relief for aliens already in the United States, provided they had entered legally prior to April 1, 1948, were legally admissible, were displaced from the country of their birth or last residence because of events subsequent to World War II, and could not return to their country because of persecution or fear of persecution. The act was amended in 1950, extending the date of legal entry to the United States to April 30, 1949.

A number of Chinese in the United States became eligible under the act when Communist forces gained victory in China in 1949, establishing the People's Republic of China. Ultimately a total of 3,465 Chinese students, officials, and seamen stranded in the United States had their status adjusted to permanent residents. Thousands more, including other Asians such as Filipinos, entered the United States as displaced persons.

The extra slots were a vent to the strict limitations of the IMMIGRATION ACT OF 1943, which repealed the Chinese EXCLUSION ACT OF 1882 and gave China an annual quota allowing 105 immigrants to enter the United States.

The Displaced Persons Act expired in 1952, but the numbers of refugees from both Europe and Asia continued to swell, resulting in the REFUGEE RELIEF ACT OF 1953, which was a continuation of its predecessor, except that many were admitted as nonquota immigrants. Under this act, more than sixteen thousand Asians entered the United States or adjusted their status. Another act, the Refugee Relief Act of 1957, allowed close to ten thousand Asians into the United States. These included refugees from China, Korea, Japan, and Indonesia, as well as other parts of Asia.

Mortgaging of the quotas under the Displaced Persons Act resulted in the unavailability of quotas to other applicants. In 1957, the numbers mortgaged were restored and unencumbered from the national quotas.

District associations: Chinese social organizations in the United States representing immigrants' native regions and unique spoken dialects. Chinese immigrants in the United States not only were socially and economically divided but also represented a variety of districts, cultures, and spoken languages.

The rich and more respectable merchants were generally the San-yi (from the three Guangdong districts of Nanhai, Panyu, and Shunde); the petty merchants, artisans, and agriculturalists were mainly among the Si-yi (from the four Guangdong districts of Enping, Kaiping, Taishan or Xining, and Xinhui); and the laboring class came from a variety of regions. Then there were the Hakkas (guest settlers), who generally dominated the barber business, and the tenant farmers, engaging in fruit growing in the Sacramento-San Joaquin Valley, who were mostly Zhongshan immigrants.

Each region spoke its own local variation of Cantonese, so there was a basic correspondence between Chinese class structure and dialect groups. The people from Canton and the San-yi spoke Cantonese, and that dialect came to be considered standard. Most people from the Zhongshan district, about thirty miles south of Canton, spoke a dialect closely resembling the standard Cantonese, but those from the surrounding countryside spoke a dialect akin to Amoy. The Si-yi people, who made up the bulk of Chinese immigrants, spoke a dialect almost totally incomprehensible to city dwellers. Finally, among the heterogeneous groups were the Hakkas. Originally migrating from North China, the Hakkas spoke a dialect more akin to Mandarin than the other groups. Though the Hakkas never constituted more than 10 percent of the Chinese population in the continental United States, they made up about 25 percent of the Chinese in Hawaii.

Among these dialect groups there was a long history of rivalry and sometimes conflict. The Cantonese called themselves Puntis, which meant "the natives," and considered the Hakkas invaders. In the United States, the Hakkas formed their district association called the Yan Wo Company (or Renhe Huigan), the Zhongshan immigrants founded the Yeong Wo Company (Yanghe Huiguan), the Taishan natives formed an exclusive organization called the Ning Yeung Company (or Ningyang Huiguan), the Kaiping and Enping

Chinese the Hop Wo Company (Hehe Huiguan), and the more affluent San-yi people organized their Sam Yup Association (or Sanyi Huiguan). By the 1860's, they combined all these district/dialect associations into the Zhonghua Huiguan, known in English as the Chinese Consolidated Benevolent Association (CCBA); it was widely known to Americans as the Chinese Six Companies. (See CHINESE CONSOLIDATED BENEVOLENT ASSOCIATIONS and HUIGUAN.)

Divination: Art of foretelling future events, frequently practiced by Chinese who believe in fortune-telling and geomancy. Divination is found in all civilizations, ancient and modern, and is practiced by interpreting omens and also with the help of supernatural powers and natural and psychological techniques.

Diwali (also, Deepawali): One of the four main Hindu festivals. It is celebrated the month of Kartika (mid-October to mid-November) on the first new-moon day when the sun reaches Libra. The word *diwali* literally means "row of lights."

For this day, the houses are thoroughly cleaned and freshly whitewashed or painted. In the evening, the women of each household worship the goddess Lakshmi and light rows of oil lamps in doorways, patios, verandas, and windows to celebrate the reappearance of the sun, which has been "hidden" during the rainy season by the malevolent water spirit. Rice-flour designs on doorsteps and threshholds as well as fireworks and illuminations in the evening make Diwali one of the most colorful and picturesque festivals in India.

Different events are celebrated on this day, pointing to the diverse and enduring appeal of this festival. Diwali is said to celebrate the marriage of Lakshmi, and Vishnu, the second of the Hindu Trinity. Lakshmi, also on this day, once a year liberates Bali, who was a prisoner in the seventh world, allowing him to roam in this world. On this day as well, Rama (an incarnation of the god Vishnu), having defeated the demon king Ravana, returns victorious with Seeta to Ayodhya after a fourteen-year exile. Expressing their joy at the return of their beloved Rama, the people illuminate oil lamps in their houses and all over the city. The day also celebrates Krishna's defeat of the demon Narakasura. According to the *Puranas*, on this day, the goddess Lakshmi dwells in oil and Ganga Devi in hot water. Therefore, a ritual bath in both brings the grace of both goddesses, cleansing an individual's sins. Such a bath is considered to be as sanctifying as a dip in the holy Ganges River.

Marking the beginning of a new commercial year, many merchants open new account books on this day. Diwali also announces the approach of winter, and winter crops are sown. Diwali is a festival of lights that dispels darkness in people's lives and offers a new beginning of hope and promise, while celebrating the victory of *dharma* over *adharma* (injustice).

Celebrated among Asian Indians in the United States, where it is often called Deepawali, the festival is very popular. In 1992, New York City's Deepawali festival, organized by the Association of Indians in America, drew a crowd of almost 250,000.

Dockworkers strike: Labor conflict involving the International Longshoremen's and Warehousemen's Union (ILWU) over the difference in the wages earned by longshoremen in Hawaii and those on the West Coast. West Coast longshoremen earned $1.82 an hour; in Hawaii, working the same ships with the same cargo and for the same company, they earned $1.40 an hour.

The Honolulu Advertiser depicted the strike, which had begun on May 1, 1949, as a communist plot to control Hawaii. On May 4, a four-column "Dear Joe" editorial appeared on the newspaper's front page, written by *Advertiser* publisher Lorrin Thurston, who would publish a series of similar pieces. "Joe" was supposed to be Joseph Stalin, the Soviet dictator. Cast in the form of a report, the editorials impliedly reflected the views of Harry Bridges, ILWU president, supposedly the leader of a communist conspiracy to dominate Hawaii.

In Hawaii the legislature passed a bill that gave the Territory of Hawaii the right to operate the docks and hire additional dockworkers at prestrike wages. The government stevedoring operation began on August 15.

The government-hired stevedores unloaded all the ships in the harbor and loaded those bound for Gulf and Atlantic ports. They did not load ships for the West Coast since there the ILWU would refuse to unload them.

The employers finally agreed to grant the laborers an increase of fourteen cents an hour on their return to work; eight cents an hour would be paid retroactively from March 1 to the end of June, 1949, with an additional seven cents payable beginning February 28, 1950. The strike officially ended on October 23, 1949. It had lasted 177 days. Research Associates of Honolulu estimated that the strike cost the islands $100 million.

By the end of the strike more than twenty-four thousand island residents were unemployed—17.6 percent of the workforce. Of those still employed some

The continuing political fallout from the dockworker's strike of 1949 included accusations of Communist Party infiltration within the ranks of the International Longshoremen's and Warehousemen's Union. Here union leader Jack Hall (right) testifies before the House Un-American Activities Committee in Honolulu in April, 1950, to answer charges of being a Communist sympathizer. (AP/Wide World Photos)

had had their pay cut by as much as half. Food prices had risen 6 percent. The strike had split the community into opposing sides, bankrupted some small merchants, caused large financial losses to industry and wage earners, and established the ILWU as a power in Hawaii.

Doho: Japanese term that refers to all ethnic Japanese at home and abroad, whatever their citizenship. The term is traditionally placed after the name of the country of residence—Hawaii *doho*, for example.

Doi, Isami (May 12, 1903, Ewa, Oahu, Territory of Hawaii—1965): Artist. Earning a B.A. degree in art studies from Columbia University, he moved to Paris to continue his training from 1930 until 1931. Back in New York, he became an important adviser to many Japanese American artists and encouraged them in their work. Later, he returned to Hawaii, where he had begun his art studies, and continued to paint. His work has been exhibited in various museums and galleries.

Doi, Nelson Kiyoshi (b. Jan. 1, 1922, Pahoa, Hawaii): Lieutenant governor of Hawaii. He is considered a prominent figure in the rise of Japanese American Democrats following the end of World War II. He was educated at the University of Hawaii and the University of Minnesota Law School, from which he earned his J.D. degree in 1948. He married Eiko Oshima in 1949. Before winning election as the state's lieutenant governor (1974-1979), he served in the Hawaii State Senate (1959-1969) and as senior justice of the Third Circuit Court, Hilo (1969-1974).

Yuriko Doi. (Asian Week)

Doi, Yuriko (b. Aug. 13, 1941, Tokyo, Japan): Theater director. Before emigrating to the United States in 1967, she studied theater at Waseda University. In 1978 she founded San Francisco's Theatre of Yugen, a company devoted to cultivating American appreciation for classical Japanese *kyogen* and No theater and to creating cross-cultural or "fusion" theater by melding classical Japanese performance techniques with Western themes and materials.

Dok guk: Korean soup of rice cakes boiled in beef broth with scallions and diced garlic; customarily served on the first day of the new year.

Dong, Arthur E.: Producer, writer, director. Educated at the American Film Institute, the Center for Advanced Studies, and San Francisco State University, he is the producer and director of numerous Asian American films and documentaries. His works include *Forbid-*

den City, U.S.A. (1989), for which he won nine awards from various film festivals, and *Sewing Woman* (1982), a short film that earned an Academy Award nomination for its portrayal of a woman's struggle to survive.

Dong-hoe (also, *tong-hoe*): Self-governing social organization in Korea. Originating in the Silla Kingdom, the institution was established on every Hawaii plantation to maintain law and order among Korean immigrants. In 1907 the separate groups united and became the Hanin Hapsong Hyop-hoe (United Korean Society), which lasted two years.

Dong-jang (also, *tong-jang*): Korean title for the elected person in charge of a Hawaii plantation *dong-hoe*, a self-governing social organization established to maintain law and order among Korean immigrants.

Donner Pass railroad tunnel: Constructed for the Central Pacific Railroad line passing beneath the Donner Summit in the California Sierra Nevada. It was constructed by Chinese workers during the 1860's with drills and explosives; the extreme hazards of the project cost many Chinese their lives.

Double Ten (Oct. 10): Celebration commemorating the Chinese Revolution of October 10, 1911, which overthrew the Qing Dynasty and established the Republic of China in 1912. "Double Ten" refers to the tenth day of the tenth month. It is a national holiday in

In a Double Ten celebration (circa 1920's), marchers parade through the streets of Chicago's Chinatown. (Asian American Studies Library, University of California at Berkeley)

Taiwan and is celebrated by many Chinese communities worldwide.

Dragon Boat Festival: Held to commemorate a famous statesman-poet of China, on the fifth day of the fifth lunar month. In the third century B.C.E., Zhu Yuan was an honest and able minister. Because of jealousy and court intrigue, however, Zhu Yuan was banished to a distant village far from the capital. Well-liked by the villagers, he brooded deeply over the conditions in China. He finally composed a beautiful poem expressing his thoughts, then drowned himself in a river. Villagers searched for him in vain, finding no trace of him. They threw rice dumplings into the river to feed his spirit, but these were soon gobbled up by the fish.

It was said that one day Zhu Yuan's spirit appeared to some villagers and told them that a monster had been eating everything they had cast into the river. The spirit suggested that they use the sharply pointed leaves of bamboo, tied securely together to form a triangular pouch. The pointed leaves and pouch will, the spirit assured them, look like a demon-dispelling sword and frighten the monster away; so the villagers could safely put rice in the pouches and toss them into the river for Zhu Yuan's spirit. This made the villagers much happier, and some of them added bits of turtle meat to the rice in the pouches.

Today, the little rice-filled pouches are available all year round, not just on the day of the Dragon Boat Festival. Each pouch contains a salted duck-egg yolk, and some also add beans and bits of salted pork.

In some areas Dragon Boat races are still held. The boats are long and sleek, decorated with a fancy dragon's head and a tail at the end of the boat. Amid much fanfare, a drummer urges the paddlers to hurry. According to tradition these boats are out searching for Zhu Yuan, the beloved Chinese patriot.

A festival boat race is held annually in Hong Kong; it is an international event, open to anyone wishing to participate.

Dragon dance: Dance performed with a long, brightly colored cloth dragon held up by large poles; usually

The traditional Chinese dragon dance is performed in order to chase away evil spirits as the next lunar year begins. (San Francisco Convention and Visitors Bureau)

performed during Chinese New Year celebrations and parades.

Draves, Victoria "Vickie" Manalo (b. 1924, San Francisco, Calif.): Diver. Born to a Filipino father and his British wife, Draves grew up in the San Francisco Bay Area. She and her twin sister enjoyed swimming at various public pools. As a sixteen-year-old, Draves was invited to join a diving club on Nob Hill. In the face of severe anti-Asian prejudice, Draves was forced

Vicki Manalo Draves recorded several historic "firsts" as a member of the U.S. Olympic diving team competing at the 1948 Games. (Filipino American National Historical Society)

to drop the Filipino name "Manalo" and adopt "Taylor," her mother's maiden name, in order to be admitted to the Nob Hill swimming facilities. She later began training with the San Francisco Crystal Plunge Swim Club under the watchful eye of Charlie Sava, a highly respected diving coach. After competing in various local competitions during the early 1940's, she began training with coach Lyle Draves at Oakland's Athens Club. When World War II broke out, she accepted a post as a secretary in a local army office. Unable to train with her coach, who had moved to Southern California, and sensitive to continuing difficulties resulting from anti-Asian prejudice, Draves went into semiretirement. After the war, she moved to Los Angeles and was married to Lyle Draves. With her husband as her coach, Draves soon returned to top form and won three consecutive ten-meter platform diving titles at the National Tower Diving Championships between 1946 and 1948 and earned the national springboard title in 1948. Selected as a member of the 1948 U.S. Olympic diving team after somewhat less than spectacular performances in the qualifying competitions, Draves went on to earn gold medals in women's platform and springboard diving—the first woman to place first in both diving competitions at the same Olympic games and the first woman of Asian ancestry to win an Olympic gold medal. In recognition of her achievements, Draves was inducted into the International Swimming Hall of Fame in 1969.

Dual citizenship: An important issue involving the Nisei, the children of Japanese immigrants, concerned dual citizenship. Japan's nationality law, like that of many European nations, followed the rule that if the father was a citizen of Japan, then so were his children, regardless of whether or not they were born in Japan. The United States, unlike Japan, did not recognize dual citizenship.

In 1914 Japanese Americans on the American West Coast asked the Japanese government to allow those Nisei wishing to do so to renounce their Japanese citizenship. The Japanese government did change the law in March, 1914, to allow the Nisei this right. Under dual citizenship the Japanese government could compel the military service of the Nisei, even though they were born in the United States. Such obligations, however, could be enforced only if a person holding dual citizenship were physically present in that country. Although Japan had no real legal claim to American citizens holding Japanese citizenship, organizations such as the Japanese American Citizens League (JACL) continued until 1942 to encourage the Nisei to renounce their Japanese citizenship.

A number of laws were passed that affected the citizenship of the Nisei. The Cable Act (1922) penalized native-born American women who married an alien ineligible for citizenship by taking away their citizenship. Through efforts by the League of Women Voters and the JACL, the act was repealed in 1936.

In 1930 fifty percent of the Nisei were dual citizens, reflecting the fact that a large proportion of those Nisei seven years of age or older had renounced their Japanese citizenship. In 1943 the U.S. War Relocation

AUTHORITY (WRA) estimated that only one out of four Nisei held dual citizenship.

Dun, Dennis (b. Apr. 19, 1952, Stockton, Calif.): Actor. Graduated with a B.A. degree from San Francisco State University in 1975, he is regarded as one of the leading Asian American actors of his generation. He began acting with the ASIAN-AMERICAN THEATRE COMPANY in 1977 and has been in more than twenty-five productions there. He has also appeared on television's *Midnight Caller* (1988-1990) and *Falcon Crest* (1981-1990) and in several films, including *The Last Emperor* (1987), *Big Trouble in Little China* (1986), *Year of the Dragon* (1985), *Prince of Darkness* (1987) and *A Thousand Pieces of Gold* (1991).

Durga: Hindu goddess associated with death, destruction, and epidemics. Durga is worshipped throughout India, but particularly in Bengal, as Divine Mother, the symbol of female power. She is but one of various manifestations that together form the consort of the god Shiva, the others being Parvati, Gauri, Uma, Kali, Devi, and Bhavani.

Leading Asian American actor Dennis Dun. (Asian Week)

E

East West Players: The United States' first Asian American theater company, founded in 1965. The goals of this organization have remained consistent throughout its history. Specifically the company seeks to establish "Asian Pacifics as a vital and dynamic component of the American Theatre community"; provide opportunities for professional writers to experiment and develop their works; serve the Asian Pacific American community as a site for the expression and preservation of its cultural life; and provide a bridge between East and West by offering performances that address the needs of American audiences. In support of these stated goals, the East West Players (EWP) has featured the best the Asian American entertainment community has to offer, while providing training and exposure for not only Asian American talent but also the broader Los Angeles community as well.

Under the guidance of MAKO, the company's first artistic director, the EWP progressed from its initial modest 1966 production of *Rashomon* in a small church on Sunset Boulevard to a space of its own

Playwright David Henry Hwang. (AP/Wide World Photos)

elsewhere. Offering from four to six main stage productions per year, with pieces ranging from modern interpretations of the classics across cultures to world premieres of works by young Asian American playwrights, the company quickly established itself as a vital theatrical force in the multicultural mix of Los Angeles. Indeed, by 1990, shortly after Mako had stepped down as the company's guiding force, the EWP had garnered some forty-nine *Drama-Logue Awards* and seven Los Angeles Drama Critics and *L.A. Weekly* Theatre Awards.

Beyond the EWP theatrical season, other programs serve to nurture Asian American and multiethnic talent. Significant among these are the acting classes, Summer Repertory, Summer Workshops, new play readings, the David Henry Hwang Writers' Institute, and the Philip Kan Gotanda Series.

Eastern Bakery: First Chinese American bakery in San Francisco (California) Chinatown, founded in 1924. The bakery serves a variety of traditional Chinese and American pastries and other baked goods, including moon cakes, the symbol of the Harvest Moon Festival holiday.

Eastwind Books and Arts: Offers a comprehensive range of English- and Chinese-language materials about China, Chinese Americans, and Asian Americans. Founded in 1979, it began as the brainchild of a group of twenty or so friends, scholars, and other investors who saw a need for such a store. Existing bookstores offered only a few copies of a limited selection.

Over the years, Eastwind has remained privately owned and is managed by one of the original founders and investors, Doroteo Ng, a multilingual third-generation Chinese from the Philippines. Though the enterprise began more as a hobby for Ng and his colleagues—all of whom shared a love for reading and a frustration over the inaccessibility of materials—it has grown to one of the largest and best-known bilingual Chinese and English bookstores in the United States.

The first store, located in San Francisco's Chinatown, attracted enough customers to warrant the opening of a second store the following year. The second location, in Berkeley, took advantage of the presence of students and scholars affiliated with the University of California, Berkeley, only a few blocks away. A third store was established in 1991, also in San Francisco's Chinatown, to relieve the overcrowded conditions of the original space. In addition to books, the stores offer a limited selection of cards and other artwork. The stores have presented readings by Chinese American authors such as Amy TAN, Gus LEE, and Gish JEN.

While the Berkeley store carries both English- and Chinese-language books, the San Francisco locations have divided most of their materials according to language. The original store focuses on Chinese-language materials, while the newest one carries primarily English-language materials about Asian Americans and China as well as a growing catalogue of items about other Asian countries as well. This store, Eastwind English Books and Gallery, also exhibits works of local artists, with priority given to works related to Asians or Asian Americans.

Customers frequenting the bookstores represent a broad mix. A large segment are first-generation immigrants and second- and third-generation descendants. Another well-represented group is made up of non-Chinese people, including many university scholars, interested in Chinese culture.

Eberharter, Herman P. (Apr. 29, 1892, Pittsburgh, Pa.—Sept. 9, 1958, Arlington, Va.): U.S. representative. Elected to the 75th U.S. Congress in 1936, as a Democrat, he served ten consecutive terms. During his term he was a member of the Dies Committee, formally called the House Special Committee to Investigate Un-American Activities. His subcommittee investigated the WAR RELOCATION AUTHORITY (WRA) and, in 1943, set out to prove the disloyalty of Japanese Americans. Eberharter later claimed that the report was prejudiced and that most of its assertions were unsubstantiated. The Dies Committee failed to verify its allegations.

Eiju dochyaku: Japanese term roughly translated as "children of the soil." The term refers to the permanent settlement of Japanese Americans in the United States.

Japanese American proprietors of a Sacramento watch shop, circa 1910. Immigrant Japanese who settled permanently in the United States were known as eiju dochyaku. *(Sacramento State Archives)*

Milton Eisenhower, president of Kansas State College, at his home in Manhattan, Kansas, 1950. (AP/Wide World Photos)

Eisenhower, Milton Stover (Sept. 15, 1899, Abilene, Kans.—May 2, 1985, Baltimore, Md.): Government official. To the world, Eisenhower was the brother of former president Dwight D. Eisenhower and a man who led a multifaceted career as an educator and as an advisor to six presidents. To Japanese Americans, however, he was best known as the first director of the WAR RELOCATION AUTHORITY (WRA).

In 1926 Eisenhower began his government career in the Department of Agriculture and stayed there for sixteen years. In 1942, during World War II, he was appointed director of the WRA largely because of his bureaucratic experience and his relationship with Dwight, then a rising star in the military. Eisenhower knew nothing about the Japanese Americans and even less about the internal government debates concerning their ultimate incarceration. The only thing of which he was certain was that it was his job to move people of Japanese ancestry away from the West Coast.

When Eisenhower started his position at the WRA, Japanese Americans were allowed to migrate voluntarily away from the West Coast and into the interior—a plan WRA officials assumed would be the means for evacuation. Eisenhower, however, thought the plan too dangerous and believed a supervised evacuation to rural areas outside Military Area No. 1 would be beneficial to all parties involved. Safety would be ensured, and the Japanese Americans could be used to work on sugar beet farms.

Karl Bendetson, the Army liaison between Provost Marshall General Allen W. Gullion and Lieutenant General John L. DeWitt, had other plans. On April 7, 1942, at a meeting of governors, attorneys, generals, and other officials of the Western states (with the exception of California) called by Bendetson, Eisenhower presented his resettlement plan and issued a plea for tolerance toward Japanese Americans. What he received was a barrage of racist responses from state leaders, which stunned him. They, along with Bendetson, the eventual architect of the Japanese American internment, wanted nothing short of a concentration camp.

Shortly after this episode Eisenhower resigned. In the 1970's he wrote in his memoirs of his regrets at having taken the job: "I have brooded about this whole episode on and off for the past three decades, for it is illustrative of how an entire society can somehow plunge off course."

El Monte berry strike (1933): Major agricultural strike that took place in the San Gabriel Valley area of Southern California. It involved many Japanese berry growers, some Japanese farm workers, and many Mexican farm workers. Moreover, elements of the larger Japanese American community as well as white landowners and the Mexican government ultimately became involved in the conflict.

In 1933 approximately 80 percent of the six to seven hundred acres of berries grown in the area were farmed by Japanese members of the CENTRAL JAPANESE ASSOCIATION OF SOUTHERN CALIFORNIA. Wages, during the Depression, had dropped to very low levels. Partly as a result of this, growers were struck by the communist-organized Cannery and Agricultural Workers' Industrial Union, whose membership was mostly Mexican American and Mexican. To help their parents harvest the highly perishable crops, Japanese Ameri-

can youth were excused from school. The El Monte JAPANESE AMERICAN CITIZENS LEAGUE (JACL) pushed for this action. In addition large numbers of relatives and friends responded to the call to help in the fields.

More generally, this conflict illustrates the relationship between Japanese farmers, white landowners, and certain public officials. At the time of the strike, a state alien land law prohibited the immigrant generation Issei from buying or leasing land. Those who continued in farming found ways to get around this legal barrier. The county district attorney was responsible for enforcing the law. If a white landowner was proven guilty of colluding with a Japanese grower to skirt the law, the landowner could have his or her land taken away. Hence, wealthy white landowners were threatened by the strike as it focused attention on their profitable illegal arrangements with Japanese growers.

White growers were also concerned that if the Mexican strikers were successful against the Japanese, the Mexicans would walk out of the white owners' fields next. It is estimated that more than six thousand Mexican American and Mexican workers eventually struck Japanese growers throughout Los Angeles and Orange County. Thus it is not surprising that white landowners, the El Monte and Los Angeles chambers of commerce, the Los Angeles Police Department, and the Los Angeles County Sheriff's Department supported the Japanese farmers rather than the strikers. Ultimately the berry pickers did win higher wages, but by then, peak harvest, and thus the need for workers, had largely passed.

Eldrige v. See Yup Company (1859): California Supreme Court ruling that the state courts were not the arbiters of whether Chinese pagan religious rituals offended public policy or morals. This case arose over a dispute in ownership of land on which a Chinese Buddhist temple had been built. The court also addressed the issue of the right of Chinese to conduct religious practice. The court, however, declined to dispose of the latter question, restricting its opinion solely to the question of ownership of the land. *Eldrige* is one of the earliest legal proceedings involving the Chinese in America.

Emeneau, M. B. [Murray Barnson] (b. Feb. 28, 1904, Lunenburg, Nova Scotia, Canada): Linguist and educator. In 1923, after graduating from Dalhousie University, Halifax, Emeneau was named a Rhodes Scholar. That same year he entered Balliol College,

Oxford, where he received his second bachelor's degree in 1926 and a master's degree in 1935. During the period 1926-1931 he studied linguistics and anthropology with eminent linguists E. H. Sturtevant and Edward Sapir, concentrating on Sanskrit, Greek, and Latin. With a Ph.D. degree from Yale, in 1935 he embarked on very ambitious fieldwork in the Nilgiris area of Central and South India on some neglected Dravidian languages. After his return from India in 1938, he taught linguistics at Yale. In 1940 he joined the University of California, Berkeley, as assistant professor of Sanskrit and general linguistics. In 1953 he became the founder-chairperson of the Department of Linguistics at the same university. In addition he held numerous distinguished positions in the field of linguistics, such as president of the Linguistic Society of America (1949) and editor of the *Journal of the American Oriental Society* (1947-1951). He received numerous honors and awards for his contributions to Indology and linguistics. Notable among these awards and honors are the Guggenheim Fellowships (1949, 1956) and a celebration to honor him along with two other scholars at the Linguistic Society of America 1978 Linguistic Institute held at the University of Illinois at Urbana-Champaign.

Among Emeneau's many contributions to Indology and linguistics, his works on various aspects of Sanskrit language and literature are especially noteworthy. In particular his translation of Kalidasa's *Shakuntala: Or, The Lost Ring* (c. 45 B.C.E. or c. 395 C.E.) is viewed as a brilliant translation of the classical Indian play into English. His works on Dravidian languages combine the theoretical and methodological insights of an interdisciplinary nature. His *A Dravidian Etymological Dictionary* (1961), co-authored with T. Burrow, represents a landmark that will impact generations to come. His work on India as a linguistic area is unique in the sense that it not only highlighted unity in diversity among the Indian languages but also made a solid contribution in the field of areal, or contact, linguistics. This work, in turn, inspired numerous other works on this topic. The depth and diversity of Emeneau's accomplishments are still being discovered and rediscovered in the field of linguistics.

Emergency Detention Act of 1950: U.S. legislation aimed at detaining those who would "commit or conspire to commit espionage or sabotage." It was passed by Congress over the veto of President Harry S Truman. It resulted from the anticommunist fervor of the time and was reminiscent of the previous internment of Japanese Americans. Camps, including TULE LAKE, which housed Japanese Americans during World War II (1939–1945), were prepared for possible use. Though repealed in 1971, it set a precedent for possible recurrence of mass internment.

Emergency Service Committee (ESC): A wartime organization founded by Japanese Americans in Hawaii to promote patriotism and improve morale within their community in the wake of the attack on Pearl Harbor. Many committee members helped support peaceful service organizations such as the Red Cross; others were active in the war effort by recruiting volunteers for Japanese American regiments and raising money for war bonds. Although many of the committee's members were accused of denigrating their Japanese heritage through their efforts to promote assimilation of Issei and Nisei within American society, the ESC did serve as a liaison with Hawaii's mainstream white community by helping preserve civil rights for Japanese Americans in Hawaii.

Emigration Convention of 1886: Agreement under which the Hawaiian government agreed to ensure the humane treatment of incoming Japanese immigrant contract laborers. This covenant followed reports of mistreatment of Japanese who had come to Hawaii under contract to work on the sugar plantations. Two groups of about 1000 each of these emigrants reached Hawaii in February and June of 1885.

After the arrival of the second boatload, the authorities in Japan charged that plantation overseers in Hawaii were treating the Japanese workers inhumanely, citing unjustified acts of violence and inadequate medical attention. Additional problems had resulted from having too few interpreters and inspectors. Japan suspended emigration pending firm assurances from Hawaiian authorities that previous wrongs would be redressed and guarantees given of full protection to the emigrants.

A combination of circumstances favored further negotiations. Hawaii's King David Kalakaua had seen his kingdom depopulated by disease and a foreign way of life. He wanted the Japanese to settle in Hawaii and help repopulate it. The sugar planters of Hawaii were desperately in need of workers to cultivate the plantations and considered the Japanese to be ideal for the purpose.

At the same time, Japan was suffering a severe economic depression that particularly affected the livelihood of its agricultural workers. Permitting large

Delos Emmons. (AP/Wide World Photos)

numbers of them to emigrate to Hawaii, would mean money sent home to their families, an attractive prospect if the abuse of Japanese workers ceased.

Soon after Robert W. Irwin (the Hawaiian minister to Japan who had accompanied the first group of emigrants) had returned to Tokyo, he was told that assurances received from Hawaii, along with developments in Japan, had cleared the way for the emigration convention requested by Hawaii. The convention was signed in Tokyo on January 28, 1886.

A third lot of immigrants arrived in Honolulu on February 14, 1886, along with the signed convention. Both governments ratified the terms of the convention in Honolulu on March 6.

The convention opened the way for large-scale emigration of Japanese contract laborers to Hawaii under the joint auspices of the Hawaiian and Japanese governments. It continued in operation until the summer of 1894. Under its terms twenty-eight thousand Japanese, in twenty-six shipments, eventually arrived in Hawaii.

Emmons, Delos (Jan. 17, 1888, Huntington, W. Va.— Oct. 3, 1965, Hillsborough, Calif.): Military official. When Pearl Harbor was bombed by Japan in December, 1941, he was a lieutenant in the U.S. Air Force; ten days later he was named military governor of Hawaii. Though Hawaii was placed under martial law, there was no mass internment of Japanese Americans in the islands.

Empress Dowager (Cixi; Nov. 29, 1835, Beijing, China—Nov. 15, 1908, Beijing, China): Ruler. A concubine to Emperor Xianfeng and the mother of Emperor Tongzhi, she held de facto power in the Qing government from the time she became regent for her son and coregent of Guangxu, Emperor Xianfeng's nephew, until her death.

Empress of China: American ship originating out of New York and used in eighteenth century commerce between the United States and China. It also became the first American ship to sail in Chinese waters.

Endo, Mitsuye (b. 1920, Sacramento, Calif.): Petitioner in Japanese American internment case. Before the Japanese bombing of Pearl Harbor, Endo had worked for the California Department of Motor Vehicles. She was a U.S. citizen, had never been to Japan, did not speak or read the Japanese language, was raised as a Methodist, and even had a brother in the U.S. Army. None of these qualifications, however, satisfied the state of California: She and other Japanese Americans were summarily fired from their jobs following Japan's attack.

In January of 1942 Saburo Kido, an attorney with the JAPANESE AMERICAN CITIZENS LEAGUE (JACL), investigated the firing of the Japanese American California state employees. He discovered that they were questioned about their knowledge of Japan and their ties to any Japanese organizations on the assumption that they possessed dual citizenship. All were charged with being Japanese citizens and belonging to organizations that aided the enemy. Immediately Kido recruited attorney James Purcell to help him fight these charges. The rapid pace of the government's exclusion program, however, forced them to change their plans. Instead they searched for an ideal candidate for a *habeas corpus* test case. Endo was the perfect candidate.

On July 12, 1942, Endo's *habeas corpus* petition was filed in the federal district court in San Francisco. In the petition former WAR RELOCATION AUTHORITY (WRA) director Milton EISENHOWER was asked to show why Endo had been detained. At the July 20, 1942, hearing the government lawyer, Alfonso J. Zirpoli, argued that there were a number of "fifth columnists" among the Japanese American population and that it was impossible to tell the loyal from the disloyal. He urged the court to dismiss the petition.

Although *habeas corpus* petitions are supposed to be handled quickly to avoid further possible undue detention, the court took close to one year to reach a decision. On July 3, 1943, the judge dismissed the petition without explanation. An appeal was filed.

By the time the Supreme Court heard arguments for the Endo case in October of 1944, Allied victory in World War II was almost assured. The government lawyers soon realized that there was no legal way to justify the continued internment of Endo and others like her—especially since the WRA had conducted its screening of the "disloyal" from among the "loyal." The government eventually called for the release of Endo and others who had passed the WRA screening so that the overall constitutional question of the internment could be avoided. On December 18, 1944, the Supreme Court unanimously decided in favor of Endo's *habeas corpus* petition.

Endo, Russell: Scholar. A professor of sociology at the University of Colorado, Boulder, Endo played an influential role in the early development of Asian American Studies. He coedited (with Stanley Sue and

Nathaniel Wagner) *Asian-Americans: Psychological Perspectives* (1973), a two-volume work which served as one of the first textbooks on Asian Americans. Endo has published articles on bibliographic materials for ASIAN AMERICAN STUDIES, the growth of Asian American Studies programs, and other topics. He was among the coeditors of *Frontiers of Asian American Studies* (1989).

Enemy Alien Control Unit: Branch of the U.S. Justice Department. It was established following the presidential proclamations of December 7 and 8, 1941, and was responsible for the prosecution and detention of aliens suspected of espionage and disloyalty in the United States, particularly the West Coast, Hawaii, and Alaska. The unit's formation was one of the earliest measures taken against the Japanese following the attack on Pearl Harbor, and it was followed by the sepa-

ration of the Japanese from other enemy aliens and their evacuation in 1942 first to assembly centers and then to internment camps.

English as a Second Language (ESL): The teaching of English to speakers of other languages. As a discipline ESL has developed from more simplistic "grammar-translation" methods of teaching to more communicative or conversational approaches.

ESL has followed the development of foreign-language teaching in general, although since the 1960's it has outstripped that broader profession in its implementation of new findings about language acquisition. Before the 1930's and 1940's the emphasis was on the Classical Method, which focused on the memorization of grammatical rules and translation of texts. In the 1940's and 1950's more behavioral approaches were used, reflecting then-current psychological pre-

The rise in Asian and other immigration to the United States has accelerated the demand for English-language instruction. Learning English is for many new immigrants the key to successful assimilation into American society. (James L. Shaffer)

ESL kindergarten class at a New York City public school. (Hazel Hankin)

occupations. "Programmed learning" became the rule of the day, and programs stressed learning of "model sentences" and repetition of vocabulary items. Conversation skills and the actual ability to function using the language were not emphasized.

The establishment of the English Language Institute (ELI) at the University of Michigan in 1941 gave impetus to serious research in teaching English to foreign speakers. In 1966 ESL teachers in the United States were given their own forum with the establishment of Teachers of English to Speakers of Other Languages (TESOL) and its journal, *TESOL Quarterly*. Real interest in the idea of "communicative competence" began around this time also, especially with the work of researchers such as Dell Hymes, who focused on teaching strategies that aimed at real functional competence in English.

The importance of English as the international language of trade, diplomacy, and research has created a great demand for competent speakers of the language, particularly in developing countries that are anxious to modernize. There is a great interest in ESL in Asia, particularly in the People's Republic of China, which sees competency in English as an important compo-

nent in its modernization drive. (It has been estimated that there are more people studying English in China than in the United States.)

The continuing influx of Asians and other immigrants into the United States has created a tremendous demand for instruction in ESL, which represents for them the key to successful assimilation into American society. Organizations such as the ELI send many native English speakers to Asia every year to teach ESL or teach Asian students and immigrants in programs developed in universities and adult education centers all over the United States. (See BILINGUAL EDUCATION.)

English Standard Schools: A set of segregated public schools in the Territory of Hawaii. The first English Standard School opened in 1924. By 1937 there were ten such schools, including one intermediate and one high school. Oral English proficiency examinations determined eligibility.

School officials created English Standard Schools in response to pressure from middle-class European Americans who objected to sending their children to public schools in which Hawaii Creole English, popu-

Segregated class of ninth-graders, 1931. (Mary Tsukamoto)

larly known as "Pidgin English," was the prevailing spoken language. Such groups also did not want their children to attend schools in which children of immigrant sugarcane plantation laborers—primarily Japanese, but also Chinese, Portuguese, Koreans, and Filipinos—predominated.

Supporters of English Standard Schools argued that these schools promoted Americanism by encouraging and safeguarding correct speech habits and that special treatment was needed for a select group of students. Opponents argued that these schools were discriminatory and contradicted the American ideal of equal opportunity. They said that it was unfair to expect children whose first language was not English to speak perfect English when they entered school.

Ostensibly based on oral English proficiency, English Standard Schools in fact segregated students by race and class. Until World War II about half of all Standard School students were European Americans, while no more than 2.5 percent of them attended non-Standard public schools. In contrast Japanese American students before World War II constituted from 3 to 8.5 percent of all Standard School students and about 55 percent of all students in non-Standard public schools. Other groups—students of Hawaiian and

part-Hawaiian, Portuguese, and Chinese descent— were better represented in the Standard Schools during this period, though in some cases only marginally so. In later years, as more and more nonwhite students succeeded in passing the oral English entrance examinations, the Standard Schools became primarily a mark of social status. Serving to encourage feelings of elitism was the fact that only a small proportion of all public school students—from 2 percent in 1925 to 9 percent in 1947—attended these schools.

Opposition to English Standard Schools grew stronger after World War II. This led the Territorial Legislature to phase them out. Beginning in the fall of 1949 the Standard Schools accepted no new students, and the last class graduated from high school in 1960.

Ennis, Edward J. (1907–1990): Attorney and government official. During World War II, Ennis served as an attorney with the U.S. Justice Department. He opposed the War Department's plan to incarcerate Japanese Americans in internment camps on the grounds that such camps were unconstitutional. Ennis was unable, however, to lobby enough support within the Roosevelt Administration to prevent the signing of the executive order that set the relocation and detention process in motion. Despite his stated opposition to internment, Ennis was placed in charge of the government's ENEMY ALIEN CONTROL UNIT, which was responsible for holding hearings regarding the loyalty of Japanese, German, and Italian residents suspected of conspiring against American interests. He was also appointed to prosecute key cases against Gordon HIRABAYASHI and Fred KOREMATSU for violation of wartime curfew regulations. Ennis ultimately supported the government's claim that detainment of Japanese Americans was lawful on the grounds of military necessity. After leaving the Justice Department in 1955, Ennis worked as an attorney with the American Civil Liberties Union (ACLU). He testified on behalf of Japanese Americans at congressional hearings held during the 1980's by the COMMISSION ON WARTIME RELOCATION AND INTERNMENT OF CIVILIANS (CWRIC).

Enryo: Japanese term that means the exercise of restraint in personal interactions in Japanese society in order to maintain cordial insider and outsider group relationships. Out of concern for not imposing oneself on outsiders who are not part of one's most intimate circle of natural or quasi-natural kin, the Japanese developed a strategy for keeping an adequate distance from outsiders and their domain. *Enryo*, which is a compound of the two Chinese character words *en* (distant) and *ryo* (consideration), originally (during the Edo period, 1600-1867) meant an act of seclusion from public places by feudal retainers and priests in repentance for their sins. Subsequently, the meaning changed to "keeping thoughtful distance" and became a rule of social conduct that applied to all members of Japanese society. In a society where the notion of *wa* (harmony) is an ideal state of life, the exercise of *enryo* is considered essential for avoiding interpersonal conflicts. Even if one is invited to enter the domain of an outsider, a great deal of hesitation customarily precedes accepting the invitation and crossing the buffer zone.

In exchanging greetings to affirm each other's wellbeing, for example, one should refrain from volunteering too much information about oneself as well as use restraint in inquiring after others. When visiting someone's house, the visitor will insist on leaving soon so as not to inconvenience the host. After repeated entreaties, the guest enters the house and is usually treated to tea and refreshment. First, the visitor ritually declines the offer, which is followed by a plea from the host to disregard *enryo*. After such polite exchanges the visitor should be certain of not appearing greedy while accepting the offer *enryonaku* (without reservation). When taking leave, apologies are expressed by the visitor for having been a nuisance to the host, who, being satisfied with the visitor's proper etiquette, may reciprocate by requesting further visits.

Not all social situations require the uniform exercise of *enryo*. For *enryo* to play a key role in successful social interactions, tact is needed for determining both the right time for using it and the extent of its use.

Esaki, Leo (Esaki Reiona; b. Mar. 12, 1925, Osaka, Japan): Physicist. Esaki shared the Nobel Prize in Physics in 1973 for his discovery of the tunneling effect in semiconductors. He performed experiments that led to the discovery of the tunnel diode—a powerful device vital to the operation of modern computers.

The son of an architect, Esaki attended a Kyoto high school that would one day be able to boast of having enrolled three Nobel Prize-winners. While working toward his Ph.D. degree at the University of Tokyo, he

Nobel laureate Leo Esaki. (The Nobel Foundation)

was an employee of the Sony Corporation in Tokyo, during which time he made his breakthrough formulations on tunneling. In 1959 he finished work on his doctorate and was married to Masako Araki, from whom he was later divorced. Arriving in New York in 1960, Esaki was employed by the International Business Machines (IBM) Corporation, with whom he would gain growing success as a noted physicist. Five years later he was made an IBM Fellow—the company's highest research honor. Other award-winning achievements include his research into superlattices. Esaki has also played a central role in establishing better relations between the scientific communities of the United States and Japan, of which he has elected to remain a citizen.

Ese: Korean term for second-generation persons of Korean ancestry residing outside Korea.

Espiritu, Yen Le (b. February 13, 1963, Saigon, Republic of Vietnam, now Ho Chi Minh City, Socialist Republic of Vietnam): Scholar. Espiritu, a Vietnamese American married to a Filipino American, is an assistant professor in the Department of Ethnic Studies at the University of California, San Diego. Her *Asian American Panethnicity: Bridging Institutions and Identities* was published in 1992. In it she explores the phenomenon "in which previously unrelated groups submerge their differences and assume a common identity." The book emphasizes that interethnic cooperation is the key to preserving the rights and interests of all Asian Americans, from the less powerful to the more prominent.

Eu, March Fong (March Kong Fong; b. Mar. 29, 1922, Oakdale, Calif.): U.S. ambassador to Micronesia; California secretary of state. In 1994, after serving for twenty years as California secretary of state (she was the first woman elected to that office), Eu resigned to accept the position of U.S. ambassador to Micronesia.

A third-generation Californian, Fong's parents were the owners of a hand laundry. She received her B.S. degree from the University of California, Berkeley, her M.Ed. degree from Mills College, and her Ed.D. de-

In 1974, March Fong Eu became the first woman to serve as California secretary of state. Here she describes to the press the robbery attempt in her home in 1986. (AP/Wide World Photos)

gree from Stanford. Before she began her career as a politician, she had been a dental hygienist and a lecturer in health education at Mills.

Fong was elected to the State Assembly in 1966 representing Oakland and Castro Valley. She won election as secretary of state in 1974 by the record-setting margin of three million votes. She began her fifth term in 1991.

In 1973 Fong married Singaporean businessman Henry Eu. His refusal to file a financial disclosure form required by federal campaign laws would cause her to drop out of the race for a U.S. Senate seat in 1988.

During her years as secretary of state, Eu implemented more than four hundred legislative bills and championed women's and human rights. These bills have included implementing voter registration by mail, getting legislative approval and funding for a new building to house all state archives and historical records, eliminating notary public abuse of power, and streamlining and automating the filing requirements and procedures mandated by various state governmental branches.

On November 10, 1986, an intruder ambushed Eu at her home in Los Angeles in a robbery attempt. After this traumatic experience, fighting crime became one of her first priorities.

Eu has a daughter, Marchesa Suyin, and a son, Matthew, an attorney who ran for the position of California state controller in 1990. In her spare time Eu plays golf and enjoys Chinese painting and calligraphy. In 1978 she published a children's book, *Sons of Chong*.

Evacuation Claims Act of 1948: U.S. law permitting Japanese Americans to seek redress against the U.S. government because of forced federal evacuation dur-

Forced evacuation of Japanese Americans living on the West Coast began not long after the Japanese bombing of Pearl Harbor on December 7, 1941. Here a tremendous explosion rocks the USS Shaw *inside the harbor.* (Hawaii State Archives)

ing World War II (1939–1945). Public Law 886 was signed by President Harry S Truman on July 2, 1948. It is sometimes referred to as the "Japanese-American Evacuation Claims Act."

This law allowed people of Japanese ancestry to file claims for real or personal property lost or damaged after December 7, 1941. The evacuation had been initiated under EXECUTIVE ORDER 9066 (1942) and had included Americans/resident aliens of Japanese ancestry from coastal military areas in Alaska, Arizona, California, Hawaii, Oregon, and Washington. A limited amount for legal fees could also be recovered as part of any allowed claim. Yet under the new act no one could claim monetary damages for insured property losses, physical hardship or injuries (including death), mental suffering, inconvenience, or loss of anticipated profits or earnings.

Claims originally were to be filed within the eighteen months following the date of enactment. Subsequent laws established additional time periods within which claims could be made. A 1956 amendment to the original law also allowed contested claims to be heard by the Court of Claims, whereas before all

claims were processed by the U.S. attorney general, with no appeals allowed. By 1981, 26,568 claims had been settled, with payments amounting to an estimated $37 million out of a total of $148 million in claims. The maximum amount payable for any one claim was then $100,000.

Finally, in 1988, forty years later, Congress passed Public Law 100-383, which was signed into law by President Ronald Reagan on August 10 as the CIVIL LIBERTIES ACT OF 1988. This law granted each surviving evacuee $20,000 and permitted surviving spouses, children, or parents of deceased evacuees to claim the $20,000 designated for the deceased.

Ewha Chinmok-hoe (Friendship Society of Ewha Plantation): Political organization founded by Koreans on May 3, 1905, on Oahu, Hawaii, to boycott Japanese goods.

Executive Order 9066 (1942): Federal declaration issued by U.S. president Franklin D. Roosevelt for the purpose of detaining Japanese Americans during World War II. As a result of the proclamation, approxi-

President Gerald Ford (foreground, right) signs the proclamation rescinding Executive Order 9066 in the summer of 1976. (White House Historical Society)

mately 120,000 Americans of Japanese ancestry were removed from the West Coast and detained in concentration camps.

According to historians, officials in the Justice and War departments disagreed over whether to order the mass removal of Japanese Americans. The War Department, with the support of the president, prevailed. Executive Order 9066 therefore began a deliberately conceived plan to exclude and detain all Japanese Americans on the West Coast.

The order authorized the secretary of war or any military commander to whom he delegated responsibility the power to designate military areas in the event of a national emergency. In these areas, the rights of any person to enter, remain, or leave could be controlled by military order.

Pursuant to the order Secretary of War Henry L. Stimson authorized General John DeWitt, the Western Defense Commander in San Francisco, to issue a series of civilian orders. Public Proclamation No. 1 on March 2, 1942, created a military area along the coastal half of the states of Washington, Oregon, and California and along the southern portion of Arizona.

Public Proclamation No. 3 on March 24 imposed an 8:00 P.M. to 6:00 A.M. curfew in the zone. The restriction applied to German and Italian aliens and all persons of Japanese ancestry. Public Proclamation No. 4 on March 27 prohibited any Japanese American from leaving the military area without permission. In addition Public Law No. 503 on March 21 provided the authority to punish any violations of any military order issued as a result of Executive Order 9066.

In 1980 Congress established the COMMISSION ON WARTIME RELOCATION AND INTERNMENT OF CIVILIANS (CWRIC) to investigate the facts and circumstances of Executive Order 9066. The CWRIC's 1983 report concludes that the presidential order was not justified by military necessity and that the decision to exclude and to detain Japanese Americans without individual hearings was based not on military reasons but on racial prejudice. Among the remedies proposed was redress to those still living who had been excluded pursuant to the order. A presidential apology and redress for Japanese Americans was enacted into law in 1988.

Exeter incident (1929): Anti-Filipino riot that broke out on October 24, 1929 in Exeter, California, a small farming community in the San Joaquin Valley. Since Filipino labor had been used to harvest Kadota figs and Emperor grapes, there was a long-standing feud be-

tween Filipino field-workers and their white counterparts. The white workers were enraged not only by the strong competition from Filipinos but also by the latter's relationship with white women.

As the picking season ended, a local carnival to celebrate the end of the harvest prompted white youths to shoot rubber bands at young Filipinos who walked with their dates. Racial taunts were shouted by a growing band, and a Filipino worker pulled a knife to protect himself from the mob. One bystander was cut, and a vigilante mob quickly formed.

An infuriated crowd of three hundred then marched upon the ranch of E. J. Firebaugh, the largest employer of Filipino labor in the area, and drove Filipinos from their makeshift camp. The mob then marched to a nearby Filipino labor camp and demanded its closure. A mob of masked, shotgun-carrying vigilantes, led by Exeter's police chief, C. E. Joyner, subsequently ran the Filipino farmworkers out of Exeter.

In its coverage of the incident, the *Exeter Sun* editorialized that Filipinos had a penchant for violence; the paper also gave credence to sexual stereotypes concerning Filipinos. Indeed, for the anti-Filipino contingent interracial dating was as large an issue as was the fear of economic competition. Other California newspapers, such as the *Stockton Record*, the *Sacramento Bee*, and the *San Francisco Examiner*, also took the anti-Filipino line. The *Stockton Record* wrote that the riot was provoked by "the insistence of Filipinos that they be treated as equals by white girls." The prestigious Commonwealth Club of California warned about the social and economic dangers of Filipino labor.

The economic argument used by those who hoped to restrict Filipino labor was that Filipinos worked too cheaply and did not understand the American system. As evidence for this conclusion, the *Watsonville Evening Pajaronian* and the *Stockton Record* attacked Filipinos for undercutting the wages of local workers. The leading California agribusiness groups demanded an end to the use of Filipino farm labor, and Republican U.S. senator Hiram W. Johnson wrote letters to leading San Joaquin Valley growers, vowing to end the influx of Filipino workers.

The publicity surrounding the Exeter incident attracted opportunistic politicians. Judge D. W. Rohrback of the Pajaro Township, located in Monterey, began delivering speeches on "the Filipino problem." Using the Northern Monterey Chamber of Commerce as his forum, he raised fears of Filipino workers, the emerging Filipino labor unions, and the possibility of violence in the fields.

The significance of the Exeter incident is that it created hysteria in the San Joaquin and Salinas valleys and in the Monterey canneries. The *Ang Bantay*, a Los Angeles-based Filipino weekly, editorialized that a double standard of justice, housing, and employment prevented Filipinos from entering the mainstream of California life. The Stockton-based *Three Stars*, another Filipino newspaper, suggested that Americans needed to understand Filipinos, not fear them.

The reaction against Filipinos was largely the result of liberalized immigration policy and the rising fear of a "third wave" of cheap Asian immigrant labor. The Exeter incident was a prelude to almost a decade of violence against Filipino farmworkers.

F

Families: Asian American families are here defined as families from Chinese, Japanese, Korean, Southeast Asian (Cambodia, Laos, and Vietnam), and Filipino backgrounds and cultures. This article discusses Asian families first in terms of historical events. It then describes values such as filial piety, obligation, and not losing face to lend an understanding of how family norms are established. It explains the family roles of the patriarch, eldest son, matriarch, and daughter-in-law, and the structure of the Asian family. The discussion of marriage and child-rearing practices focuses on discipline techniques, socialization methods, and interracial marriages. The article describes the problem of identity for children and youth, as well as aging issues such as intergenerational tensions. The final section, on family problems, considers a number of issues, including dilemmas faced by recent immigrant families of Chinese and Southeast Asian cultures.

History. The first Asians to come to the United States as immigrants were the Chinese. They came as individual fortune seekers and as contract laborers to work on the sugar plantations of Hawaii, in the gold mines of California, on the railroads that spanned the Western part of the United States, and as launderers, shopkeepers, and agricultural laborers.

The Chinese began to come in the late 1840's. Most were single men from two provinces of southeast China—GUANGDONG and FUJIAN—that had for centuries sent laborers overseas. Some of these men were married and left wives behind in China. When gold was discovered in California in 1848, thousands of young Chinese men, like men from many parts of the world, were enticed to leave their homes and families and try their luck in the United States. They were not

Family Types in U.S. Western Region Population, 1990

All American Families

Female householder

Other

15%

6%

79%

Married couples

Asian American Families

Female householder

Other

14%

7%

79%

Married couples

Source: U.S. Bureau of the Census, *1990 Census of Population: General Population Characteristics: United States,* 1992.

A family of Japanese American flower growers in Oxnard, California. (Michael Yamashita)

immigrants in the strictest sense; few intended to live out their days in the United States. Like many who came from Southern and Eastern Europe, they were SOJOURNERS. They left China and came to the United States hoping to make enough money to return to China, rejoin their families, buy land or a business, and live a prosperous life. A long campaign by white racists, however, resulted in increasingly severe restrictions against Chinese immigration, beginning with the CHINESE EXCLUSION ACT OF 1882.

Many Chinese went back to China, but most had not yet saved enough money to go back in the style that they had set as their goal. In the late nineteenth century, the Chinese men moved to the growing cities of the American West—San Francisco, Seattle, Los Angeles, and a host of smaller towns. There they were segregated from the white population, and, for self-protection as well, they came to live close together in CHINATOWN communities.

Not the least of their problems was that they were destined to remain members of a bachelor society. ANTIMISCEGENATION LAWS in most western states forbade Chinese and other Asians to marry white persons. With the passage of the exclusion acts, any hope of being reunited with their families depended on them making enough money to return to China as they had hoped, for alien Chinese laborers were not allowed to bring their wives to the United States. The Chinese bachelors coped with their isolation by playing MAH-JONGG, re-creating Chinese plays and operas, and visiting prostitutes. Some of the prostitutes were European Americans; others were Chinese women sold or kidnapped into slavery and then brought to the United States, ostensibly as the wives of men of the merchant class.

Japanese immigrants, who began to come to the United States in significant numbers in the 1880's, were similar to the Chinese in certain respects: Both groups were overwhelmingly young and male in the early years, both sought economic improvement, both came primarily to the West Coast and Hawaii, and both intended to return to their homeland once their fortunes were made. The Japanese, however, were determined to learn from the mistakes of the Chinese. The Japanese government carefully screened those men who would go to the United States and—during the early period of immigration—actively intervened on behalf of its citizens in the United States. Seeking to avoid the pitfalls of a bachelor society, where prostitution, gambling, and drunkenness, prevailed, the Japanese government in time to came to promote the emi-

gration of Japanese women and the establishment of family life in the United States.

Although the GENTLEMEN'S AGREEMENT (1907-1908) restricted immigration of male Japanese laborers, it permitted the entry of wives and children of laborers already in the United States. At this point, the Japanese American community began to change from a bachelor society to a family society. Some Japanese men went back to Japan, married, and returned with their wives. Others arranged by letter to acquire spouses in the famous "PICTURE BRIDE" system. Many of the women in question were shocked to find on arrival that the successful businessmen they had been led to believe they were marrying were actually laborers and keepers of tiny shops. They had cast their lot, however, and there was no going back. Men who had wandered throughout the American West, following the crops and working in mines, canneries, and fishing operations, now settled down and started families. This period in the development of the Japanese American community ended with passage of the restrictive IMMIGRATION ACT OF 1924, which barred further immigration from Japan.

Korean Americans, who began to come to the United States at the beginning of the twentieth century, were victims of the same anti-Asian movement that harassed and finally excluded the Japanese (in fact, since Koreans were officially represented by the Japanese consul, most non-Asians never knew of their separate identity). In addition to economic motivation, many of the early Korean immigrants came to escape from the oppressive domination of the Japanese. Thus for political reasons they were reluctant to return to their homeland.

Unlike Koreans, Filipinos had the choice to stay in their home country or come to the United States as U.S. nationals because of the colonial relationship between the Philippines and the United States. Coming to the United States was presented to them as an option around 1905, when the importation of Japanese and Korean laborers ended. From 1906 to 1946, the HAWAIIAN SUGAR PLANTERS' ASSOCIATION heavily recruited Filipinos to work in the sugar plantations. Unrestricted Filipino immigration to the continental United States ended with passage of the TYDINGS-MCDUFFIE ACT OF 1934, limiting Filipino immigration to an annual quota of fifty. This effectively cut off further immigration and stranded Filipino men in the United States, unable to bring over Filipino wives.

Lonely and missing family life, some Filipino men, unlike the earlier Chinese, Japanese, and Korean immigrants, sought to marry European and Mexican American women. Although U.S. nationals, Filipinos were still discriminated against because of their race. Since Filipinos were not "Mongolians" like Chinese, Japanese, and Koreans, they were not under the jurisdiction of the antimiscegenation laws. In 1931, however, a county clerk in Los Angeles, California, refused to issue a marriage license to Salvador Roldan, a Filipino man, and Marjorie Rogers, a Caucasian woman. In *SALVADOR ROLDAN V. LOS ANGELES COUNTY* (1931), that action was contested. The county superior court ruled in Roldan's favor, on the grounds that Filipinos were "MALAYS," not "Mongolians," a decision upheld on appeal in 1933. Less than three months after this decision, however, the California state legislature amended the civil code to prohibit intermarriage between Caucasians and "Malays." In addition, existing Filipino-Caucasian marriages were retroactively invalidated. These prohibitions remained in effect until 1948, when

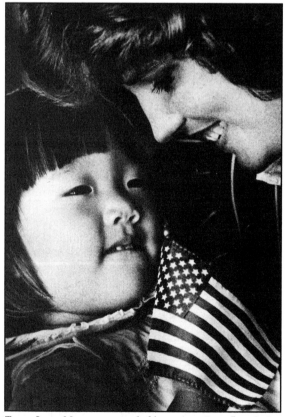

Tracy Lynn Max, age two, holds an American flag during naturalization ceremonies in a Northampton County, Pennsylvania, courtroom. With her is Cynthia Max, Tracy's adoptive mother. The youngster was born in Korea but adopted by Joseph and Cynthia Max at seven months of age. (AP/Wide World Photos)

the state's antimiscegenation laws were ruled unconstitutional by the California Supreme Court.

Unlike other Asian immigrants, Filipinos could become naturalized citizens through service in the military during World War II. (The American-born children of all immigrants, regardless of race or ethnicity, were American citizens by right of birth.) Many Filipino men became citizens after military service. The LUCE-CELLER BILL OF 1946 made Filipino (and Asian Indian) immigrants in general eligible for naturalization.

The MCCARRAN-WALTER ACT OF 1952 extended the right of naturalization to Asian groups not covered by previous legislation. (The Chinese had received this right through the IMMIGRATION ACT OF 1943, which repealed the Chinese exclusion acts.) In addition, the 1952 act, in conjunction with the acts of 1943 and 1946, eliminated the exclusionary barriers to Asian immigration. Nevertheless, the immigration quotas allotted to Asian nations by these acts were extremely small.

Actual immigration, however, greatly exceeded the quota levels. Some families were formed, for example, when Chinese American men who served in the U.S. military were permitted to bring back wives as WAR BRIDES, outside the quota. Other soldiers, Asian and non-Asian, brought back wives from other Asian countries, such as Japan and Korea.

The quota system which had been in place without essential changes since 1924 ended with passage of the IMMIGRATION AND NATIONALITY ACT OF 1965. Thereafter, large and increasing numbers of Chinese, Filipinos, and Koreans came to the United States each year. Unlike earlier waves of Asian immigration, they came, often, as families. Southeast Asians—especially Vietnamese, Cambodians, Laotians, and Hmong, as well as ethnic Chinese from Southeast Asia—began to come to the United States in large numbers after 1975, with the fall of the government of South Vietnam and continuing turmoil in the region. Many of their families had been destroyed or separated by war and flight, but most Southeast Asian refugees managed to reconstitute families, indeed extended clans, in the United States.

Values and Norms. The values and norms for traditional Chinese, Japanese, Korean, and Vietnamese families are similar. All are based upon Confucian concepts and principles, which emphasize specific roles and proper relationships between people. Filipino culture is not based on Confucianism, although it has some values in common. CONFUCIANISM focused on the hierarchical, cardinal relationships in five areas: between the ruler and his subjects, between father and son,

Traditional family structure for many Asian American families is based on filial piety, with children taking care of parents and with both parties often living under the same roof. This Asian family is vacationing together at Lake Tahoe, California.
(Robert Fried)

between husband and wife, between elder and younger brothers, and between older and younger friends.

Filial piety is a prime Confucian virtue. According to Confucius, filial piety involved love, respect, and fear. It is one of the main manifestations of *li*, or propriety—proper attitudes and behaviors toward others as defined by the five cardinal, hierarchical relationships.

The Confucian ideal of filial piety emphasizes taking care of parents. This is not an option but an obligation. Under all circumstances and even to the extent of denying oneself while showing no resentment, children, particularly sons, are to observe the precepts of filial piety. The Japanese version of filial piety, *oyakoko*, demands a child's obligation and loyalty to lineage and parents. In the Filipino culture, *utang na loob* is a value similar to filial piety that implies reciprocity and a sense of obligation that children feel toward their parents.

Filial piety is obligatory for parents, too. It is their duty to rear their children, particularly the sons, mor-

ally and in accord with acceptable societal standards. Daughters are not exempted from being filial because of gender. Historically in societies shaped by the Confucian tradition, the expectation for the daughter to be filial to her natal parents continued even after she was married and had joined her husband's family. Her obligations to her husband's family were even more onerous.

In the filial piety model, men are to venerate ancestors and have sons to carry on their family names. Women are to be submissive to their husbands and marry out of their families to become a part of the husband's family. Children are to be an asset to the family and to behave in a way that avoids shaming the family or losing face, a concept that regulates social behavior for all family members. The family comes first, before the individual, in all the Confucian cultures. Values of harmony and obligation are strongly emphasized.

These concepts of filial piety have shaped Chinese, Japanese, Korean, and Vietnamese cultures. Filipino culture has had a different model upon which to build values and beliefs. Some of their family values and norms are based upon Roman Catholicism. Others are based upon fatalism or animism, with practices and beliefs focused around nonhuman spirits. The fatalistic beliefs stem in part from an ancient Malay tradition predating the coming of Roman Catholicism to the Philippines. Fatalism encourages utter submission to those in a superior station and to supernatural powers. Faced with obstacles, one adjusts to them or resigns oneself to them, believing that they will pass in time.

BUDDHISM has also influenced Asian family values. Harmonious living, moderation in behavior, self-discipline, modesty, and selflessness are Buddhist principles observed by many Asian families. The Japanese value *enryo* requires that a family member be modest in behavior, humble in expectations, and appropriately hesitant in intruding on another's time and energy. The Japanese family also practices *kenshin*, which demands submission to group interests in order to obtain harmonious family life. Other Japanese values are *on* (obligation) and *gaman* (perseverance).

Structure. The structure of many Asian families is based on the Confucian ideal of filial piety and the "big family ideal"—the extended family with clan connections. This big family ideal is more true of Chinese and Vietnamese cultures than of Japanese, Korean, and Filipino. The big family ideal suggests an *esprit de corps* with a unity of purpose among family members and a goal to share honors and maintain harmony. Traditionally the focus of the big family ideal was on the father-son relationship, where all the sons were expected to stay under the same roof, forming an extended family. Families were to be extended by generation as well, with grandparents, parents, and children all inhabiting one address. In Japanese and Korean families, the big family ideal was modified so that younger sons typically would split and form their own households, while recognizing the primacy of the household of the oldest son.

In Asian families, it is not uncommon for several generations to live under the same roof. Traditionally, the bride would move into the husband's house and would find her role within the husband's family structure. In the second and third generations, Asian American families tend to be more nuclear, because of acculturation to American patterns and the ever-increasing mobility of American life. There are urban and rural differences: Nuclear families tend to exist more in urban areas, and role distinctions are often not as clear-cut in urban families. Still, many Asian American families are extended families, and this extended family structure plays an important role in the socialization of children.

In Filipino culture, the definition of extended family differs from that in Chinese, Japanese, Korean, and Vietnamese cultures in that Filipino family structure is characterized by bilateral equality, with relatives of both parents included in the extended family. Filipino culture is not patrilineal but bilateral; the kinfolk of the father and the mother are equal in status. The extended family in Filipino culture also includes ritual kin, *compadres*. (See FICTIVE KINSHIP.) Through this system of ritualized kinship, or *compadrazgo*, deeply rooted in Catholic ceremonies of baptism and marriage, Filipino friends and allies can serve as godparents to children. These godparents help the parents with financial, moral, and spiritual matters.

Roles. The roles of Asian family members are dictated by cultural norms guided by patrilineal, patriarchal, and patrilocal principles in the Chinese, Japanese, Korean, and Vietnamese cultures. Historically there were four major roles in these traditional Asian families: those of the patriarch, eldest son, matriarch, and daughter-in-law.

The role of the patriarch was to be the head of the family, the household, and in the Chinese case, the clan. He was to provide for his sons, educate them in the ancestral tradition, and see to it that they were suitably married. He was obliged to do this, not because he owed it to his sons but because he was obliged to his ancestors.

The role of the eldest son was to show respect to his parents, particularly his father, and take responsibility for the family name. He was to maintain authority in the home and teach his sons obedience and respect. He was also a role model to his younger siblings. The oldest sibling provided guidance and continuous instruction to the younger siblings. The eldest son owed his father absolute obedience. He was required to support his parents, mourn them, bury them (according to social station and financial ability), provide for their needs in the other world, and take all the necessary steps to ensure perpetuation of the male line.

The powerful female role belonged to the matriarch, the wife of the patriarch. The matriarch was in charge of daughters-in-law, daughters, and children, and she was both a nurturant caretaker and stern taskmistress.

The role of the wife, as daughter-in-law, was to serve the mother-in-law, produce a male heir, be subservient to the husband, and be the primary person to rear the children. The mother's role was more affec-

Asian American Household Size and Composition, 1990-1991

Household Size, 1991

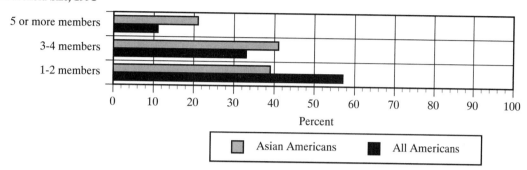

Average Persons Per Household, 1990

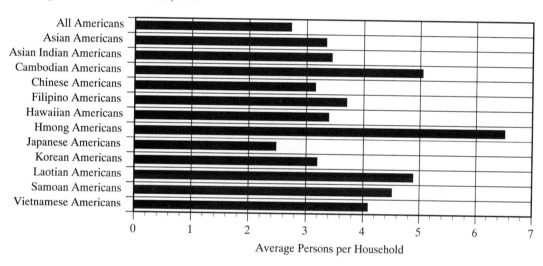

Living Arrangements, 1990

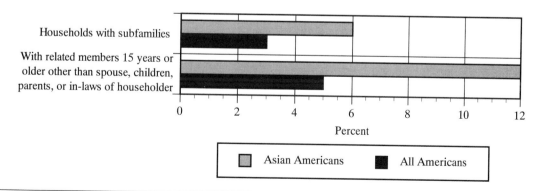

Sources: Susan B. Gall and Timothy L. Gall, eds., *Statistical Record of Asian Americans.* Detroit: Gale Research, Inc., 1993. U.S. Bureau of the Census, *1990 Census of Population: Asians and Pacific Islanders in the United States,* 1993.

Asian American Youth, Selected Characteristics, 1989 and 1991

Comparative Percent of Births to Teenagers, 1989

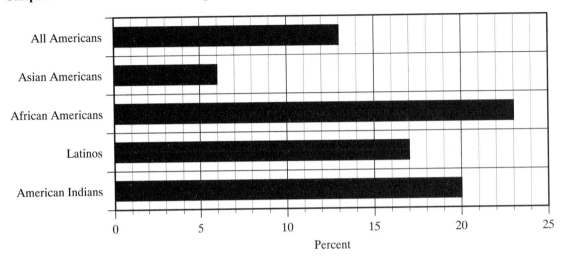

Comparative Activities for Youths 16-24 Years, 1991

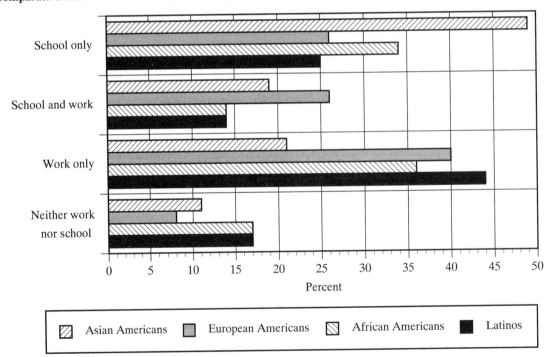

Sources: U.S. Bureau of the Census, *1990 Census of Population: Asians and Pacific Islanders in the United States,* 1993. U.S. Bureau of the Census, *1990 Census of Population: General Population Characteristics: United States,* 1992. William O'Hare, "America's Minorities: The Demographics of Diversity." *Population Bulletin* 47:4 (1992).

tionate toward the children than the father's. She often acted as mediator, earning the children's respect and affection. This role of the mother in the children's training was not only in the interest of the welfare of the children but also in the mother's self-interest. Her relationship, particularly to her sons, tended to afford protection from her dominating mother-in-law and other intrusive extended family members. It also guaranteed her a favored position during widowhood. By contrast, a woman who failed to produce a son was in a most vulnerable position.

Marriage. Marriage in Asian families was an expected event in the life of the family and the young adult. Traditionally, it was the father's responsibility to see that a suitable woman was chosen for the son. Determining suitability frequently involved checking into family background—social status, financial endowment, health, and mental health of family members.

Traditionally, families arranged marriages with very little say from the young adults. Often the parents employed a go-between who would work out the negotiations to meet the requirements of both families. Marriages were arranged to acquire wealth, obtain beneficial social connections, and maintain harmony.

Such a system guaranteed much family stability in Asia, and the first generation of each Asian immigrant group has sought to import its practices to the United States. In the 1930's, for example, first-generation Japanese Americans hired matchmakers to find marriage candidates for their children and check out their backgrounds. Frequently, the children, imbued with American ideals of romantic love, objected. Sometimes the children won out, sometimes the parents; in some cases there was a compromise, with a young woman, for example, choosing her mate but the family having the matchmaker go through the rituals anyway. By the latter part of the second generation, arranged marriages were uncommon. Other Asian groups, less far along the generational ladder, seem to be going through a similar transition from arranged to romantic mate choice.

Divorce rates among Asians have been relatively low, partly because marriage in traditional Asian cultures is defined not as something for individual fulfillment but rather as duty. Also, traditionally there is great shame in divorce along with serious ostracism. In traditional Vietnamese culture, for example, divorce is highly stigmatized and considered dishonorable. The husband is supposed to be responsible for his wife for the duration of their lives.

INTERRACIAL MARRIAGE is rising among all the Asian groups except Filipinos. Before the second wave of Filipino immigration, the rate of interracial marriage among Filipinos was very high. As with the Chinese, changes in immigration law had made them a bachelor society without women from their home country, but unlike the Chinese, they were not forbidden by law to intermarry. More than half the marriages by Filipino men before World War II (1939-1945) were interracial. In the period of family immigration since 1965, Filipino intermarriage patterns have more nearly resembled those of other Asian groups.

Probably about one in four Chinese Americans in the 1990's married someone who was not Chinese. The rate for Koreans was about the same, for Southeast Asians somewhat lower. The highest rate of interracial marriage is among Japanese Americans—more than half marry non-Japanese. This is primarily a result of their generational structure—marriageable Japanese Americans are mainly members of the fourth generation—as well as geographical dispersion and entry into the middle class. For all the Asian groups, more Asian women than Asian men marry outside the group, which leaves some Asian men without partners.

For the Vietnamese, interracial marriages or liaisons were not uncommon during the Vietnam War (1965-1975). These relationships resulted in Amerasian children, some of whom in the 1980's and 1990's sought their roots and identity in the United States.

Child-rearing Practices. Traditionally, Asian American children were subjugated to filial piety restrictions. Behavior of children and youth operated on the principle of bringing honor to the family and not incurring shame or loss of face. Children were reared, generally, under close supervision by family members or extended family members. In the Filipino culture, children were encouraged to be reciprocally dependent on kinship groups.

In traditional Confucian cultures, discipline is administered seldom by corporal punishment and hardly ever through verbal reasoning. In the early years, the children are indulged or pampered. When they are older, however, and are able to understand obligations, complete obedience is expected of them. They have to follow rigid guidelines and family expectations in order to adopt a role in the family structure.

The primary techniques of discipline are shaming and withdrawing of affection. It is assumed that a child will not take seriously the guidance of a loving adult but will obey the commands of a stern, feared parent. Even if a father is pleased with the accomplishments of his son, the father will show no pleasure in the pres-

Asian Americans Under 18 Years Living with Two Parents, 1990

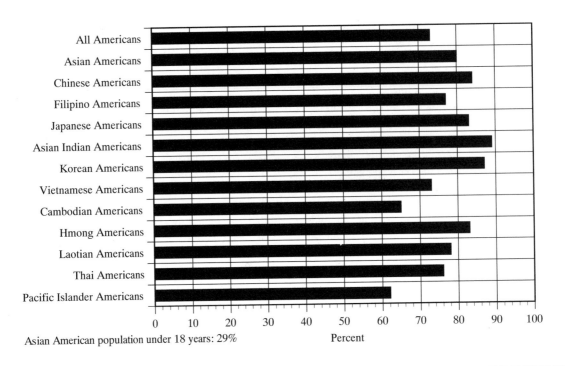

Asian American population under 18 years: 29%

Percent

Sources: U.S. Bureau of the Census, *1990 Census of Population: Asians and Pacific Islanders in the United States,* 1993. U.S. Bureau of the Census, *1990 Census of Population: General Population Characteristics: United States,* 1992. William O'Hare, "America's Minorities: The Demographics of Diversity." *Population Bulletin* 47:4 (1992).

ence of the son, although he might express his pride in the son's absence. Teasing and gossiping by extended family members are other means used to control behavior.

Children are socialized by parents, extended family members, and teachers. Children are viewed as an economic investment, a safety net for one's retirement in old age. In TAGALOG, one of the Filipino languages, children are called *kayamanan*, which means "wealth."

Although children are highly valued in Asian cultures, as they grow up in the United States, the influence of their peers is great and very often conflict with their parents intensifies, especially for those families who try to maintain traditional family values. Asian American children and youth face different issues depending on their age, racial identity, geographic location, and generation level. Some second- and third-generation American-born youth struggle with identity issues, whereas some first-generation immigrant youth struggle with language comprehension and peer ridicule and rejection.

Aging. The aged have always played a prominent role in Asian families. Confucius gave status to the elderly by declaring wisdom to be affiliated with age. In Asian cultures, in contrast to prevailing attitudes in the West, the elderly are to be respected and revered as their age increases. They play important roles in decision-making in all matters. Their wishes often supersede those of other family members.

Respect for the elderly is often reflected in the use of a proper form of address. In the Filipino culture, *manong* is the proper address for a man older than oneself, *manang* for a woman. The responsibility of caring for the elderly falls upon the children: The children were cared for when young by the parents; the elderly parents are to be cared for when old by their children. This sense of reciprocity and obligation is ingrained in Asian family values.

Family Problems. Asian families are faced with dilemmas that revolve around assimilation and acculturation to American culture. Traditional Asian cultural values are threatened, for example, when financial pressures force Asian parents to choose between paying high medical costs for elderly parents and high tuition costs for children's education.

Financial pressures can also undermine the extended family structure. In the American economy, Asian families often must move to where it is feasible to make a living. Professional couples move to locations where elderly parents may not want to go and so must leave family and roots. This situation results in families being spread throughout the United States and puts strain on extended family ties. In addition, as more women are employed outside the home, the traditional expectation that women will take total responsibility for children and serve mothers-in-law becomes increasingly difficult to fulfill.

The value of filial piety is challenged as the youth become acculturated and abandon traditional values and customs. Lack of respect toward parents results in loss of face, poor communication, and alienation. Tra-

Asian mother and daughter at play. Increasingly among Asians living in America, the realities of modern life—single parenthood, for example—are threatening to undermine traditional family organization. (David S. Strickler)

ditional cultural values are also threatened as rates of intermarriage increase. Asian families may feel that their distinctive cultural values and traditions are in danger of being lost.

Family roles are also affected by language barriers. Immigrant parents must depend on their children when language proficiency is required; children, even young ones, are forced to supplant their parents as decision-makers. This role reversal undermines the traditional family structure. At the same time, the immigrant parents' patterns of discipline and socialization may be challenged by officials who inform parents that such practices are not acceptable in the American social environment.

Asian families are known for their resiliency. Despite the problems they face, they share a strong belief in perseverance, which helps families to adapt to their environment without compromising other significant cultural values.—*Rowena Fong*

SUGGESTED READINGS:

- Asian Women United of California, eds. *Making Waves: An Anthology of Writings By and About Asian American Women.* Boston: Beacon Press, 1989. A collection of essays, poems, short stories, and memoirs of Chinese, Japanese, Korean, Filipino, South Asian, and Southeast Asian women. The anthology provides valuable insights into issues of immigration, war, work, identity, and injustice.

- Ho, Man Keung. "Family Therapy with Asian/Pacific Americans." In *Family Therapy with Ethnic Minorities.* Newbury Park, Calif.: Sage, 1987. This chapter reviews cultural values in relation to family structure, extended family ties, husband-wife and parent-child relationships, family help-seeking behaviors, and the impact of immigration and cultural adjustments.

- Huang, Larke Nahme. "Southeast Asian Refugee Children and Adolescents." In *Children of Color*, by Jewelle Taylor Gibbs, et al. San Francisco: Jossey-Bass, 1989. Describes the migration history of Southeast Asian refugee youth and provides culturally sensitive information on sociocultural issues in assessing and treating the youth.

- Huang, Lucy Jen. "The Chinese American Family." In *Ethnic Families in America: Patterns and Variations,* edited by Charles H. Mindel and Robert W. Habenstein. New York: Elsevier, 1976. Covers historical background, marriage and intermarriage, divorce, family process and socialization, and problems of aging, with suggestions for changes and adaptations.

- Kim, Bok-Lim C. *Korean-American Child at School and at Home.* Washington, D.C.: Administration for Children, Youth, and Families, U.S. Department of Health, Education, and Welfare, 1980. This monograph explores the relationship between school and community in Chicago and Los Angeles. Offers useful information about marginality and biculturality issues for Korean American children.

- Kitano, Harry. *Japanese Americans.* 2d ed. Englewood Cliffs, N.J.: Prentice-Hall, 1976. A comprehensive book on Japanese Americans, covering such topics as war experiences, family and community, culture, and social deviance. Japanese in Hawaii are also mentioned. Offers useful discussions of assimilation, acculturation, and cultural and structural pluralism.

- Okamura, Jonathan, and Amefil Agbayani. "Filipino Americans." In *Handbook of Social Services for Asian and Pacific Islanders,* edited by Noreen Mokuau. New York: Greenwood Press, 1991. Provides historical background, a sociodemographic overview, and a profile of social and psychological problems, values, and behavioral norms, providing insightful suggestions for helping Filipinos solve these problems.

- Shon, Steven, and Davis Ja. "Asian Families." In *Ethnicity and Family Therapy*, by Monica McGoldrick, John Pearce, and Joseph Giordano. New York: Guilford Press, 1982. The chapter describes family structure, family roles, the communication process, marriage, and cultural norms, such as issues of obligation and shame. Important issues for treatment include developing a therapeutic alliance and the race of the therapist.

- Sue, Stanley, and James Morishima. "Understanding the Asian American Family." In *The Mental Health of Asian Americans.* San Francisco: Jossey-Bass, 1982. The chapter discusses Francis Hsu's and George DeVos's theories of Chinese and Japanese culture, respectively. These theories offer frameworks for understanding the social, cultural, religious, and role dimensions of Asian American families in the context of mental health concerns.

- Takaki, Ronald. *Strangers from a Different Shore.* Boston: Little, Brown, 1989. A comprehensive history of Chinese, Japanese, Koreans, Asian Indians, and Filipinos in the continental United States and Hawaii from the 1800's to the 1980's. Offers wide-ranging observations on the development of Asian American cultures and social structures, including many family issues.

Family associations (also, clan associations): Chinese immigrant organizations with membership based on having the same surname or the same several surnames. These associations are an extension of the concept of the ancestral hall of a particular lineage.

Because of the need to socialize as well as to secure mutual aid and protection in a hostile environment, Chinese immigrants to America often sought the company of others from the same clan-village. Such groupings, known as *fang*, had existed since the early days of Chinese settlement in California.

In any one locality abroad, however, immigrants from the same village were comparatively limited in number. Expanding on the concept, Chinese immigrants formed family associations that enrolled members on the basis of surname. The sole criteria was and is descent from an alleged common ancestor, with no limitation on the village of origin.

Family associations seem to have appeared in the United States in San Francisco around the 1870's, where their formation was spurred by the necessity for collective defense against external threats. Later, numerically smaller clans also banded together into multisurname family associations in order to gain collective strength to counter the domination of the more numerous clans. Generally the rationale for such alliances of several surnames was based on some alleged common ancestor or event in Chinese mythology or history. The best-known association of this type is the Lung Kong Tin Yee Association, which enrolls members from four different clans—Liu, Guan, Zhang, and Zhao—based on the story of the four sworn brothers with these surnames in the *Romance of the Three Kingdoms* (1522).

During the nineteenth century and early twentieth century, when the threat of *tong* fights was ever present, family associations often had an organization called a *tang*, which was led by elders and had jurisdiction over clan affairs. A separate organization called a *gongsuo*, consisting of younger members, acted as the clan association's defense unit against outside threats.

When the threat from TONG WARS diminished after the 1920's, many associations began merging the two branches. Since the end of World War II the trend has been for single surname organizations to change their name to *zongqinhui*. Today family associations are primarily centers for social events such as annual spring banquets. Many also provide benefits for members such as awarding scholarships to members' children.

Fan-Tan: Popular Chinese gambling game as well as a type of card game. In the former a square is first drawn upon a table, with each of its sides designated 1, 2, 3, and 4. The banker spreads on the table a pile of small objects or playing pieces. The players then bet as to what they think the number of leftover pieces will be after the pile has been reduced to a total of four or less by being divided by four repeatedly as necessary. The bets are placed on the side of the square that bears the number being selected. The number of pieces in the final batch determines the winning number: For example, if three pieces remain, "3" wins the game. There are several varieties of Fan-Tan.

Fang, John T. C. (May 27, 1925, Shanghai, China— Apr. 27, 1992, San Francisco, Calif.): Publisher. A pioneer in bringing Asian American news to the community and mainstream American society, he studied journalism in China, served as associate editor of the *New Life Daily News* in Taiwan, and came to the United States in the early 1950's. He was managing editor of the *Chinese Daily Post* in San Francisco; president of Pan Asia Venture Capital Corporation; and founder/publisher of ASIAN WEEK, a community-based newspaper.

John Fang. (Asian Week)

Farrington v. Tokushige (1927): U.S. Supreme Court ruling that struck down a series of regulations in Hawaii inhibiting operation of the state's Japanese-language schools. Such legislative restrictions, the Court declared, are unconstitutional. Under the regulations, foreign-language schools were required to obtain a written permit from the state and pay a fee of one dollar per student. In late 1922 a petition initiated by newspaper publisher Kinzaburo MAKINO was filed asking the court to enjoin the enactment of further restrictive laws, which, the petitioners contended, deprived them of liberty and property without due process of law as guaranteed by the Fifth Amendment to the Constitution.

There were at the time more than 160 foreign-language schools in Hawaii. The great majority of these were Japanese schools, with total enrollments of about 20,000 pupils. The schools, moreover, were not publicly funded.

On appeal, the Supreme Court affirmed the constitutional right of Japanese parents—or those of any other race or nationality—to direct the education of their children without undue restrictions.

February 28 incident (1947): Occurrence in which a soldier of the Chinese Nationalist army shot to death a Taiwanese woman street vendor suspected of selling contraband cigarettes. The killing triggered a series of clashes between native Taiwanese and Nationalist militia who had recently arrived from the Chinese mainland, during a period of martial law. Thousands of local residents were killed during the riots, which broke out in February, 1947. Public discussion of the massacre remained taboo in Taiwan until the late 1980's. In 1992 the Taiwanese government issued an official report that concluded that the incident was the result of human errors that could have been avoided.

The Chinese Nationalist army occupied the island of Taiwan following the defeat of Japan in World War II and imposed a military government over the island. Resentment of the newly arrived military authorities grew among the local Taiwanese population, especially among the elite who had lived under Japanese rule for the previous fifty years. The February 28 incident occasioned the expression of this resentment. Protests over the street vendor's death turned into a two-week uprising. Overreacting to the riots, the Nationalist governor-general ordered an island-wide crackdown to quell the rioting. Several months of Nationalist army reprisals followed. The military justified this action out of fear that the Chinese Communists would take advantage of the unrest to spread their revolution from the mainland to Taiwan.

Memories of the February 28 incident have perpetuated animosity between the island's native-born Taiwanese population and mainland immigrants who fled from the Chinese mainland to Taiwan after the Chinese Nationalist army was defeated by the Chinese Community Red Army in 1949. After the government lifted martial law in 1987, the ban on discussing the incident in public was also ended. Relatives of the victims called on the government to make a full disclosure of the incident. The government responded by issuing a report and also sought to foster reconciliation and to bridge the cultural gap between the local population and mainland immigrants by sponsoring commemorative activities and erecting memorials.

Federated Agricultural Laborers Association: Filipino labor union chartered by the AMERICAN FEDERATION OF LABOR (AFL) in 1940. AFL recognition followed the union's successful representation of thousands of asparagus cutters and other farm workers during a series of labor strikes in central California.

Feleo-Gonzalez, Marina (b. July 22, 1932, Santa Rosa, Philippines): Playwright, screenwriter, and media consultant. Founding president of the screenwriters guild of the Philippines and founding chair of the Radio/TV Writers Guild of the Philippines, her scripts have received numerous accolades, including Filipino equivalents of the United States' Academy and Emmy Awards. In the United States, she has lectured widely on Asian and Asian American film, video, and culture and taught for independent film organizations including Third World Newsreel, the Film News Now Foundation, and Women Make Movies.

Feng shui: Members of diverse cultures now and in the past often seem to share a similar intuitive association of their personal well-being and avoidance of misfortune with their being "in the right place at the right time." Chinese civilization has responded to this source of universal anxiety by inventing and promoting an art of human placement known as *feng-shui*. *Feng shui* is the Chinese vernacular term (Mandarin pronunciation; various spellings) for a comprehensive body of theories and practices that have superficial characteristics of a terrestrial astrology; that is, some aspects of *feng shui* involve divining the future or discovering hidden knowledge by using Earth surface features (for example, mountains and streams) as sur-

A fenh shui map of an auspicious tombsite on Cheju Island, Republic of Korea, c. 1200.

rogates for celestial features (for example, planets, stars, and asterisms).

Definition. The term is composed of two Chinese ideographs for "wind" and "water." These are described by Herbert Chatley (1917) as "outward and visible signs of celestial Yang and Yin"; he continues with a concise English-language working definition for *feng shui* that is still widely accepted as authoritative and accurate: "The art of adapting the residence of the living and the dead so as to co-operate and harmonize with the local currents of the cosmic breath."

In accepting this definition, one must eventually interpret *feng shui* within a more complex and comprehensive Song Dynasty (960-1279) neo-Confucian cosmology. Otherwise, it becomes convenient but misleading for skeptics and the uninformed to dismiss *feng shui* as "geomancy." Such glossing over of the term has tended in the past to reduce *feng shui* discourse in the West to culturally insensitive anecdotes involving Asian occult searches for lucky places and presently tends to promote myopic speculations about the magical efficacy of interior design strategies. Thus little progress has been made toward increasing any

cross-cultural understanding of the larger ethical and environmental implications of *feng shui*'s complex integration with neo-Confucian cosmology.

Historical Development. Feng shui origins likely spring from early Taoist preoccupations with universal philosophical questions involving humankind's place in nature and its relation to all things in the universe. Proto-*feng shui* in the early dynastic period associated abstract ideas about order, chaos, and change with solving more practical problems of hydraulic engineering, agricultural productivity, and social control.

Consolidation of the entire *feng shui* system as applied to propitious sitings for temples, cities, and imperial burials was well underway by the end of the Han Dynasty (206 B.C.E.-220 C.E.), and it soon spread beyond the "Middle Kingdom" to the Korean peninsula, to Vietnam, and to Japan. During the ensuing "golden age" of Buddhism in East Asia, temples and pagodas were located according to *feng shui* principles. Later, during the Song Dynasty, the Chu Hsi school of neo-Confucianism formulated its "bureaucratization of nature," which tacitly endorsed *feng shui* logic within a new synthesis of classical Confucian ideas about society and government, and Taoist and Buddhist ideas about nature and the universe. Chu Hsi neo-Confucianism subsequently became state cults in Ming Dynasty (1368-1644) and QING DYNASTY (1644-1911) China and in YI DYNASTY (1392-1910) Korea.

Owing to these developments, *feng shui* became popularized throughout the Chinese neo-Confucian cultural realm, as reverence for ancestors merged with anxieties about "correct" ethical procedures involving burial practices and grave siting (except in Japan, where popular *feng shui* evolved to emphasize regulation of journeys rather than placement of tombs). Although *feng shui* had ceased to be the exclusive possession and preoccupation of emperors and aristocrats, its grip on the public mind had conveniently secured for those in power their social control of the masses. Growth and prosperity ensued, and by the eighteenth century neo-Confucian civilization had achieved perhaps the highest standard of living in the world for that time. Its success rested on the backs of millions of farmers simultaneously cultivating their virtues through hard work and, except in cases of extreme poverty, diligent adherence to *feng shui* conventions.

Despite the general decline of state neo-Confucianism in East Asia during the nineteenth and twentieth centuries, the *feng shui* epiphenomenon has survived there. One may anticipate encountering both former impacts and the continuing presence of *feng shui* practices wherever neo-Confucianism remains entrenched in rural folklife or as part of the culture of rural migrants settling in East Asian cities. Overseas emigrants from East Asia have also carried neo-Confucianism abroad; as a result, *feng shui has transcended its East Asia regional incubator to become a dynamic new element in world popular culture and is attracting attention and adherents among Western peoples. This has been demonstrated in the 1990's, for example in the United States and Canada, by the increasing and widespread influences of feng shui* on real estate markets, architecture, and interior design.

Relations to Geography. Conventional wisdom among medieval neo-Confucian peoples long dictated that *feng shui* practices govern site selections and construction plans for all "human habitations," which are broadly defined through past and present practices to include graves, houses, cities, shrines, and even business establishments. As a locational theory involving surveying practices, *feng shui* can be accurately characterized as an interpretive and applied art. It is neither science nor religion but rather a systematic body of indigenous geographical-locational theories and practices involving trained scholar/technicians ("earth doctors"), their surveying devices (featuring enigmatic compasses), and associated artifacts (manuals and maps). In *feng shui* as it is known today, these objects are only the most obvious indicators preserving complex underlying thought patterns that operate according to their own internal logic and that adapt to specific circumstances.

Feng Shui Logic. The logic of *feng shui* assumes that people have inherent tendencies to move toward certain places. These places are auspicious points of reference that coincide favorably with the points of reference for cosmic events. Thus *feng shui* through its surveys allows people to adapt their houses and living spaces to "local currents of the cosmic breath" (*qi,* in Chinese). *Feng shui* theory holds that these vital currents originate in heaven, descend to earth through its highest mountain, and diverge to the four quarters through "dragons" (celestially charged mountain chains). Cosmic currents may also well up beneath the earth surface as "yellow springs," at which places *feng shui* experts will attempt to discover and exploit the springs for specific clients (who may or may not have the appropriate virtue and natal astrology to reap the benefits). Arguably neo-Confucian society and the environment may have benefited the most from *feng shui* practices during premodern times, as the system once operated to engage humankind into a place-specific

spirit of cooperation with the universe while dissuading individuals from selfish, unethical, and rapacious settlement practices.

SUGGESTED READINGS: • Chatley, Herbert. "Feng Shui." In *Encyclopaedia Sinica,* edited by Samuel Couling, p. 175. Shanghai: Kelly and Walsh, 1917. • Feuchtwang, Stephan D. R. *An Anthropological Analysis of Chinese Geomancy.* Vientiane, Laos: Editions Vithagna, 1974. • Needham, Joseph. *Science and Civilisation in China: History of Scientific Thought.* Vol. 2. Cambridge, England: Cambridge University Press, 1956. • Rossbach, Sarah. *Interior Design with Feng Shui.* New York: E. P. Dutton, 1987. • Wheatley, Paul. *The Pivot of the Four Quarters: A Preliminary Enquiry Into the Origins and Character of the Ancient Chinese City.* Chicago: Aldine, 1971. • Yoon, Hongkey. *Geomantic Relations Between Culture and Nature in Korea.* Taipei: Chinese Association for Folklore, 1976.

Fenollosa, Ernest Francisco (Feb. 18, 1853–Sept. 21, 1908, London, England): Art historian, curator, and poet. Amid the national modernizations of the MEIJI RESTORATION (1868-1912), a period in which much of Japan's artistic heritage began to fall into neglect, Fenollosa strove to preserve the country's classical art. Through his writings and lectures, he introduced Oriental art to the West, opening the door to further scholarship on the subject. He was the son of a Spanish musician who had landed in the United States in 1838, settling in Salem, Massachusetts. Fenollosa matriculated at Harvard, studying philosophy and sociology, graduating first in his class in 1874, and being elected class poet. During that time he also began painting. A fellowship enabled him to enter postgraduate study in philosophy and theology at Cambridge in England.

Fenollosa spent 1877 taking classes at the Boston Museum of Fine Arts. In 1878 he married Lizzie Goodhue Millett and began teaching at Tokyo Imperial University, where he was a lecturer in political science, philosophy, and economics until 1886. Taking note of the decline to which Japan's ancient temples and their artworks were exposed as a consequence of modernization, Fenollosa enthusiastically championed preservation and set about learning the history, themes, and methods of classical Japanese art. He financed a Tokyo exhibition of classical works in 1881. The following year he delivered a lecture entitled "The True Theory of Art." As his opinions and ideas assumed greater popularity and influence, others were inspired to embrace this facet of their culture, including several

Nineteenth century street scene depicts a mingling of Japanese and Western culture. (Library of Congress)

painters who pioneered a movement to revive Japanese painting. Fenollosa also completed a study comparing Greek drama and the traditional No theater of Japan. Under the sponsorship of the Japanese government, he and an official of the education ministry traveled throughout Europe in 1886 in an effort to learn the methods of teaching and preserving the fine arts. Fenollosa returned to Japan and in 1887 cofounded the Tokyo Art Academy; he also helped draft a law to preserve the temples and their artistic contents.

While living overseas, Fenollosa converted to BUDDHISM and was baptized under the name of Tei-Shin. He was also apprenticed to the ancient academy of the Kano, which gave him the Japanese name of Kano Yeitan Masanobu. In addition, the emperor of Japan awarded him the third classes of the Order of the Rising Sun and the Order of the Sacred Mirror.

Not until 1890 did Fenollosa return to the United States, specifically to the Boston Museum of Fine Arts as its curator of Oriental art. During his tenure there he wrote assorted monographs on Oriental art and published several books. In addition to his devotion to the visual arts, Fenollosa retained a lifelong love of poetry; his recital of his poem "East and West" at Cambridge in 1892 was followed by the publication of *East and West: The Discovery of America and Other Poems* (1893). *The Masters of Ukioye* (1896) is a nonfictional volume describing an exhibition of Japanese paintings and color prints at the New York Fine Arts Building. Following his divorce from Lizzie, he married Mary McNeil in 1895.

Fenollosa left the museum in 1897 to become an English-language instructor and professor of English literature at a school in Tokyo, staying for three years before returning to the United States and a professorship at Columbia University. He completed *An Outline of the History of Ukiyo-ye* in 1901; a description of the famous seventeenth century woodblock prints of the Edo period's (1600-1867) Ukiyo-e (pictures of the floating world) school, it is considered a classic. Fenollosa died in London en route to Japan. Works that appeared after his death include the two-volume *Epochs of Chinese and Japanese Art: An Outline History of East Asiatic Design* (1912), compiled by Mary McNeil Fenollosa, and *The Chinese Written Character as a Medium for Poetry* (1920), edited by Ezra Pound, a work which exercised a significant influence on modern poetry.

Fiancees Act of 1946: U.S. legislation that permitted American servicemen to bring foreign-born fiancées into the United States. On June 26, 1946, the Fiancees Act expanded provisions of the 1945 WAR BRIDES ACT by exempting a maximum of five thousand alien women engaged to marry American servicemen from national-origins quotas. Chinese fiancées constituted a portion of the female immigrants who took advantage of this opportunity, and most of them married Chinese American men. Thus, the Fiancees Act helped to correct a generations-old gender imbalance, which past anti-Chinese immigration laws had forced upon Americans of Chinese ancestry.

Fictive kinship: Also known in literature as "ritual" kinship, forms of fictive kinship range widely from the Masai blood brotherhood to legal adoptions and fosterages to mock marriages. Any form of fictive kinship is best seen as alternative and/or supplemental to "real" kinship relations. Participants in fictive kinship are expected to behave "like real kinsmen or better."

A most elaborate development of fictive kinship is best exemplified in the *compadrazgo* institution of Latin America, and by extension, the Philippines. In Europe it is known as "godparenthood." Made official by the Roman Catholic church in the Council of Trent (1545-1563 C.E.), the Sacrament of Baptism is the medium by which the basic fictive ties in Christian cultures are created: between baptismal sponsor(s) or godparent(s) and godchild, and between the child's parents and godparent(s). Major ethnographies have demonstrated that in Latin America a child's parent-godparent ties take priority over the ties between godchild and godparent. The reverse applies in Europe. Ritual sponsors are also required for the Confirmation Sacrament at adolescence, allowing the baptismal sponsor(s) to serve again. Choice of sponsors tends to be more social than moral or theological and reflects the range of networks that participants are willing to accommodate. The largely Christian Philippines has created its own style of *compadrazgo* closer to Latin America, perhaps more expanded and suitable to the bilateral kinship structure.

At the heart of the social network is the sponsored individual (*inaanak*, or Spanish *ahijado/ahijada*); the ritual sponsor (*ninong*, if male, or *ninang*, if female), the latter as modification from the Spanish terms *padrino* and *madrina*; and the sponsored's parents. Ritual and real parents address and refer to one another as *compadres* for males and *comadres* for females—hence the term *compadrazgo*. Biological children of the sponsors are ritual siblings (*kinakapatid*) to the sponsored and are addressed in the senior-junior hierarchy of sibling terminology. Sometimes the fictive kin terms are also applied to the spouses of the ritual kinsmen or to anyone with whom a person wishes to validate already existing closer ties. Among Filipino Muslims, ritual brotherhood is fairly common between males who grew up together and shared a woman's milk when infants (salususu). In adulthood ritual brotherhood may be entered into regardless of ethnic differences. Other forms such as child borrowing (*piging*) and social adoption (ampon or hingi) occur in literature.

Fifteen Passenger Bill of 1879: Congressional legislation that proposed to limit to fifteen the number of Chinese on any ship destined for the United States. Though passed by both the House and the Senate in 1879, President Rutherford B. Hayes vetoed it as a violation of the Burlingame Treaty (1868).

Fijian Indians: Term referring to those who, directly or indirectly, trace their ancestry to an Asian Indian settlement in Fiji.

When the Fiji Islands became a part of the British Empire in 1874, the British government was confronted with a massive responsibility to free Fiji from all debts and to organize and develop its economic activities. Failing to integrate the indigenous population and other Pacific Islanders into the plantation economy, the Fijian government had to look elsewhere for hardworking laborers. Having previously served in Mauritius and Trinidad and being well aware of the Asian Indians' capacity for hard work, Sir Arthur Gordon, the first governor of Fiji, requested that the imperial government negotiate with the Indian government for indentured laborers.

A group of five hundred indentured laborers first arrived from India on May 15, 1879, and by 1915, there were approximately sixteen thousand indentured Indians working the sugar plantations in Fiji. Reports of unscrupulous recruiters abducting men, women, and children and forcing them to travel to Fiji against their will were common. Referred to as "coolies," the indentured laborers lived and worked under the most inhumane conditions. In 1914, in response to Mahatma Gandhi's campaign against the indenture system, motions were introduced in the Indian Parliament to dismantle it and in 1916, the system finally came to an end. While some former indentured laborers returned to India, a large majority of them exercised their options to remain in Fiji, having been assured that they would be granted the full rights of permanent residents.

Approximately 80 percent of Indians in Fiji are descendants of indentured laborers, while other Indian residents arrived as a result of free migration. From the outset of their arrival in Fiji, the indentured laborers were concerned with the education of their children and with ways of improving the living conditions on the plantations. Several Indian religious, linguistic, and cultural organizations emerged to address these needs.

By the 1920's, the evolving structure of the Indian settlement had begun to reflect the Indo-Aryan traditions of India itself. In 1922, a residential tax was levied on all community members between the ages of eighteen and sixty. After a decade of taxation without representation, in 1929 the Indians were finally granted representation in the Legislative Council. Since then, the Asian (East) Indians have continued to contribute actively to Fiji's political, social, and economic development.

In the 1950's, Fijian Indians began to emigrate overseas, and today, successful enclaves of Fijian Indian settlements are found in the United Kingdom, New Zealand, Australia, Canada, and the United States. Since October 10, 1970, when Fiji became an independent nation, the greatest challenge for the Fijian Indians has been to secure and maintain a political parity in a multiracial and multiethnic democracy in the Pacific.

Fijians: Indigenous population of the Sovereign Democratic Republic of Fiji, more commonly known simply as "Fiji." An archipelago comprising more than three hundred islands, Fiji is located in the South Pacific, east of Australia and north of New Zealand. Its total land area of about 7,056 square miles contains a 1992 population of about 748,000.

History. Exhibiting distinct negroid physical features, Fijians are believed to have been a part of the Melanesian migration dating back to 7,000 B.C.E. and the Polynesian flow of several thousand years later. While there is a lack of empirical archaeological evidence, the diffusionist tradition in anthropology argues that there are sufficient similarities to link the Fijian linguistic patterns to those found in the east African region of what is now known as "Tanzania." A more direct link to Africa has located the Fijian customs in the ancient traditions of Thebes. It has been speculated that the Fijians' ancestors may have been introduced into Egypt as slaves and that they may have escaped from there to roam the oceans until they found themselves in the South Pacific.

The islands in the Fiji archipelago were discovered

FIJI ISLANDS

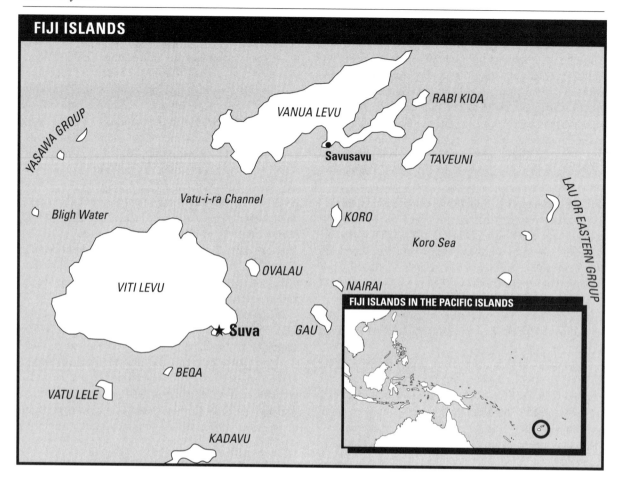

in a period covering approximately two hundred years; however, the Dutch navigator Abel Tasman is believed to have first sighted the islands in 1643 when his small ship ran aground on the Nanuku Reef, northeast of the island of Tavenui. Tasman's accounts of cannibalism, savagery, and treacherous coral reefs kept mariners and explorers away from the Fiji Islands until 1774, when Captain James Cook sailed through the southern islands in the Fiji group. Captain William Bligh's discoveries, which included nearly all the important islands, were the direct consequences of the events leading to the mutiny on the HMS *Bounty* in 1789. Subsequently Bligh returned to Fiji in 1792, confirmed discoveries made earlier, and accurately charted the islands on a map. During the closing years of the eighteenth century, Captain James Wilson in 1797 extended the discoveries of Tasman, Cook, and Bligh.

By 1805 the lure of profitable trade in sandalwood and later the beche-de-mer (sea cucumber, a marine animal consumed mainly by the Chinese) had attracted the first European settlers, who were either merchants or missionaries, to Fiji. Early settlers encountered an indigenous society fragmented into a handful of tribal kingdoms. The European introduction of firearms disproportionately shifted the balance of power among the rival tribes. Consequently intertribal warfare became more intense, and increased cannibalism plagued the islands for the next four decades. While missionaries were instrumental in converting some of the natives to Christianity, abolishing the practice of cannibalism and reducing the Fijian language to writing, the continued bloody civil war resulted in murderous chaos for the natives and destruction of property for the foreign settlers on the islands.

National Unification and Later Independence. Movement toward unification of the Fiji Islands was first initiated when a tribal chief of the Bau island group, Ratu Cakobau, assumed leadership of his tribe after deposing rebels from within his own tribe in the Battle of Kaba. After restoring order and civility to his own kingdom, Cakobau undertook to do the same for the rest of the islands. Unable, however, to resolve the country's secular and religious problems and to free Fiji from all debts owed to the Americans, Cakobau, a

Fijian villagers, in traditional native clothing, using bamboo sticks to beat a rhythm while performing at the Polynesian Cultural Center, Oahu, Hawaii. (Brigham Young University, Hawaii)

converted Christian, sought to make Fiji a British protectorate. In 1862 he first made an offer of cession to Great Britain but the offer was rejected. The next offer was made to the United States. Since that country was engaged in its own Civil War, this offer was also ignored. The island kingdom was then forced to formulate its own governmental structure. A confederation was created, but a rivalry between Cakobau and Chief Ma'afu soon led to its collapse within a five-year period, in 1867. In 1871 Cakobau was finally declared king of the Fiji Islands, and a constitution was developed and a government established. The viability of the Cakobau Kingdom was, once again, of very brief tenure and collapsed in 1873. This failure threw the country into economic chaos, civil disorder, and anarchy. Once again an offer of cession was made to Great Britain, and this time the offer was accepted. Fiji was ceded to Queen Victoria of Great Britain on October 10, 1874. In a spirit of mutual trust, an unconditional Deed of Cession was prepared and was formally signed by Ratu Cakobau, the other tribal chiefs, and the queen's representative, Sir Hercules Robinson. Fiji was annexed as a British Crown Colony.

The Native Affairs Ordinance of 1876 gave the Fijians a coherent administrative structure that permitted the country to be governed by Britain through a Legislative Council. The Council assumed greater local authority as its elected membership increased steadily. Almost a century later Fiji achieved full independence, and on October 10, 1970, it became a member of the British Commonwealth with Dominion status and joined the United Nations as its 127th member. Early experiments in a multiracial and a multiethnic democracy profoundly advanced the political consciousness among Fijians. Politically the greatest challenge for Fijians is to preserve their democracy; to share power and maintain harmony in a society that is fundamentally fragmented along racial and ethnic lines.

Communal Life. Traditionally Fijian life is rooted in small rural villages known as *koros*. Each *koro* is comprised of fifty to two hundred kin-based groups known as *tokatoka*. The social and political structure of a *koro* is generally a hierarchy of a patrilineal clan, or *matagali*. The patriarch of the clan is the chief who holds the title of *tui*. Each chiefdom is referred to as a *vanua*.

A *koro* consists of several thatched-roof huts called *bures* arranged around and spreading away from the village green. Since the majority of Fijians are Christians, a *bure kalou* (church) is prominently located in the center of the green. The chief and the spiritual leaders occupy structures along the green while commoners take up residence in *bures* away from the green. Relationships within and between villages are based upon the concept of *kere-kere*, or mutual begging and/or borrowing. Subsistence economy is characteristic of village life in Fiji, and each village grows garden crops including *dalo* (taro), *kumala* (yams/sweet potatoes), and *cassava* (tapioca) for its own consumption. After a long day of *taitai* (gardening) or fishing, the men gather in the public *bure* around a *tanoa* (a large wooden bowl with legs) for a drink of *yaqona* (a solution prepared from the roots of Piper methysticum, a mildly narcotic plant) and swap yarns as the *bilo* (a cup made of half a coconut shell) is passed around. On special occasions the village community shares a communal meal prepared in a *lovo*, or pit/earth oven, made of hot stones along with which the meat, fish, and vegetables are buried. Traditional ethnic dress for the Fijian men includes a *sulu*, or a calf-length loincloth, a kiltlike skirt, and a brightly flower-printed, loose fitting *bula* shirt. Women's *sulus* are generally ankle-length and are augmented with a thigh-length Western-type flower-printed dress. Easy going and fun-loving Fijians have developed a passion for sports and have distinguished themselves in international rugby competitions, soccer tournaments, and boxing and wrestling matches.

As the rapidly encroaching Western civilization transforms the rich traditional life patterns among tribal peoples around the globe, the Fijians have managed to meet the challenges of modernization without becoming victims of this process. They have cautiously embraced innovation and novelty while at the same time retaining the traditional core of their existence. Fijians have entered the modern world without compromising their racial and ethnic identity.—*Richard A. K. Shankar*

SUGGESTED READINGS: • Lasaqa, Isireli. *The Fijian People Before and After Independence.* Canberra: Australian National University Press, 1984. • Lawson, Stephanie. *The Failure of Democratic Politics in Fiji.* New York: Oxford University Press, 1991. • Roth, G. K. *Fijian Way of Life.* 2d ed. Melbourne: Oxford University Press, 1973. • Thomson, Basil. *The Fijians: A Study of the Decay of Custom.* 1908. Reprint. London: Dawsons, 1968. • Tippett, Alan Richard. *Fijian Material Culture.* Honolulu: Bishop Museum Press, 1968. • Wright, Ronald. *On Fiji Islands.* New York: Viking, 1986.

Fil-Am: Term used to describe the children resulting from the intermarriage of American soldiers and Filipinos during World War II. It is also the abbreviation for Filipino American.

Filipinas: National general-interest magazine, founded in 1993, with a focus on Filipinos and Filipino Americans. The magazine includes feature stories, profiles of prominent Filipino Americans, and news of relevance to the Filipino community.

Filipino American National Historical Society: Nonprofit organization founded in 1982 to collect, preserve, and disseminate information about the Filipino experience in the United States. In 1987, the organization established the National Pinoy Archives in order to gather and index materials that will provide the public with access to information about the PINOY— the first-generation immigrants from the Philippines to the United States. Printed documents such as newspaper and magazine articles, research reports, government documents, letters, diaries, and political pamphlets have been gathered along with graphic materials such as posters, slides, and photographs; audio tapes of oral history interviews have also been collected and transcribed. Headquartered in Seattle, Washington, the society has begun to coordinate the cataloging of satellite archives that have been established in areas where active regional chapters of the society exist. Historians Fred CORDOVA and Dorothy Laigo CORDOVA were among the society's founders.

Filipino American press: The development of Filipino American newspapers in the United States can be compared to the cycles of growth in a garden: Some of these newspapers sprout, blossom, wither, and die; others—a few—last a long time.

Each has its own history and agenda. Some are weekly, biweekly, fortnightly, monthly, and bimonthly. Some are political, some are nonpolitical. Some were opposed to the Marcos regime while others supported it. Most are or have been printed in English, although some have been printed in TAGALOG or Ilocano alone, or in a combination with English. In brief, it is difficult to generalize about these publications, as it is with any mass communications medium, whether in the mainstream or the ethnic press.

Before discussing the extent of Filipino American publications, a caveat must first be offered. Accurate information is difficult to obtain. Established journalism directories such as *Editor & Publisher Yearbook* and *N. W. Ayer & Sons Directory* are marginally helpful. The Philippine embassy in Washington, D.C., with

its eight regional consulates, provides the most current and useful data.

Extent. In 1992 there were an estimated fifty-five Filipino American newspapers. The breakdown included eleven in the San Francisco Bay Area; seventeen in Los Angeles County; four in San Diego County; three in the Seattle area; three in Chicago; one in New Jersey; four in New York; two in Florida; three in Texas; two in Virginia; one in Maryland; one in Portland; two in Honolulu; and one in Guam. There were also six Filipino American magazines: *Bridges*, *Community Advocate*, *Fil-Am Image*, *The Filipino*, *Heritage*, and *Mabuhay*. Another magazine, *Filipinas*, was founded in 1993. Donn V. Hart noted that in 1976 there were a total of only twenty-eight publications, with nine in California. About 80 percent of those were started after 1969, an indication of the recency of those newspapers. He notes that when martial law was declared in the Philippines, a "spate of newsletters appeared, all of them anti-Marcos." Many were "hastily written, irregularly issued and erratically distributed."

In 1977 Amelita Besa had traced a total of 124 news publications since 1900, which was "only a fraction of what may have been published." Some newsletters were published by Filipinos in Alaska salmon canneries. In 1976 there were seventeen newspapers. Some 65 percent of these were established in 1970. "The computed average number of years a publication exists is 8.2 years. There may be periods of profuse journalistic productivity, but for the most part, they are short-lived. Thus we may characterize the Filipino press as in constant flux." She added that the picture of the Filipino as a compulsive publisher is not an exaggeration.

Seattle author and journalist Fred CORDOVA also reached the same conclusion. He wrote: "Their numbers have been too many and too short-lived. Hawaii alone had accounted for approximately 30 published in the 1930s and discontinued shortly after their starts. The average life span of Filipino American periodicals has been estimated to last about seven years, most of those famine rather than feast."

About 40 percent of Filipino American publications were started in California in 1976, which then had a Filipino population of 135,248. In 1990 there were 1,051,000 Filipinos and thirty-two publications, or about 58 percent of the total Filipino American publications in the United States. Even though the number of Filipinos living in California has grown considerably in sixteen years, the number or percentage of such publications has not grown in proportion to the population.

Staff members of the Filipino Forum. (Filipino American National Historical Society)

Reasons for Publication. Why do Filipino Americans publish newspapers? There are several reasons. As Besa observed, first there is a need to organize and affiliate with one another. One of the first U.S. publications was the *Philippines Review*, published by students in Boston in 1905. The *Philippines Journal* in Stockton, in 1939-1941 played a role in organizing farm workers.

Second, newspapers provide linkage among Filipino Americans and their home country. The *PHILIPPINE NEWS* in south San Francisco began in 1961 as the U.S. edition of the *Manila Chronicle* in the Philippines. With six editions, it is one of the more successful U.S. publications.

Third, newspapers offer a forum for discussing issues affecting Filipino Americans. Such publications can help advocate a cause. One of the oldest continuous Filipino American newspapers in the United States is the *PHILIPPINES MAIL*. It was published first in Salinas in 1921 by Luis Agudo as the *Philippine Independent News*. Over the years, with Delfin Cruz as editor, the newspaper campaigned on a number of issues to help improve the conditions of Filipinos. Such issues included the right to buy lands, working conditions, and intermarriage with white women.

Finally, some publishers want an outlet to express their views. As noted earlier, some newspapers were born during martial law in the Philippines. These newspapers (and newsletters) were strongly anti-Marcos. One source notes that Ferdinand MARCOS' money was "generally suspected of underwriting newspapers like the *Filipino Reporter* in New York and the *Filipino American* in the San Francisco Bay Area. Opposition papers such as the *Philippine News* in Daly City, California, were picked out for destabilization" that involved pressuring advertisers to boycott such papers.

The Mainstream. In addition to the number of Filipino Americans who publish and edit their newspapers, there are a growing number of Filipino American journalists working for the mainstream American news media. They include Lloyd LaCuesta, former president of the ASIAN AMERICAN JOURNALISTS ASSOCIATION (AAJA); Leslie Guervarra, Phil Manzano, Benny Evangelista, Ed Diokno, Victor Marina, and Gary Reyes.

One conclusion that can be drawn from this subject is that Filipino American newspapers tend to reflect the Filipino American population in general. The numbers will always change. In observing ethnic newspapers in the United States, there are usually two general problems: lack of advertising revenue and a declining readership. As new immigrants become more acclimated and "Americanized," their interest in ethnic news and news of the homeland declines. In the case of Filipino American newspapers, however, the latter factor may not be as valid, given the increase in the Filipino population in recent years.—*Donald L. Guimary*

SUGGESTED READINGS: • Besa, Amelita. "A History and a Contemporary Survey of Filipino-American Periodicals, 1900-1976." M.A. thesis. Temple University, 1977. • Bogardus, Emory. "The Filipino Press in the United States." *Sociology and Social Research* 18 (1934): 582-585. • Cordova, Fred. *Filipinos: Forgotten Asian Americans*. Dubuque, Iowa: Kendall/Hunt, 1983. • Hart, Donn V. "The Filipino-American Press in the United States: A Neglected Resource." *Journalism Quarterly* 54 (1977).

Filipino American women: Filipino women are also known as "Filipinas" or "PINAYS." Less than twenty thousand Filipinas emigrated to the United States before 1946, but these women played a significant role in the development of the then largely male Filipino American community. Since 1965, however, Filipino women immigrants have outnumbered Filipino male immigrants. Contemporary Filipino women face many of the same issues as other Asian women in the United States: They must maintain the balance between family and career responsibilities while trying to keep cultural traditions alive.

Women in the Philippines. It has been argued that before colonization, people in the Philippines practiced bilateral or even matriarchal cultures. Unlike women in other parts of Asia, women in the Philippines could become rulers and priestesses and own and inherit property and other resources. One Filipino creation myth describes the first Filipino man and woman emerging simultaneously from a piece of bamboo that has been pecked by a large bird. The woman even frightens away the bird when it tries to bother the man. This myth highlights the place of women in Filipino culture: The first woman was not created out of man's rib, but emerged as a being in her own right, equal to man; additionally, the first woman protected the first man from harm. Although Spanish and American colonization affected Filipino culture, some ves-

Filipino Women's Club, Seattle, circa 1949. (Filipino American National Historical Society)

tiges of the indigenous culture, with respect to the place of women, remain. Filipino women in the Philippines have equal status with men. A woman (Corazon AQUINO) was elected president of the Philippines, a breakthrough that most Western countries have yet to achieve. Filipino women worldwide are commonly characterized as controlling the family finances and having equal or even superior authority to the men when it comes to running the household.

History of Filipinas in the Untied States. The presence of Filipinas in North America can be traced back to the days when Spain colonized the Philippines. Manila was one of the major ports of call for the Spanish galleon trade. Filipinas were sometimes present on those galleons, as "companions" for the crew. The women who became pregnant were often left in Mexico or other places at the journey's end. Other early Filipino women in North America were the wives and daughters of the "Louisiana Manilamen," present in the bayous around New Orleans since the mid-eighteenth century. These women were the ancestors of today's "Filipino Cajuns." Filipinas were also the first Asian war brides, as exemplified by Rufina Jenkins, the wife of Sergeant Francis Jenkins, a Spanish-American War veteran who settled in Seattle after the war.

Like their male counterparts, many Filipino women came to the United States for an education, adventure, or better job opportunities. During the major immigration waves of Filipinos to the United States from 1900 to 1946, however, it is the absence, rather than the presence, of Filipinas that is most notable. Women did not emigrate for various reasons. Many poor families would have only enough resources to send sons to America, not daughters. Spanish cultural influences made it necessary for "decent" women to be accompanied by chaperones wherever they went. During the years 1907 to 1929, the ratio of men to women emi-

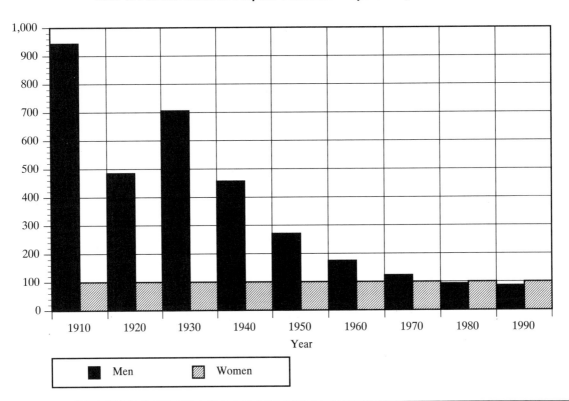

Male-to-Female Ratio of Filipino American Population, 1910-1990

Sources: Herbert Barringer, Robert W. Gardner, and Michael J. Levin, *Asians and Pacific Islanders in the United States.* New York: Russell Sage Foundation, 1993. U.S. Bureau of the Census, *1990 Census of Population: Asians and Pacific Islanders in the United States,* 1993.

Note: Data show number of Filipino American males per 100 Filipino American females.

Filipino American hospital lab technician. After U.S. legislation in 1965 opened the doors to greater immigration, many Filipino women entered the United States as professionally or technically trained workers. (Martin A. Hutner)

grating from the Philippines to Hawaii was about 11 to 1. During the same period, the ratio for Filipinos emigrating to the continental United States was no better than 20 men to 1 woman. Thus, Filipino communities of that time were overwhelmingly male. In the 1920's women were encouraged to go to Hawaii to take care of domestic duties for the working men, and between the years 1909 to 1946 about ten thousand Filipinas immigrated there. In Hawaii, some Filipinas worked on the plantations in the sugarcane fields. Other women provided necessary domestic services for the workers: They ran boardinghouses, restaurants, and grocery stores, did laundry and sewed clothing, took care of the children, and farmed vegetables for peddling at the open market. Filipinas in the continental United States often had the same responsibilities, working alongside the men in the fields and running small businesses that served the community. Addition-

ally, some women were professionals—teachers, nurses, and pharmacists. Women also came to the United States as "pensionadas," students sponsored by the government or a particular school to get an education in the United States and return to the Philippines.

Role of Women in the Community. Because of their scarcity, Filipinas were often the focal points of the community. One woman would become a surrogate mother or aunt or sister to many men. A young Filipina coming of age in the United States would sometimes have ten or more men trying to court her. Children born in the United States would have several men named as "godfather" or "uncle." In this manner, single men were able to be included in extended family networks. Filipino women took the lead in organizing fund-raising events such as queen contests and box socials and cultural activities such as JOSE RIZAL DAY celebrations. They were responsible for keeping Fili-

Educational Attainment, Labor Status, and Occupation of Filipino American Women, 1990

Education of Women 25 Years or Older	
	Percent
High school graduate	16%
Some college or associate degree	24%
College graduate	35%
Advanced or professional degree	7%
Total high school graduate or more	82%

Women 16 Years or Older	
	Percent
In labor force	72%
(Unemployed	5%)
Not in labor force	28%

Employed Civilian Women 16 Years or Older

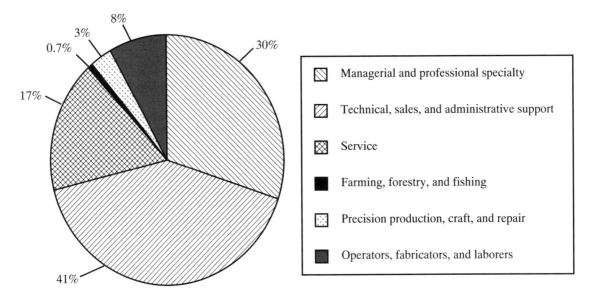

Managerial and professional specialty

Technical, sales, and administrative support

Service

Farming, forestry, and fishing

Precision production, craft, and repair

Operators, fabricators, and laborers

Source: U.S. Bureau of the Census, *1990 Census of Population: Asians and Pacific Islanders in the United States,* 1993.

pino culture alive in the United States.

Contemporary Issues. Relatively small numbers of Filipinas (about twenty thousand) had come to the United States by 1934, when the TYDINGS-MCDUFFIE ACT was passed, severely curtailing Filipino immigration. After World War II some sixteen thousand Filipinas came to the United States as war brides. This new infusion of women revitalized Filipino American communities. After the IMMIGRATION AND NATIONALITY ACT OF 1965 went into effect, Filipino women started emigrating in large numbers, outnumbering male immigrants. Many women qualified under the family reunification categories of the act as the wives, daughters, sisters, and mothers of American citizens. Many

others came under occupational categories such as "Professional, Technical, and Kindred Workers." These latter women are doctors, nurses, scientists, lawyers, teachers, and other professionals. They emigrate because salaries in the United States are much higher than those in the Philippines and there are more job opportunities. Many women send money to the Philippines to help support extended family members. Filipino women immigrants are among the most highly educated of America's immigrants. Despite their educational background, however, Filipinas often find themselves in service industry or clerical positions, working two jobs to earn enough money. Studies show that Filipino women receive only half the income of

Caucasian men. Other problems that Filipino women face in the job market are gender discrimination and sexual harassment. Some Filipinas have filed grievances or lawsuits because of discrimination in the workplace, and some have won their cases. Continued immigration and the growth of the resident Filipino American community ensure that the population of Filipinas and the diversity of their experiences will continue to expand.—*Linda Revilla*

SUGGESTED READINGS: • Cabezas, Amado, Larry Shinagawa, and Gary Kawaguchi. "New Inquiries into the Socioeconomic Status of Pilipino Americans in California." *Amerasia Journal* 13, no. 1 (1986-1987): 1-21. • Cordova, Dorothy. "Voices from the Past." In *Making Waves*, edited by Asian Women United of California. Boston: Beacon Press, 1989. • Cordova, Fred. *Filipinos: Forgotten Asian Americans.* Dubuque, Iowa: Kendall Hunt, 1983. • Pido, Antonio. *The Pilipinos in America.* Staten Island, N.Y.: Center for Migration Studies of New York, 1985. • Teodoro, Luis, ed. *Out of This Struggle: The Filipinos in Hawaii.* Honolulu: University of Hawaii Press, 1981. • U.S. Commission on Civil Rights. *Civil Rights Issues Facing Asian Americans in the 1990's.* Washington, D.C.: Author, 1992.

Filipino Americans: With a population of 1.4 million in 1990, Filipino Americans are one of the fastest-growing Asian American groups and the second largest (after Chinese Americans). Filipinos have a long history of immigration and settlement in the United States that dates back to the eighteenth century, although most immigrants have arrived since the 1965 changes in United States immigration laws. Prior to World War II (1939-1945), the great majority of Filipinos who immigrated to the United States came as agricultural workers and were primarily single young men with little formal education. While many of them returned to the Philippines, many settled permanently in the United States, especially in California and Hawaii.

The liberalization of U.S. immigration laws in 1965, allowing the entry of skilled workers and the reunification of families, resulted in a tremendous increase in the Filipino American population. In contrast to Filipinos who came to the United States prior to World War II, the post-1965 immigrants on the whole were highly educated, having held white collar positions in the Philippines before leaving. They have contributed substantially to the social and economic development of the Filipino American community, although they, along with American-born Filipinos, remain subject to widespread prejudice and discrimination from society at large, which attempts to restrict their social mobility.

The post-1965 immigration from the Philippines has resulted in a revitalization of Filipino culture, language, values, beliefs, religious rituals, and other social activities. Filipino American ethnic identity and culture are being expressed and maintained in various ways and contexts in communities across the United States. In particular, cultural values that are centered on family relationships are especially important to Filipino Americans. Distinct Filipino American communities have also emerged in various parts of the United States, particularly Hawaii and California; they are distinguished by residential enclaves and small business establishments. The challenge facing the Filipino American community is to transform its growing population into a political power having socioeconomic mobility.

Early Arrivals. Although Philippine immigration to the United States did not formally begin until the early 1900's, Filipinos have been present in what eventually became the United States since the late eighteenth century. Filipino sailors are reported to have settled in the bayous around Barataria Bay, south of New Orleans, as early as 1763, one year after Spain gained possession of what later became the state of Louisiana. These early Filipino settlers had been sailors aboard Spanish ships in the galleon trade between the Philippines (then a Spanish colony) and Acapulco, Mexico. The Filipino American community in Louisiana is thought to be the oldest continuously settled Filipino community in the United States.

Filipinos were also present in California before it became part of the United States. Antonio Miranda Rodriguez, perhaps also a former sailor on a Spanish galleon, was part of a forty-four person expedition, sent by the Spanish government from Mexico, that founded what later became the city of Los Angeles in 1781. Other Filipinos may have settled in Southern California during this period, since Spanish galleons landed there for provisions before continuing to Acapulco.

Filipinos were also in Hawaii before it became a U.S. territory. The 1853 census of the Hawaiian kingdom recorded the presence of five Filipinos who may have been sailors aboard American or European trading ships. It is also known that in 1888 a troupe of twelve Filipino musicians and acrobats chose to remain in Honolulu rather than proceed with their tour of the United States.

Following the annexation of the Philippines by the United States in 1898 as a result of the SPANISH-AMERICAN-PHILIPPINE WAR, the first Filipinos to come to America were college students. These *pensionados*, as they were called, began attending American universities on colonial-government scholarships in 1903. The first group of one hundred students was selected from twenty thousand applicants, and by 1907, 180 Filipinos were studying at almost fifty colleges and universities. In addition to the *pensionados*, other Filipino students—most of whom had to fund their education themselves—enrolled in American colleges and universities.

Immigration to Hawaii. As a result of the annexation of the Philippines, Filipinos could freely enter the United States as nationals rather than aliens, although they lacked the full benefits and privileges of American citizenship. Thus, in 1906, Filipinos were recruited to work on the sugar plantations in Hawaii, when a group of fifteen ILOCANOS (people of northern Luzon in the Philippines) was brought by the HAWAIIAN SUGAR PLANTERS' ASSOCIATION (HSPA) for a short tour of plantation working and living conditions. After a few unsuccessful efforts in the succeeding years, Filipino labor recruitment to Hawaii became more firmly established in 1909. The first recruits were primarily from the Visayan Islands, particularly Cebu, in the central Philippines, and were followed by Ilocanos from the northwest of the country. By 1923, Ilocanos comprised the largest group of annual plantation labor recruits.

Philippine immigration to the United States contin-

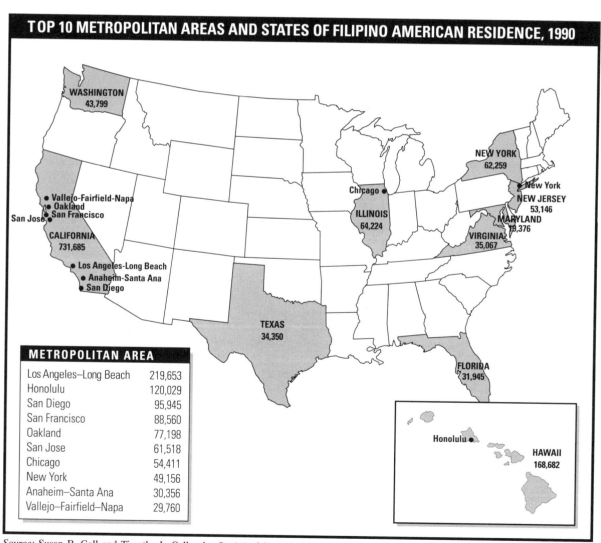

TOP 10 METROPOLITAN AREAS AND STATES OF FILIPINO AMERICAN RESIDENCE, 1990

WASHINGTON 43,799

NEW YORK 62,259

New York

NEW JERSEY 53,146

MARYLAND 19,376

VIRGINIA 35,067

Chicago

ILLINOIS 64,224

Vallejo-Fairfield-Napa
Oakland
San Francisco
San Jose

CALIFORNIA 731,685

Los Angeles-Long Beach
Anaheim-Santa Ana
San Diego

TEXAS 34,350

FLORIDA 31,945

METROPOLITAN AREA	
Los Angeles–Long Beach	219,653
Honolulu	120,029
San Diego	95,945
San Francisco	88,560
Oakland	77,198
San Jose	61,518
Chicago	54,411
New York	49,156
Anaheim–Santa Ana	30,356
Vallejo–Fairfield–Napa	29,760

Honolulu

HAWAII 168,682

Source: Susan B. Gall and Timothy L. Gall, eds., *Statistical Record of Asian Americans.* Detroit: Gale Research, 1993.

Filipino American female members of the Teodoro Alonzo Lodge No. 123, in a group photograph dated 1938. (Filipinos: Forgotten Asian Americans by Fred Cordova)

ued until 1934, when the TYDINGS-McDUFFIE ACT limited the entry of Filipinos to fifty persons per year. This act, which also provided for Philippine independence in 1946, allowed for the importation of Filipino agricultural workers in the event of a labor shortage. The HSPA, concerned about the unionization of plantation workers by the INTERNATIONAL LONGSHOREMEN'S AND WAREHOUSEMEN'S UNION (ILWU), was able in 1946 to recruit another 6,130 Filipino men, who were accompanied by 450 women and nine hundred children. Thus, between 1909 and 1946, about 126,000 Filipinos immigrated to Hawaii, the great majority of them single young men from rural barrios with little or no formal schooling. Most of these men came with the hope of saving some of their earnings in order to buy some land upon their return to the Philippines. Slightly more than one-third of the Filipinos remained in Hawaii, while more than sixty-one thousand went back to the Philippines, and about nineteen thousand continued on to the continental United States. With immigration limited to a one-hundred-person quota, established when the Philippines attained independence, between 1946 and 1965 only thirty-four thousand Filipinos entered the United

States. After World War II and through the 1950's, many former labor recruits returned to the Philippines because of the difficulty in bringing their families to join them.

Life on the Hawaiian plantations was quite difficult for Filipino and other sugar workers because of the poor working and living conditions. Labor recruits signed a three-year agreement stipulating that they would receive free transportation to Hawaii, housing, medical care, and wages, which were one dollar per day in 1915. On their part, the recruits agreed to work a ten-hour day in the fields or twelve hours in the mill for six days each week. The plantation maintained strict paternalistic control of the daily life of workers, particularly to prevent them from engaging in labor-organizing activities. By 1922, Filipinos had become the largest ethnic group (41 percent) on the plantation work force, and in the 1930's, they represented 70 percent of the workers.

Filipinos in Hawaii had an especially difficult period of adjustment because of the lack of employment opportunities other than plantation labor. The immigrant plantation groups that had preceded them, Chinese and Japanese, had established economic niches

Filipino American Statistical Profile, 1990

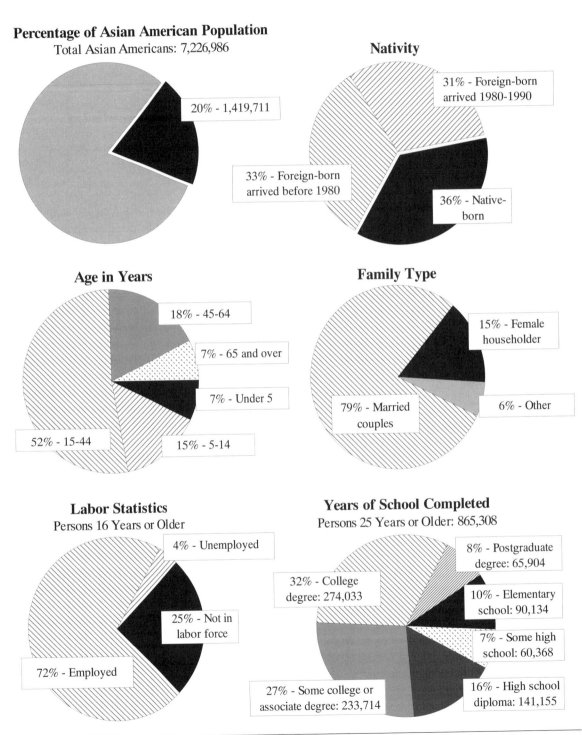

Percentage of Asian American Population
Total Asian Americans: 7,226,986

20% - 1,419,711

Nativity

31% - Foreign-born arrived 1980-1990

33% - Foreign-born arrived before 1980

36% - Native-born

Age in Years

18% - 45-64

7% - 65 and over

7% - Under 5

52% - 15-44

15% - 5-14

Family Type

15% - Female householder

6% - Other

79% - Married couples

Labor Statistics
Persons 16 Years or Older

4% - Unemployed

25% - Not in labor force

72% - Employed

Years of School Completed
Persons 25 Years or Older: 865,308

8% - Postgraduate degree: 65,904

32% - College degree: 274,033

10% - Elementary school: 90,134

7% - Some high school: 60,368

16% - High school diploma: 141,155

27% - Some college or associate degree: 233,714

Source: U.S. Bureau of the Census, *1990 Census of Population: Asians and Pacific Islanders in the United States,* 1993.

for themselves in Honolulu in wholesale and retail trade and in skilled and semiskilled work, and the Depression severely restricted Filipinos to agricultural labor. As a result, Filipinos were unable to develop a significant urban population; less than 8 percent of the sixty-three thousand Filipinos in Hawaii in 1930 resided in Honolulu. The preponderance of Filipino men over women (5 to 1 in 1930) resulted in a variety of aggressive behaviors as the men competed for female attention. This led to much negative stereotyping of them as violent, ignorant, uneducated, and "flashy." Another consequence of their gender imbalance was the slower and smaller development of the second generation of Filipino Americans, which retarded their socioeconomic mobility as a community.

Immigration to the Continental United States. The

Occupation

Employed Persons 16 Years or Older	Percentage
Managerial and professional specialty	27%
Technical, sales, and administrative support	37%
Service	17%
Farming, forestry, and fishing	1%
Precision production, craft, and repair	7%
Operators, fabricators, and laborers	11%

Income, 1989

Median household income	$43,780
Per capita	$13,616
Percent of families in poverty	5%

Household Size

Number of People	Percentage
1	12.4%
2	19.2%
3	18.1%
4	20.2%
5	14.6%
6	8.1%
7 or more	7.4%

Source: U.S. Bureau of the Census, *1990 Census of Population: Asians and Pacific Islanders in the United States,* 1993.

Filipino American historical experience in the continental United States, particularly on the West Coast, differs in some respects from that in Hawaii. Since no organized labor recruitment agency similar to the HSPA existed in the continental United States, most of the early arrivals in the Western states were former plantation laborers from Hawaii. Almost sixteen thousand Filipinos moved from Hawaii to the West Coast between 1907 and 1929, until there were more than thirty thousand Filipinos in California in 1930. The West Coast states had no established Filipino communities comparable to the plantation "Filipino camps" in Hawaii. Filipino laborers on the West Coast traveled for most of the year following the ripening crops in pursuit of work. At the start of the year, they harvested asparagus, an activity for which Filipinos became especially noted. In spring and summer, some Filipinos went to Alaska and Puget Sound in Washington State to work in the salmon canneries, while others picked lettuce in the Salinas Valley, and various fruits throughout California. In the fall, Filipinos traveled to the Yakima Valley in Washington State to harvest apples. During the winter, some moved to the city and worked in hotels and restaurants as service workers.

Another significant difference between the Filipino American experience in Hawaii and in the continental United States was the far harsher treatment they received on the mainland, although there was also considerable prejudice and discrimination against Filipinos in Hawaii. Between 1928 and 1930, in several farming towns in California, Washington, and Oregon, there were outbreaks of ANTI-FILIPINO race riots as a culmination of the bigotry and hostility toward them. The most publicized of these riots occurred in Watsonville, California, in 1930, when a mob of several hundred white people attacked Filipino farm workers and killed one of them.

Because of their willingness to work for lower wages, Filipino laborers were viewed as "unfair competition" by white agricultural workers. Filipinos were also despised because of their supposed immoral character, involvement in crime, and frequent relationships with white women, the latter an outcome of their especially unbalanced sex ratio on the mainland (fourteen males to every female in California in 1930). As a result, a movement to terminate Filipino immigration to the United States was initiated by organized labor and other conservative groups. Antimiscegenation laws (ruled unconstitutional in 1948) were also passed in the 1930's to restrict Filipino men from marrying white women.

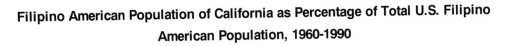

Filipino American Population of California as Percentage of Total U.S. Filipino American Population, 1960-1990

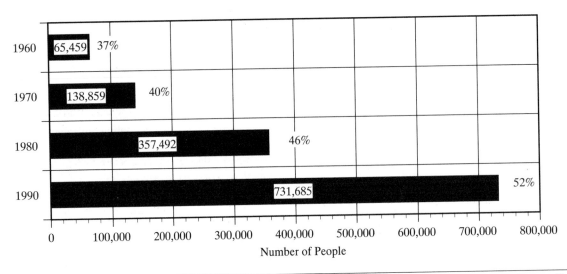

Source: Lorraine Jacobs Crouchett, *Filipinos in California: From the Days of the Galleons to the Present.* Cerritos, Calif.: Downey Place Publishing, 1982.

Pre-World War II Filipino immigrants settled not only in California, but also in other parts of the United States. Some went to Washington State and Alaska, while others moved to cities in the Midwest and the East. In Chicago, Filipinos obtained civil service positions in the postal service or were, along with Filipinos in Philadelphia, in the U.S. Navy. Filipinos in Detroit, New York, and Washington, D.C., took temporary jobs as service workers in restaurants and hotels or as domestic servants.

Filipino Contributions to the Labor Movement. Filipinos made significant contributions as leaders and workers in the labor movement in Hawaii and in California. In Hawaii, they actively participated in numerous strikes in the sugar and pineapple industries and organized their own labor unions, such as the Filipino Federation of Labor, beginning in the 1920's. As the largest ethnic group in the sugar and pineapple industries since the 1920's, Filipinos made great sacrifices during strikes and in the labor movement in general for the ultimate benefit of all working people in Hawaii. Over the years, Filipino Americans have held prominent leadership positions (including the long-held directorship of Carl Damaso) in the ILWU, the union that succeeded in organizing all plantation workers in 1946. In recognition of their significant contributions to the labor movement and to the Democratic Party in

Hawaii, Filipino Americans have been appointed as directors of the state Department of Labor and Industrial Relations for more than twenty years, starting in 1962.

In California, Filipino farm workers in the Salinas Valley formed their own Filipino Labor Union (FLU) in 1933. Led by Rufo Canete, the FLU organized several strikes in the 1930's against lettuce growers. Filipinos, along with Chicanos, formed the bulk of agricultural labor until the 1960's, and together they led the movement to organize farm workers, establishing a joint union, the Field Workers Union, as early as 1936. In 1959, a Filipino American, Larry D. ITLIONG, led the AGRICULTURAL WORKERS ORGANIZING COMMITTEE (AWOC) in recruiting union members. In 1965, AWOC organized a strike against grape growers in Delano and was soon joined by the National Farm Workers Association headed by Cesar Chavez, a Mexican American. The strike was a success, and the two unions subsequently merged into the UNITED FARM WORKERS ORGANIZING COMMITTEE, of which another Filipino American, Philip VERA CRUZ, served as vice president. Through these and previous unions, Filipino Americans played a major role in enhancing wages and working conditions for agricultural workers in California.

Post-1965 Immigration. The tremendous growth in

the Filipino American population, from 337,000 in 1970 to 782,000 in 1980 and to 1.4 million in 1990, is essentially a result of the increased immigration from the Philippines. This movement has been made possible by the 1965 IMMIGRATION AND NATIONALITY ACT, which provided for the reunification of families and for the entry of skilled workers needed in the United States. More than eight hundred thousand Filipinos have emigrated to the United States since the act was passed. The Filipino American diaspora, the largest overseas Filipino population, annually sends nearly one billion dollars to relatives in the Philippines.

In the first five years after enactment of the 1965 immigration law, more than seventy-three hundred Filipino doctors, surgeons, engineers, and scientists were admitted into the United States as skilled workers. After the 1970's, however, the great majority of Filipino immigrants entered under the family reunification provisions. Nevertheless, several thousand skilled and technical workers, primarily nurses, are recruited from the Philippines each year for employment in the United States on a contractual basis.

In the 1980's, the Philippines represented the second largest source of immigrants to the United States after Mexico. During that decade, a total of 474,000 Filipinos settled in America, more than fifty-seven thousand in 1989 alone. The extent of Philippine immigration is such that about two-thirds of the Filipino American population was born abroad. There is an estimated backlog of six hundred thousand visa applications at the U.S. Embassy in Manila, and Filipino immigration to the United States is expected to continue at its relatively high level. In addition to legally admitted immigrants, there are also thousands of undocumented Filipino immigrants residing the United States.

Filipinos emigrate to the United States primarily to join family members. Survey studies of Filipino immigrants generally have found that family factors are most frequently reported as the principal reason for emigrating and are usually followed by economic reasons. Filipino immigration to the United States is a classic example of "chain migration," the process in which family members in the home country are assisted by relatives who have gone before them. In addition to submitting a petition to the U.S. Immigration and Naturalization Service, previously settled family members generally provide the airfare, initial accommodations, and job search help for their newly arrived kin. This support and assistance given to relatives is an indication of the strong value placed on family ties by Filipino Americans.

Family ties also account for the destination of Filipino immigrants in the United States. The great majority of immigrants settle initially with their relatives, usually those who had petitioned them from the Philippines. These include parents, spouses or fiancées, children, and siblings. In terms of selecting their intended destination in the United States, economic factors are of much less significance than kinship ties for immigrants.

It is not surprising then that Filipino immigrants tend to settle in Filipino American population centers. A slight majority of immigrants have settled in California, with smaller numbers in Hawaii, Illinois, New York, New Jersey, Washington, and Virginia. These same states and in roughly the same rank order are the primary states of residence of Filipino Americans.

In contrast to Filipinos who came to the United States before World War II, the post-1965 immigrants have a much higher level of education. The majority of adult Filipino immigrants in the mid-1980's were college graduates with a substantially higher educational status than the general adult population in the Philippines. A major problem faced by these better educated Filipino immigrants, however, was obtaining a job commensurate with their previous education and employment in the Philippines. Many immigrants who held professional or managerial positions in the Philippines had to accept lower-status occupations in the United States. Filipino immigrants are frequently found in blue-collar craft and service work.

Socioeconomic Characteristics. Filipino Americans rank relatively high on various socioeconomic indicators compared to other ethnic groups and to the total American population. Both men and women have high median levels of education, which reflects the great value placed on higher education in Filipino culture. There is much concern, however, about the significantly high dropout rate of Filipino American high school students in California and the underrepresentation and attrition of Filipino college students. While post-1965 immigrants arrived with relatively high levels of education, the offspring of immigrants and American-born Filipinos are generally not following this pattern. Given the strong cultural value placed on college education among Filipino Americans, it has been suggested that certain institutional barriers may be having a chilling effect on the educational aspirations of young Filipino Americans.

In relation to employment, Filipino Americans have a rate of labor-force participation which is considerably higher than that of the total American population. More than two-thirds of Filipino women are employed, the highest proportion for any group of women in the United States. The substantial percentage of Filipino Americans in the labor force reflects the willingness of immigrants to take employment even though it may not be equivalent to their previous occupation or training in the Philippines.

A majority of employed Filipino Americans are in white-collar positions as professional, administrative, technical, and clerical workers. Significant percentages of Filipinos are also service workers, craft workers, operatives, and laborers. In Hawaii, Filipino Americans tend to hold primarily blue-collar occupations, particularly in service and construction work. Substantial numbers of Filipino immigrants are employed in the tourist industry in Hawaii as hotel maids, food-service workers, and maintenance workers.

The median family income of Filipino Americans is above the national figure, perhaps because of the significant percentage of Filipino families with three or more workers and the larger size of Filipino households compared to those of Americans. In terms of per capita income, Filipino American men rank below the national median for males, although Filipino women have a higher median income than that of American women. Filipino Americans, compared to other ethnic groups, appear to receive smaller economic returns in terms of income and occupational status for their educational qualifications, a factor that may be a result of discriminatory employment practices.

Because of historical and ongoing immigration, social and cultural diversity with respect to language, generation, and degree of assimilation is a distinct characteristic of the Filipino American community. The three major ethnolinguistic groups in the Philippines, that is, TAGALOGS, VISAYANS, and ILOKANOS, are well represented among Filipino Americans, as are smaller groups such as Pampangans, Pangasinanses, and Ilonggos. Generational differences are also significant within the Filipino American community. First generation Filipinos can include "oldtimers" or MANONGS (older brothers), who came prior to World War II as labor recruits, as well as "newcomer" post-1965

Although transplanted to the United States, many Filipino Americans retain some form of ties to their native land. Here a Philippine American cultural association participates in a parade commemorating Philippine Independence Day in New York. (Richard B. Levine)

Filipino American Population in the U.S. and Hawaii by Census Year, 1910-1990

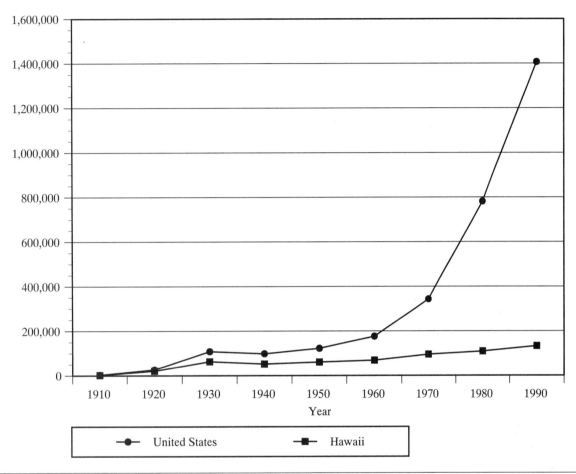

Source: Susan B. Gall and Timothy L. Gall, eds., *Statistical Record of Asian Americans.* Detroit: Gale Research, Inc., 1993. Harry H. L. Kitano and Roger Daniels, *Asian Americans: Emerging Minorities.* Englewood Cliffs, N.J.: Prentice Hall, 1988.

Note: Filipinos were counted under "other race" for the U.S. in 1900 and for Alaska in 1920 and 1950.

immigrants. Second-generation Filipino Americans similarly can differ considerably in age and length of residence in the United States.

Population Distribution. While Filipino Americans reside in every state, they tend to cluster in a few regions of the United States. More than 60 percent of them live in the Western states, particularly California, Hawaii, and Washington. Filipinos in California form the largest Asian American group (732,000), while the second largest Filipino American community is found in Hawaii (168,000). Other states with significant numbers of Filipinos, although much fewer than in California and Hawaii, are Illinois, New York, New Jersey, and Virginia.

Filipino Americans tend to reside in urban areas.

Metropolitan areas with sizable numbers of Filipinos include Los Angeles-Long Beach, San Francisco-Oakland, and San Diego in California; Honolulu, Hawaii; and Chicago, Illinois. Daly City in Northern California and the Kalihi area of Honolulu have substantially large Filipino American communities. These communities are distinguished by houses with Spanish-style embellishments, such as balustrades and wrought iron fences and railings, and by Filipino-owned small business establishments such as restaurants, video rental shops, bakeries, travel agencies, and money-exchange shops.

Cultural Values and Norms. Filipino culture provides the basis for the expression and maintenance of Filipino American ethnic identity. In particular, Filipino cultural values and behavioral norms that are centered on family and kinship relationships serve as an important means of maintaining a sense of distinct group identity in American society. For a Filipino, one's family is the source of individual and social identity and of material and emotional support and security. Kinship and family norms and values that are especially important to Filipino Americans include respect for and deference to one's parents and older relatives in general, maintenance of close family relations, including with extended family kin; and love and concern for one's children. These family values are evident in the assistance provided to relatives in the immigration process from the Philippines to the United States and in the sacrifices that parents make for their children's well-being and future security.

Another significant value among Filipino Americans is education, particularly higher education. This is valued because it is viewed as a means of socioeconomic mobility, especially for one's children. The Filipino emphasis on higher education can be seen in the encouragement and support, including financial assistance, that parents give to their children.

Future Prospects. By the early twenty-first century, Filipino Americans may emerge as the largest Asian American group, with a population of more than two million, primarily because of continuing immigration from the Philippines. The arrival and settlement of these immigrants will contribute to the continued affirmation and expression of Filipino American culture and identity. Because of its majority immigrant population and because of prevalent anti-immigrant attitudes, however, the Filipino American community can expect continuing prejudice and discrimination, particularly in employment, that will restrict Filipinos' socioeconomic mobility.

Given the ongoing growth and development of the Filipino American community, a social arena that might bear watching in the future is Filipinos' participation in politics, particularly in local communities in California. Because a majority of the Filipino American population is concentrated in major urban areas of that state, there should be viable opportunities for them to hold elective office. As yet, Filipinos have had a significant presence in electoral politics only in Hawaii, as evidenced in its lieutenant governor, a few state legislators, and several county council persons. Political empowerment of Filipino Americans may provide a collective means for fostering their greater and more equitable participation in American society.—*Jonathan Y. Okamura*

SUGGESTED READINGS:
• Alcantara, R. R. *Sakada: Filipino Adaptation in Hawaii.* Washington, D.C.: University Press of America, 1981. Based on oral historical interviews with former plantation laborers, or *sakadas*, this book presents a social history of the Filipino American community in a plantation town in rural Oahu from the 1920's to the 1970's. Filipino men and women who first came to Hawaii describe their lives and personal histories in their own words. Enlivening the text are extended quotes and descriptions of individual experiences.

• Almirol, E. B. *Ethnic Identity and Social Negotiation: A Study of a Filipino Community in California.* New York: AMS Press, 1985. This unrevised version of the author's Ph.D. dissertation in anthropology (1977), provides, from theoretical perspectives of ethnic identity and relations, a full ethonographic account of the Filipino American community in Salinas. It describes and analyzes the historical development of the community, family and kinship ties, voluntary associations, socioeconomic status and occupational activities, political participation, and relations with other ethnic groups in Salinas.

• *Amerasia* 13 (1986-1987). The entire issue is devoted to the study of Filipino Americans. It contains a number of well-written articles that encompass the diverse range of areas in Filipino American studies, including education, socioeconomic status, politics, history, literature, and folklore. In particular, four articles on socioeconomic status and mobility represent a cogent analysis of the structural constraints that restrict Filipino American occupational and educational access.

• Carino, B. V., J. T. Fawcett, R. W. Gardner, and Fred Arnold. "The New Filipino Immigrants to the United States: Increasing Diversity and Change." *Papers of the East-West Population Institute,* no. 115 (May, 1990). This study provides useful quantitative data on Filipinos who were issued immigrant visas to the United States in 1986 or who changed their visa status in the United States from nonimmigrant to permanent resident that same year. Contains abundant information on immigrants' backgrounds before immigration, their demographic and socioeconomic characteristics, their plans and expectations concerning life in the United States, the use of family networks in the immigration process, and factors related to occupational choices.

• *The Filipino American Experience in Hawaii: Social Process in Hawaii* 33 (1991) Published in commemoration of the eighty-fifth anniversary of Filipino immigration to Hawaii, the thirteen articles (including a bibliography on Filipinos in Hawaii) in this special issue address diverse aspects of the Filipino American community in Hawaii, for example, politics, social change, labor history, educational status, post-1965 immigration, ethnic identity, and religious movements. It is especially useful for courses on Filipino Americans or Asian Americans.

• *The Filipino American Experience in Hawaii: Social Process in Hawaii* 33 (1991): 12-38. The article entitled "The Filipino Community in Hawaii: Development and Change" is an excellent overview of the historical and contemporary dimensions of the Filipino American community in Hawaii. Discusses such issues as plantation life, labor organizing, post-1965 immigration, and community institutions. It is highly recommended as a concise yet comprehensive introduction to the community.

• Pido, Antonio J. A. *The Pilipinos in America: Macro/Micro Dimensions of Immigration and Integration.* New York: Center for Migration Studies, 1986. This broadly conceived study focuses on a range of political, economic, and legal issues in the immigration and settlement of Filipinos in the United States in terms of macro and micro structural factors. Its reference value lies in its incorporation of historical and contemporary material on the Philippines, on Filipino immigration to the United States, and on the relations and social status of Filipinos in American society.

• Takaki, Ronald. "Dollar a Day, Dime a Dance: The Forgotten Filipinos." In *Strangers from a Different Shore: A History of Asian Americans.* New York: Penguin Books, 1990. This chapter on pre-World War II Filipino American history is accessible while providing much descriptive information on the experiences, particularly the hardships, encountered by the first generation of Filipino immigrants, especially in California. The chapter also includes a discussion of Carlos Bulosan's experiences as a migrant worker and writer.

Filipino Federation of America: Mutual aid, fraternal organization founded in Los Angeles in 1925 and established in Hawaii in 1928. In the 1920's and 1930's, the federation competed against two other major fraternal associations with Philippine origins, the Caballeros de Dimas Alang and Legionarios del Trabajo.

Established as a "quasi-religious" organization with roots in Filipino folk beliefs, the federation was formed by twelve men and their charismatic leader, Hilario Camino MONCADO. A key founding member and close associate of Moncado was Lorenzo de los Reyes. Trained in the tradition of Philippine folk mysticism, Reyes became the federation's spiritual leader.

The organization recruited aggressively as a unique "twelve by twelve" organization—composed of twelve divisions of twelve lodges each, each lodge having twelve members. Its membership base came from the Filipino farm workers in California and contract laborers in Hawaii.

Members were required not to drink, gamble, or smoke and were encouraged to lead "moral" lives. Officers and managers of the different federation branches in California and Hawaii—and a majority of the members who were active in the political agenda of the federation—were identified as "material" members. The "spiritual" members chose to lead "ascetic" lives (for example, fasting) and established their separate colony in Hawaii in 1930.

The organization sponsored popular activities: banquets, parades, and golf tournaments celebrating RIZAL DAY, July 4th, and the organization's many anniversaries. It published a monthly magazine, *The Filipino Nation.* It promoted the "fight for Philippine independence"—a cause that appealed to the nationalistic spirit of expatriate Filipinos and that the members equated with "Moncado's mission."

The federation evolved into a messianic movement as members developed the belief that Moncado was the reincarnation of Jesus Christ, a rebirth that they believed had occurred earlier in the person of Jose RIZAL, the Philippine national hero who was executed by the Spaniards in 1896. Critics of Moncado openly accused him of "hocus-pocus" leadership and of "stealing" his members' hard-earned money.

Loyal members continued to support Moncado's travels and activities, especially his involvement in Philippine politics starting in 1934 until 1946. The membership dwindled after World War II and following Moncado's death in 1956. First-through-third-generation followers, however, still exist today in California, Hawaii, and the Philippines.

Filipino Federation of Labor. *See* **Filipino labor unions; Manlapit, Pablo**

Filipino immigration to the United States: Filipino immigration to America formally began in the early 1900's after the United States took possession of the Philippines following the Spanish American War in 1898. Before embarking on their American journey, however, the Filipinos had already found their way to the continent during the earlier centuries of Spanish colonial rule.

Pre-1898 Filipino Settlements. The history of Filipino "immigration" to the New World during the first centuries of Spanish rule is largely undocumented. However, the pre-nineteenth century presence of Filipinos in the Americas has been widely accepted based on isolated sources. It begins, for example, with the passing mention in Philippine history textbooks of the names of native chieftains who were sentenced to be exiled to Mexico as punishment for participating in a rebellion against the Spanish authorities in the Philippines in 1587. It was also historically very logical for the natives of the islands to have been transported by their Spanish masters to the New World during the more than two centuries of the MANILA-Acapulco Galleon trade (1565-1815) as seamen, soldiers, indentured servants, and slaves. Recent unpublished research, for instance, has referred to incidents in which "indios" from the Philippine archipelago onboard trade ships, set foot on the coast of California in Morro Bay, Monterey, Carmel, and San Francisco. Some Filipinos also made their way to the Hawaiian kingdom in the nineteenth century: "5 Filipinos" were listed in the Hawaiian census of 1853.

The most popular of these semihistorical accounts center on the "Manila men" settlements, believed to have been started in the eighteenth century by Filipino seamen who jumped ship to escape Spanish enslavement and who eventually made their way to the Louisiana coast. However, the body of published materials about the pre-1898 Filipinos, to date, is not supported by sufficient evidence to establish when and how the colonists settled in southern Louisiana. There is also disagreement as to why the Filipinos came. The notion that these early immigrants were "escaping to freedom" in order to avoid heavy taxes, forced labor, and military enlistment, is contested, for example, by a theory that a substantial number of Filipinos were brought over by the Spaniards for the purpose of introducing rice cultivation technology in the Louisiana lowlands.

Journalists and travelers in the nineteenth century

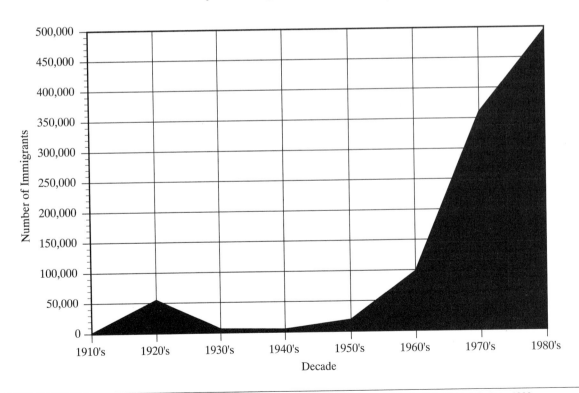

Filipino Immigration to the U.S., 1911-1990

Source: Susan B. Gall and Timothy L. Gall, eds., *Statistical Record of Asian Americans.* Detroit: Gale Research, Inc., 1993.

Manila Village, a Filipino settlement in Barataria Bay, southeastern Louisiana. (Filipino American National Historical Society)

wrote about the existence of the old Filipino colonies in Barataria Bay and St. Malo. American writer Lafcadio Hearn published his account of the "Manila men" in *Harper's Weekly* in 1883. When the United States took control of the Philippines at the end of the nineteenth century (see SPANISH-AMERICAN-PHILIPPINE WAR), Americans—conscious of their newly acquired island possession and their Filipino subjects—rediscovered the story of the early Filipino colonists. A newspaper article which appeared in 1901 in the *Washington Post* (and was reprinted in the *Manila Times*) played to this interest, and in 1907, the Manila press heralded the "discovery of a new colony of Filipinos" in Louisiana by an American businessman in the Philippines who personally "investigated" the Filipino settlements. Filipino expatriates and *pensionados* also visited and wrote about the "century-old" Filipino community in the 1930's. More recent writings on the subject have rekindled interest and great pride in this legacy, particularly among the new generations of Filipino Americans.

The Beginning of Immigration. As the Filipinos faced the arrival of the Americans on the eve of the twentieth century, they entered the second phase of their colonial history, leaving behind more than three centuries of Spanish domination and being subjected, this time, to American "benevolent imperialism." President William McKinley assured the Filipinos that America's mission was one of "benevolent assimilation" with the intent "to win the confidence, respect,

and affection of the inhabitants of the Philippines . . ."

Desirous of preserving their independence, the Filipinos resisted American rule leading to a brief but bloody war, which the Americans won. On July 4, 1902, President Theodore Roosevelt declared the war officially over and the American government in the Philippines began in earnest to win Filipinos, particularly members of the elite class, over to their side. The promise of independence was withheld, however, until a time when the Americans became convinced that the Filipinos were "fit" to govern themselves, politically and economically. Until then, Filipinos had the status of American nationals, ineligible to become citizens but having the right to move freely between the Philippines and the United States. This liberty of movement facilitated the way for Filipino immigration to America.

Two major factors contributed to shaping the character of this immigration experience, converging with other forces that pushed and pulled Filipinos to leave home and come to America. One impetus was education; the other catalyst was labor. The former originated in relation to the American education policy in the Philippines; the latter started out from the labor recruitment policy of Hawaii's plantation industry.

Americans saw education as essential in preparing Filipinos for the "duties of citizenship" and for the economic development of the islands. Education also became an effective instrument for Americanization and goodwill, which resulted in winning Filipino friendship and loyalty. To the elite, U.S. education pol-

The possibility of strategic military installations in the Philippines appealed to American military officials as early as the Spanish-American-Philippine War. The U.S. naval base at Subic Bay, shown here, was not legislatively established until 1947. It was abandoned, by order of the Philippine government, in 1992. (Library of Congress)

icy presented opportunities for advancement, including preparation for government office and other national leadership positions. To the masses, exposure to American education in the public schools offered the hope that they too might benefit from education in the same way that members of the privileged class traditionally had. The common people believed that the fruits of education were attainable under an American regime that spoke of democratic ideals and equality.

The Pensionados *and the "Student Movement."* In 1903, the colonial administration under then Governor William Howard Taft passed the PENSIONADO ACT. This legislation established government support for sending the "best qualified" Filipino students, including a small number of women, to study in the United States. The first one hundred students were chosen islandwide. Most of them came from the families of the *ilustrado* (educated) class, and ranged from sixteen to twenty years of age. Later *pensionados*, particularly those who were sent beginning in 1919, were chosen from a pool of young and bright Filipino government employees and were sponsored by their respective agencies.

Initially conceived as an American goodwill strategy, the *pensionado* program became the mechanism for the advanced training of the personnel needed to run the government bureaucracy. It was consistent with the policy of preparing the Filipinos for "self-government" and satisfied the American desire for educational reforms.

The prestige that came with being chosen as a government scholar to study in renowned universities and colleges in the United States was only half of the reward for the *pensionados*. The other half came with the exciting promise of a government job or a promotion when they returned home. This combined achievement gave the *pensionados* very high status. It also created a new Americanized generation from the *ilustrado* class, reenforcing *ilustrado* involvement and leadership in the "nation-building" and "Filipinization" efforts of the American colonial government.

Often referred to as the "*pensionado* movement," the elite program reached only a small number of about five hundred to perhaps no more than seven hundred students (including those who received only partial scholarships) during the pre-World War II decades. However, it had a far-reaching, long-lasting impact on the building of Philippine institutions, particularly the educational system, in which returned *pensionados* played key roles in reformulating policies and in the writing of local textbooks for the schools.

The program also succeeded in producing powerful pro-American Filipino leaders and policymakers.

Because of the highly selective nature of the *pensionado* program with a limit on the number of scholarships awarded each year, many more students from the wealthy class and from the provincial *inquilino* (middle-class) families aspired and ventured to study in America on their own. Members of the peasantry also followed with similar dreams. A study by a YMCA/YWCA-sponsored Commission on Survey of Foreign Students in the United States reported in 1925 that the movement of private Filipino students to America "began almost as early as the American occupation itself" and that the majority of them supported themselves by working just like "the self-supporting American students."

This "student movement" to America had its local counterpart in the Philippines. Starting with the establishment of the University of the Philippines in 1911, the importance of getting an education as a means to economic and social advancement had spread throughout the archipelago and "Manila emerged as the national center for university education in the 1920's." That commentary from a volume featuring a collection of Philippine political cartoons published in the *Philippine Free Press* is followed by a quotation from the magazine's sarcastic editorial describing a 1929 cartoon, which showed a conceited provincial or barrio student returning from MANILA during the summer vacation: "Does he not come from the great city, with all the latest there is in dress and fashion? . . . everything about him becomes the object of emulation and envy. Even his manner of walking, of carrying himself, are studied and aped."

The same criticism greeted the returning *pensionados*, who were accused of having brought back from the United States an "American accent" along with an "Americanized" superior attitude. Yet, as the *Free Press* editorial suggested, this "student class" was emulated by those with similar hunger for education and aspirations for success and status. Undoubtedly, thousands of Filipinos headed for America to further their studies, following—and alongside—the *pensionados*. Many, too, had learned to believe that American institutions were "better" than those that existed in the Philippines.

Although there was a local "student movement" impetus in the Philippines, the powerful image of the successful and accomplished *pensionado* from America created an indelible impression on the Filipinos. Particularly affected were members of the large rural class whose families saved and borrowed to give their children an education, preferably in Manila or, ideally, the United States. After all, the returning *pensionados* gave passionate testimony to America as "the greatest country on earth . . . because it seeks to elevate all men regardless of creed, belief, background and tradition, color and nationality." Manuel BUAKEN heard such a speech from a returning *pensionado* honoree in his hometown in Ilocos Sur and recalled many years later, in *I Have Lived with the American People* (1948), that the speech "fired in me the urge to go to America."

Although the student exodus to America started early, the number of Filipinos who were enrolled either fulltime in degree programs or were taking courses parttime in the United States was small. In 1922, the Bureau of Insular Affairs listed 1,156 Filipino students in the United States, including 192 who were in high school and 120 unclassified students. A list compiled by the Committee on Friendly Relations Among Foreign Students for the academic year 1929-1930 showed 896 Filipino students enrolled in American colleges and universities nationwide: 48 percent in western states, 35 percent in the central region, and 17 percent in the east.

In contrast, thousands of Filipinos left annually for Hawaii as plantation workers beginning in the early 1900's.

The Sakadas. Three years after the first cohort of *pensionados* left for the United States, a special representative of the HAWAIIAN SUGAR PLANTERS' ASSOCIATION (HSPA), A. F. Judd, made an unpublicized visit to the Philippines for the purpose of bringing back three hundred Filipino families to Hawaii to work on the plantations. It took Judd eight months to accomplish a gargantuan task which included first securing the permission of the American colonial government in MANILA to approve the HSPA's recruitment plans, then traveling in different provinces to do the actual recruitment with the help of American contacts in Manila. On December 20, 1906, Judd returned to Honolulu, not with the three hundred families he had set out to recruit but with only fifteen Filipinos. He was warned by Americans who lived in the Philippines that he would have great difficulty persuading Filipinos to leave the islands. He was also told that the Filipinos were not ideal workers to begin with because they were "lazy."

The HSPA persisted in its efforts to entice the Filipinos to come because they represented an ideal source of cheap and stable labor. The Filipinos came from an agrarian background and had experience in sugar pro-

duction; they were also perceived to be docile and willing workers. With the U.S. annexation of both Hawaii and the Philippines, the diplomatic and legal barriers to recruiting Filipinos were nonexistent or greatly minimized, particularly the immigration hurdle. It was also beneficial to the HSPA at this time to bring in a new national group to counter its predominantly Japanese workforce, which had begun to press for higher wages and reforms.

In 1907, the HSPA managed to bring in an additional 150 Filipino recruits (*sakadas*), but no similar attempt was made the following year. The Japanese strike of 1909 led the HSPA to resume importing Filipino laborers that year and to create a better recruitment organization in the Philippines. It established a main office in Manila, opened HSPA stations which concentrated on recruiting in the VISAYAN and Ilocos provinces, and employed local recruiting agents. As a promotional strategy, the HSPA brought the earlier *sakadas* back to the Philippines to help convince potential recruits of the benefits of plantation work; it also showed a film in rural centers depicting an enticing life in Hawaii.

Filipinos in Hawaii. Thus, from 639 recruits in 1909, the number of those who signed up increased to 2,915 in 1910, including a minimal number of women and children. In a ten-year period, from 1911 to 1920, the average number of arriving *sakadas* reached close to 3,000 annually. Returning workers who managed to bring back their savings and those who wrote home and sent money orders and positive news about working in Hawaii became the most effective promoters for the sugar industry.

Between 1921 and 1931, 83,938 *sakadas*, again with a small number of women and children, came through the HSPA, averaging 7,630 each year. Hundreds more not recruited in the Philippines traveled

Filipino Immigration to Hawaii	
Date	Number of Immigrants
1907-1919	28,500
1920-1924	29,200
1925-1929	44,400
1930-1935	20,000
TOTAL: 1907-1935	122,100

Source: Sucheng Chan, *Asian Americans: An Interpretive History.* Boston: Twayne Publishers, 1991.

Note: Hawaii was a U.S. territory during this period.

Immigrant Philippine laborers in the San Joaquin Valley, central California, circa 1930's. (Filipino American National Historical Society)

directly to Hawaii, and others used Hawaii as a stepping stone to America. Successful in its recruitment efforts, the HSPA stopped paying for the Filipinos' passage to Hawaii by 1926. Due to the Depression, the HSPA suspended recruitment and repatriated 7,300 *sakadas* in 1932. By this time, however, the Filipinos had become the largest ethnic group of workers on the plantations, replacing the Japanese.

The passage of the TYDINGS-McDUFFIE ACT of 1934 gave the go signal for Philippine independence in ten years time, but it also limited Filipino immigration to the United States, which had previously been unrestricted, to fifty persons annually. However, through congressional lobbying, a specific provision in the act exempted the Territory of Hawaii from the quota and allowed the HSPA to continue to recruit Filipino laborers until the Philippines became a sovereign state.

In July, 1945, with that deadline looming, the HSPA—having lost part of its labor force to military service during the war, and faced with a newly organized labor union (the INTERNATIONAL LONGSHOREMEN'S AND WAREHOUSEMEN'S UNION, or ILWU) and an impending island-wide strike—hurriedly sent its representatives to the Philippines to install the machinery for its final recruitment. From Port Salomague, near the HSPA cuartel in Vigan, Ilocos Sur, six thousand male workers and their families, including 446 women and 915 children, sailed to Hawaii in six con-

tinuous shuttle voyages of the SS *Maunawili* and the SS *Marine Falcon* between January 14 and June 19, 1946.

This crossing of the " '46 *sakadas*" was a milestone in Filipino immigration to Hawaii. It marked the end of organized labor importation from the Philippines. It brought in a new breed of postwar immigrant workers who had more education and who became actively involved in organized labor. It contributed to stabilizing the composition of the family in the Filipino immigrant community because many of the '46 *sakadas* were married or formed families in Hawaii after their arrival. It added to the development of a more integrated Filipino community in Hawaii and to the dynamics of post-1965 immigration.

The "Filipino Invasion" of California. The Filipino *sakadas*—their early history, and their significantly large and continuous waves of arrival over an extended period—essentially ushered in Filipino American immigration. Between 1909 and 1946, 126,831 Filipinos came to Hawaii via the HSPA. More than half stayed in Hawaii and about 32 percent returned to the Philippines. Roughly 16 percent, perhaps more, moved to the mainland, headed specifically for California.

The movement of Filipinos to the West Coast started in the early 1920's. The State of California's Department of Industrial Relations pointed to 1923 as the year "when the Filipino invasion began," with the arrival of 2,426 Filipinos, 85 percent of whom came from Hawaii. In 1929, 5,795 landed in California; this time, only half came from Hawaii and the other half originated from MANILA. From 1920 to 1929, California counted 31,092 Filipinos who were admitted to the state through the ports of San Francisco and Los Angeles. Not included in these statistics were Filipinos who sailed from the Philippines directly to Seattle, for instance, and migrated down to California from there.

A few thousand women who arrived during this period came mostly from the *sakada* population in Hawaii; a majority of them were second-generation, born in Hawaii. The women who came were younger on average than the men; 57 percent of the women were under the age of twenty-two. While 43 percent of the women were married, only 23 percent of the men were married. The gender imbalance was more pronounced on the mainland than it was in Hawaii. Among Filipinos in California in 1930, the ratio of men to women was 14 to 1, while in Hawaii at the same time the ratio was 5 to 1.

The Filipino exodus to the West Coast was precipitated by conditions in Hawaii and the Philippines and the labor situation in California. Hundreds of *sakadas* led and participated in an active Filipino labor movement. Hundreds also left Hawaii after the strikes of 1920 and 1924 to avoid an unsettling situation and to seek better opportunities in the United States, starting with higher wages. The IMMIGRATION ACT OF 1924, which excluded "aliens not eligible to citizenship" (i.e., Asians), also eliminated sources of cheap labor. Since the act did not apply to Filipinos, who were U.S. nationals, Americans on the mainland looked to the value and accessibility of the Filipino labor force already in Hawaii; labor agents from California actively recruited the *sakadas* to work in the state's farm industry.

Although economic conditions in the Philippines were a major factor for emigration, the desire of Filipinos to experience personally the promise of America—as articulated to them by American teachers, returning *pensionados*, and in letters received from relatives and townmates abroad—simply became contagious. As more Filipinos from the rural areas traveled to the United States, the thin layer of the earlier student population on the West Coast easily gave way to the weight of the heavy influx of labor immigration.

Roughly 85 percent of the 31,092 Filipinos who entered California by ship between 1920 and 1929 disembarked in San Francisco; 15 percent were admitted in Los Angeles. Most Filipinos immediately headed for their central destination, Stockton, which became known as "Little Manila." They also concentrated in other communities, such as Salinas; many settled in San Francisco and Los Angeles, preferring urban life, but were confined, just the same, to low-paying menial jobs. Filipino farm workers followed the crops throughout California; some Filipino immigrants went to Alaska during the summer to work in the canneries and to Arizona, Utah, Colorado, Montana, and North Dakota for more seasonal farm work.

Immigrant Life in Other Places. Many of the West Coast Filipinos also headed for the central and eastern regions of the country—to escape from the cruel conditions in which they found themselves, to see other parts of the country, or to continue their perennial search for better opportunities. Such was the situation for Philip VERA CRUZ, who had previously moved around in North Dakota and Minneapolis on farmwork contracts. In 1934, he and his friend, Frank Valdovino, left Spokane for Chicago. "We heard, you see, that some Filipinos in Chicago were working in the post office and that sounded like a good job." Instead, Philip Vera Cruz worked for one restaurant in Chicago for seven years and "gave up my ideas about finishing my education . . . [to be] able to send money home on a regular basis."

Vera Cruz returned to the West Coast and moved to Delano when the war started. He may or may not have been counted in the 1940 Census among the 1,740 Filipinos living in Chicago at that time and about whom very little has been known, until the publication of work about the prewar Filipino immigrants in Chicago—Midwest immigrants whose lives differed from those of their West Coast counterparts.

These findings reveal that "the story of Chicago's early Filipinos . . . is the story of the transition from a student community to an immigrant community in the years before World War II." This student community consisted of the early, successful *pensionados* who returned to the Philippines, followed by others who didn't, a community which changed after the 1930's with the arrival of cohorts of students who were "self-selected and self-supporting" and exhibited the pattern of the "immigrant ways of life." Although their original intention in coming to the United States was to study, these new arrivals had to support themselves through school, which now also included trade school education. Many had to postpone their education or give up on their studies altogether. The Great Depression contributed to the decline of the student-based community, as shown by the decline in enrollment of

Filipino-owned produce stand along a highway in San Lorenzo, California, in 1942. World War II altered the way Americans viewed Filipinos, a positive development that encouraged this man to advertise his nationality to increase business. (National Archives)

Filipino full-time students at the University of Chicago from forty-six in 1926-1927 to ten in 1933-1934.

Many of the Chicago Filipinos opted for employment with the post office and the Pullman Company instead of service jobs. They were also very involved in social and community organizations. Unlike their countrymates on the West Coast, a number of them married interracially, resulting in Filipino mestizo families.

Although the Filipino immigrant communities evolved in different ways in different parts of the country, the TYDINGS-McDUFFIE ACT and World War II gave them a common experience: The flow of new immigrants into their communities was cut off, giving the Filipinos time and opportunity to "become Americans."

War and Citizenship. The years prior to World War II produced legislation which established the sovereign destiny of the Philippines and the legal status of the Filipinos in the United States. Although "Filipino exclusion" laws could not be passed on constitutional grounds, the TYDINGS-McDUFFIE ACT solved this "problem" for the anti-Filipino interest groups in California. Not only did the bill limit Filipino immigration to fifty annually after 1934; it also stipulated that those who left the country after this period, regardless of length of U.S. residency, could not return except under the same quota.

The Tydings-McDuffie Act was followed by the FILIPINO REPATRIATION ACT OF 1935, authored by the same San Francisco congressman, Richard Welch, who had introduced "Filipino exclusion" bills earlier. In the words of a historian, the 1935 act "was an outright push to eliminate Filipino immigration," intertwined with a humanitarian concern for the plight of the thousands of unemployed and destitute Filipino workers affected by the Depression. The act provided free transportation to the Philippines for Filipinos in the continental United States who wished to return to their homeland. Although the deadline was extended from the original date of December, 1936 to December, 1940, only 2,190 Filipinos repatriated. The 1930 census counted 108,424 Filipinos. By the next census, in 1940, the figure had dropped to 98,535, demonstrating the effect of the Tydings-McDuffie Act and possibly suggesting self-initiated repatriation.

WORLD WAR II changed American attitudes toward Filipinos. The bravery of the Filipinos and the unwavering loyalty and trust they showed toward the United States, led many Americans to regard Filipinos as their "brown brothers." The war also had a liberating effect for the Filipinos in the United States, prompting Fernando Taggaoa—a Filipino student at Stanford University who had come to America in 1932 and was about to be inducted into military duty—to write in 1942: "Oh Emancipating War! Gone will be the thousands of Filipinos, particularly in California, relieved of the brunt of prejudice and injustice. No more shall the illiterate workers be oppressed, exploited and made to live in shacks and hovels, for they will have gone to fight and die for their freedom."

Being "ineligible to citizenship," Filipinos were barred from enlisting in the military service. However, in 1942 President Franklin Delano Roosevelt signed executive orders allowing Filipino noncitizens to enlist or be drafted in the military and to work in the government and the defense industry. (Earlier, the 1ST FILIPINO INFANTRY REGIMENT had been formed in San Luis Obispo under the command of Lieutenant Colonel Robert H. Offley, who spent his boyhood in the Philippines and knew the TAGALOG language. Other Filipinos chose to join the regular army.)

An amendment to the Nationality Act of 1940, the Act of March 27, 1942, made noncitizens who served in the military eligible for U.S. citizenship. To take advantage of this amendment, Filipinos in the military service had to apply for citizenship within three months after enlistment, or file during a six-month period after the end of the war, or after an honorable discharge during the war. Nearly ten thousand Filipino veterans and those still in active service took advantage of this opportunity before the filing deadline of December 31, 1945. (A subsequent amendment to the Nationality Act of 1940, Public Law 567, Act of June 1, 1948, superseded the December 31, 1945 filing deadline and provided for naturalization of any person not a citizen who had served in the U.S. military "during either World War I or during a period beginning September 1, 1939, and ending December 31, 1946." This amendment, however, specifically excluded those who enlisted in U.S. forces in the Philippines—an exclusion not redressed until the IMMIGRATION ACT OF 1990. See FILIPINO VETERANS AND NATURALIZATION.) Many of those who enlisted, still single, also benefited from the WAR BRIDES ACT OF 1945; they married in the Philippines, and their Filipina wives followed them to America.

On July 2, 1946, two days before Philippine independence, the U.S. Congress passed the Luce-Celler Bill (also known as the Filipino Naturalization Act; see LUCE-CELLER BILL OF 1946), authorizing "admission into the United States of persons of races indigenous to India, and . . . to the Philippine Islands, to make them racially eligible for naturalization." This law also raised the immigration quota for each country to one hundred.

For the Filipinos who had come mostly as immigrant workers in the 1920's and 1930's, the aftermath of the war brought changes and opportunities which gave them the dignity that had been denied them, individually and collectively, and the rights to good education, better employment, property ownership, citizenship, and family building.

Postwar Immigration and Filipino Women. If Filipino women were conspicuously absent in the early prewar decades of Filipino immigration, postwar immigration showed the reverse phenomenon. Apart from the tiny annual quota of one hundred, there was a steady flow of nonquota immigration, including a significant number of Filipinos who were citizens or enti-

Filipino Immigrants' Occupational Profile, 1991

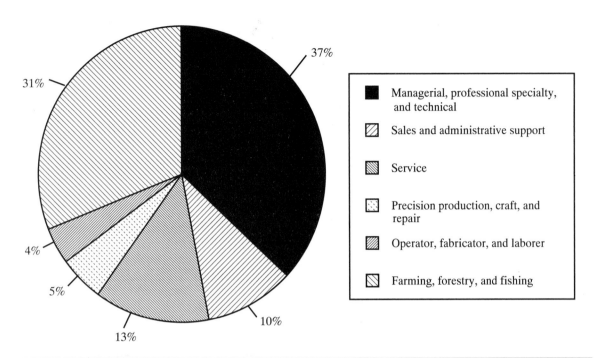

Managerial, professional specialty, and technical

Sales and administrative support

Service

Precision production, craft, and repair

Operator, fabricator, and laborer

Farming, forestry, and fishing

Source: Susan B. Gall and Timothy L. Gall, eds., *Statistical Record of Asian Americans.* Detroit: Gale Research, Inc., 1993.

tled to citizenship. In this way, many Filipinos who were the wives or children of U.S. citizens entered the United States.

In 1950, the Filipino population in the United States reached 122,707. Between 1951 and 1959, approximately 2,000 Filipinos became naturalized citizens annually, and soon petitioned spouses and children to join them. Among these exempt groups were also the Filipina wives and children of Caucasian Americans who had been longtime residents in the Philippines and were now returning to the United States. In 1959, 2,633 Filipinos were admitted, 65 percent of whom were women; a similar pattern was evident in 1961, in which close to 50 percent of Filipino immigrants were wives of U.S. citizens, many of whom were servicemen. By 1960, the Filipino population in the United States had reached 176,310, in large part as a result of the growth of the American-born segment of the Filipino American community.

Many of the early "old-timer" immigrants had remained single. Bienvenido Santos' stories echo the loneliness of their lives wherever they lived—in San Francisco, Kansas, or Washington, D.C. Postwar immigrant conditions encouraged these men to return to the Philippines to "procure" brides. The arrival of single Filipinas wishing to relocate to the United States also provided them with the opportunity to marry, even at a late age; in most cases, their wives were much younger than they were. These unions gave the "old timers" the families deprived them during the prime of their life in America.

The next wave of Filipinas came after the IMMIGRATION AND NATIONALITY ACT OF 1965 revamped U.S. immigration policy. This time, many of the women who came were professionals who entered under the third (professional) preference. Mostly concentrated in the medical professions, particularly nursing, these women played a major part in creating a separate chain of migration based on occupation after 1965.

Post-1965 Immigration. The 1965 immigration law reunified the families of the earlier cohorts of Filipinos who came to America. This "kinship" character of Filipino immigration is particularly pronounced in Hawaii, where the chain of migration started from a long-established and large population base of Filipino U.S. citizens or permanent residents.

Referring to this pattern as "relative-selective immigration" in a "dual chain" system of immigration, a

1991 study states that "more than 62 percent of the Filipinos arriving between 1966 and 1970 came to join other family members" in Hawaii and that "three quarters of these immigrants were relatives of U.S. citizens, i.e., Filipinos who had arrived before 1960." And because of the rural roots of the Filipinos in Hawaii, subsequent family members in this immigration chain also show the same sociodemographic background. The absence of a sizable professional-based immigrant population correlates with the lower educational, occupational, and income levels among Hawaii Filipinos compared to their mainland counterparts.

A separate "occupational" chain of immigration evolved in response to the secondary purpose of the 1965 immigration law: to bring much-needed professionals to the United States, especially in the medical field. "Between 1966 and 1976, occupational immigrants accounted for nearly fifty percent of all people entering the U.S. under the preference system" with "about one-third of all Filipinos admitted to the United States during these ten years." This second chain of the "dual immigration" began with the arrival of Filipino professionals who took jobs in the bigger metropolises, such as the New York-New Jersey area. These professional cohorts also tended to enter as "complete" families, with more than half of them between 1967 and 1977, for example, coming with spouses and children.

In general, the pattern of difference in the occupational distributions for Hawaii and the New York-New Jersey areas shows that "over time, the two regions have continued to lure basically the same type of immigrant they first attracted after the 1965 act. Hawaii has continuously attracted Filipinos who are generally service, urban industrial, and agricultural workers, whereas New York-New Jersey still receives a disproportionate number of health and other highly trained professionals."

In 1976, Congress passed a law which required that professionals entering under the third preference should be at the request of potential employers; additional restrictions also required "foreign medical graduates" to pass an examination before they could be admitted to the United States. These restrictions reduced the entry of occupational immigrants under the third preference by 1978, prompting many to enter the United States on a temporary visa in order to first find potential employers willing to sponsor them. While only about 25 percent of Filipino health professionals in 1973 entered on a visitor visa as a way of acquiring immigrant status, the figure increased to al-

most 75 percent in 1975 and "was still about 45 percent in 1985."

A significant finding about this "dual chain immigration" is that the post-1965 immigration phenomenon has relatively few ties with the pre-1965 immigration experience. This fact is reflected in a remark made by a college-age Filipino American from New York, a statement echoed by others like him born in the 1970's to post-1965 immigrants: "Our parents think that Filipino immigration history began in 1965."

The Filipino American population has risen significantly as a result of the 1965 Immigration Act. In 1970, there were 343,060 Filipinos in the United States; in 1980, 781,894; and in 1990, 1,406,770. Demographers continue to predict that Filipino Americans will become the largest Asian American group early in the twenty-first century.

The current geographic distribution of the Filipino American population reflects the historical and sociodemographic dimensions of Filipino immigration. Filipino Americans are heavily concentrated in California and Hawaii, where Filipino immigration had its beginnings; these top two states claim more than half of the total Filipino American population. Washington state also has a significant number of Filipinos.

The next heavy clusters of Filipinos are in Illinois, New York, and New Jersey, with Texas not too far behind. These states reflect the professional/occupational character of post-1965 Filipino immigration. The third cluster consists of West Virginia, Florida, and Maryland. The concentration of Filipinos in these states, with major naval and military bases (a factor in California as well), points to the prominent role that Filipinos in the military have played in the immigration process. This is an unexplored area of Filipino immigration that needs further study.

Immigration and Filipino Americans. Filipinos occupy a major place in the history of Asian American immigration. Their arrival in the United States in large numbers immediately following the exclusion of Chinese and Japanese labor placed them as the third major Asian group of workers upon whose toil the life of the agricultural industry in Hawaii and California depended for many decades.

With the high proportion of male Filipino immigrants came the disadvantageous and threatening "bachelor" syndrome; the dominant white society perceived the young and single Filipinos as inherently and contagiously "immoral" and therefore, a "threat" to the social fiber of America. Thus, the flow of prewar Filipino immigrants was met with determined efforts

Ferdinand and Imelda Marcos were eventually forced to flee the Philippines following the disastrous general elections of 1986. They headed for Hawaii, in the United States, which had granted them political asylum. Here Marcos addresses the Honolulu press not long after his arrival. (AP/Wide World Photos)

to stop them from entering the United States or to "eradicate" their presence by forbidding the male-dominant population to propagate itself outside their group through legislation and social restrictions.

The inability of the pioneering Filipino immigrants to form families—whether as a result of restrictions or because of the absence of Filipino women—contributed greatly to the delay in the development of a viable Filipino American second-generation constituency. Instead, the Filipino American community which evolved from the prewar immigrants consisted of a small number of Filipino families with children and a disproportionately larger population of "bachelor PINOYS," some of whom were fortunate to have been "adopted" by Filipino families, but the majority of whom lived isolated lives in small communities, cities, or on the road while "following the crops." In addition, the Filipino population occupied a low socio-economic position. Poverty prevented most Filipino

Americans, especially the families with mouths to feed, from pursuing their aspirations—for themselves or their children.

The small cohort of second-generation Filipino Americans born before World War II maintained their ties with their parents' immigrant culture. The arrival of the postwar immigrants, with a significant percentage of women, nurtured the Filipino American community, which was also strengthened by the existence of many more families and a growing number of college-educated American-born Filipinos.

However, it was not until after the liberalization of U.S. immigration policy in 1965 that the Filipino American community experienced explosive growth and began to command the attention of the larger community. Composed of American-born and immigrant Filipinos, Filipino Americans became involved in the Civil Rights and antiwar movements of the 1960's, the ethnic studies movement of the 1970's, and the community and political activism (partly ignited by a strong opposition to U.S. government support for the MARCOS regime) that extended into the 1980's. The long-established activism of the Filipinos in the Asian American labor movement also became prominent at this time, even though Larry ITLIONG's role in the United Farm Workers movement was overshadowed by Cesar Chavez's popularity.

Post-1965 immigration has had an empowering, replenishing effect on the Filipino American community, providing the numerical strength needed to push for minority rights. However, the dual chain immigration has also begun to highlight the diversity of the Filipino American community, reflecting conflicting values and concerns based on the differing perspectives and interests of the American-born and the immigrant Filipinos. Many Filipino Americans lament their "disunity" and are convinced that this is the main hindrance to their political empowerment.

As this debate goes on in the Filipino American community, the children of the post-1965 immigrants—now an increasingly visible and articulate force on college campuses throughout the country—are embracing a commitment to a long-established but unfulfilled goal of achieving recognition and full participation for Filipinos in American society. Confronted by their personal and generational struggle with the paradoxes of their Filipino American identity, they have nevertheless begun to reclaim and pay homage to the heritage of the MANONGS, the early immigrants who pioneered a painful journey to America.

Immigration created the Filipino American experience, and it continues to shape the character and direction of this legacy. Today, immigration occupies a major and ongoing chapter in the history of the Filipino people. Once a people reluctant to immigrate, the Filipinos now play a prominent part in the phenomena of human migration and the global diaspora. It all started with their immigration to America.—*Steffi San Buenaventura*

SUGGESTED READINGS:
• Alcantara, Ruben. "1906: The First Sakada." In *Filipinos in Hawaii . . . the First 75 Years*, edited by Juan C. Dionisio. Honolulu: Hawaii Filipino News Specialty Publications, 1981. Alcantara's works have focused on the *sakada* experience in Hawaii, which was the subject of his dissertation. His research has added significantly to the pioneering work of Dorita Clifford. This article is part of a longer piece in this anniversary magazine, a volume which contains much useful information about the Filipinos in Hawaii.

• Beechert, Edward D. *Working in Hawaii: A Labor History*. Honolulu: University of Hawaii Press, 1985. Beechert provides a good overview of Hawaii's labor history. The author devotes sufficient discussion on the role of Filipinos in organized labor, particularly their role in the 1924 and 1937 "Filipino strikes" and their relationship with the Japanese labor movement after the 1920 strike. He does not touch on the role of the '46 *sakadas* in the postwar multiethnic labor movement.

• Buaken, Manuel. *I Have Lived with the American People*. Caldwell, Idaho: Caxton Printers, 1948. Buaken has not been given the recognition he deserves for documenting the early history of Filipino immigration in California. A contemporary of Carlos Bulosan, Buaken presents an accurate account of the life of the Pinoy in America, similar in structure to Bulosan's story. Buaken lived in Los Angeles and was married to a Caucasian, Iris Buaken, who wrote about their interracial marriage in the context of the anti-miscegenation law of California.

• Bulosan, Carlos. *America Is in the Heart*. Seattle: University of Washington Press, 1946. This classic work was given posthumous recognition with the advent of the ethnic studies movement in the 1970's. It has continued to inspire Filipino Americans and sensitize them to the struggle of the first Filipino immigrants against racism and economic exploitation. Originally accepted as an autobiography and social history, Bulosan's book has now been established to be a fictive narrative based on a combination of biographical account, the experiences of his cohorts, and events which underscored their painful encounter with America.

• Clifford, Sister Mary Dorita. "The Hawaiian Sugar Planter[s] Association and Filipino Exclusion." In *The Filipino Exclusion Movement*, edited by J. M. Saniel. Quezon City, Philippines: Institute of Asian Studies, University of the Philippines, 1967. Clifford provided the seminal work on the HSPA and the Filipino plantation workers in her master's thesis in the 1950's. The figures she compiled on the Filipinos recruited by HSPA from 1909 to 1946 have become the standard reference for researchers, and her work on this subject remains unchallenged.

• Lasker, Bruno. *Filipino Immigration*. Chicago: University of Chicago, 1931. Reprint. New York: Arno Press, 1969. This now classic work by Lasker was first commissioned by the American Council of the Institute of Pacific Relations at the height of the debate on Filipino exclusion and a few years before the passage of a Philippine Independence Act. Lasker based this excellent and comprehensive study on data from Hawaii and California, government documents and research studies, numerous interviews, and academic journal and newspaper citations. Lasker also made use of Philippine government documents and reports and Philippine press accounts.

• Melendy, H. Brett. *Asians in America: Filipinos, Koreans, and East Asians*. Boston: Twayne Publishers, 1977. Melendy pioneered scholarly study of Filipino American history in the 1970's. Working as a history professor in California and also in Hawaii made Melendy very familiar with the history of Filipinos in both states. This volume contains significant and very informative chapters on the Filipinos; he also wrote numerous articles on discrimination against Filipinos, citizenship status, and problems of accommodation. Melendy's works deal primarily with pre-1965 Filipino immigration.

• Pido, Antonio J. A. *The Pilipinos in America*. New York: Center for Migration Studies, 1986. Pido's work comes from a post-1965 Filipino immigration perspective and with an analytic, social science framework. The volume presents an abbreviated history of the Filipino people, touches on some aspects of their psychocultural traits as background, gives minimal treatment of earlier waves of Filipinos, and concentrates the discussion on the Filipino American experience which has developed from the post-1965 immigration.

• Posadas, Barbara M., and Roland L. Guyotte. "Unintentional Immigrants: Chicago's Filipino Foreign Students Become Settlers." *Journal of American Ethnic History* 9 (Spring, 1990): 26-48. Posadas has pioneered the documentation of the Filipino American experience in the Midwest, with a particular emphasis on the "old-timer" generation in Chicago. Her articles have included pieces on the Filipino families in Chicago, interracial marriages among the early immigrants, and Filipino employment in the railroad company. Her scholarship expands Filipino American history beyond the traditional Hawaii-California concentration.

• *Post-1965 Filipino Immigration Studies.* Most of the information on the Filipino immigration experience after 1965 has been drawn from sociodemographic studies and census statistics. The East West Center in Honolulu has published valuable studies based on census data and on special surveys conducted through its Filipino Immigration project (now discontinued) in the early-mid 1980's. Examples of Center Population Institute studies published in 1990 are "The New Filipino Immigrants to the United States: Increasing Diversity and Change" and "Recent Filipino Immigration to the United States: A Profile." Publications in *International Migration Review* and by the Center for Migration Studies have also included Filipino immigration articles. A study by John Liu, Paul Ong, and Carolyn Rosenstein, "Dual Chain Migration: Post-1965 Filipino Immigration to the United States," *International Migration Review* 25, no. 3 (1991): 487-513, provides a very good source in understanding the logic and dynamics of the post-1965 Filipino immigration phenomenon.

• Santos, Bienvenido. *Scent of Apples*. Seattle: University of Washington Press, 1979. Santos has documented the Filipino immigrant experience in his writings, particularly in his now-famous short stories, such as "Immigration Blues" and "The Day the Dancers Came." Through his literary works, he has articulated the loneliness of the postwar Pinoys, and the "old timers' " alienation and their nostalgia for the home country.

Filipino immigration to the United States, sources of: Filipino immigrants come from virtually all regions of the Philippines. During the period of labor recruitment prior to World War II, however, a substantial majority of immigrants were from the Ilocos and Visayas areas. With the liberalization of U.S. immigration laws in 1965, there has been much greater diversity in the regional background of Filipino immigrants, with increased representation from the Tagalog region, including Metro Manila. Through processes of chain migration facilitated by the 1965 immigration act, certain regions, particularly Metro Manila, have emerged as the primary source areas of Filipino immigration to the United States. The result has been greater cultural, linguistic, and socioeconomic diversity within the Filipino American community.

Pre-World War II Immigration. During the labor recruitment period of Filipino immigration before World War II, the great majority of Filipinos who came to Hawaii and the West Coast of the United States were ILOCANOS and Visayans. The former come from the northwest corner of the main Philippine island of LUZON, particularly the provinces of Ilocos Norte, Ilocos Sur, La Union, and Abra. Some Ilocanos also are from Pangasinan Province, which lies adjacent to Ilocos Sur, as a result of previous Ilocano migration into Pangasinan.

Visayans are from the islands in the central region of the Philippines (such as Bohol, Cebu, Leyte, Negros,

PRINCIPAL SOURCES OF POST-1965 FILIPINO IMMIGRATION

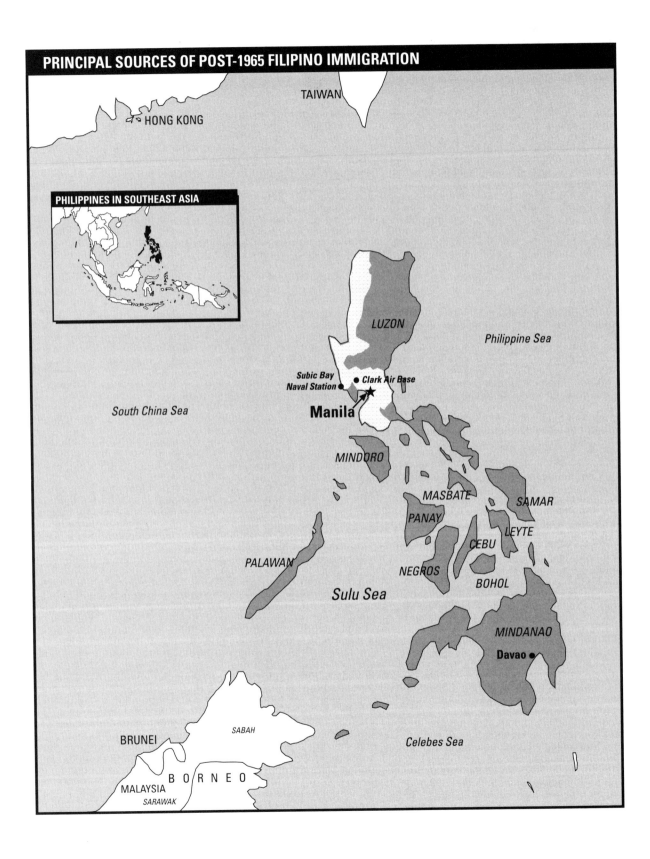

PHILIPPINES IN SOUTHEAST ASIA

TAIWAN

HONG KONG

LUZON

Philippine Sea

Subic Bay
Naval Station • • Clark Air Base

South China Sea

Manila

MINDORO

MASBATE

SAMAR

PANAY

LEYTE

CEBU

PALAWAN

NEGROS

BOHOL

Sulu Sea

MINDANAO

Davao •

BRUNEI

SABAH

Celebes Sea

MALAYSIA

B O R N E O

SARAWAK

Panay, and Samar). They were the first large group of Filipinos brought to Hawaii to work on the plantations by the HAWAIIAN SUGAR PLANTERS' ASSOCIATION (HSPA). Between 1916 and 1928 (the period for which data are available), Visayans, especially from Cebu and Bohol, represented 31 percent of the 74,000 Filipinos recruited by the HSPA to work in Hawaii. This percentage also can be considered a rough estimate of the Visayan proportion of the 119,000 Filipinos who arrived in Hawaii between 1907 and 1934 during the period of labor migration. This estimate is based on Visayans having constituted a majority of the more than 18,000 Filipinos recruited to Hawaii before 1916, while Ilocanos represented the bulk of the 22,000 laborers arriving after that year.

Ilocanos constituted more than one-half (53 percent) of the Filipinos who were brought to Hawaii between 1916 and 1928. Of these 39,500 Ilocanos, almost 60 percent were from the single province of Ilocos Norte and another 30 percent were from Ilocos Sur. Ilocanos quickly developed a reputation on the plantations for their hard work, which contributed to their further recruitment as laborers.

Very few Filipinos from MANILA, the capital of the Philippines, and the surrounding Tagalog provinces were recruited to Hawaii as plantation laborers. Between 1916 and 1928 only 129 Filipinos from Manila and another 320 from the provinces of Bataan, Batangas, Bulacan, Cavite, Laguna, and Rizal around the capital city were brought to Hawaii. The HSPA did not recruit or eventually stopped recruiting workers in regions where a labor shortage would have disrupted the local sugar industry, such as in central and southern Luzon and on Negros and Panay, since American corporations, including several sugar factories based in Hawaii, had financial investments in that industry.

Between 1916 and 1928, similarly small numbers (717) of Filipinos from MINDANAO in the southern Philippines were brought to Hawaii, almost two-thirds (64 percent) of whom were from Misamis Province. This also may have been because of restrictions on the regions where the HSPA could recruit laborers.

Other Filipinos went directly to the continental United States without first working in Hawaii. They included greater numbers of Tagalogs and former Manila residents, especially among students who came to study at American universities.

Post-World War II to 1965 Immigration. The last recruitment of Filipinos to work on the sugar and pineapple plantations in Hawaii occurred in 1946. Because most of the plantation laborers at that time were Ilo-

cano and had been given the opportunity to request that their relatives in the Philippines be recruited, the great majority of the approximately 7,500 Filipinos who arrived in 1946 also were Ilocano. Other Filipinos, particularly the wives and children of previous immigrants who had become U.S. citizens, continued to arrive in the United States in comparatively small numbers during the postwar period.

Post-1965 Immigration. This phase of Philippine immigration was initiated by the IMMIGRATION AND NATIONALITY ACT OF 1965, which allowed for the reuniting of families and for the entry of skilled workers needed in the United States. As a result Filipino immigrants originate from throughout the Philippines but tend to be concentrated in a few regions. A survey of 1986 Filipino immigrants to the United States found that more than one-third (36 percent) of them had resided in Metro Manila, while another 13 percent came from the surrounding Tagalog provinces (Batangas, Bulacan, Cavite, Laguna, and Rizal). About 16 percent of the immigrants were from the Ilocos region (including Pangasinan) since the family reunification provisions of the 1965 act provided for the resumption of Ilocano immigration through chain migration processes in which previously settled immigrants help their relatives in the Philippines emigrate. Approximately the same percentage (15 percent) of immigrants had resided in the two provinces where the former U.S. military facilities in the Philippines were located: Pampanga (Clark Air Force Base) and Zambales (Subic Naval Base). A considerable number of these immigrants enter the United States as a result of American military personnel having met their Filipino spouses while stationed at the bases. After settling in the United States, these spouses can petition their relatives to join them.

The remaining 20 percent of the 1986 Filipino immigrants were from the various other regions of the Philippines. MINDANAO and the Cordillera area in northern LUZON appear to be much less represented than the other parts of the country, a historical consequence of pre-1965 immigration patterns.

The greater regional diversity represented among the post-1965 immigrants has contributed significantly to the increased socioeconomic, cultural, and linguistic diversity within the Filipino American community. On the whole the post-1965 immigrants, particularly those from Metro Manila, with their urban background, are highly educated, with substantial percentages of college graduates and professionally skilled workers. Their arrival thus has enhanced the overall socioeconomic status of Filipino Americans.—*Jonathan Y. Okamura*

SUGGESTED READINGS: • Carino, B. V., J. T. Fawcett, R. W. Gardner, and F. Arnold. *The New Filipino Immigrants to the United States: Increasing Diversity and Change.* Papers of the East-West Population Institute, No. 115. Honolulu: East-West Center, 1990. • Dorita, Sister Mary. *Filipino Immigration to Hawaii.* Master's thesis, University of Hawaii, 1954. San Francisco: R and E Research Associates, 1975. • Lasker, Bruno. *Filipino Immigration to Continental United States and to Hawaii.* Chicago: University of Chicago Press for the American Council, Institute of Pacific Relations, 1931. • Sharma, Miriam. "The Philippines: A Case of Migration to Hawai'i, 1906 to 1946." In *Labor Immigration Under Capitalism: Asian Workers in the United States before World War II*, edited by L. Cheng and E. Bonacich. Berkeley: University of California Press, 1984.

Filipino labor unions: There has been a long tradition of Filipino labor union activity in American labor experience. A wide variety of Filipino labor unions have dominated the fields in Hawaii and California. In July, 1909, the HAWAIIAN SUGAR PLANTER'S ASSOCIATION (HSPA) announced that several hundred Filipino laborers were en route to Hawaii to work in the local fields. For a decade Filipino sugarcane workers toiled for low wages under miserable working conditions. This oppressive treatment led to the birth of Filipino labor unions.

Union Birth. Pablo MANLAPIT, a young fieldworker who came to Hawaii from the Phillipines in 1910, and who later became the first Filipino to practice law in Hawaii, played an important role in organizing Filipino workers and making them aware of the need for a united union front. The repressive atmosphere on the plantations, coupled with the HSPA's arrogant attitude toward Filipinos, made local fieldworkers increasingly militant, and this prompted the emergence in Hawaii of union activity long established in the Philippines.

In 1919, Manlapit and other Filipino labor leaders organized a movement for higher wages and improved working conditions, which included a demand for recognition of the Filipino Federation of Labor, the fieldworkers' union, by the HSPA. After a year of attempting to improve conditions in the fields through negotiation, the Filipino Federation of Labor was ready to strike. On January 19, 1920, Manlapit issued a strike order and urged Japanese workers to join them. Manlapit strongly believed in interethnic labor organizations.

The HSPA responded by evicting 12,000 Filipinos from company housing, including 4,000 children.

Founding officers of the Filipino-dominated Cannery Workers and Farm Laborers Union, founded in Seattle, Washington, in 1933 and chartered by the American Federation of Labor a year later. (Filipinos: Forgotten Asian Americans by Fred Cordova)

Soon mobs of angry whites demanded an end to Filipino unions in the fields. The prospect of Filipino and Japanese workers uniting in a strike frightened C. Brewer & Company, a leading sugar plantation. The company therefore attempted to drive a wedge into union unity by talking separately with each group. By isolating Filipino and Japanese workers from one another, the major plantation managers hoped to end the strike. When that strategy did not succeed, Hawaiian, Portuguese, and Korean strikebreakers were brought into the fields.

Although the Filipino workers were defeated in the 1920 strike, they learned valuable organizational lessons. Manlapit emerged as a respected union leader, and Filipinos did cooperate with Japanese, Spanish, Puerto Rican, and Chinese laborers in the 1920 strike. The 1920 strike firmly established the concept of ethnic labor unionization. Not only were Filipinos in the forefront of Hawaii labor activity, but they also helped to publicize the need for better housing, improved working conditions, and an end to the paternalistic attitude of the plantation managers.

Filipino Labor Unions in California. The poor working conditions and fluctuating wages in the Imperial, San Joaquin, and Salinas valleys created the proper conditions for Filipino unionization. In 1933 the Filipino Labor Union was formed after the AMERICAN FEDERATION OF LABOR (AFL) refused to organize Filipino farmworkers.

D. L. Marcuelo, a Filipino businessperson in Stockton, California, founded another organization, also called the Filipino Labor Union, to better the wages, working conditions, and fringe benefits of Filipino workers. Since 1930 Marcuelo had urged Filipino farmworkers to organize a workable union. In August, 1934, the union called a strike in the Salinas lettuce fields. During the one-day strike, 700 workers staged a walkout to demonstrate Filipino labor union strength. Since Filipinos represented 40 percent of the total workforce, the union hoped to renegotiate their present wages. The walkout failed when Mexican, East Indian, and other Asian laborers were brought in to replace striking Filipino workers.

As a result of this strike, a wave of anti-Filipino sentiment surfaced in California. The *San Francisco Chronicle* reported that dynamiting and mob violence took place in Lodi, Gilroy, and throughout the smaller towns in the Salinas Valley.

The Filipino Labor Union continued to press growers for recognition as a mainstream union. The Associated Farmers of California responded by labeling the

Filipino boy harvesting cauliflower in Santa Maria, California. Photograph by Dorothea Lange, 1937. (Library of Congress)

union a "communist front group" and calling Filipino labor leaders "unrepentant radicals." Marcuelo urged Filipinos to select a strike site so that the union could win a major labor confrontation and receive recognition under U.S. president Franklin D. Roosevelt's National Industrial Recovery Act. The provisions of this New Deal legislation required employers to recognize a union during a strike. Section 7a of the act guaranteed binding arbitration, and if the union could win this concession it would be a recognized force in the California fields.

The Salinas lettuce strike of 1934 was the event that established Filipino labor unionization. In cooperation with the white-dominated Vegetable Packers Association, an AFL affiliate, the union in late August, 1934, struck with a united front and stopped agricultural production in the fields and sheds around Monterey County. Once the strike was concluded Filipino labor unions were an established part of the California labor scene.

After another successful strike in Salinas in 1936, the AFL granted a charter to the Field Workers Union,

Alaskan salmon cannery workers, 1939. (Filipino American National Historical Society)

Local 30326, a combined Filipino-Mexican labor union. In 1940 the AFL chartered the FEDERATED AGRICULTURAL LABORERS ASSOCIATION, a Filipino union, which had successfully represented thousands of asparagus workers, brussel sprout pickers, celery cutters, and garlic harvesters in a series of strikes in the central San Joaquin Valley.

By the late 1930's Filipinos were active in the Alaska salmon canneries. In 1938 Filipino salmon cannery workers organized to rid themselves of labor contractors. Soon Filipino workers were being hired from an AFL union hall.

The evolution of Filipino labor continued, and in 1941 the Filipino Agricultural Laborers Association had won a number of asparagus strikes. Soon this union emerged as the key post-World War II Filipino labor organization. In 1959, Larry ITLIONG formed the AGRICULTURAL WORKERS ORGANIZING COMMITTEE, and by the mid-1960's Itliong's Filipino union had combined with César Chavez' Chicano labor union to dominate the San Joaquin Valley. The result was to bring ethnic labor unions together in a position of solidarity in the California fields.—*Howard A. DeWitt*

SUGGESTED READINGS: • Chan, Sucheng. *Asian Americans: An Interpretive History.* Boston: Twayne,

1991. • Crouchett, Lorraine Jacobs. *Filipinos in California: From the Days of the Galleons to the Present.* El Cerritos, Calif.: Downey Place Publishing House, 1982. • DeWitt, Howard A. *Anti-Filipino Movements in California: A History, Bibliography and Study Guide.* San Francisco: R and E Research Associates, 1976. • DeWitt, Howard A. *Images of Ethnic and Radical Violence in California's Politics, 1917-1930: A Survey.* San Francisco: R and E Research Associates, 1975. • DeWitt, Howard A. *Violence in the Fields: Filipino Farm Labor Unionization During the Great Depression.* Saratoga, Calif.: Century Twenty One Publishing, 1980. • Melendy, H. Brett. *Asians in America: Filipinos, Koreans and East Indians.* Boston: Twayne, 1977.

Filipino locality or hometown organizations: Voluntary associations established and maintained by Filipino immigrants who share common origins in a community or larger region in the Philippines. Filipinos began forming these associations in the 1920's and 1930's on the sugar plantations in Hawaii and in farming communities in California. During this period locality organizations primarily served mutual aid and social functions for their members, and they generally continue to serve these as well as other purposes. As a result of the greater numbers of Filipinos immigrating to the United States since 1965, locality associations have increased substantially in number with the establishment of new organizations and the revival of previously existing groups. These associations provide an organized means for immigrants to develop and maintain relationships with one another and for aspiring individuals to assume leadership roles in the Filipino American community.

Historical Origins. Locality organizations were started by Filipino agricultural workers in both California and Hawaii after their arrival in substantial numbers. Laborers joined these groups for the social and security benefits that they provided, which were especially valued given the prevailing harsh living and working conditions. In Hawaii plantation workers organized *saranay*, or mutual assistance associations, among "townmates" (immigrants from the same hometown in the Philippines) or the larger Filipino plantation community. Hometown associations organized dances, celebrations of the feast day of the town's patron saint, and other social gatherings for their members. If a member became ill or died, the "club," as these groups often were called, gave to his or her family a monetary donation contributed by the other members. Hometown associations also served as rotating credit groups (*HULUGAN*) and thereby enabled Filipino laborers earning low wages to remit significant amounts of money to their families in the Philippines.

Basis of Membership. Locality organizations draw their members from among immigrants with a common place of origin in the Philippines, generally a town or province. Hawaii is notable for the prevalence of hometown associations of immigrants from the Ilocos provinces (such as Ilocos Norte, Ilocos Sur, and La Union) in the northeast Philippines. Examples of the more than forty of these associations are the Bacarra Aid Association, Pasuquineos of Hawaii, and Sadiri ti San Nicolas. In contrast immigrants from other areas in the Philippines tend to be represented by provincial or regional organizations or may not be represented by

Membership in locality or hometown organizations has remained popular among Filipino immigrants in America. (Filipino American National Historical Society)

any such association. A majority of the locality organizations in Hawaii represent communities in the Ilocos region, and most of these Ilocano groups are hometown associations. Many of them were started on the plantations prior to World War II.

The significant number of Ilocano hometown associations reflects both plantation labor recruitment and post-1965 immigration to Hawaii. Since the mid-1920's, ILOCANOS were the largest group among Filipino plantation labor recruits and in 1946 were the last sugar workers brought to Hawaii. Ilocanos also constitute the majority of Filipino immigrants who have settled in Hawaii since the 1965 liberalization of U.S. immigration laws that fostered the reunification of families. Also prevalent in Hawaii are hometown associations of immigrants from Pangasinan Province, many of whom are Ilocano since Pangasinan is adjacent to the Ilocos region.

Other Filipino locality organizations represent whole provinces in the Visayas region of the Central Philippines (such as Bohol, Cebu, Panay, Samar, and Siquijor) or provinces in central LUZON (such as Batangas, Bulacan, Cavite, Nueva Ecija, and Pampanga). The smaller number of immigrants from any one hometown in these provinces who have settled in a particular area in the United States tends to encourage provincial rather than hometown associations. Most of these province-based associations were established after the arrival of post-1965 immigrants. Locality organizations representing provinces and regions in MINDANAO in the Southern Philippines are not common given the comparatively smaller number of immigrants from that area.

Association Activities. Locality organizations generally provide various mutual aid benefits for their members, particularly in times of illness or death. The most common entitlements are death benefits for the deceased member's family, which may be a predetermined amount or the collected contributions from members. This mutual assistance function of locality associations has now become less important since most Filipino immigrants have close relatives to assist them in times of need.

Monetary or other charitable contributions to the hometown or province in the Philippines also are made by locality organizations, although not necessarily on a regular basis. These donations have been for a variety of purposes, such as to assist schools, churches, and hospitals; to repair municipal buildings, and to build water tanks. In gratitude for such contributions, the names of individual donors or of the locality organization may be prominently displayed on a plaque or in some other way in the home community. Assistance also is sent to home areas at times of natural disasters such as floods or earthquakes.

Locality associations organize social activities to celebrate their town fiesta; these often culminate on or near the feast day of the town's patron saint. Activities include beauty queen contests, dances, and banquets, which may also serve as fund-raisers. Associations usually sponsor at least one large social gathering each year for their members, such as a potluck picnic or banquet to commemorate the founding of the organization or to install its new officers.

Social Significance. The widespread proliferation of locality organizations following the post-1965 immigration of Filipinos might be assumed to indicate their social significance in the Filipino American community. Most associations are not especially active, however, even in organizing social functions for their members, and the latter tend to limit their participation in the association. The establishment and continuity of these organizations lie essentially with their leaders who may desire social recognition and prestige for themselves.

Like other Filipino voluntary associations, locality organizations primarily provide a formal setting for immigrants to establish and sustain ties with one another. Through their various office-holding positions, associations also provide opportunities for those who would like to establish themselves as leaders in the Filipino American community—particularly the younger, college-educated post-1965 immigrants.—*Jonathan Y. Okamura*

SUGGESTED READINGS: • Alcantara, Ruben. *Sakada: Filipino Adaptation in Hawaii, pp. 57-59, 146-151. Washington, D.C.: University Press of America, 1981.* • Almirol, E. B. "Filipino Voluntary Associations: Balancing Social Pressures and Ethnic Images." *Ethnic Groups 2, no. 1 (1978): 65-92.* • Ave, Mario. *Characteristics of Filipino Social Organizations in Los Angeles.* Master's thesis, University of Southern California, 1956. San Francisco: R and E Research Associates, 1974. • Okamura, J. Y. "Filipino Hometown Associations in Hawaii." *Ethnology 22, no. 4 (1983): 341-353.*

Filipino music and dance: The study, performance, and support of Filipino music and dance genres in the United States are important markers of ethnic identity for Filipino Americans. Genres perpetuated by Filipino Americans may be understood in relation to four historical periods in the Philippines: precolonial,

Spanish colonial, United States colonial, and postindependence. These historical periods inform the origins, characteristic features, and social context of music and dance forms pertinent to the formation of Filipino American identity.

Precolonial. In the United States, the most widely practiced indigenous musical genre at present is called *kulintang*. The *kulintang* is a gong ensemble that was introduced to the southern Philippines before the arrival of Islam and that has long been played by Muslims in MINDANAO and Sulu. Like other Southeast Asian gong traditions, the instruments used are primarily

The Singkil *is a narrative dance that portrays the grace of young Maranaw aristocratic girls in the southern Philippines.* (Samahan Philippine Dance Company)

bossed gongs and idiophones; the forms are cyclic; each instrumental part has a specific musical function; and improvisation is based on melodic and rhythmic formulas.

On the West Coast of the United States, where the majority of Filipino American immigrants have settled, university music departments and community-based organizations encourage the study of traditional music including *kulintang*. California-based organizations, such as the *World Kulintang Institute* in Los Angeles and *Kulintang Arts* in San Francisco, employ traditional teaching methods in which Filipino and non-Filipino students learn from acknowledged masters via oral transmission and by imitation. In addition to traditional styles, neotraditional *kulintang* styles emphasize innovation and modernization of the tradi-

The Tinikling *is one of the most popular yet difficult Philippine dances, requiring that its participants exercise grace, rhythm, and agility.* (Filipino American National Historical Society)

tion. Filipino musicians and other Asian American musicians have produced fusions of *kulintang* with other musical genres as expressions of panethnic Asian American solidarity.

Indigenous dances are performed at Filipino American cultural events to promote awareness of Filipino culture and to foster community participation. In the United States, the popular Tinikling and Singkil dances are presented primarily in entertainment contexts. Tinikling is a programmatic dance in which the dancers imitate the quick steps of the tikling bird. The dancers skillfully avoid being struck on the feet by two bamboo poles, manipulated on each side in highly rhythmic patterns. Singkil is a narrative dance that depicts the grace of young Maranaw aristocratic girls in the southern Philippines. BIBAK refers to associations of ethnic upland Filipinos in Los Angeles and Hawaii whose members present music and dances of their own respective regional traditions.

Spanish Colonial. The Spanish introduced new instruments, harmonically based music, new melodies, and new music/dance forms including the *habanera*, *danza*, *polka*, and *martsa*. The main influence of the Spanish was the *rondalla*, a string band. *Rondalla* is derived from the Spanish/Mexican tradition of *cumparasa* (string band). During the pre-World War II period, early immigrants to the United States, primarily single men, played *rondalla* as a form of entertainment, socialization, and solace. The *rondalla* played for dances, serenades (*harana*), "taxi dances," and other social events. The string band sound and diverse repertoire were ideally suited for dancing and partying. *Rondalla* ensembles in California, Texas, and Hawaii play for Filipino and non-Filipino cultural events and parties.

The basic *rondalla* instrumentation consists of plucked-string instruments. The repertoire includes Spanish, Latin American, and American instrumental dance pieces as well as arrangements of Philippine folk songs. The repertoire of songs derives from different geocultural regions, and songs are sung in a variety of languages. Although the home language may no longer be spoken by Filipino Americans, it has been maintained in song. In this respect, music plays an important role in the maintenance and assertion of Filipino identity for American-born Filipinos.

United States Colonial: During the United States colonial period, changes in the public educational and administrative systems stimulated new musical developments. Local as well as foreign songs were taught in the public education system. Each town formed its own *banda*, a marching band and/or symphonic band based on U.S. models. The famous Philippine Constabulary Band, formed in 1902, toured the United States on several occasions, the earliest dating to the St. Louis Exposition in 1904.

Although the study of European classical music performance and composition was introduced during the Spanish colonial period, its greatest flowering occurred later. In 1916, a conservatory of music was founded at the University of the Philippines. New compositions conformed to Western musical idioms (including the art song, or *kundiman*; concerto; symphony; symphonic poem; and chamber music) and often incorporated traditional melodies. The *sarsuwela*, an operetta derived from the Spanish *zarzuela*, was introduced by Spanish officials and merchants but gained its greatest popularity during the early decades of the twentieth century. The *sarsuwela* is a dramatic performance based on topical themes, interspersed with songs and dances, and sung in a *bel canto* style. Although the popularity of *sarsuwela* decreased in the Philippines after World War I, it was still being produced during the 1930's in the United States.

Popular dance forms introduced during the American colonial period include the fox-trot, cakewalk, and Charleston. These dances were popular at taxidance halls during the 1920's and 1930's in the United States. *PINOYS* in the United States worked as musicians in these dance hall bands, as well as performing for traveling shows and live radio broadcasts.

Postindependence. The international success of Filipino artists in concert music, opera, ballet, and modern dance is a source of pride for Filipino Americans. In the field of classical music performance, the Philippines has produced international artists including composer-conductor Lucrecia Kasilag, pianists Rowena Arrieta and Cecile Licad, and operatic tenor Noel Velasco. New music composition and modern choreography show efforts to incorporate indigenous elements within contemporary idioms. Compositions by avant-garde composer Jose Maceda brought into prominence native musical concepts such as drone, melody, and timbre (for example, the 1975 composition "Udlot-Udlot"). The Ballet Philippines, the national theater group, presents modern dance choreographies based upon indigenous themes and movement vocabularies and/or repertories.

For Filipino Americans, contact with the Philippines is maintained partly through the mass media. The latest trends in popular music and dance are disseminated via videocassettes, audiocassettes, Filipino-language radio and television broadcasts, Tagalog films, and tours by leading popular artists. Musical styles include 1970's *Pinoy Rock*, the fusion of a rock beat with the national language TAGALOG or a mixture of English and Tagalog (Taglish). Some of the top proponents include the Juan de la Cruz Band, Mike Hanopol, and Freddie Aguilar. Aguilar scored an international hit in 1978 with "Anak" ("Child"), which has been translated into many East Asian and Southeast Asian languages. Opposition to the MARCOS regime sparked the composition of protest music during the 1970's and 1980's by folksingers including Jess Santiago, Joey Ayala, and Heber Bartolome. Other popular styles that incorporate themes and lyrics drawn from Filipino life include local manifestations of pop, jazz, disco, and country and western.—*Andrew Weintraub*

SUGGESTED READINGS: • Cadar, Usopay. "The Role of Kulintang Music in Maranao Society." *Ethnomusicology* 17, no. 2 (1973): 234-249. • Dioquino, Corazon C. "Musicology in the Philippines." *Acta Musicologica* 54 (1982): 124-147. • Maceda, Jose. "Drone and Melody in Philippine Music Instruments." In *Traditional Drama and Music of Southeast Asia*, edited by Mohd. Taib Osman. Kuala Lumpur: Kementerian Pelajaran Malaysia, 1974. • Trimillos, Ricardo D. "Music and Ethnic Identity Among Overseas Filipino Youth." *Yearbook for Traditional Music* 18 (1986): 9-20.

Filipino Naturalization Act. *See* **Luce-Celler Bill of 1946**

Filipino Repatriation Act of 1935: U.S. legislation that provided free transportation for Filipinos in the continental United States who wished to return home to the Philippines but were unable to afford the cost. The act was backed by both humanitarians concerned about the impoverished condition of Filipinos and anti-Asian exclusionists who wanted Filipinos out of the United States.

In the 1920's anti-Asian exclusionists, predominantly members of labor organizations and groups such as the NATIVE SONS OF THE GOLDEN WEST, began calling for the exclusion of Filipinos from the United States. Newspapers picked up and amplified the outcry. Chinese, Japanese, Korean, and Indian immigration had previously been curtailed, but Filipinos, as "American nationals," were free to come to the United States. In 1929 the California legislature passed a resolution asking Congress to consider a ban on Filipino immigration.

A survey conducted by the Philippine Society found that thousands of Filipinos were unemployed and wanted to go back to the Philippines. In 1931 the Society actively lobbied the U.S. government to fund the return of Filipinos to their homeland. Filipinos in the United States and in the Philippines supported this idea. Their hope was that if enough of the poor Filipinos left the United States, legislation preventing immigration would be unnecessary.

In 1933 Samuel Dickstein, chairman of the Committee on Immigration and Naturalization, submitted a report to the House on joint resolution 577, which provided for Army and Navy transports to be used to ship Filipinos back to the Philippines, and for the U.S. government to finance this operation. According to Dickstein's report, justification for the United States' financing of the proposed operation existed because the situation of the Filipinos was perceived as a "national emergency." Furthermore removing Filipinos would relieve the communities in which they lived of a great financial burden. The committee had evidence that 30 to 60 percent of the approximately forty-five thousand Filipinos in the United States were unemployed. The committee assumed that many of those poor Filipinos would take advantage of a free trip back home.

The goals of the humanitarians and exclusionists were met with the passage of the FILIPINO REPATRIATION ACT, signed into law by President Franklin D. Roosevelt on July 11, 1935. The act provided for the free transportation of Filipinos back to the Philippines. (Filipinos in Hawaii were not eligible.) Once Filipinos were repatriated, they would be readmitted to the United States only as part of the 50-persons-per-year quota, set under the prevailing terms of the TYDINGS-MCDUFFIE ACT of 1934. Relatively few Filipinos repatriated under the new act—only 2,190, despite the fact that the dealine, originally set for December, 1936, was extended to December, 1940. The Filipinos' reasons for lack of interest in the Filipino Repatriation Act included the difficulty of later returning to the United States, the poor economic conditions in the Philippines, and the shame of returning to the Philippines in poverty.

Filipino rites of passage: Predominantly Roman Catholic, the people of the Philippines generally follow the rites of passage prescribed by the Roman Catholic church in conjunction with the sacraments. Of these, baptism, marriage, and death are most prominent. Preparation for and commitment to the celebration of

Families attending a baptismal service, California, circa 1950's. (Filipino American National Historical Society)

these occasions in one's life are universally shared across social classes and provincial boundaries.

Baptism. As mandated by the church, baptism marks the transition from being a non-Christian to becoming a Christian. The ritual, involving the pouring of water over a newborn's head, is performed by a priest typically over a font in one section of the church in the presence of the child's parents and sponsors. This ritual cleansing, dramatized in Jesus Christ's baptism in the river Jordan is designed to "wipe out" the original sin of humanity, a fundamental concept in Christian theology. At the social level, the child is introduced not only to relatives and friends but also to the wider social milieu of the Christian community. In this connection the child acquires new relationships—those with the baptismal sponsors, whose role is to serve as moral mentors for the child.

Although the ritual is intended by the church to be performed in the first month of life, compliance often takes several years. The feast that accompanies the celebration can take a tremendous toll on the family economy; therefore, the preparation for the event takes time. Often baptism and confirmation are timed to coincide with the community fiesta, incurring only one expense. The baptism of a first son, however, is most festive and given special attention. Thus in the period prior to actual baptism, two things often happen: One, a child may be given a provisional baptism (*buhos*) performed by a layperson; and two, confirmation may be conducted immediately after the official baptism. In the first situation, the newly born child is ritually washed in the house by a midwife or a curer, and the ritual is not recorded in the church's registry; in the second, the celebrant, usually close to teen years, undergoes two rituals on the same occasion using the same or separate sets of sponsors for each ritual. As generally practiced, confirmation, an important and carefully scheduled sacrament of the church, takes on a secondary emphasis to baptism, despite the presence of a bishop, who is required to perform confirmations. Faithful adherence to church rules is typically observed by the elite.

Marriage. Preceded by a period of courtship and engagement, proper marriage is marked by a wedding ceremony held in church with an array of participants (the entourage) and with a priest officiating at some point during the wedding Mass. Mass is foregone in cases of mixed marriages. A less than proper wedding is a civil ceremony conducted by a justice of the peace, and entered into hastily as the result of an elopement. The latter occurs when parental consent is withheld for any reason. Since a church wedding is highly desired, those who marry in the civil ceremony hope to be eventually married in the church at some future time. Each ceremony is usually followed by a wedding feast provided by the groom's family in the bride's household or elsewhere. All other expenditures related to the wedding are usually shouldered by the groom's family. Variations in this practice depend on the degree of acculturation to Western conventions.

Preparation for marriage involves interfamily negotiations, marshaling of economic resources, and setting the wedding date. A month prior to the wedding, the priest announces the forthcoming marriage to the congregation to inform the community and solicit any just cause to stop it. After the wedding, the couple moves briefly into the groom's family home, then later into the bride's, for an indefinite period, before achieving independence. Emancipation from the parental households is directly related to social class and modernity.

Marriage brings together in new alliance a variety of people from the groom's and bride's respective, extended families with sometimes complex in-law relationships. It may affect property transfer from the groom's family to that of the bride in a transaction called "donation." It also establishes new connections with the wedding sponsors. The latter are chosen for a number of reasons, not the least of which are the patronage and assistance they are able to provide to the newlyweds as the latter assume adult roles.

Death. In the Filipino people's worldview, death represents a transition from the life on earth to that of the other world. Nevertheless the inevitability of death is always met with sadness and resignation. A much wider range of emotions and attitudes are evoked when death is unexpected and premature. Comparatively the details of the observances connected with death receive greater attention for an adult than for a child. Prior to the funeral Mass and burial are a series of ritual and social imperatives: rosary recitations, novenas, and visitations by relatives and friends. The ideal death is one that receives the rite of extreme unction from a priest. The wake held in the house of the deceased lasts from three to seven days, providing that relatives from distant places attend. Each day of the wake involves constant food preparation for the guests; nightly games of MAH-JONGG and various card games are organized to keep "corpse watchers" awake. The idea is for the corpse not to be left unattended until its final disposition.—*Enya P. Flores-Meiser*

SUGGESTED READINGS: • Jocano, F. Landa. *Growing up in a Philippine Barrio.* New York: Holt, Rinehart and Winston, 1969. • Kasman, Edward Salkiya. "Birth and Death Rituals Among Tausugs of Siasi." Master's thesis, University of Santo Tomas, 1962. • Nurge, Ethel. *Life in a Leyte Village*. Seattle: University of Washington Press, 1965. • Nydegger, William F., and Corinne Nydegger. "Tarong: An Ilocos Barrio in the Philippines." In *Six Cultures—Studies of Child-rearing*, edited by Beatrice B. Whiting. New York: John Wiley & Sons, 1963.

Filipino values: Indicative of their agrarian base and a pervasive religious ideology, Filipino values tend to rest on a broad framework of sociability and obligations attending human relationships. Filipino values are easily discovered and understood in the general context of social psychology. In short, interpersonal relationships assume priority over connections between persons and things, or between persons and the supernatural. At the center of an individual's relationship with others is the family, the kinship, and the community, in relation to which key values are articulated in varying degrees.

Family and Utang Na Loob. First noted by Charles Kaut as a fundamental value among Filipinos, *utang na loob* may be translated as "a recognized indebtedness felt from within" by one person toward another. Implied in the concept is the permanency of the indebtedness whose repayment can only be attempted and approximated but never fully canceled. In this connection the prototype is found in the parent-child relationship in which a child's indebtedness toward the parents endures forever as a result of his/her being born, and such indebtedness may be partially repaid in one's becoming a parent at some future date. Thus other imperatives such as respectful behavior, obedience, cooperation, and personal sacrifice for the family, to name a few, are best understood in the context of *utang na loob*. The latter, however, must be distinguished from plain *utang*, a simple debt. This can be repaid and thus restores the relationship between two individuals in ongoing equal and reciprocal terms. *Utang na loob* as a concept has parallels, in Japan and to some extent China and, by implication, lies outside the scope of simple reciprocal relationships.

Kinship, Egalitarianism, and Pakikisama. Social expectations demand that an individual acknowledge kin beyond the sphere of the family. The Filipino bilateral kinship system ideally requires equal treatment of both sets of relatives, paternal and maternal. Favoritism for one side over the other, real or imagined, is negatively viewed though begrudgingly accepted as a practical measure and consequence. Overt discrimination for or against one side is known as *kabilaanin* (imbalanced) and is seen as a negative value, especially when class considerations enter into the equation. The individual who successfully meets the social expectations of individuals and groups in the many levels of his/her connections is highly regarded for embodying the Filipino value *pakikisama*. Although this value has been equated with *amor propio* (personalismo, self-esteem, and, in a sense, personal charisma), *pakikisama* goes beyond these and maximizes sociability as an end in itself. It elevates the consideration of the other over one's personal gain and interest and endures in the presence of other loyalties. The sphere of *pakikisama* is typically gauged outside the immediate family, whose primacy is a given. That is, *pakikisama* is most comprehensible in connection with extended family, neighbors, and friends.

Community and Pakikipagkapwa. Within the rubric of social relations and the community, many more concepts associated with "sociability" have been sought by some native social scientists of the Philippines in the linguistic domain of the local culture. Some of those concepts that have been linguistically derived and juxtaposed to the concept of *pakikisama* are *pakikibaka* (joint struggle), *pakikibagay* (conforming), *pakikisalamuha* (interacting), *pakikiisa* (being one with), or *pakikipagkapwa* (identifying with another/sharing one's humanness). Virgilio Enriquez assigns priority to *pakikipagkapwa* over *pakikisama* (adjusting) as a concept broader in scope and more fundamentally rooted: "*pakikipagkapwa* is much deeper and profound in its implications. It also means accepting and dealing with the other person as an equal. The company president and the clerk in an office may not have an equivalent role, status and income but the Filipino way demands and implements the idea that they treat one another as fellow human beings. . . . This means having a regard for the dignity and being of others." Elsewhere, Enriquez further explains: "In meaning, the Filipino word *kapwa* is the unity of the 'self' and 'others.' In English the word 'others' is actually used in opposition to the 'self' and implies the recognition of the self as a separate identity. In contrast, *kapwa* is a recognition of shared identity." By extension from the human condition, one might even suggest that this sharing of identity may be seen as analogous to the relationship between Christ and humanity. From another perspective, *kapwa* may be seen as the best representation of the Filipino "generalized other" in its most universal and developed sense.

One notion that has also been suggested as a Filipino value is *hiya*. *Hiya* translates as "shame" and constitutes a major form of sanction in Filipino communities. Socialization literature on the systematic inculcation of this concept illustrates its relevance to the cautious encounters at the interclass, intergenerational, and insider-outsider levels. *Hiya*, therefore, ensures appropriate behavior, demarcates areas of deviation, and lends support to the higher ideals of the community. Failure to uphold those values and social expectations in their proper contexts necessarily invokes shame. To have no shame (*walang hiya*) is to admit to a defective socialization and portrays a person as entirely worthless.

Superimposed on these fundamental Filipino values and notions is an equally desirable Western-derived agenda: class mobility for both the individual and the family, modernization of outlook and worldview, and full participation in the "market culture." Built on the values of competition, individualism, and material success, the Western (primarily American) agenda inevitably must confront traditional Philippine values. In effect, such a collision is presumed to occur in the personalities of individuals whether in their home communities or abroad, even as it poses the question of survival of those values created for agrarian communities against the onslaught of industrial values.—*Enya P. Flores-Meiser*

SUGGESTED READINGS: • Bulatao, Jaime C. "Hiya." *Philippine Studies* 12 (1964). • Enriquez, Virgilio G. "Kapwa: A Core Concept in Filipino Social Psychology." In *Philippine World-View*. Singapore: Institute of Southeast Asian Studies, Pagir Panjang, 1986. • Kaut, Charles. "Utang Na Loob: A System of Contractual Obligation Among Tagalogs." *Southwestern Journal of Anthropology* 17 (1961): 256-272. • Lynch, Frank, ed. *Social Acceptance: Four Readings on Philippine Values*. Quezon City: Ateneo de Manila University, 1964.

Filipino veterans and naturalization: When the U.S. entered World War II in December, 1941, resident Filipino immigrants, being noncitizens, were not eligible for military service. Soon, however, as the demand for manpower increased, their status changed. Thousands of Filipinos in the United States, previously denied the right to become naturalized citizens, attained citizenship through military service.

Filipinos became eligible for U.S. military service in 1942, following an executive order by President

Members of the 1st Filipino Infantry Regiment, a World War II U.S. Army unit. By the war's end, ten thousand Filipino veterans had won their American naturalization rights. (Filipino American National Historical Society)

Franklin Delano Roosevelt. Some Filipinos were made citizens prior to induction in mass naturalization ceremonies. Many who attained citizenship through military service, however, had to apply individually for naturalization on the basis of an amendment to the Nationality Act of 1940, the Act of March 27, 1942, which made noncitizens who served in the military eligible for citizenship. By December 31, 1945, the filing deadline following the end of the war, nearly ten thousand Filipino veterans had become citizens through military service. Soon thereafter, the U.S. Congress passed the LUCE-CELLER BILL OF 1946 (also known as the Filipino Naturalization Act), an amendment to the Nationality Act of 1940 which made Filipino immigrants to the United States eligible for naturalization.

For Filipinos in the Philippines who served with U.S. forces there against the Japanese, the situation was much different. Early in the war, Roosevelt had issued an executive order which incorporated the Philippine armed forces into the U.S. military. Accordingly, Filipino veterans in the Philippines should have been eligible for naturalization, just as their Filipino American counterparts had been.

A subsequent amendment to the Nationality Act of 1940, Public Law 567, Act of June 1, 1948, superseded the December 31, 1945 filing deadline and provided for naturalization of any person not a citizen who had served in the U.S. military "during either World War I or during a period beginning September 1, 1939, and ending December 31, 1946." This amendment, however, specifically excluded those who had enlisted in U.S. forces in the Philippines.

This exclusion left many Filipino veterans with a sense of betrayal. Not until the IMMIGRATION ACT OF 1990 was this injustice redressed. Section 405 of the 1990 law provided for naturalization of Filipino veterans who served in the U.S. military in the Philippines or with allied Philippine forces during World War II.

An estimated sixty thousand Filipino veterans were expected to apply for naturalization under this provision. By the beginning of 1994, fewer than half that number had applied, in part because many of the veterans lack official U.S. records of their service, and the U.S. Immigration and Naturalization Service (INS) had refused to accept substitute documents, such as Philippine government records. In March, 1994, however, the U.S. Ninth Circuit Court of Appeals, affirming a lower court ruling, found that the INS policy violated the intent of the 1990 law. As a result of this decision, veterans with Philippine documents became able to apply for naturalization.

Filipino weddings: Commonly include a mix of Christian, predominantly Catholic, rituals and indigenous traditions. For the most part, however, contemporary Filipino weddings are similar to American weddings.

In old-style, traditional weddings, the groom "pays" the bride's family for the bride, and the families of both the bride and groom are expected to pay for the cost of the wedding. The bride's family pays for her dress and may have to pay for church costs, while the groom's family bears the financial burden for the food served at the wedding reception. Since the majority of Filipinos are Catholic, wedding services are usually held in a Catholic church, accompanied by a full or abbreviated Mass. Traditionally, the bride wears a *tierna*, a decorated Filipino dress, and the groom wears a special wedding shirt and pants. Included in the wedding party are a cadre of godparents or sponsors, who can be as few as one or two couples or as many as fifty. Being asked to be a sponsor or godparent is an honor, and their roles vary. Generally, godparents are expected to advise the newlyweds in their marriage and may pay for certain wedding expenses. For example, one set of godparents may sponsor the rope or the veil used in the ceremony or contribute food for the wedding banquet, perhaps in the form of a pig or goat.

During a Catholic ceremony, the wedding couple often says a silent prayer and leaves a bouquet at the altar of the Virgin Mary. The couple is later bound by a large rope and covered by a veil. After the ceremony, the reception is held at someone's house or at the church or community hall. Guests, many of whom do not attend the wedding ceremony, may number in the hundreds or even thousands. Filipino food predominates at the banquet. Offerings of food, generally a small portion of most types of food present, are made to significant ancestors at a makeshift family altar. The family altar may include photographs of the deceased and lighted candles. After a blessing, the wedding feast may proceed. The bride and groom and wedding party are served first; guests get their food buffet-style.

Entertainment at Filipino weddings is similar to that at American ones. Variations may include performances by some of the guests of traditional Filipino dances or songs, or other displays of talent. There is always music, usually live, and dancing. "Fund-raising" for the newlywed couple often takes the form of a variety of money dances. In one, the bride and groom dance encircled by the guests, who shower them with money. In another, guests take turns placing coins or folded bills onto the lips of the bride, who passes the

Philippine wedding customs include placing the veil and cord over the head and shoulders of the bridal couple. Such traditions are commonly carried over into Filipino American weddings. (Filipino American National Historical Society)

money to the groom by a kiss. The groom takes the money with his lips and drops it to the floor. A more contemporary version is to have the male guests line up to pin money on the clothes of the bride and then dance with her a few moments. The same procedure occurs with female guests and the groom. The next day, a much smaller party is held, at which the newlyweds open their wedding gifts.

Filipinos and the Alaska canned salmon industry:
Employment in the salmon canneries in Alaska played a major role for tens of thousands of Filipinos in the United States. For decades, from the early 1900's to the 1980's, Filipinos, both newly arrived and established residents, traveled to far-flung salmon processing plants scattered along the Alaska coastline.

Thousands of Filipinos would annually migrate from California, Oregon, Washington, and other West Coast states to spend a season, usually about two months, working at isolated canneries from Bristol Bay to Southeast Alaska. Many of these male workers were new immigrants from the Philippines, with limited English-language skills, and most were single and

without permanent jobs. Some were college students, and working at the canneries enabled them to save money for their studies. Most, however, were unskilled migrant workers who spent the rest of the year working in hotels, restaurants, or the agricultural fields of California or other Western states doing "stoop labor."

The first Asian workers in the Alaska canneries were Chinese, who started in 1878. Many had recently finished working in railroad construction camps on the West Coast. A few of the early Chinese workers became foremen and labor contractors. Later came Japanese workers. As Congress in 1882 restricted Chinese immigration to the United States, however, and in 1924 limited Japanese entry, salmon cannery owners began hiring more Filipinos, Mexicans, Koreans, African Americans, and Pacific Islander workers. Packers preferred hiring nonwhite help, known as the "China Gang." Each cannery employed from fifty to about two hundred workers, and eventually, as demand for canned salmon grew, there were about 150 canneries in Alaska in the 1930's.

Of the canneries' workforce, Filipinos became the largest ethnic group, supplanting the Chinese and

Japanese. Early Chinese foremen and labor contractors trained their Filipino understudies, who would later take over their jobs. In 1910, there were 406 Filipinos living in the United States, and 16 went to Alaska that year. In 1920, there were 1,587 who worked in Alaska out of a U.S. Filipino population of 5,603. Ten years later, in 1930, there were 45,208 Filipinos in the United States, and 4,200 worked in the Alaska plants.

Because of high unemployment during the Great Depression and racial discrimination (Filipinos could not vote, own property in some states, or have government jobs), working in Alaska enabled many Filipinos to have at least some employment. Alaska cannery jobs did provide transportation, room and board, and a chance to work with other Filipinos and save money during the summer.

Workers were recruited initially by Chinese and later by Filipino labor contractors. Some of the major contractors in Seattle were Pedro Santos, Valeriano Sarusal, and Pio de Cano, who was trained by Charlie Soon, an early Chinese contractor. Because of the harshness of the working and living conditions at many remote canneries, abuses and exploitation of the workers did occur. Poor food, long work hours, gambling, fights, and cold damp rooms were some of the conditions that led to the creation of the CANNERY

WORKERS' AND FARM LABORERS' UNION in 1933. It was formed by Filipinos who dominated the union for decades. They also continued hiring mainly Filipino workers.

After 1964, when the U.S. Congress passed the Civil Rights Act, more white college students and females began working at the canneries. Third- and fourth-generation Filipinos continued working in the industry but not to the extent that the first generation did. Of that generation, some remained in Alaska rather than returning to Seattle. They married native Alaskan women and became permanent residents of Alaska.

Film: Asian Americans have been a part of the film industry since its beginnings in the first decades of the twentieth century. During much of that history, film images of Asians and Asian Americans have been crudely stereotypical. Moreover, Asian characters have frequently been portrayed by white actors rather than by Asians, especially in leading roles. The 1990's, however, showed significant signs of change. As Asian American producers, directors, actors, and others in the film industry made an increasingly visible impact, they continued a tradition established by earlier generations of Asian American filmworkers who achieved much under adverse conditions.

The salmon canneries of Alaska have provided a major source of employment for scores of Philippine immigrants to America since the early years of the twentieth century. Filipino men are among the Alaskan cannery workers pictured here, in a photograph dated 1926. (Filipino American National Historical Society)

Stereotypes and Stock Characters. In surveying the history of Asian Americans in film, it is important to note that cinematic images of Asians have historically been linked to negative social and political circumstances surrounding the Asian presence in the United States, from the exclusionary legislation of the nineteenth century through America's various military engagements with Asian nations.

Depictions of Asians in film have depended largely on a limited repertoire of stock characters. In the silent era, Richard Barthelmess was cast as a Chinese laundryman who rescues an abused girl played by Lillian Gish in D. W. Griffith's *Broken Blossoms* (1919). In the 1920's, Lon Chaney made it his specialty to play Asian parts. In *Bits of Life* (1921), Chaney played a San Francisco opium overlord. He followed this with the role of a doomed Chinese in the 1922 film *Shad-*

ows, in which his character is shipwrecked near a New England village and subsequently persecuted by the town's people. Chaney went on to star in several other movies in which he was cast as an Asian. These stock roles seldom represented Asian Americans as fully human, fully developed characters, yet over time, such depictions came to be accepted by both the viewing public and filmmakers as realistic representations of Asian people.

The racist stereotype of the "YELLOW PERIL" also perpetuated images of Asians as disease-ridden and degenerate. Representations of first Chinese, and later Japanese, were based on nineteenth century cartoons characterized by the exaggeration of Asian physical features and the attribution of negative personality traits. During the era of silent movies, films such as *Chinese Rubbernecks* (1903), *The Yellow Peril* (1908),

Chinese American film director Wayne Wang, outside the Cannery Theater, San Francisco, 1981. Into the 1990's, perhaps the most successful Asian American filmmaker in the United States. (Nancy Wong)

Early Chinese American actor Anna May Wong. (Library of Congress)

and *What Ho the Cook* (1921), promoted the stereotype of Asians as buffoons. *Chinese Rubbernecks* featured a chase scene involving Chinese laundrymen, while the Chinese servant in *The Yellow Peril* disrupts a home and is subsequently thrown out of a window, beaten up by a policeman, and finally set on fire as part of a supposed attempt at comedy. Another film of the period, *Hashimura Togo* (1917), which can be viewed with some irony today, featured Sessue HAYAKAWA as a technologically inept Japanese.

Asian detectives, often portrayed as "clever" aphorism-spouting individuals, had their earliest prototype in the 1912 silent film, *The Adventures of Boe Kung*, "the Chinese Sherlock Holmes." This genre came into its own with the Charlie CHAN films, beginning with the 1926 film House Without a Key, with George Kuwa in the lead role, followed by *The Chinese Parrot* (1928), starring Kamiyana Shojin, and *Behind That Curtain* (1929), starring E. L. Park. Significantly, though, the popularity of the Charlie Chan series really began in 1931, at the point when the lead character began to be played by non-Asian actors. The role of Charlie Chan was played by Warner Oland, Sidney Toler, Roland Winters, J. Carrol Naish, and Peter Ustinov. More than thirty Charlie Chan movies were made

in a period spanning the 1930's to the 1950's.

Films depicting Asian Americans as violent and scheming members of Asian secret societies or as dissipated purveyors of opium and sex are also standard fare in the canon of film history. The actual places inhabited by Asians are also often cinematically represented as locales which engender evil deeds. From *War of the Tongs* (1917) through *Chinatown Nights* (1929) and *The Hatchet Man* (1932) to *The Year of the Dragon* (1985), as well as in the popular martial arts movies (*Enter the Dragon*, 1973; *The Big Brawl*, 1980; *Enter the Ninja*, 1982; *Revenge of the Ninja*, 1983; *The Protector*, 1985), Chinatowns or Asian milieus are consistently depicted as murky backdrops for crime, vice, and violence. In these environments, Asian men are frequently seen as power-hungry, cruel, and lustful. In one of the more sensational moments in film history, Sessue Hayakawa tears the gown off the shoulder of a white woman who refuses his advances and then brands her in the 1915 film, *The Cheat*. The same motif recurs in films as varied as *Mr. Foo* (1914), *The Thief of Bagdad* (1924), *Old San Francisco* (1927), *The Bitter Tea of General Yen* (1933), and

Japanese American silent screen veteran Sessue Hayakawa, in a publicity still for The Bridge on the River Kwai *(1957). The film captured multiple Academy Awards, including the Best Supporting Actor prize for Hayakawa.* (AP/Wide World Photos)

Ensemble cast members of The Joy Luck Club. (Museum of Modern Art/Stills Archive)

Daughter of the Dragon (1931), not to mention the FU MANCHU and Flash Gordon movies featuring Ming the Merciless; in all of these, Asian men are portrayed as lusting over hapless white women.

The distorted images of Asian males has its parallel in the film stereotypes of Asian women. Whether they are portrayed as long-suffering women enduring ill-fated love relationships, "Dragon Ladies," prostitutes, or peasants, Asian women have historically been rendered as exotic stereotypes. As with the portrayal of Asian males, roles for Asian women have frequently been played by white actresses. Sylvia Sydney, Myrna Loy, Louise Ranier, Katherine Hepburn, Agnes Moorehead, Gene Tierney, Jennifer Jones, Shirley Maclaine, and Bette Davis are among the many white actresses who have played Asian women.

A Long Tradition. While white actors have dominated the portrayal of Asians, persons of Asian descent have worked in film from the earliest days of this medium's history. The 1914 film *The Chinese Lily*, for instance, had an all-Chinese cast. In this era, Leong But-jung, better known as James B. Leong, started the Wah Ming Motion Picture Company in Los Angeles. Financed by Chinese American businesses, the company intended to produce films based on Chinese themes using all-Chinese casts. Both Leong and another Chinese American, Moon Kwan, were involved in D. W. Griffith's *Broken Blossoms*. Moon served as the film's technical director, while Leong worked as Griffith's assistant director. Another Chinese American, James Wang, worked as the technical director for the 1919 film *Red Lantern*, with its cast of more than five hundred Chinese American extras.

In front of the camera, the two Asian American actors who gained the widest attention in the early history of film were Anna May WONG and Sessue HAYAKAWA. Wong's film credits, which extended for more than thirty years, included *The Red Lantern* (1919), *The Toll of the Sea* (1922), *The Thief of Bagdad* (1924), *Daughter of the Dragon* (1931), and *Shanghai Express* (1932). Hayakawa's career, which began in silent films in 1914 with his appearance in *Wrath of the Gods*, also stretched into the era of sound with roles in *Tokyo Joe* (1949) and *The Bridge over the River Kwai* (1957). Less is remembered today of Hayakawa's wife Tsuru Aoki, who in the early days of film starred in several movies, including *The Courageous Coward* (1919). Aoki enjoyed both a film and theater career and was known as a director as well.

A number of Asian American actors have also had

unusually long careers by virtue of their ability to find a niche in supporting roles. They include Keye LUKE, who began his acting career in the 1930's in movies such as *The Painted Veil* (1934), starring Greta Garbo. Luke continued his acting career into the television era with the *Kung Fu* series. Likewise, actors such as Philip AHN, James SHIGETA, Nobu MCCARTHY, Buelah Kwoh, James Soo, and Victor Sen YOUNG have all enjoyed a certain degree of public visibility through their long and varied careers.

In the 1990's, the successes of Wayne WANG (*The Joy Luck Club*, 1993), Joan CHEN, Jason Scott LEE, the late Brandon Lee, and many others have given Asian Americans an increasingly prominent presence in film. At the same time, many films from Asia are introducing American moviegoers to Asian perspectives.—*Patricia Lin*

SUGGESTED READINGS: • Gussow, Mel. "Beyond the Dragon Lady and No. 1 Son." *The New York Times*, September 3, 1990. • *Renee Tajima Reads Asian Images in American Film*. Video. Paper Tiger Television, 1984. • Tajima, Renee. *The Anthology of Asian Pacific American Film and Video*. New York: Film News Now Foundation, 1985. • West, Woody. "Boos for a Bogus Morality Play." *Insight* 6 (September 3, 1990): 64. • *Yuki Shimoda: Asian American Actor*. Video. Visual Communications, 1985.

1st Filipino Infantry Regiment: World War II U.S. Army unit made up chiefly of Filipinos living in the United States. After Japan attacked PEARL HARBOR and invaded the Philippines, thousands of Filipino American residents volunteered for military service. Six months later twenty thousand Filipinos wore the American uniform despite experiencing legal discrimination. Many composed the 1st Filipino Infantry Regiment and saw action in the Visayas and on LUZON.

Immediately following the outbreak of the Pacific war, Filipinos across the United States rushed to recruiting stations. Initially, would-be volunteers faced rejection. Beginning in November, 1941, Filipinos had been required by law to register as aliens. In 1942, however, President Franklin Delano Roosevelt signed an executive order allowing Filipino noncitizens to enlist or be drafted in the military. In the same year, an amendment to the Nationality Act of 1940 made noncitizens who served in the military eligible for U.S. citizenship. By 1943, a thousand soldiers of the 1st

Cannon company unit of the 1st Filipino Infantry Regiment, March, 1944. (Filipino American National Historical Society)

Filipino Infantry Regiment had been naturalized.

The 1st Filipino Infantry Regiment consisted of Filipino conscripts and was organized in the United States. It drilled for ninety days in various California encampments and was under American officers as well as Filipino junior officers. The TAGALOG-speaking Colonel Robert H. Offley was commander. Offley had been reared in the Philippines, where his father had been governor of Mindoro, an island south of Luzon.

Once trained, the regiment was dispatched to New Guinea, where it formed Philippine Civil Affairs Units (PCAU). In a freed Philippines, these units would aid the Filipino population in promoting civilian administration, medical and educational programs, and relief distribution.

The regiment joined MacArthur's 6th Army invasion of Leyte in October, 1944. Before that invasion force landed, a Japanese aircraft inflicted a few losses on the unit. Nevertheless the first soldier to raise an American flag on the beach was an Ilocano member of a PCAU. This team later helped civilians at Palo Alto on Leyte and in 1945 assisted liberated Filipinos on Luzon in the provinces of Pangasinan, Tarlac, Pampanga, Laguna, and Cagayan.

Besides aiding civilians, the 1st Filipino Infantry Regiment braved combat. It shared patrol duties with the American Division on Leyte and Samar and cooperated with Filipino guerrillas as well on the latter island.

First Korean Independence Air Force: Flight-training school established in Willows, California, in 1919, at the height of the Korean independence movement. (See MARCH FIRST MOVEMENT.) Founded by Hahn Chang Ho, a young Korean who had come to the United States in 1916, and several likeminded friends, the school was conceived to supply pilots to fight the Japanese, who had annexed Korea in 1910. Not long after its founding, the group moved from Willows to Redwood City, where their instructor was Frank Bryant, the chief instructor at the Redwood Aviation School.

The quixotic venture ended in 1920 after about a year of training. It had been funded by a prominent Korean rice farmer in the Willows area, but a disastrous drought forced him to withdraw his support.

5 Ks. *See* **Gobind Singh; Khalsa; Sikhism**

Flowing Stream Ensemble: San Francisco-based musical group that used Chinese and Western instruments to play classical, folk, and contemporary Chinese music, founded in 1972. The group, one of the first to perform outside San Francisco Chinatown, played for Chinese Premier Zhao Ziyang when he visited the United States in 1983. Its music was featured in Arthur DONG's Oscar-nominated film *Sewing Woman* (1984).

FOB: Abbreviation for "fresh off the boat," used by Chinese Americans and other Asian Americans to refer to Asian immigrants who have only recently arrived in the United States.

Fong, Hiram L. (b. Oct. 15, 1906, Honolulu, Territory of Hawaii): U.S. senator. Fong ranks among the most distinguished Americans of Chinese ancestry. Born to poor, illiterate Chinese immigrants, Fong became a symbol of the wealth that the United States possesses in its diversity of peoples and cultures—and of the opportunities that exist for persons of genuine ability and discipline living in a democracy. Through intelligence, hard work, education, and perseverance, he achieved great success in law, local and national politics, and business. He became the first Asian American elected to the U.S. Senate (1959-1977), the first Chinese American in Congress, and the first Chinese American to be nominated for U.S. President at a national convention (1964). He won the Horatio Alger Award in 1970 for his outstanding success despite humble beginnings. He became a multimillionaire but forgot neither his immigrant heritage nor his friends.

Early Life. As one of eleven children, Fong worked from age four to help his father, Lum Fong, an indentured sugar plantation worker, laborer, and night watchman, and his mother, Chai Hai Lum, a housewife who had been a governess for a wealthy family. The home in which Fong was born was an unpainted, low-rent house in a poor rural area. Growing up with neighbors of Chinese, Hawaiian, Japanese, or Portuguese ancestry, he became tolerant of others. He liked to be busy and was often outdoors. Whether he picked algaroba beans, fished, caddied, or worked at a small store, Fong gave his earnings to his parents. Yet he never felt deprived or envious of others.

Education/Family. Studious, self-confident, and a good public speaker, Fong was the first of his family to graduate from high school (1924). Ambitious for a Harvard Law School degree, he still had to help support the family and save for his education. Not until 1930 did he graduate (Phi Beta Kappa) from the University of Hawaii. In 1932 he entered Harvard. Study-

Hiram L. Fong. (Library of Congress)

ing long hours and living as cheaply as possible on borrowed funds, Fong achieved his law degree in 1935. After three years as Honolulu deputy attorney general, he paid off his debts, married Ellyn Lo, opened a private law office, and was elected to the territorial House of Representatives as a member of the Republican Party (GOP).

The Fongs had four children: Hiram, Jr., Rodney, and twins Merie-Ellen and Marvin-Allan. During World War II Fong became a major in the U.S. Seventh Air Force. Later he retired from the Air Force Reserve with the rank of colonel.

Law. By taking in law partners of Japanese, Korean, or English-Hawaiian ancestry, Fong started the first multicultural law firm: Fong, Miho, Choy & Robinson. It often represented minority clients and became very successful in immigration and other cases. He left the law firm after being elected senator.

Politics. From 1900 to 1954 the mostly white GOP controlled Hawaii's political, economic, and social life, but Fong cooperated with Democratic Party legislators. In multicultural Hawaii there is no single ethnic group big enough to make up a majority of voters. Politicians must therefore have wide appeal. Fong enjoyed political success for more than thirty years, but in his first territorial election, the GOP kept him from taking office for one week because he opposed their choice for Speaker. The resulting publicity made Fong a hero among minority voters. He favored statehood, and as sponsor of many bills to help workers, he gained labor-union support. Between 1949 and 1953 he was Hawaii's first Chinese American Speaker of the House until defeated in the Democratic takeover of 1954. He then retired from politics.

Hawaii became a state on August 21, 1959. In a surprising comeback, Fong was elected one of two statehood senators. When Congress recessed, Senator Fong and a small group traveled at his expense to a number of Far East countries (some that were attracted to Communism) and to Hong Kong. He thought if Asians saw him in person, it would prove to them that U.S. democracy did work.

Fong served under Presidents Dwight D. Eisenhower, John F. Kennedy, Lyndon B. Johnson, Richard M. Nixon, and Gerald R. Ford. He was active on major Senate committees such as Appropriations, Judiciary, and Post Office and Civil Service. He successfully nominated qualified persons of Asian, Hawaiian, and Caucasian ancestry to become judges, commissioners, and other high officials.

Known as a man who kept his word, Fong also believed in the one man-one vote principle. He gave bipartisan support for civil rights, voting rights, agriculture, education, highways, ocean and tropical research, labor, the military, anti-Communist activities, and other important matters. A fiscal conservative, he also looked beyond party loyalty to vote against GOP nominees to high office who he felt were unqualified. He proudly supported the landmark 1965 IMMIGRATION AND NATIONALITY ACT that eliminated quotas favoring Western nations, so that East Europeans, Asians, and Pacific peoples could emigrate in equal numbers.

When President Johnson won a landslide victory in 1964, Fong set an all-time record in Senate elections by running 31.8 percent ahead of the GOP presidential candidate. Undefeated, Fong retired from the Senate in January, 1977.

Business. In 1952 Fong and several cofounders started Finance Factors, a privately owned industrial loan company that in forty years diversified into a multimillion-dollar family of companies that included financial branch offices on the major islands, real estate development, home building, securities, investments, and insurance. Fong headed Finance Factors, but he gave credit to a smart, hard-working team of cofounders, codirectors, managers, and loyal employees for its growth. Finance Factors later became part of Finance Enterprises.

Fong's Plantation and Gardens. Fong became Honolulu's fourteenth largest private landowner. As a retirement project he developed more than one hundred of the seven hundred acres of hilly land he owned on windward Oahu into a beautiful tourist attraction. There are sweeping vistas, exhibits, flowering plants and fruit trees, and experimental projects. He named valleys and plateaus after Presidents Eisenhower, Kennedy, Johnson, Nixon, and Ford. Fong loved pulling weeds, working in the gardens, and making plans for the family to continue his project.

The winner of many local and national awards, Fong also achieved international honors, such as the Order of the Brilliant Star with Grand Cordon from the Republic of China, and the Order of Diplomatic Service Merit, Gwanghwan Medal (the highest diplomatic award) from the Republic of Korea. He was a role model for minorities, an American of Chinese ancestry born into humble circumstances who rose through education and perseverance to live the American Dream.—*Michaelyn Chou*

SUGGESTED READINGS: • Chou, Michaelyn P. *"The Education of a Senator: Hiram L. Fong from 1906 to 1954."* Unpublished Ph.D. dissertation (American Studies). Honolulu: University of Hawaii at Manoa, 1980. • Chou, Michaelyn P. "New Insights into the Political Career of Hiram L. Fong." In *The Chinese American Experience: Papers from the Second National Conference on Chinese American Studies* (1980), edited by Genny Lim. San Francisco: Chinese Historical Society of America: Chinese Culture Foundation of San Francisco, 1984. • Chou, Michaelyn P. *Oral History Interview with Hiram L. Fong, Senator from Hawaii, 1959 to 1977.* Washington, D.C.: Former Members of Congress, Inc., 1979, 1980. • *Tributes to the Honorable Hiram L. Fong of Hawaii in the United States Senate, upon the Occasion of His Retirement from the Senate.* Washington, D.C.: U.S. Government Printing Office, 1977.

Fong, Walter: Entrepreneur. Owner of the Farmer's Market chain of supermarkets, he played an important role in the building of the Confucius Church of Sacra mento, which was founded for religious, social, cultural, and educational activities in February, 1961. A cultural and religious landmark, the church housed a school and the CHINESE CONSOLIDATED BENEVOLENT ASSOCIATION (CCBA).

Fong Yue Ting v. United States (1893): U.S. Supreme Court ruling that as a function of national sovereignty Congress can rightfully force aliens to have certificates of residence (the GEARY ACT OF 1892) and can deport or expel those who lack them. On a broader scale, the Court affirmed the plenary power of Congress to pass laws restricting the rights of aliens in the United States—the principle expressed in the earlier Supreme Court case of CHAE CHAN PING V. UNITED STATES (1889).

Fong Yue Ting involved three Chinese laborers who had emigrated to the United States in 1874, 1877, and 1879. None of them possessed the certificate of residence required by the Geary Act. Only one had applied to the collector of internal revenue for a certificate but had been rejected because he was not able to obtain the testimony of a white person to the fact of his residence. The three men were arrested by U.S. marshals, brought before a federal judge, and ordered deported. Their cases were appealed to the Supreme Court.

In the majority opinion, written by Justice Horace Gray, no distinction was made between the right of Congress to exclude Chinese laborers from entering the United States and the right to expel them. Both were attributes of American sovereignty, and the procedure for expulsion was to be determined by Congress and was not reviewable by a court of law. "It is," Gray said, "but a method of enforcing the return to his own country of an alien who has not complied with the conditions upon the performance of which the government of the nation, acting within its constitutional authority and through the proper departments, has determined that his continuing to reside here shall depend."

Justices David J. Brewer and Stephen J. Field filed dissenting opinions. Exclusion of Chinese laborers and expulsion are two different things, they wrote. A Chinese laborer, resident in the United States, is entitled to the protections of the due process clause of the Fifth Amendment to the federal Constitution. Expulsion is a form of punishment: "It involves first an arrest, a deprival of liberty; and, second, a removal from home, from family, from business, from property." Therefore, before a resident alien may be deported, he or she is guaranteed a trial in a court of law.

Ben Fong-Torres. (San Francisco Chronicle)

Fong-Torres, Ben (b. Jan. 7, 1945, Alameda, Calif.): Writer. The first Asian American writer to appear regularly in a national magazine, he served as senior editor of *Rolling Stone*, a national music magazine; and editor of *East/West*, a bilingual weekly community newspaper. He has also been published in numerous national magazines and is the author of *The Motown Album: The Sound of Young America* (1990) and *Hickory Wind: The Life and Times of Gram Parsons* (1991). His autobiography, *The Rice Room: Growing Up Chinese-American—from Number Two Son to Rock 'n' Roll*, was published in 1994.

Foot-binding: Chinese practice of severely constricting the feet of females. Tradition dates the origin of foot-binding to a Five Dynasties (907-960 C.E.) palace concubine who bound her feet and twirled about on a lotus platform for the emperor's pleasure. The practice became popular during the Southern Song Dynasty (960-1279 C.E.), when Neo-Confucian values promoted chaste behavior by restraining women's mobility to keep them housebound. Foot-binding was widespread in the Ming (1368-1644 C.E.) and QING (1644-1911 C.E.) dynasties because of renewed emphasis on female chastity. Bound feet also came to signify wealth and status since only well-to-do households could support women with crippled feet.

The foot was bound by drawing the four smaller

toes up into the insole and winding the wrapping tightly about the toes and the heel to force them together, leaving the big toe unbound. If the practice was begun when the girl was from five to seven years old, and if it was properly performed, "golden lotus" feet attained an ideal three-inch length in about a year. Tiny feet were considered beautiful and necessary for arranging a good marriage. In a society where modesty required the body to be fully covered, bound feet took on erotic connotations.

Although widespread, the practice was not universal. In an effort to assert the ethnic MANCHU separateness of their women and to discourage their intermarriage with Chinese, Qing rulers prohibited foot-binding. The HAKKAS, who did not bind their feet, probably influenced the prohibition against foot-binding and the forcible unbinding of feet by means of the TAIPING REBELLION (1850-1864) forces in areas under their control.

Nineteenth century reformers urged abolition of foot-binding and established antifootbinding societies. The practice was so deeply entrenched, however, that the EMPRESS DOWAGER's Anti-footbinding Edict of 1902 and a decree issued in 1912 by the republic's provisional president, SUN YAT-SEN, proved ineffective. The practice continued in conservative rural areas into the 1930's. Both economic opportunities for women and modern education helped to change attitudes on foot-binding. Overseas Chinese communities also gradually ended the practice.

Foran Act of 1885: U.S. legislation outlawing the practice of contract labor. While the 48th Congress was in session, Ohio Congressman Martin A. Foran introduced a bill that made it unlawful to assist alien contract laborers prior to their emigration to the United States by subsidizing their transporation costs. The bill was aimed at halting the flow of immigrant workers to Hawaii and the U.S. mainland; its passage provoked labor recruiters to employ various schemes to circumvent the new law. Transportation assistance, meanwhile, continued under cover of secrecy.

Forbidden City: Chinese nightclub with dancing and a floor show. Officially opened on December 22, 1938, in San Francisco, California, it featured Chinese American dancers and performers and later became a popular place for Chinese Americans, as well as public officials, movie stars, and even heads of state. It closed its doors in 1961, after twenty-three years of entertainment. The club is the subject of *Forbidden City, U.S.A.*

(1989), a documentary film by Academy Award-nominee Arthur DONG.

Foreign Commission of the Korean Overseas Association (also, United Korean Committee in America): A Washington, D.C.-based nationalist organization of Korean Americans that in 1941 created the Korean Commission, the only diplomatic agent of the Korean provisional government in China. During heightened anti-Japanese sentiment in the United States, the commission convinced authorities that since Korean Americans were not Japanese citizens they should have the same rights as those of the Allied nations. During World War II the commission served as the official liaison between Korean Americans and the U.S. government.

Foreign Miners' Tax (1850): First in a series of discriminatory California mining taxes imposed on Mexican and Chinese miners during the late nineteenth century. The California legislature passed the first such tax following the California gold rush and the onslaught of thousands of gold seekers from around the world. This first Foreign Miners' Tax imposed a $20 monthly mining tax on noncitizens of the United States who were mining in California. It was printed in Spanish and English, and despite its wording and the large presence of foreign miners in California, the tax targeted only Mexican miners. The legislature passed it in response to the economic and racial resentment among the white majority of miners toward the Mexican minority of miners in the California goldfields.

For their part the Mexican miners continued to mine in California, while declining to pay the discriminatory and prohibitive mining tax. In response the white miners began gathering in protest and threatening to collect the tax forcibly. After a brief period of tension, many Mexicans departed from the California goldfields and returned to Mexico.

With the Mexican departure the Chinese soon became the target. The Chinese, like the Irish and the Germans, had flocked to California seeking gold. By 1852 the population of Chinese miners had substantially increased. In response to this increase the white miners began viewing the large Chinese minority as an economic and racial threat. The California legislature, in support of the growing anti-Chinese sentiment and because of the political clout of the white miners, reintroduced the Foreign Miners' Tax. Its reenactment lowered the monthly mining fee to $3, printed the tax law in English, Spanish, and Chinese, and targeted Chinese miners.

The revamped Foreign Miners' Tax, with variations enacted over the years, was enforced and collected from Chinese miners in California for almost twenty years. Until its demise in 1870, after being declared a violation of the U.S. Constitution, it provided significant tax revenue for California and its mining counties. The Foreign Miners' Tax, in conjunction with other anti-Chinese activity during the 1850's, marked the birth of the ANTI-CHINESE MOVEMENT in California.

Formosa: Former name of TAIWAN. The name "Formosa," which means "beautiful," was given to it in the late sixteenth century by Portuguese explorers who journeyed to the region. For years, "Formosa" was the name by which Taiwan was known to the West. Other ancient names for Taiwan are "Pokkan" and "Pekiand."

Fortune cookie: A thin, ear-shaped sugar cookie containing a slip of paper on which an aphorism or brief prediction is written regarding the recipient's future, usually served at the end of a meal in a Chinese restaurant. It was created by the Kay Heong Noodle Factory in San Francisco in the 1930's to attract tourists.

Forty-niners: Prospectors who went to look for gold in the Western United States during the California gold rush of 1849.

Immigrant Chinese miners were among the thousands of Forty-niners who traveled West in search of instant wealth during the California gold rush days. (California State Library)

4-C: U.S. military draft classification for enemy aliens. NISEI were not eligible for the draft because they were classified as enemy aliens during World War II (1939-1945). After the attack on PEARL HARBOR (December 7, 1941), nearly all Nisei who had volunteered for the U.S. armed forces were discharged and reclassified as 4-C. Before being classified as 4-C, however, they were classified as 4-F, the category for those not qualified to serve because of their physical condition.

442nd Regimental Combat Team: Japanese American combat team formed of NISEI volunteers from the U.S. mainland and Hawaii. It was organized by presidential decree in January, 1943, and, combined with the all-Nisei 100TH INFANTRY BATTALION from Hawaii, it became the most highly decorated unit of its size in American military history.

Following the anti-Japanese hysteria that accompanied the attack on Pearl Harbor, the U.S. military removed all Japanese Americans from National Guard units and transferred them to the Corps of Engineers as common laborers. In April, 1942, the Japanese Americans on the West Coast were placed in RELOCATION CENTERS.

In subsequent months, pleas from the Japanese American community that it be given a chance to prove its loyalty convinced U.S. government authorities and the military that a separate unit composed of Japanese American volunteers should be formed. Although only fifteen hundred men were initially called for, more than ten thousand volunteered, from which approximately three thousand were selected to form the 442nd Regimental Combat Team.

Basic training began at Camp Shelby, Mississippi, in February, 1943. The newly organized unit adopted a Hawaiian gambler's phrase "go for broke," meaning "shoot the works," as its regimental motto.

Leaving the United States for Italy, the troops arrived in May, 1944, and were attached to the 34th (Texas) Division. In September, 1944, they joined in

Japanese Americans militia served in the U.S. armed forces with distinction during World War II. Here several troops, all residents of Hawaii and serving with the Allied 5th Army in Italy, visit an Italian town they helped liberate. (National Archives)

the invasion of southern France. In the Vosges Mountains, they rescued the lost battalion of the 141st Infantry Regiment. As a result, all members of the 442nd were declared "honorary Texans."

The achievements of this combat team are legendary. None of the elite U.S. Army Airborne or Ranger units came close to the 442nd's record 18,143 medals for valor, including 1 Medal of Honor, 52 Distinguished Service Crosses, 1 Distinguished Service Medal, 588 Silver Stars, 5,200 Bronze Stars, and 9,486 Purple Hearts.

Considering that the 442nd never carried more than three thousand men on its roster, the 9,486 Purple Hearts represent a casualty rate of more than 300 percent.

French rule in Indochina (1858-1954): French rule of the area consisting of Vietnam, Laos, and Cambodia. From the occupation of the Saigon Delta in 1858 until the withdrawal of French forces from Indochina in 1954, France progressively occupied the territories that would become Vietnam, Laos, and Cambodia. France, unlike Great Britain, professed to value native institutions and chose to rule through them. This policy produced a small native elite that admired French culture but was widely separated from popular movements.

From the late eighteenth century, French Catholic missionaries were active in Annam, where they enjoyed local support until 1820. When Emperor Tu Duc attempted to destroy Christianity, the Saigon Delta was occupied. In 1874, Annam (central Vietnam) was made a French protectorate and Cochin China (southern Vietnam) a full colony. Between 1884 and 1893, Tonkin (northern Vietnam), Cambodia, and Laos were occupied. British opposition to further westward expansion forced France to recognized the independence of Siam in 1896.

French colonial policy was based upon the theory of assimilation, suggesting full integration of colonies and mother country, including representation in the French assembly. Among the Southeast Asian possessions, however, only Cochin China was represented, for it alone was a colony (rather than a protectorate). Because cultural assimilation proved ineffective, by World War I (1914-1918), a policy of indirect rule had been adopted, utilizing native institutions and administrators whenever possible.

Seeking assimilation, the French vigorously suppressed nationalist movements. The most active of these, the VIET MINH in Vietnam (Cochin China, Annam, and Tonkin), gained strength during the period of Japanese occupation (1941-1945) and hoped to be rewarded with independence by the allies after the war. Instead, the French were reinstalled, leading to a bitter civil war (1946-1954). The Viet Minh's capture of the fortress of DIEN BIEN PHU (May, 1954) in northwestern Vietnam led to the Geneva Accords (July, 1954), which provided for French withdrawal and division of her former territories into North and South Vietnam, Cambodia, and Laos.

Fresno Rodo Domei Kai (also, Fresno Labor League): Socialist Japanese labor union formed in 1908. It lasted only two years but had a big impact on the lives of ISSEI laborers. At its height, the organization boasted two thousand members. It unified workers who suffered from wage cuts, wretched working conditions, and corrupt labor contractors. In this era, Issei workers were excluded from traditional organized labor unions in America. The league's main figure was Takeuchi Tetsugoro, a member of the Social Revolutionary Party.

Frick v. Webb (1923): U.S. Supreme Court ruling that upheld the constitutionality of California's ALIEN LAND LAW OF 1920. The case was sponsored by the JAPANESE ASSOCIATIONS, which wanted to challenge the legality of the law.

Under the act, aliens ineligible for American citizenship (such as the ISSEI) could not own shares of stock in California agricultural land companies unless expressly permitted to do so under the provisions of a treaty. Raymond Frick wanted to sell shares of stock in a land company to Nobutada Satow, an Issei. After the state attorney general's office informed Frick of the violation and threatened to confiscate the shares, Frick filed a court petition to enjoin the state from enforcing the law. He claimed that the statute violated not only his constitutional rights but also the U.S.-JAPAN TREATY OF COMMERCE AND NAVIGATION (1911).

The Supreme Court found otherwise. Although the treaty of 1911 allowed Japanese citizens to conduct trade in America, the Court concluded, it did not give them the right to own stock in land companies. Moreover, the Court ruled, the California Alien Land Law violated neither the treaty nor the Constitution.

Fu Manchu: Villainous fictitious Chinese character created by English adventure novelist Sax Rohmer in 1913 with the publication of *Dr. Fu Manchu*. The character was later featured in films and on television and radio. In the Fu Manchu series of stories, the title character is an inscrutable, evil genius bent on world domination. Rohmer also employed many negative stereotypes in portraying the other Asian male characters of his stories. Chinatown itself was depicted as mysterious, exotic, and criminal.

Stephen S. Fugita. (Charles Barry)

Fugita, Stephen S. (b. Apr. 6, 1943, Jerome, Ark.): Scholar. As director of the Ethnic Studies Program and associate professor of psychology at the University of Santa Clara, California, he has studied mental-health issues relating to the Asian American community, especially those relating to the World War II internment of Japanese Americans. He received his Ph.D. degree in psychology at the University of California, Riverside and was director of the Pacific/Asian Mental Health Research Center at the University of Illinois, Chicago from 1987 to 1990. He coauthored *The Japanese American Experience* (1991) and wrote *Japanese American Ethnicity: The Persistence of Community* (1991).

Fujian: Coastal province in southeastern China. Situated immediately north of the Tropic of Cancer and between two other seaboard provinces, Zhejiang to the north and GUANGDONG to the southwest, Fujian is hemmed in from the interior of China by the Wuyi Mountains and is bounded on the east by the China Sea and the Taiwan Strait. More than 90 percent of its total area (47,529 square miles) is mountainous. The population, about 32 million in 1993, is densest in the coastal plains and estuaries where the major cities, Fuzhou (the capital), Quanzhou, Zhangzhou, and Xiamen are located. The inhabitants speak four main Chinese dialects (three Min languages and HAKKA), but the province is so linguistically fragmented that virtually every prefecture or county has retained its own distinctive subdialect.

The fortunes of Fujian have been influenced by its ready access to the sea. Quanzhou was described by Marco Polo as one of the world's greatest ports of the late thirteenth century. Subsequently Fujian suffered from Ming Dynasty bans on overseas trade and from the Manchu takeover in the seventeenth century, when coastal portions of southern Fujian and TAIWAN, controlled by powerful Zheng-family merchant seafarers, resisted QING rule for nearly forty years. Coastal and overseas trade resumed after the Zheng surrender in 1683. Xiamen then emerged as Fujian's chief port, and Taiwan came under Fujian's jurisdiction until 1887. Following the end of the First OPIUM WAR in 1842, Fuzhou and Xiamen were selected as two of the first five treaty ports established in China.

Overseas emigration from Fujian began to follow the maritime routes established by southern Fujianese traders during the thirteenth and fourteenth centuries. Major Fujianese communities abroad flourished by the seventeenth century, most notably in Manila, Batavia, and Nagasaki. The overseas Fujianese population in the insular or "South Sea" (Nanyang) regions of Southeast Asia increased dramatically during the nineteenth century because of the exodus of Chinese laborers. The illicit COOLIE TRADE, carried on briefly in Xiamen from 1847 to 1853, also brought shiploads of Fujianese immigrants to Australia, Cuba, Peru, and the British West Indies, as well as to California and Hawaii. Nevertheless, the millions of overseas Chinese claiming Fujianese ancestry have remained concentrated in countries of Southeast Asia.

Despite modern innovations, Fujian stagnated during much of the twentieth century. Militarists ruled the province under the early Chinese Republic, and the Japanese occupied its coastal sections between 1938 and 1945. In 1949 Communist forces gained control of Fujian, but the Nationalist government, after its evacuation to Taiwan in that year, continued to hold strategic offshore islands, including Jinmen and Mazu. Fujian suffered from the war zone prevailing in the Taiwan Strait and from a lack of investment. After Xiamen was declared a special economic zone and Fuzhou's seaport area a development zone in the early 1980's, however, Fujian began to attract considerable investment, particularly from Taiwan by the end of the decade.

In the late 1980's and 1990's, Fujian—chiefly the area around Fuzhou—has been the primary source of illegal immigration from China to the United States. Highly organized rings of human smugglers carry on this trade, which received widespread attention in 1993, when a ship full of illegal immigrants, the

Golden Venture, ran aground near New York, and several other ships were apprehended at sea. Most of the illegal immigrants from Fuzhou enter the United States via Mexico; some settle in California, but the majority settle in New York's Chinatown, where a Fuzhounese community has sprung up.

Fujii Sei v. State of California (1952): Landmark California Supreme Court ruling that the state, by means of the ALIEN LAND LAW OF 1913, could not prevent aliens ineligible for U.S. citizenship from owning land. The court struck down the statute for violating the constitutional guarantee of equal protec-

An Issei woman displays photographs of her grandson and great grandson. California Issei were once prohibited under state law from attaining U.S. citizenship. (National Japanese American Historical Society)

tion under the law regardless of race or nationality.

Significantly, prior to this case the U.S. Supreme Court had issued several major opinions—COCKRILL V. PEOPLE OF STATE OF CALIFORNIA (1925), for example—upholding the constitutionality of the land laws. In OYAMA V. CALIFORNIA (1948), however, the Court ruled that the land laws could not violate the rights of U.S. citizens solely on the basis of race or nationality; there the laws were found to deprive a citizen of his constitutional rights.

In the wake of the *Oyama* decision, which declared the Alien Land Law to be unconstitutional, Fujii Sei, a Japanese alien ineligible for citizenship, purchased land in violation of the statute. Authorities then moved to confiscate the property and annul title. The state supreme court, however, overruled them and upheld Fujii's right as an ISSEI to hold title to land in California.

Fujinkai: Japanese women's association or club. Many were formed by ISSEI women, usually through churches. These associations had many roles in the community, such as teaching English skills and homemaking skills.

Fukoku kyohei: Japanese phrase meaning literally, "wealth combined with military strength." It became the political slogan "Enrich the nation and Strengthen the army," a motto popular during the Meiji Era after 1870.

Fukuda, Mitsuyoshi (b. 1917): Corporate officer. In 1966 he was named vice president of industrial relations for the Honolulu company Castle & Cooke, becoming the first-ever Japanese American vice president of a BIG FIVE corporation. He had been hired by the company in 1946. Before that he had served in the all-Nisei 100TH INFANTRY BATTALION, where he rose to the rank of infantry major—the highest level of any Nisei combat officer.

Fukunaga, Myles (d. Nov. 19, 1929, Honolulu, Territory of Hawaii): Convict. The son of plantation workers who fell into poverty, he was convicted of the 1928 kidnap/murder of Gill Jamieson, son of the vice president of the Hawaiian Trust Company, the family's primary creditor. The crime sparked a manhunt. During the trial the Japanese community rose to Fukunaga's defense to ensure a fair trial. Later the community protested what it believed was an unfair trial that resulted in a death sentence, even though a psychiatrist testified that the defendant was insane. Appeals were unsuccessful and Fukunaga was executed.

Fukuoka: Prefecture on KYUSHU, Japan's southernmost major island. Fukuoka was the place of origin of many Japanese who emigrated to the United States from the 1880's to 1924. It occupies an area of about 1,912 square miles and had a population of about 4,831,000 in 1991. Its major industries are agriculture in the south and coal mining in the north. The prefecture's capital, Fukuoka, is located on Hakata Bay and in ancient times was one of the three trading ports of Japan. This seaport city developed into a commercial and cultural center and is the seat of Kyushu University.

Fukuyama, Francis (b. Oct. 27, 1952, Chicago, Ill.): Scholar. Fukuyama's provocative article "The End of History?" drew international attention when it was first published in *The National Interest* in 1989.

The son of Yoshio Fukuyama, a Congregationalist minister and an educator, and Toshiko (Kawata) Fukuyama, Francis Fukuyama received a B.A. from Cornell University in 1974. Following graduate study at Yale University in 1974-1975, Fukuyama worked as a consultant for a Los Angeles-based company, Pan Heuristics, in 1978-1979. Since 1979 he has been with the RAND Corporation. He received a Ph.D. from Harvard University in 1981.

Fukuyama's thesis, developed at book length in *The End of History and the Last Man* (1992), is that following the collapse of communism in the Soviet Union, there are no significant global challengers to liberal democracy and capitalism. Thus history, defined as the evolving competition between political, social, and economic ideologies, has come to an end. While Fukuyama's conclusions have been vigorously debated, he has undeniably made an impact on policymaking in the post-Cold War world.

Fukuzawa Yukichi (1835—1901): Educator. His opinions on Japan's political future, expressed principally in his many writings, were greatly influential as the nation emerged from centuries of ironclad feudal reign into the modern period of Westernization. A prolific writer on many subjects, he also established schools, including Keio University—a prestigious private institution—and a Tokyo-based newspaper. Yet above all he became prominent for his efforts to instill in the Japanese a sense of the merits of Westernization. Through his enormously popular books, he urged his countrymen to consider these ideas, which, he contended, would only serve to make Japan a stronger world power. His writings also influenced many Japanese to immigrate to the United States.

Fun kung: Chinese term used to describe the share-cropping arrangement between Chinese laborers and Hawaiian landowners. Literally translated as "divide work," *fun kung* was a system by which Chinese workers were organized under the leadership of a manager of their own choosing. This manager was responsible for negotiating the terms of the group's employment: the percentage of profits to be paid to the laborers, the housing arrangements, and the working conditions. A prevailing employment system in the wake of Hawaii's annexation by the United States, *fun kung* was an early form of collective bargaining among Chinese workers whose negotiating stance was strengthened by the landowners' inability to recruit and transport new laborers directly from China under cheaper contract terms.

Furo (also, *o-furo*): Japanese-style bathing. In Japan, the bath consists of a deep square bathtub filled with very hot water, into which bathers immerse themselves by sitting or squatting. Strictly speaking, the clean hot water is meant for long, leisurely hours of soaking and relaxation. Bathers therefore soap and rinse their entire bodies thoroughly before actually stepping into the bath. The word *furo* means the wood or charcoal fire beneath the traditional bathtub by which the water was heated. The bathtub itself is known as the *yubune* (hot-water ship). In more modern times, bathtub water is heated typically by means of a gas range. Also, while older-style tubs were built of wood, modern tubs are made of artificial materials.

Public bathhouses (*sento*) have been at the center of Japanese culture since the time of the TOKUGAWA shogunate (1600-1867). While visiting these popular establishments, many hours would pass as patrons ate, drank, played games, and so forth. Nowadays, although bathhouses are fewer in number, bathing is still a prime social activity, as attested by the continuing popularity of Japan's hot spring resorts, which occupy many Japanese vacationers annually.

Bathing, moreover, has from the earliest times been endowed with religious significance, specifically with respect to SHINTO, the native religion of Japan. Shint holds that goodness is associated with cleanliness and evil with impurity.

G

Gaman: Japanese term translated literally as "endurance" or "patience." This word is used to describe the suppression of anger and emotion. For Japanese Americans it is employed primarily to connote the endurance of Japanese in America in the face of racism, violence, and discrimination.

Ganbatte: Japanese term meaning "stick to it." It was employed by Japanese Americans to connote their struggle for social, political, and economic advancement in the United States. *Ganbatte* (1983) is also the title of Karl Yoneda's autobiography about his life as a Kibei worker and member of the Communist Party.

Gandhi, Mahatma (Mohandas Karamchand Gandhi; Oct. 2, 1869, Porbandar, Gujarat, India—Jan. 30, 1948, Delhi, Republic of India): Nationalist and spiritual leader. Considered the father of independent India, Gandhi led the Indian National Congress from 1919 to independence in 1947 and challenged the then all-powerful British Empire. Also known as the *Mahatma* (great soul), as his followers called him, Gandhi was a major twentieth century social and political thinker. His advocacy and practice of peaceful and nonviolent struggle against the British rule, his effort to involve the masses in the struggle for India's independence, his commitment to greater social justice, his effort to bring about greater understanding between Hindus and Muslims, and his crusade to uplift the condition of millions of untouchables in India made Gandhi an exemplary and inspiring figure within and outside India.

Around the world, people have responded to Gandhi's example and adopted his method of political protest without violence; Martin Luther King, Jr., Lech Walesa, and the European peace movement are only a few examples. In 1983, Richard Attenborough made the epic motion picture *Gandhi*, which depicted the career of this world-historical figure who began in South Africa as an assimilationist and ended in India as a nationalist.

Early Life. Born into a middle-class Hindu family, Gandhi attended school in his native Porbandar and later in Rajkot, a small princely state, where his father had become a *dewan* or prime minister. Mohandas was the youngest child of his father's fourth wife and was more attached to his mother, a devout adherent to Jainism, than to his father. Young Gandhi was deeply influenced by his mother's saintliness and her deep moral and religious nature, both of which affected his thinking and shaped his political style.

Gandhi's school records indicate that he was a mediocre student. While his marriage with Kasturbai, arranged by his family at age thirteen, interrupted his studies for one year, Gandhi attended the University of Bombay and Samaldas College in Bhavnagar before going to London, at age eighteen, to study law at the Inner Temple. During his three years' stay in London, Gandhi came in contact, mainly through the London Vegetarian Society that he had joined, with a variety of people representing different religions and ideology. In London, he was also introduced to the Bible and read Bhagavadgita for the first time, which later became his "spiritual dictionary" and "infallible guide of conduct."

After returning to India in 1891, Gandhi tried, without any success, to practice law in a Bombay court. Thereafter, he took to drafting petitions for litigants at Rajkot until he left for South Africa in 1893 to work as a lawyer for an Indian firm; there, he had a successful law practice for twenty years. The racial discrimination that Gandhi experienced in South Africa, including being thrown out of the first-class railway compartment while traveling from Durban to Pretoria—which he later described as one of the most creative experiences of his life—transformed the introverted and shy Gandhi into an activist and a civil rights leader fighting racism and discrimination against Indians in South Africa.

Gandhi founded the weekly newspaper *Indian Opinion* in South Africa in 1904 and established two *ashrams* or religious retreats for community living, Phoenix Farm and Tolstoy Farm. He also led the Indian community, composed mostly of indentured labor, in their fight against the discriminatory race legislation of 1906. His effort resulted in the signing of the Smuts-Gandhi agreement—the "Magna Charta" of South African Indians—in 1914.

Leader of the Nationalist Movement. When Gandhi returned to India in January, 1915, he was already known to Indian leaders for his novel techniques of political struggle in South Africa. In the beginning, Gandhi established an *ashram* in Sabarmati, near Ahmadabad, and traveled, upon the advice of his mentor

Mahatma Gandhi. (AP/Wide World Photos)

G. K. Gokhale, all over India to familiarize himself with India and its problems. Gandhi started his first public campaign in 1917 on behalf of the indigo workers of Champaran in Bihar. In 1919, he launched a nationwide *hartal* (closing of businesses) against the Rowlatt Bills, which began his twenty-eight years of struggle against the British rule in India. The Amritsar massacre of April, 1919, at Jallianwalla Bagh, in which British troops opened fire on an unarmed crowd of Indians killing 379 and injuring more than twelve hundred, brought Gandhi to the forefront of the nationalist movement in India. In the aftermath of the Amritsar massacre, Gandhi emerged as the undisputed leader of the Indian National Congress.

Under the leadership of Gandhi, the congress became a truly national instrument; he transformed the hitherto urban middle-class coterie into a movement of Indians of all classes. Gandhi identified with the poor masses by leading the life of a saint and using religious language and symbols. Thus he could reach millions of poor peasants and mobilize them in a manner other congress leaders could not. Under Gandhi's charismatic leadership, the independence movement in India resembled a pilgrimage.

Gandhi led three major campaigns between 1920 and 1947: The noncooperation movement, which was started in 1920 but was canceled in 1922 because of incidents of violence and which was Gandhi's response to the Amritsar massacre; the civil disobedience campaign (1930-1934), in which he first launched a Salt March against the tax on salt in 1930 and then attended the disappointing Second Round Table Conference (1930) in London; and the "Quit India" movement of August, 1942, which demanded that Great Britain should immediately hand over power to Indians or confront mass civil disobedience. During these campaigns, Gandhi and other nationalist leaders were arrested and sent to jail several times.

Toward Independence and After. Gandhi wanted a united independent India and opposed the idea of partition of the country along religious lines. He worked tirelessly toward bringing a Hindu-Muslim accord by meeting with M. A. Jinnah and other Muslim leaders, appealing to congress leaders to arrive at a compromise, and observing a fast. He failed in his effort, however, mainly because of the stubbornness of the Muslim League; India was partitioned into two sovereign states (India and Pakistan) on August 15, 1947.

Gandhi did not hold any public office in independent India. When communal violence broke out in different parts of India, Gandhi worked toward healing the scars of communal conflict. It is ironic that he was shot and killed by Nathuram Godse, a Hindu fanatic, in Delhi on January 30, 1948. His death was mourned as a personal loss by millions around the world.

Gandhi's importance lies as much in his leadership of the nationalist movement as in leading a social revolution that empowered the poorest people in India. Gandhi's legacy continued in the form of the constitutional ban on the practice of untouchability and affirmative action policies for the lower castes and tribes in independent India. Gandhi and his ideas continue to inspire people within and outside India.—*Sunil K. Sahu*

SUGGESTED READINGS: • Brown, Judith M. *Gandhi: Prisoner of Hope.* New Haven, Conn.: Yale University Press, 1989. • Chatterjee, Margaret. *Gandhi's Religious Thought.* Notre Dame, Ind.: University of Notre Dame Press, 1983. • Copley, Anthony. *Gandhi: Against the Tide.* New York: Basil Blackwell, 1987. • Fischer, Louis. *The Life of Mahatma Gandhi.* New York: Harper & Row, 1983. • Gandhi, Mahatma. *An Autobiography: The Story of Experiments with Truth.* Translated by Mahadev Desai. Harmondsworth, Middlesex, England: Penguin Books, 1982. • *The Essential Gandhi: An Anthology of His Writings on His Life, Work, and Ideas.* Edited by Louis Fischer. New York: Vintage Books, 1962. • Rothermund, Dietmar. *Mahatma Gandhi: An Essay in Political Biography.* New Delhi: Manohar, 1991. • Rudolph, Susanne Hoeber, and Lloyd I. Rudolph. *Gandhi: The Traditional Roots of Charisma.* Chicago: University of Chicago Press, 1983.

Gannen-mono: Japanese phrase translated as "people of the first year." The *Gannen-mono* got their name from the fact that they came to Hawaii in 1868, the first year of the Meiji period in Japanese history. Although the *Gannen-mono* were the first group of Japanese laborers recruited to work in Hawaii, they are not celebrated as the beginning of Japanese immigration because they left Japan without proper government approval. That distinction belongs to the KANYAKU IMIN (contract laborers), who did leave lawfully.

The *Gannen-mono* left Japan without approval because the recruiter, Eugene Van Reed, an American merchant serving as Hawaii's consul, got caught in the uncertainties of the last days of the Tokugawa shogunate and the beginning of the Meiji government. For about 250 years, until 1866, the Tokugawa shogunate did not allow any Japanese to emigrate. Foreign pressure changed that policy, and Van Reed was able to receive approval from the shogunate to take a group of

Japanese to Hawaii. Unfortunately for him, however, the Meiji government came into control before the group left and refused to honor the shogunate's decision. In defiance Van Reed ordered the ship carrying the recruits to sail without permission.

Of the almost 150 recruits, a mix of children and adults, few were farmers. The rest represented assorted occupations. Unaccustomed to working long hours under the scorching sun, and feeling that they were mistreated, the immigrants found life in Hawaii difficult. They registered their complaints with the Hawaii Board of Immigration, and in December 1896, the Japanese government sent investigators to look into the situation. The employers, needing workers, promised better working conditions and allowed those who wished to return to Japan to do so. Forty did.

For seventeen years no more laborers were sent to Hawaii because of a climate of distrust. The Meiji government did not want Japan to be viewed as another China, a supplier of cheap labor to be mistreated in foreign lands. When Japan eventually did decide to send immigrants to Hawaii once again, the Japanese government was better prepared to handle immigration and the recruits were more carefully selected.

Gardena: Suburban city in southern Los Angeles County, notable for its large concentration of Japanese Americans. Settled in the 1880's, the area attracted many Issei growers and nurseries and other small businesses. Incorporated in 1930 and comprising the communities of Gardena, Moneta, and Strawberry Park, the city of Gardena would grow to become one of the most substantial Japanese communities in the United States.

Japanese Americans began moving to the Gardena area around the beginning of the twentieth century. Issei farmers found that conditions there were particularly favorable to the cultivation of strawberries. They began to plant strawberry fields, opened nurseries, and engaged in truck farming. In the aftermath of the San Francisco earthquake and fire of 1906, many more Japanese Americans chose to resettle in Southern California. Eventually, a Japanese American community was established in Gardena, with a town meeting hall, a Japanese-language school, and various cultural and professional associations. The number of small businesses, too, began to grow. By 1907 the city was home to more than 250 Japanese Americans.

In the following decades, while the number of Japanese Americans in Gardena remained relatively small, the community was solidly established. In 1940 there were more than twenty Japanese American nurseries in

CALIFORNIA

Gardena. The forced evacuation of Japanese Americans during World War II broke the continuity of the Japanese American community in Gardena. Beginning in the 1950's, however, the community enjoyed a resurgence. As Gardena was transformed into a suburban residential city, it began to attract large numbers of Nisei as well as immigrants fresh from Japan. The Japanese American population in Gardena increased from 741 in 1950 to 4,372 in 1960 to 8,412 in 1970. In 1970, when Japanese Americans made up only a little more than one-quarter of 1 percent of the total U.S. population, 20 percent of Gardena's residents were Japanese Americans—the highest percentage for any city in the United States, excluding Hawaii. In 1978 the number of Japanese Americans in Gardena exceeded 9,100, about 21 percent of the city's population. Between 1980 and 1990, however, the Japanese American population declined slightly, from 9,489 to 9,217. Among California cities with the highest concentration of Asian Americans in 1991, Gardena ranked ninth.

Gardeners Associations: Japanese immigrant community organizations formed by Issei gardeners to promote economic empowerment during the Great Depression. The first was organized in 1932 to fight racist and nativist employment practices. In 1937 three smaller Japanese American groups formed the Southern California Gardeners Federation, representing a third of all Japanese American gardeners in Southern California. Associations varying in size continue to serve an array of functions from social to political and economic.

Gay and lesbian issues: Asian Pacific lesbians and gay men are emerging as visible members of the Asian Pacific communities. Homosexuality, considered a taboo, unspoken topic within Asian Pacific communities has gained attention given the disclosure of many Asian Pacific lesbians and gay men in addition to the progress of the lesbian and gay rights movement. Asian Pacific lesbians and gay men have been actively working and gaining acceptance in Asian Pacific communities through writing, participating in sensitivity panels, speaking in classrooms, working in various causes, and educating others about homophobia (the irrational fear of someone who loves and is attracted to another person of the same sex).

Lesbian and gay issues have surfaced in the Asian Pacific ethnic press, in political, social, and cultural organizations, and in conferences as a subject that demands attention and warrants discussion. Workshops, panels, and articles delineating the experiences and concerns of Asian Pacific lesbians and gay men continue to appear on a regular basis in conferences and newspapers. Some of these concerns include the denial of the existence of homosexuality within Asian Pacific communities; the lack of representation and racism in mainstream lesbian and gay organizations; identity politics; family dynamics; ethnic and cultural diversity; immigration issues; and internalized self-hate. Acquired immune deficiency syndrome (AIDS) is also a major concern for gay and lesbian as well as heterosexual Asians and Pacific Islanders.

Because Asian Pacific lesbians and gay men could not find support and resources in Asian Pacific and gay and lesbian organizations, they created groups to affirm their existence. Asian Lesbians of the East Coast (New York); Asian Pacific Lesbians and Gays (Los Angeles); Asian Pacific Lesbians and Friends (Los Angeles); Asian Pacifica Sisters (San Francisco); Gay Asian Pacific Alliance (San Francisco); and Gay Asian Pacific Support Network (Los Angeles) formed in the 1980's when the climate was conducive to "come out" and a critical mass of interested people was available ("coming out" refers to the disclosure of one's lesbian or gay sexual identity). New groups formed in the late 1980's and early 1990's such as Alliance of Massachusetts Asian Lesbians and Gay Men (Boston); Trikone (San Francisco); South Asian Lesbians and Gays Association (New York); and Gay Asian Pacific Islander Men of New York. These organizations have made a significant impact on the broadening of the Asian Pa-

Asian gay males—the T-shirt reads "Queer 'n Asian." (Bob E. Myers)

cific experience in the United States by recognizing the activities and contributions of lesbian and gay members of Asian Pacific communities.

Writers helped increased the visibility of Asian Pacific lesbian and gay lives, experiences, and histories. Willyce Kim, Canyon Sam, Kitty Tsui, Chea Villanueva, and Merle Woo, among others, helped pave the way for other Asian Pacific lesbian writers to emerge within an evolving body of literature. Arvind Kumar, Han Ong, Vince Sales, Joel B. Tan, and Henry Tran have published in journals and newsletters. Two published anthologies that chronicle experiences of Asian Pacific lesbians and gay men include *Between the Lines: An Anthology of Pacific Asian Lesbians* (1987) and *A Lotus of Another Color: An Unfolding of the South Asian Gay and Lesbian Experience* (1993). A lesbian of color anthology, *Piece of My Heart* (1993), includes Asian Pacific lesbian writers from the United States and Canada. Two journals that dedicate entire issues on Asian Pacific lesbian and gay literature and critical writings are the *Asian/Pacific American Journal* (1, no. 2, Spring/Summer, 1993) and *Amerasia Journal* (Spring, 1994). Newsletters such as *Phoenix Rising* (Asian Pacifica Sisters), *Lavender Godzilla* (Gay Asian Pacific Alliance), and *Trikone* also serve as important resource guides. These written materials and organizations help educate, validate, and inform Asian Pacific lesbians and gay men as well as greater Asian Pacific communities.

Geary Act of 1892: Stringent law aimed at limiting Chinese immigration to the United States. The American violation of the BURLINGAME TREATY (1868), which recognized reciprocal privileges for Chinese and American citizens, and the failure to protect and provide for Chinese immigrants on American soil strained China-U.S. relations to the breaking point, and the extravagant hopes for rapid expansion of trade with China faded.

Democrat Thomas Geary of California had already driven the Chinese out of Sonoma County. He proposed the Geary Act to drive them out of the United States. The act extended all bills in force (including the CHINESE EXCLUSION ACT OF 1882) for another ten years. It required all Chinese to obtain a certificate of eligibility with a photograph within the year. If arrested without such a certificate, the burden of proof fell upon the person in question. These certification procedures were similar to those required of free black persons and itinerant slaves in the antebellum South and those stipulations once in force in czarist Russia

In the United States, anti-Chinese hysteria was fueled by, among other things, the fear that immigrant Chinese were taking over the economy, putting whites out of business and out of jobs. (Asian American Studies Library, University of California at Berkeley)

and later in South Africa's system of apartheid. The act also denied bail to the Chinese in *habeas corpus* proceedings. It prescribed a prison term of one year for all violators, followed by deportation upon completion of the term of confinement.

Such an act, in violation of the Burlingame Treaty of 1868, outraged political spokespersons for the local Chinese community and evoked a severe reaction from the Chinese government. Seeing it as unconstitutional and unjust, the Chinese were advised not to register. Eighty-five thousand of the 106,688 Chinese in the United States refused to register, and wholesale deportation seemed imminent. Meanwhile, twenty-three appeals urged the fifty-second Congress to repeal the Exclusion Act and fifty more to repeal the Geary bill.

Chief Justice Stephen Johnson Field acknowledged the Geary Act to be in violation of the Burlingame Treaty. Nevertheless, he declared it "constitutional" on the grounds of public interest and necessity. The

Genthe photograph, "The New Toy," San Francisco Chinatown, 1904. The man standing in the center is demonstrating a noise-making papier-mache animal figure. (Library of Congress)

McCreary Amendment of 1893 extended for six months the one-year grace period for registration. It averted an impasse for the time but did little to ameliorate the rigors of the Geary Act itself.

General Sherman: American trading ship. In 1866, in an effort by the U.S. government to establish contact with Korea, the ship sailed up the Taedong River to Pyongyang, but it was set on fire and its entire crew massacred by a Korean mob. Western vessels during this period were regarded by the ruling Korean dynasty as a menace to its security. The burning of the ship marked the failure of the United States to end Korea's policy of seclusion from the West.

Genthe, Arnold (Jan. 8, 1869, Berlin, Germany— Aug. 8, 1942, New York, N.Y.): Photographer. Genthe received his doctorate from the University of Jena. He arrived in New York in 1895 and traveled on to San Francisco as tutor to the son of a baron. After completing his duties as a tutor Genthe turned his professional attention to photography. He established himself as a society photographer and developed a school of portraiture that came to be known as the "Genthe" style.

During his lifetime, Genthe shot numerous pictures of San Francisco's Old Chinatown district. In his autobiography, *As I Remember*, published in 1936, Genthe states that he quickly became fascinated by Chinatown and its people. He began venturing into what he romantically referred to as the "Canton of the West." His first Chinatown photographs so pleased him that he ventured back frequently over the next few years to capture a variety of subjects. His first volume of Chinatown photographs, *Pictures of Old Chinatown*, with text by Will Irwin, was published in 1908. A second collection, *Old Chinatown*, came out in 1913. Overall 200 of Genthe's Chinatown photographs are known to have survived, and 130 are reproduced in John Tchen's *Genthe's Photographs of San Francisco's Old Chinatown*, published in 1984.

Unlike those who used photography as social commentary, Genthe used the camera as a means of artistic expression. By his own admission he was a mediocre painter, and for him photography represented "a new and exciting medium—one by which [he] could interpret life after [his] own manner in terms of light and shade."

Genthe's photos capture rich details of early twentieth century Chinese life: There are photographs of grocery stores, street vendors, and cobblers as well as men, women, and children going about their daily routines. At the same time, however, many of his photographs were clearly meant to cater to the expectations of white Americans. Photographs of "The Opium Fiend," "Doorways and Dim Shadows," "The Peking Two Knife Man," along with selective photos of subjects in Chinese New Year finery all tended to perpetuate the notion of an exotic community immediately within the United States.

Gentlemen's Agreement (1907-1908): Executive agreement defusing tension between the United States and Japan over widescale Japanese immigration to California.

By the first decade of the twentieth century, a substantial anti-Japanese movement had developed in California and the West. The California legislature, dominated by anti-Japanese sentiment, was calling for exclusion of Japanese immigrants and other discriminatory measures. This was a matter of concern to President Theodore Roosevelt, who wished to maintain good relations with Japan.

A local decision fulfilled Roosevelt's fears. In October, 1906, the San Francisco Board of Education

Japanese Entering and Leaving the U.S. Under the Gentlemen's Agreement, 1909-1924

Total Japanese entering the U.S.:118,000

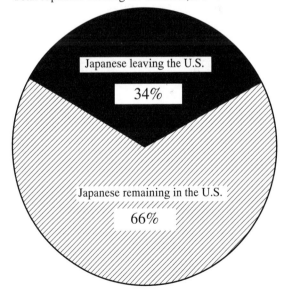

Japanese leaving the U.S.

34%

Japanese remaining in the U.S.

66%

Source: Bill Hosokawa. *Nisei: The Quiet Americans.* New York: William Morrow, 1969.

passed an order segregating Japanese students, requiring them to attend the school where Chinese students were already segregated. (See SAN FRANCISCO SCHOOL BOARD CRISIS.) This decision, which compounded racism with ignorance in its lumping together of Chinese and Japanese students, provoked a strong reaction in Japan.

Roosevelt, seeking to resolve not only this particular incident but also the larger threat to U.S.-Japan relations, invited the California congressional delegation to the White House, where his personal powers of persuasion helped resolve the crisis. At Roosevelt's urging, the delegation summoned the leaders of both houses of the California legislature and key San Fran-

Japanese-owned general store in the Lodi area of the Sacramento Valley, circa 1910. The racial climate in California at the time of the Gentlemen's Agreement was heavily anti-Japanese. (City of Sacramento Archives)

cisco school officials to Washington. In the compromise worked out by Roosevelt, the school board agreed not to segregate suitably aged Japanese students (overage students, one of the original sources of complaint, were not covered by the agreement) and the California legislature agreed not to go forward with proposed anti-Japanese legislation. In return, Roosevelt promised to secure assurance from the Japanese government that immigration from Japan would be significantly reduced.

The outcome was the Gentlemen's Agreement: a series of six diplomatic notes between the United States and Japan in 1907 and 1908. The Japanese government agreed to issue no more passports to laborers coming directly to the mainland of the United States. (The possibility of Japanese laborers entering indirectly—via Mexico, for example—was treated separately. See IMMIGRATION ACT OF 1907.) The agreement permitted passports to be issued to "parents, wives, and children of laborers already resident" in the United States. As a result, the ratio of men to women in the growing Japanese American community was much more balanced than it was in the Chinese American community during the same period.

Geomancy. *See* **Feng shui**

German-Hindu Conspiracy: The so-called "German-Hindu Conspiracy" centered on the involvement of the German government in support of Indian nationalists in World War I (1914 to 1918) as part of the global strategy to destabilize Germany's enemy, Great Britain. At the time, it was common to refer to all Indians, no matter what their regional or religious affiliation, as "Hindus," or more quaintly "Hindoos."

The Indian independence movement was well-suited to German aims. It offered Germany the opportunity to tap into a highly politicized and organized expatriate/immigrant community in Europe and the United States which had its own lines of communication. The Ghadr Party, for example, had been formed in Berkeley as early as October, 1913, and other organizations predated that by six years.

The "Hindoo" operations, as well as parallel ones with Irish nationalists, such as Roger Casement, or the *Sinn Fein*, were planned and directed from the German foreign office in Berlin by two men, Otto Guenther von Wessendonck and Max von Oppenheim. The scope of these activities was global: Europe, North America, South Asia, the Pacific, Japan, and China. Virtually from the onset of the war in August 1914,

Germany used its embassies and consulates in the United States and Mexico as bases of operation for supply of money and weapons to Indian nationalists. In the United States, German money paid for Indian nationalists to travel and organize in many states (especially on the West Coast) and to travel abroad (to the Netherlands, Germany, Switzerland, Cuba, the Canal Zone, Chile, the Dutch East Indies, the Philippines, and Hawaii, to name a few locations where the peripatetic Indian Nationalists showed up); to publish materials in a variety of Indian languages promoting Indian identity and armed resistance to the British; and to ship men and weapons back to Asia. In addition to this financial and material support, directly involved were intelligence operatives of the German army (such as Franz von Papen, Wilhelm von Brincken, and Hans Tauscher) and navy (Karl Boy-Ed, Frederik Jebsen, and Admiral Paul Hintze, among others). Some of these intrigues made their way into literature through the writings of British ex-secret agents such as A. E. W. Mason and W. Somerset Maugham (*Ashenden: Or, The British Agent* [1928]).

Overall, the targets were India and Indian troops abroad, such as those based in Singapore; however, there were a few covert operations directed toward Canada that had an Indian component. Direct German operations in the then-neutral United States, such as the sabotage of munitions facilities at Black Tom in New Jersey, were restricted to German diplomatic and military personnel and conducted independently of the Indian nationalists.

In response, the American government activity related to German/Indian matters became so intense that it spurred on the expansion of American intelligence agencies. The Office of Naval Intelligence (ONI) branch office in San Francisco became apparently so obsessed with the Indians to the exclusion of other topics that local naval commanders complained. The army created a special branch devoted to "Hindoo Agitators," M.I. 4b-23. As young men, Walter Lippmann, George Marshall, the Dulles brothers, and J. Edgar Hoover all were involved in the investigation and pursuit of the German-Indian intrigues.

Immediately after the United States entered the war on April 6, 1917 (after three years of neutrality), there were arrests of Germans and Indians that led to the several "German-Hindu conspiracy" trials in the federal courts. These were in New York, Chicago and, the most famous, San Francisco, where there were ninety-seven defendants.

In Courtroom One of the federal courthouse at 7th

498 — Getting Together

and Mission Streets, the San Francisco German-Hindu Conspiracy trial started on November 20, 1917 and ended in April, 1918. While the trial explored many side plots and personalities in colorful detail, it focused on the efforts in 1915 to smuggle weapons and men from California to Bengal on the American ships *Annie Larsen* and *Maverick*. This was presented as a violation of the Neutrality Act. The intent of the American prosecutors (with the direct assistance of British intelligence agents) was to demonstrate to the American public the vast scale and ostensibly perfidious nature of the German threat.

With a daily ritual that included some of the defendants arriving by boat from detention cells on Angel Island, Alcatraz Island, the Presidio, and other jails, the trial was highly dramatic. Some witnesses for the government were sequestered in Sonoma County to the north of the city for their protection. Armed soldiers bracketed a courtroom filled with Indians and German diplomatic staff in formal attire. Each day's events were reported in detail in all the newspapers. At noon on April 23, 1918 near the end of the trial, Ram Chandra, the leader of the Ghadr party, was assassinated by another Indian, Ram Singh, who, in turn was shot down and killed by federal marshal James Holohan (later a warden of San Quentin state prison and known as father of the electric chair). The verdicts were delivered at midnight. Sentencing was made on April 30.

As a result of the trials and subsequent convictions, the most active nationalist members still at large departed to continue their activities abroad, especially in Japan and Germany. (One exception was Lala Lajpat RAI who continued his activities in the United States for a few years with his India Home Rule League.)

As exotic as these adventures may now sound, the various plots and subplots must be viewed in their wider context, one of a set of many gambits by a major imperial power to destabilize another. Imperial Germany hardly cared about the independence of India.

The possible fruits of these efforts were twofold. The first was to destabilize India, which, while it was a significant supplier of economic resources for the British Empire, could also be a terrible drain on the military resources of that empire if Britain were confronting an armed nationalist revolutionary struggle while conducting a war around the world. Vital troops would have to be diverted from other fronts in Europe, Africa, and the Middle East. Secondly, if substantial numbers of Indian troops serving with the British forces could be suborned, that would be a critical blow to Britain's fighting capacity. Indian troops under British officers

were among the first in the European front lines of 1914. They garrisoned and fought in Africa, the Middle East, and China. In a similar manner, German support of Irish nationalists led to the Easter Uprising in Dublin and also to efforts to suborn Irish troops in the British Army. Better to tie down troops on the streets of Belfast than to have them fighting in France. A very successful German maneuver in this context was the delivery back into Russia of Vladmir Lenin, who repaid his debts to the Germans by taking Russia out of the war and giving territorial concessions to Germany.

One legacy of the German-Indian interlude in World War I was that in World War II, both Germany and Japan would again play the nationalist card. Once more Germany supported Irish and Indian nationalists, most notably Subas Chandra Bose, otherwise known as the leader, "Netaji." Bose was installed in Germany by Joachim von Ribbentrop, the German secretary of state, with his own Indian ministers, radio service, uniforms, even postage stamps and money. Indian prisoners of war were recruited into an Indian unit in the German army (the 950th Regiment, otherwise known as the *Freis Indien* Regiment). The Japanese in 1943, in turn, would do the same. When Bose moved from Germany to Japan by submarine, the Japanese rewarded him with the creation of another Indian government in exile based in Singapore. Once again it would have its own military arm, the Indian Nationalist Army (INA). Bose and his armed forces not only fought the British, but at one point briefly entered India under their own flag. Today, he is enshrined as a legendary hero of the independence movement.—*Elliot Einzig Porter*

SUGGESTED READINGS: • Dignan, Don K. "The Hindu Conspiracy in Anglo-American Relations During World War I." *Pacific Historical Review* 40, no. 1 (1971): 57-76. • Dignan, Don K. *The Indian Revolutionary Problem in British Diplomacy, 1914-1919.* New Delhi, India: Allied Publishers, 1983. • Jensen, Joan. "The 'Hindu Conspiracy': A Reassessment." *Pacific Historical Review* 48, no. 1 (1979): 65-83. • Raucher, Alan. "American Anti-Imperialists and the Pro-India Movement, 1900-1932." *Pacific Historical Review* 43, no. 1 (1974): 83-110.

Getting Together: Bilingual newspaper. The first issue of *Getting Together* appeared in New York City's Chinatown in February, 1970. Issued in English and Chinese, it was published by members of I WOR KUEN (IWK), an Asian American Maoist collective, and functioned as the party's official political organ. In

1971, the newspaper's editorial staff moved to San Francisco. Its peak national circulation numbered four thousand.

IWK used *Getting Together* as a vehicle to educate and organize in the Chinese American community and in the larger Asian American community. With *Getting Together*, IWK members wanted to offer an alternative news source that would challenge what they believed was a news monopoly held by outlets dominated by the GUOMINDANG (GMD) and other traditional forces in Chinatown. News sources used by the newspaper's editorial staff included the New China News Agency, Afro-Asian Journalist, Pacific News Service, and Liberation News. Members and friends of IWK reported and wrote the local news, mainly from San Francisco and New York. In subsequent years, local coverage branched out to Boston, Hawaii, Los Angeles, and Oakland.

Articles in *Getting Together* reflected the views of IWK on international, national, cultural, and regional issues. Coverage included the role of women in socialist Vietnam, the high tuberculosis rate in New York's Chinatown, garment factory conditions, youth and gang issues, martial law in the Philippines, and an interview with China's premier Zhou Enlai. Each issue dedicated significant pages to developments in the People's Republic of China.

Getting Together's coverage of China represented a significant development for the Chinese American community. During the eight years when the newspaper was being published, the American government did not recognize the People's Republic of China and instead maintained that the Taiwan government established by Chiang Kai-shek and GMD was the legitimate government of the Chinese.

The American government's nonrecognition policy toward China resulted in a virtual news blackout of developments in China and of the lives of its billion people. For a large portion of Chinese Americans who saw China as their ancestral homeland, the news blackout created a vacuum that *Getting Together* fulfilled.

Ghadr movement: Urdu word meaning "revolt," "mutiny," or "revolution." Within a few years after their arrival on the Pacific coasts of the United States and Canada, immigrants from the Indian subcontinent began organizing themselves around the issue of independence for their homeland, which was then under British rule. In 1913 they formed the Ghadr Party. It became the West Coast's central organization coordi-

nating nationalist activities among Asian Indian immigrants for the next three decades. With its headquarters in San Francisco, the party published a weekly newspaper and developed international strategies to overthrow British rule in India. Although there were other Asian Indian nationalist organizations in North America during the early part of the twentieth century, Ghadr Party was the most far-reaching and well known of these groups. Asian Indian nationalist activities and aspirations in North America became known as the Ghadr movement.

Background. Political activists were among the earliest immigrants to North America from the Indian subcontinent. While the majority of Indian immigrants at the beginning of the twentieth century came from the Punjab province in search of economic opportunity, political dissidents came from various parts of the subcontinent seeking a safe haven to conduct their nationalist activities. Activists and immigrants joined Asian Indian students enrolled in local universities to establish a succession of community organizations and periodicals concerned with immigration rights, economic and social welfare issues, and Indian independence.

In 1913 one of these organizations, the Hindustani Association, held a series of meetings on the Pacific coast, wherever there were numbers of Asian Indians. At these gatherings, the popular activist Har DAYAL urged his fellow Asian Indians to focus their attention and resources on political objectives. These meetings led to the formation of the Ghadr Party by the middle of 1913. The group soon established headquarters in San Francisco, where it installed a printing press. On November 1, 1913, it published the first issue of the weekly newspaper *Gadar*. By the year's end they were regularly printing the weekly in two South Asian languages, Urdu and Punjabi.

The varied constituents of the Ghadr Party devoted themselves to a militant nationalist agenda. Although the political activists, immigrants, and students did not always agree on organizational structure and strategies, their common grievances against the British colonials held the diverse group together with some cohesion for at least the first three years. Another binding force was the hostile reception Asian Indians experienced in the Untied States and Canada. The Asiatic Exclusion League and other anti-immigrant organizations had instigated riots against Asian Indian and other Asian workers in areas such as Vancouver, British Columbia; Bellingham, Washington; and Live Oak, California, during 1907 and 1908. Additionally, both the United States and Canada began imposing exclusionary measures on Indian immigration by the end of the decade. The British Indian government protested both the hostilities and restrictions directed toward Asian Indians in North America but did little else. The colonial government's apparent unwillingness to negotiate aggressively on behalf of its citizens deepened the immigrants' nationalist convictions and sense of unity.

Individuals. Among the founding members of the party were Har DAYAL, who became the general secretary and editor of the *Gadar*; Sohan Singh Bhakna, a lumber-mill worker who served as the organization's first president; and Gobind Bihari Lal and Kartar Singh Sarabha, who were students attending the University of California, Berkeley. Community leaders such as Jawala Singh, a farmer from California's San Joaquin Valley, and lumber merchant Kanshi Ram from Portland, Oregon, provided material support. Political activists such as Tarak Nath Das, Pandurang Sadashiv Khankhoje, Maulvi Barkat Ullah, and Bhagwan Singh functioned as strategists and spokespersons for the organization. In 1914 Ram Chandra, another political exile, succeeded Har Dayal as editor of the weekly paper, which was renamed the *Hindustan Gadar*.

Objectives. The organization's objectives were fourfold. First, the group aimed to build a large membership among expatriate Asian Indians around the world. Branches of the party were established in immigrant enclaves in North, Central, and South America, as well as in East and Southeast Asia. Second, the group appealed to British Indian troops in India and stationed abroad to rebel against their officers and use their military skills to help their nation gain independence. Third, the party forged connections with other nationalist organziations abroad such as the Berlin India Committee. In 1916 members of both gorups, with monetary assistance from Germany, which was then at war with Britain, attempted to smuggle arms into India. Fourth, the Ghadr leadership sought to gain support and recognition from the U.S. government and the international community for the Indian demand for independence.

The Attempted Revolution of 1915. During the summer of 1914, Ghadr strategists announced through their weekly newspaper and at their meetings that the time was near to launch an armed revolt against the British in India. Two events precipitated the call for volunteers to begin returning to India. The first was the onset of World War I, which quickly involved Great Britain. Ghadr leaders had been waiting for the time when Britain's attention and resources were being diverted elsewhere. The second event occurred in Vancouver Harbor, where the ship *Komagata Maru* had arrived to challenge Canadian immigration law. (See *KOMAGATA MARU* INCIDENT.) The Asian Indian community in North America closely watched the standoff between the mainly Punjabi passengers of the ship and the Canadian government. The passengers attempts to gain entry into Canada failed. When the ship was forced to leave the harbor on July 23, 1914, Ghadr leaders appealed to the angered immigrant community to commit itself more fully to the revolution, which would restore independence and dignity to their homeland. Within weeks Ghadr supporters began leaving for India.

By the end of 1914, hundreds of volunteers began arriving at Indian ports. They were to proceed to Punjab and spread their revolutionary message throughout towns and villages and among army troops. In the meantime, Ghadr leaders would work with local activists in India to instigate and support a revolt by Indian troops against the British. Plans were immediatley undermined, however, by the government's elaborate intelligence network, which had used British agents and Indian informers to follow nationalist activities in North America and India. Many of the returned immigrants were arrested as soon as they reached Indian ports, while others who had made their way to Punjab were soon tracked down. With the help of their informers, the government easily diffused the planned revolt.

In order to discourage further Ghadr activites in India, the colonial government passed the Defence of India Act in March, 1915, allowing the authorities to maintain tighter control and justify more extreme punishment. Those arrested during this period were put on trial in Lahore, the capital of Punjab. Of the 291 persons prosecuted in a series of three trials, 42 were sentenced to death, 114 were sentenced to life in prison, and 93 were given lesser prison terms. The majority of those convicted and sentenced were Ghadr volunteers who had returned from North America.

Ghadr Movement, 1917-1947. The party's revolutionary efforts outside India continued throughout World War I. In 1917, members of the groups were charged in the GERMAN-HINDU CONSPIRACY case and were tried in San Francisco during 1917-1918. Fifteen Asian Indians were convicted and sentenced to prison for colluding with the Germans, the enemy, during wartime. After serving prison terms some of the Ghadr activists dropped out of political life, while others relocated to different parts of the United States or moved to other expatriate centers around the world.

By 1920, Ghadr operations in San Francisco were being conducted largely by fewer political activists and more volunteers from the immigrant community. The group continued to publish political tracts and monthlies, though sporadically, throughout the 1920's and 1930's. With funds raised in the community, the party supported activities in the Punjab such as the AKALI MOVEMENT, the Desh Bhagat Parivar Sahaiyik Committee (the Committee to Assist Families of Revolutionaries), and rural education programs. The organization also continued some clandestine activities such as sending volunteers to the Soviet Union to be trained as revolutionaries. During the 1920's and early 1930's, approximately eighty Ghadr recruits received such training before going on to India.

After 1935, Ghadr headquarters functioned primarily as a community center and meeting hall. The party did not officially suspend its activities, however, until British colonial rule on the Indian subcontinent had ended and the two independent nations of India and Pakistan had emerged in 1947.

Like other expatriate communities, Asian Indians found a certain amount of support and tolerance for their nationalist activities in the United States. Nationalist organizations among the Chinese, Koreans, and Irish also flourished in the United States. Yet popular support for independsence movements did not necessarily reflect U.S. foreign policy. The U.S. government officially recognized India as a British colony and endorsed Britain's right to rule the subcontinent. This position allowed the British to conduct surveillance of Ghadr activities in North America. It also enabled the British to pressure the U.S. government to bring conspiracy charges against members of the party. Despite the U.S. government's official stance on British colonialism, many Americans continued to sympathize with Asian Indian efforts to gain national independence for the Indian subcontinent.—*Jane Singh*

SUGGESTED READINGS: • Brown, Emily C. *Har Dayal: Hindu Revolutionary and Rationalist*. Tucson: University of Arizona Press, 1975. • Jensen, Joan M. *Passage from India: Asian Indian Immigrants in North America*. New Haven, Conn.: Yale Unviersity Press, 1988. • Josh, Sohan Singh. *The Hindustan Gadar Party: A Short History*. 2 vols. New Delhi: People's Publishing House, 1977-1978. • Puri, Harish K. *Ghadar Movement: Ideology, Organization and Strategy*. 2d ed. Amritsar, Punjab: Guru Nanak Dev University Press, 1993. • *South Asians in North America: An Annotated and Selected Bibliography*. Berkeley: Center for South and Southeast Asia Studies, University of California, Berkeley, 1988.

Gibson, Walter Murray (1824, S.C.—Jan. 21, 1888, San Francisco, Calif.): Government and political leader. The son of English immigrant parents, Gibson arrived in Honolulu in 1861, eventually settling on the island of Lanai. He moved to Lahaina in 1876 and won a seat in the legislature two years later. From there he rapidly ascended the political ladder and began to exert a powerful influence over King David Kalakaua, the reigning Hawaiian monarch.

An advocate of the contract-laborer immigration system, Gibson supported the importation of "Japanese peasants" as a means of boosting the kingdom's diminishing labor pool. He also became the self-appointed champion of the native Hawaiian people, a one-man army determined to save them from disease and despair. He favored replenishing the native island population by importing Malaysians. One of Gibson's earliest legislative triumphs was to repeal the prohibition laws preventing natives from buying or drinking alcohol. Yet despite his banner policy of "Hawaii for the Hawaiians," he unwittingly sowed feelings of racial prejudice that would infect islanders for years to come. His extreme insular views won for him many enemies.

In 1882 Gibson was named premier for the entire Hawaiian kingdom, further enlarging his sphere of recklessly used, unscrupulously gained partisan power. He was finally toppled, however, by a brief, bloodless revolution in 1887 by about four hundred white businessmen deeply unhappy over Kalakaua's excessive, indulgent ways. The men, armed with weapons, imposed the restrictive "Bayonet Constitution" upon the king, who was forced to expel both Gibson and the royal cabinet. The exiled Gibson ended up in San Francisco, where he died.

Gidra: Newspaper that served as the voice of the ASIAN AMERICAN MOVEMENT in Los Angeles from 1969 to 1974. A tabloid published by an all-volunteer staff, it carried the radical political tone of the 1960's student generation. A majority of the staff and the contributors were Japanese Americans, but the paper sought to address the concerns of the Asian American community as a whole. Articles harshly condemned U.S. military actions in Southeast Asia, supported ethnic studies, and strongly identified with revolutionary nationalist organizations such as the Black Panthers.

The paper also published literature and other writings that explored Asian American politics and identity. A twentieth anniversary issue was published in 1990.

Gila River: One of ten U.S. government camps under the administration of the WAR RELOCATION AUTHORITY (WRA) used to house Japanese American evacuees during World War II. Officially the camps were designated as "relocation centers." Gila River was operational from July 20, 1942, until November 10, 1945.

The Gila River relocation center was situated on unused American Indian land southeast of Phoenix, Arizona. The terrain was hot, barren desert and the camp consisted of rudimentary barracks quickly assembled in symmetrical linear patterns of rows and streets. Surrounding the camps were barbed-wire fences and guard towers. The camp housed some thirteen thousand men, women, and children, who were assigned family quarters in the barracks. Each barrack was divided into four to six rooms averaging twenty feet by twenty feet. Furnishings within the rooms were minimal—a potbellied stove, a single suspended bare electric light bulb, and an army cot and blanket for each person.

As Gila River filled up, activities began that eventually mitigated the starkness and harshness of the surroundings and the experience of internment. Working within the WRA guidelines, the internees did all the work of maintaining the camp itself. Flower and vegetable gardens were planted, the latter providing a substantial portion of the daily diet of the internees. Schools and a variety of educational activities were established, recreation programs were conducted, and the camp published its own newspaper. Beginning in July, 1942, a "seasonal leave program" permitted volunteers to leave the camp on a temporary basis and work for Western farmers and employers experiencing war-related labor shortages. Other internees enlisted in the armed forces to get out of the hot desert and away from the barbed-wire fences. In the fall of 1942, "indefinite leaves" were permitted for those who could pass stringent security tests and who could find jobs and communities, usually in the Midwest, willing to receive Japanese.

Gradually, the camp population declined while at the same time the remaining residents established a certain pattern of life. By the fall of 1945, the camp had closed; some of its occupants returned to their former homes, while others established themselves elsewhere.

Ginger and red egg party (also, full-month party; one-month-old baby party): Coming-out party given

Warning on barbershop near a Japanese American relocation center in Arizona. (National Archives)

for a month-old Chinese baby. Ginger cooked with vinegar and sugar is eaten by the mother and guests for health, and red egg is consumed for good luck.

GMD. *See* **Guomindang**

Go for Broke: Slogan for the combined 442ND REGI-MENTAL COMBAT TEAM/100TH INFANTRY BATTALION, the all-Japanese American unit of the U.S. armed forces during World War II.

Gobind Singh (Gobind Rai; Dec. 26, 1666, Patna, India—Oct. 7, 1708, Nander, India): Tenth and last guru of the Sikh religion. He transformed the Sikh community in India from a small, persecuted sect into a force to be reckoned with.

After his father, the ninth guru Tegh Bahdur, was executed by the Mughal emperor Aurangzeb in 1675, Gobind Rai became the new Sikh leader. In an atmosphere of persecution, he embraced a more militant spirit and set about creating an army of soldier-saints.

At a gathering of his followers in 1699, Gobind Singh called on devoted disciples to give their heads to him, then disappeared with five of them inside a tent, reemerging with his sword dripping with blood. After revealing that the blood was goats' blood, Gobind Singh consecrated the five brave men as *khalsa*, or pure ones, in a ceremony wherein they drank specially prepared water from a single bowl. Thus was born the military brotherhood of the Sikhs, Khalsa.

Gobind Singh gave his closest followers and himself the new family name of "Singh" (lion) and exhorted them always to display five emblems of their new identity: long hair (*kais*), a steel bracelet on the wrist (*kara*), short pants (*kachha*), a comb in the hair (*kangha*), and a saber (*kirpan*), sometimes referred to as "the 5 Ks."

The creation of this formidable force alarmed the local Hindu chiefs as well as the Mughal authorities, and Gobind Singh's community was forced to leave their settlement at Anandpur. His two youngest sons, however, were caught and executed on orders of Aurangzeb, prompting Gobind Singh to send a defiant letter to the emperor; the letter became renowned as the *Zafarnama*, or "Epistle of Victory."

In 1707, Aurangzeb died, and Gobind Singh backed one of the princes, who later ascended the throne as Bahadur Shah. While the guru accompanied the new emperor on a campaign in Nander, two assassins entered his tent and stabbed him. Before he died from his wounds, the leader declared that there would be no

more gurus and that his followers should regard the sacred book of the Sikhs, the *Adi Granth*, as their teacher.

To the Sikh community, Gobind Singh remains the archetypal hero of their faith, combining equally the qualities of valor, artistic sensitivity, and compassion.

Godzilla: Activist art organization—its full name is Godzilla: Asian American Art Network—founded in New York in 1990. The organization, which serves as a forum for Asian American artists, grew out of dissatisfaction with the mainstream art community and its institutions. Godzilla holds meetings for discussion and debate and provides an opportunity for artists to present their work to their peers; the organization also publishes a newsletter.

Golden Dragon Restaurant massacre (1977): Gang-related shooting that took place in San Francisco's Chinatown. In the early morning hours of the Labor Day weekend, on September 4, 1977, the Golden Dragon Restaurant, located in the center of Chinatown, was busy serving late meals to an estimated one hundred patrons. The customers included gang members, college students, churchgoers, tourists, and a police officer. At approximately 2:40 A.M., three masked gunmen walked into the restaurant and opened fire on the patrons with a .38-caliber revolver, two shotguns, and a .45-caliber semiautomatic rifle. They left the scene within a few minutes. The shooting spree resulted in the death of five people and the injury of eleven others. All the victims were innocent bystanders. The gunmen's targets were the gang members eating in the restaurant; none of them was injured.

This shooting event received national attention and was referred to as the "Golden Dragon massacre." The massacre was the culmination of a long-standing Chinatown gang war between two of the major Chinese gangs at that time, the Joe Boys and the Wah Ching. The restaurant shooting represented the latest retaliatory and disabling tactic by the Joe Boys for the injuries and death of some of its members two months prior.

Although the community had been in the midst of gang fights and shootings since the late 1960's, the massacre represented a turning point in San Francisco's Chinatown. The gang violence took the lives of innocent bystanders. It threatened the livelihood of one the main tourist attractions in the city. The larger community immediately began to respond to the event. Mayor George Moscone took the first step and

The Golden Temple at Amritsar. (Government of India Tourist Office)

announced a $25,000 reward for information resulting in the arrest and conviction of the gunmen. Two more gang retaliations occurred within a few weeks and left two people dead. The mayor increased the reward to $100,000. The city also created a special Gang Police Task Force to control the gang problem. During the next year, the police arrested all but one of the gang members involved in the massacre. Chinatown was quiet for the next several years.

Golden Temple incident (1984): Storming of the SIKHS' most holy shrine at AMRITSAR, Punjab, India, by the Indian army. Prime Minister Indira Gandhi ordered the attack in June, 1984, to flush out Sikh separatists who had occupied the temple and turned it into a heavily armed fortress. Known as Operation Blue Star, the army action, which was meant to deliver a decisive blow to the separatist movement, became instead a symbol of government ham-handedness and religious persecution.

The assault was a landmark in the history of Sikh separatism. The leader of the Sikh group was a relatively unknown religious extremist, Jarnail Singh Bhindranwale. Indira Gandhi herself pushed Bindran-wale into prominence to destabilize the Sikh Akali Dal Party (see AKALI MOVEMENT), her principal political opposition in the Punjab. Bindranwale's popularity grew uncontrollably, however, and his followers began to kill Hindus and demand a separate state. Running from the law, they sought sanctuary in the Golden Temple, refusing to leave until the Sikhs were granted an independent state.

Alarmed by this challenge to the authority of the central government, Gandhi ordered an assault on the heavily fortified temple. The army moved in on June 6, 1984, deploying tanks and artillery in the face of unexpectedly fierce resistance. Days and nights of heavy and bitter fighting ensued. Bindranwale and many of his followers were killed, and with them hundreds of innocent pilgrims caught in the cross fire. Conflicting reports placed the Sikh death-toll anywhere between 450 and 1,200; in addition, at least two hundred Indian soldiers died in the battle.

The Golden Temple incident had far-reaching and disastrous consequences for India's political stability. It alienated the entire Sikh community, who were outraged not only by the loss of life but also by the desecration of their holiest temple. In revenge, two

Indira Gandhi at a New York hotel in 1983. (AP/Wide World Photos)

Three armed Sikh occupiers pose outside the heavily fortified Golden Temple, only days before Indian troops stormed the temple. The siege killed hundreds on both sides. (AP/Wide World Photos)

Following the Indian army's bloody siege of the Golden Temple, a thousand Sikhs staged a mass demonstration in New Delhi on June 11. Here a demonstrator waves a plank pulled from a soft-drink stand destroyed by protesters. (AP/Wide World Photos)

Sikhs who were among Gandhi's bodyguards assassinated the prime minister. Gandhi's assassination in turn led to a vicious backlash of anti-Sikh rioting, in which thousands of innocent Sikhs were killed. The cry for a separate Sikh state of Khalistan, which until the incident had found little support in the Sikh community, arose louder than ever amid a surge in terrorist activity.

Goleta: Community located on the California coast near Santa Barbara. On February 23, 1942, a Japanese submarine fired on local oil-drilling operations but left without inflicting serious damage. Although the evacuation and relocation of residents of Japanese descent living on the West Coast were undertaken in part because of concerns regarding the protection of coastal military installations, the attack on Goleta was the only known assault made by the Japanese against the mainland United States during World War II.

Gompers, Samuel (Jan. 27, 1850, London, England—Dec. 13, 1924, San Antonio, Tex.): Labor union leader. Gompers became the first president of the AMERICAN FEDERATION OF LABOR (AFL). He was also noted for his anti-Chinese and anti-Japanese immigration position.

In 1863, when Gompers was thirteen years old, the family emigrated from London to the United States. They settled in New York City, and the young Gompers found work as a cigar maker. At age fourteen he joined a cigar makers local, at age seventeen he married, and at age twenty-one he became a naturalized U.S. citizen.

In the mid-1870's, he helped organize the Bohemian, German, and English cigar makers into one local and in 1877 led them in a successful strike. In 1881 he helped organize the national union known as the Federation of Organized Traders and Labor Unions. It was later renamed the American Federation of Labor, and in 1886 Gompers became its first president.

As president of the young AFL, Gompers promoted unionism, a Euro-American viewpoint, and a pragmatic agenda. He supported traditional goals such as the eight-hour day and child labor laws but avoided difficult issues such as the integrating of African-American and Euro-American locals. During his tenure he declared that immigration was a major labor issue and argued that the then-open U.S. immigration policy, which was generally favored by business, hurt white wages and unionism and threatened the Euro-American cultural hegemony of the United States.

During the national debate over Chinese exclusion in the 1880's, Gompers sided with white labor in California, which condemned Chinese labor as a threat to white wages, Euro-American traditions, and democracy. In 1902 Gompers actively supported renewal of the Chinese exclusion laws and an amendment prohibiting Chinese emigration from the recently acquired Hawaiian Islands. During this period Gompers resorted to xenophobic appeals to promote his anti-Chinese position. Gompers later supported Japanese exclusion and during the 1920's called for a moratorium on all immigration. In 1924, shortly before his death, he gave his support to the IMMIGRATION ACT OF 1924 restricting Eastern and Southern European immigration.

Gompers was president of the AFL for thirty-seven years (1886-1924, except for one year, 1895). His legacy was the establishment of a powerful labor union. In 1955 the AFL merged with the Congress of Industrial Organizations (founded in 1935 under a different name) to become the American Federation of Labor-Congress of Industrial Organizations (AFL-CIO).

Gong Lum v. Rice (1927): U.S. Supreme Court ruling that affirmed the right of states to segregate Chinese Americans from public schools exclusively for white children. In *Gong Lum* the Court announced its most racist decision since the Civil War. Ironically the case did not involve African Americans but was brought by Gong Lum, a Chinese grocer in Rosedale, Mississippi. His older daughter Martha had attended the white public school for a morning in September, 1924, but the superintendent told her not to return after lunch.

Larger towns in the Mississippi Delta had barred Chinese Americans from white institutions since their

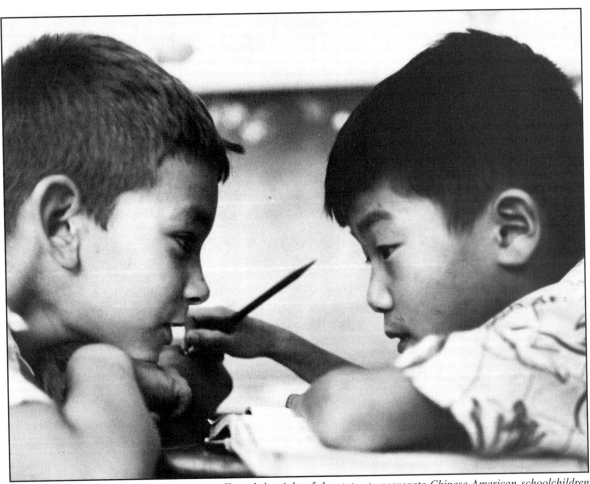

The Supreme Court decision in Gong Lum affirmed the right of the states to segregate Chinese American schoolchildren from white American students in the public schools. (David S. Strickler)

importation in 1870. (See CHINESE IN THE MISSISSIPPI DELTA.) Black schools were not, however, a real option: White administrators paid black teachers less than one-fifth what white teachers received and kept black public schools open for fewer than four months a year.

Lum filed suit the next month. His lawyers argued that "she [Martha] is not a member of the colored race nor is she of mixed blood, but that she is pure Chinese." Since Rosedale maintained no school for Chinese children, "separate but equal," required by *Plessy v. Ferguson* (1896), was not satisfied. The circuit court agreed, whereupon school officials appealed to the state supreme court. The latter reversed, citing the state constitution. Since Chinese are not white, the court reasoned, they must fall under the heading "colored races."

Lum now appealed to the U.S. Supreme Court. His lawyers boldly asserted that everyone knew the white race was "the law-making race." "If there is danger in the association [with blacks], it is a danger from which one race is entitled to protection just the same as another," they argued. "The white race creates for itself a privilege that it denies to other races."

The Supreme Court agreed that white administrators had set up schools for white persons alone. Yet, because Lum had not claimed that the black schools were inferior, Chief Justice William Howard Taft wrote, citing *Plessy v. Ferguson*, requiring Chinese children to attend them did not infringe the rights of these individuals.

The Lum family moved to Elaine, Arkansas. Not until after World War II did most Chinese children gain admission to white public schools.—*James W. Loewen*

Gonzalez, N. V. M. [Nestor Vicente Madali] (b. Sept. 8, 1915, Romblon, Philippines):

Short-story writer, journalist, and educator. Son of a school district supervisor who left academia to make his living from harvesting and homesteading, Gonzalez received a thorough education before pursuing a career in journalism. Gonzalez worked as a staff writer for *Graphic Weekly*, a Manila-based newspaper, between 1934 and 1941 before joining the staff of the *Manila Evening News Magazine* as editor in 1946. During the course of his writing career, Gonzalez produced some novels but earned his international reputation as a short-story writer; many of his stories saw publication in various magazines and literary journals. His first collection of short stories, *Seven Hills Away*, was published in 1947. Gonzalez was offered a one-year academic fellowship

N. V. M. Gonzalez. (Filipinos: Forgotten Asian Americans by Fred Cordova)

in 1949; he traveled to the United States and studied writing at Stanford University with Wallace Stegner. Upon returning to his homeland in 1950, González joined the faculty at the University of the Philippines as a visiting lecturer and professor and served in the university administration as an assistant to the president between 1962 and 1967. He continued to publish stories throughout this period in collections ranging from *Children of the Ash-Covered Loam and Other Stories* (1954) and *The Bamboo Dancers* (1961) to *Look, Stranger, on This Island Now* (1963) and *Selected Stories* (1964). In 1969 Gonzalez returned to the United States to accept a post as professor of English at California State University, Hayward. Upon being named professor emeritus, Gonzalez accepted a position as international writer-in-residence at the University of the Philippines. Considered to be the dean of modern Philippine literature, Gonzalez has been praised for his realistic portrayal of ordinary Filipinos, for his lively and distinctive prose style, and for his masterful handling of universal themes. *The Bread of Salt and Other Stories* (1993), a collection of sixteen stories that originally appeared between 1954 and 1990, offers a retrospective of Gonzalez's literary career.

Gospel Society: Earliest Japanese immigrant association established in the United States, founded in San Francisco in 1877. The group, started by Christian students, was created to spread Christianity among the Japanese immigrant population but also served to teach them about their new land, America. Among the earliest activities organized by the society were weekly Bible studies led by the Reverend Otis Gibson at the Chinese Methodist Episcopal Mission.

The society's nondenominational membership list originally comprised Methodists and Congregationalists. Dissenters (many of them Congregationalists) left the organization in 1882 and 1883 and joined with a local Presbyterian congregation to establish the First Japanese Presbyterian Church of San Francisco in 1885. In the following year, this splinter group founded the Japanese Young Men's Christian Association (YMCA).

Members of the Gospel Society elected to remain separate from the Methodist church after a merger between the two was proposed in 1890. Those opposed to a merger stressed the organization's separate role apart from the church in serving the community. A short while later, Kyutaro ABIKO was named president of the society. Over time, the group changed from a Christian organization with a strong evangelistic mission to a nonsectarian community-based agency assisting Japanese immigrants in finding jobs and lodging and teaching them English. The Gospel Society ceased to exist shortly after the San Francisco earthquake and fire of 1906.

Gotanda, Philip Kan (b. Dec. 17, 1949, Stockton, Calif.): Playwright, theater director, and filmmaker. One of Asian America's preeminent playwrights and theater directors, Gotanda has been most widely acclaimed for his Japanese American family sagas.

After earning his B.A. degree in Japanese art in 1973 from the University of California, Santa Barbara, Gotanda left for Japan, where he studied Japanese at the International Christian University and learned pottery-making in the village of Machiko. Returning to the United States, he was graduated from Hastings Law School in San Francisco in 1978.

Gotanda's first play, a musical entitled *The Avocado Kid*, was based on the Japanese folktale about Momotaro, the little boy found inside a peach. For this work, Gotanda collaborated with Dan Kuramoto, one of the founders of the jazz fusion group Hiroshima. Premiered by the EAST WEST PLAYERS in Los Angeles, *The Avocado Kid* was produced by San Francisco's

ASIAN AMERICAN THEATRE COMPANY in 1980.

Among Gotanda's many other plays and musicals are *A Song for a Nisei Fisherman* (pr. 1982), *The Wash* (pr. 1986), *Yankee Dawg You Die* (pr. 1988), *Fish Head Soup* (pr. 1991), and *Day Standing on Its Head* (pr. 1993). Among the productions Gotanda has directed are the world premiere of *Uncle Tadao* (pr. 1992), by the Japanese Canadian playwright R. A. SHIOMI; *The House of Sleeping Beauties* (orig. pr. 1983), by Tony Award-winning playwright David Henry HWANG; and *Fish Head Soup*. He has also served as dramaturge at the Asian American Theatre Company in San Francisco.

After establishing himself firmly in the stage world, Gotanda ventured into the world of film. He penned the screenplay for the 1989 American Playhouse/Lumiere production of the movie version of *The Wash*. In 1993 he wrote and directed a short film, *The Kiss*, which screened at the Sundance Film Festival and premiered in San Francisco. Besides playing the role of the protagonist in that piece, he also made a brief appearance as one of the sunglasses-wearing guitar players in Wayne WANG's film *Dim Sum* (1987).

In recognition of his achievements, Gotanda has received a Gerbode Foundation Grant; a Lila Wallace-Reader's Digest Writer's Award, a three-year grant given to artists established in their fields; a TCG/NEA Directing Fellowship; and fellowships from the Guggenheim, Rockefeller, and McKnight foundations.

Goto, Yasuo Baron (Nov. 20, 1901, Japan—Nov. 19, 1985, Honolulu, Hawaii): Businessperson and scholar. He was an agriculture expert and a vice chancellor of the Institute for Technical Interchange at the East-West Center in Honolulu, for seven years before retirement in 1969. A professor of agriculture at the University of Hawaii, he headed the Hawaii Agricultural Extension service from 1955 to 1962, before joining the East-West Center. He helped many Third World economies with agricultural development and served on the boards of many businesses and organizations.

Gramm, Wendy Lee (b. Jan. 10, 1945, Waialua, Territory of Hawaii): Economist, educator, and political appointee. A third-generation Korean American whose grandparents had worked as contract laborers on Hawaii sugar plantations, Gramm grew up on the island of Oahu and received a scholarship to attend Wellesley College. After earning her bachelor's degree in 1966, Gramm pursued graduate studies at Northwestern University and completed her Ph.D. degree. Upon graduation, Gramm joined the faculty at Texas A&M University, where she met and was married to fellow economics professor Philip Gramm in 1970. In 1976, Phil Gramm launched his political career with an unsuccessful bid to represent Texas in the U.S. Senate. With his wife's support, he ran for a seat in the House of Representatives in 1978 and was elected. Wendy Gramm gave up her tenured teaching position at Texas A&M to join her husband in Washington, D.C. Once there, she accepted a research position with the Institute for Defense Analyses, a Washington-based think tank. Gramm overcame her initial reluctance to accept a government post and joined the staff of the Federal Trade Commission (FTC) in 1982, where she advanced to become director of the commission's Bureau of Economics in 1983. In 1983, Gramm and her husband switched their political affiliation from the Democratic Party to the Republican Party. After serving as administrator of the Office of Information and Regulatory Affairs at the Office of Management and Budget (OMB) from 1985 to 1987, Gramm was appointed by President Ronald Reagan to serve as chair of the Commodity Futures Trading Commission (CFTC). She was sworn in on February 22, 1988. As head of the CFTC, Gramm was given the authority to regulate trade in commodity futures such as pork bellies, soybeans, lumber, and oil and to license and regulate the activity of brokers and salespeople involved in these financial transactions. In recognition of her expertise, she was approved to serve a second two-year term beginning in August of 1990.

Granada (Amache): One of ten U.S. government camps under the administration of the WAR RELOCATION AUTHORITY (WRA) used to house Japanese American evacuees during World War II. Officially the camps were designated as "RELOCATION CENTERS."

The Granada relocation center (also known as Amache) took its name from a nearby farming comunity in the southeast corner of Colorado. The camp was officially opened on August 27, 1942, with the first arrival of West Coast evacuees from the Merced assembly center in California. The center's population reached 7,620 at its peak, making it the tenth largest city in Colorado.

The center was located on a square-mile plot of prairie land along the Arkansas River. Housing for the evacuees consisted of thirty blocks of twelve army-style barracks, each of which was divided into six apartments. They were assigned to families with seven persons or less. In addition each block had a commu-

nity mess hall, laundry, and other facilities. There were also schools, warehouses, living quarters for WRA personnel, administration buildings, a military police station, and a 150-bed hospital.

The evacuee city was governed by an elected Community Council. Education was provided from preschool to senior high school levels in cooperation with the Colorado State Department of Education. More than 3,200 evacuees were employed by the city's own offices and enterprises such as the post office, a biweekly newspaper, and the Amache Consumer's Enterprises. The main industries of the center were agriculture and ranching, which produced vegetables and meat on 9,783 acres of land. Thus Granada, which had been designed as a prison for the forced wartime evacuees, superficially came to look like an autonomous community. From early spring of 1943 on, the evacuees who were judged as loyal Americans were permitted to leave the center and settle in the Midwest and the East. The others remained at the center until its closure in October, 1945. Still remaining at the former camp site are the concrete foundations of the camp structure, a small cemetery, and a stone memorial.

Grand Trunk Road: Road built in the mid-sixteenth century by the North Indian emperor Sher Shah of Sur. It connected Khyber Pass, located on the border of what is now Afghanistan and Pakistan, with the Bay of Bengal and covered nearly fifteen hundred miles.

Sher Shah of Sur constructed the road in order to defend his state better, to provide an infrastructure for trade, and to render traveling more convenient for the people. The road joined Peshawar, Lahore, Amritsar, Delhi, Agra, Lucknow, Allahabad, Patna, and Murshidabad and became the major communication link in North India.

By using the Grand Trunk Road as a spine, Sikh and British rulers of India constructed an extensive network of secondary roads. For the British, in addition to railroad construction, improved metal-surfaced roads such as the Grand Trunk Road were essential for maintaining imperialist control over the vast area of North India.

The Grand Trunk Road greatly contributed to the economic development of North India, and by linking villages to market towns and market towns to cities, it became the center of thriving commercial enterprises. The energetic activity on this road was captured and immortalized by Rudyard Kipling in his novel *Kim* (1901).

Various historical sites have developed along this

Nobel laureate Rudyard Kipling, in a painting dated 1907. His novel Kim *vividly described the Grand Trunk Road.* (The Nobel Foundation)

route. The Grand Trunk Road passes through AMRIT-SAR, home of the Golden Temple; reaches the confluence of the Ganges and Yamuna rivers, where the famous Indian festival Kumbha Mela is held; goes through the village of Buddh Gaya, the site where Buddha achieved his enlightenment; and passes through a host of other equally important cities.

The partition of the Indian subcontinent into India and Pakistan in 1947 severed the link provided by the Grand Trunk Road from Calcutta to Peshawar. Within the boundaries of modern India and Pakistan, however, the Grand Trunk Road continues to be important. Today, it forms the backbone of the complex road network system in North India and Pakistan. A number of smaller roads have been built around it, and small towns and villages have also developed along the route. Although primarily used for transportation, it is also widely used by pilgrims and tourists.

Great Mahele (1848): Major redistribution of King Kamehameha III's land in the Hawaiian Islands. The division and reallocation of all Hawaiian land, until then owned solely by the king, marked the end of traditional feudalistic land tenure in Hawaii.

Of all the momentous changes that were brought about in Hawaii following Western contact, the *Mahele* (division) ranks in significance with the arrival of

Captain James Cook in 1778 and the overthrow of the monarchy in 1893. The net effect of the *Mahele*, although envisioned to give the royal family, the nobility, and commoners an unalienable ownership of the land, was one of dispossession and a breakdown of complex socio-political relationships that had tied the people to their ruling chiefs for centuries.

The intent of the *Mahele* was to provide fee simple title to lands traditionally held by individuals only at the pleasure of a ruling chief. The demands of a monetized economy, stimulated by Western business interests and Christian missionary ideals, pressured land-tenure change. In 1848, King Kamehameha III was persuaded to redistribute the lands, all of which were traditionally in his care. The king was also advised that reform would help secure Hawaiian independence. Initially, Kamehameha III divided the land between himself and 245 chiefs. Crown lands would pass to the ruling monarch. Other current royal family members were given vast estates in their own right. Crown lands were later divided into crown, government, and fort lands. In the 1850 Kuleana Act, commoners could claims lands that they had traditionally used for subsistence and residence. Right of access to their former landlords' lands for gathering forest products and channeling water was theoretically guaranteed.

Unfortunately, many of the commoners were un-

Ceremony marking the one-hundredth anniversary of the birth of Kamehameha III, at Keauhou, north Kona, Hawaii, 1914. Passage of the Great Mahele marked the end of the Hawaiian monarchy's land monopoly in the islands. (Lyman House Memorial Museum)

aware of their rights and failed to file claims. Others had no access to the cash required for the official surveys of their claims. Many lands that were fallow were not recognized by the Land Commission. The government largely failed to protect the commoners' rights of access.

Once land had become an alienable cash commodity, most of the Hawaiian population, already decimated by introduced diseases, was driven from its ancestral lands. Of about five million acres distributed in the Great *Mahele*, less than thirty thousand acres were eventually granted to the bulk of the native Hawaiian population.

Gresham-Yang Treaty (1894): Treaty between China and the United States. In the wake of the GEARY ACT OF 1892, which mandated official registration of all Chinese immigrants in the United States, the Chinese government sought to renegotiate an immigration treaty with the United States in order to lessen the restrictions on Chinese attempting to enter the United States and to reduce the mistreatment of Chinese already residing in the country. The Chinese minister to the United States, Yang Ju, and the American secretary of state, Walter Gresham, negotiated the new treaty, which went into effect in late 1894.

As far as the Chinese were concerned, this treaty was only a minor improvement over previous regulations concerning immigration. It allowed for the reinstatement of reentry permits originally voided by the SCOTT ACT OF 1888, but it also allowed for the continued registration of Chinese immigrants in the United States, as stipulated by the Geary Act, and it continued the prohibition on Chinese laborers from entering the United States for another ten years. In the name of compromise, it also required American workers in China to register with the Chinese government. This, however, was mainly symbolic, since there was only a small number of American workers in China. The treaty also guaranteed that the Chinese in the United States were to be given the privileges of citizens of a most favored nation (except the right to become naturalized citizens), but it also allowed the American government to restrict Chinese activities in the United States under the undefined term of "necessary regulation." In effect, this treaty offered the Chinese little or no new protection from discriminatory measures.

A failure to achieve a more equitable treaty after the expiration of the Gresham-Yang Treaty in 1904 contributed to the beginning of the Chinese boycott of American goods in 1905.

Grove Farm Plantation (Kauai, Hawaii): Subsistence vegetable farm established by, and for, Asian workers and their families in the late nineteenth and early twentieth centuries. Each family on the plantation was provided with a small plot of land and water for irrigation to grow vegetables for personal consumption. Each plot provided enough vegetables for the family throughout the year.

Guamanians: Residents of Guam, the largest and most heavily populated island in Micronesia. Because Guam is an American territory, Guamanians are fully enfranchised U.S. citizens, except that they may not vote in American presidential elections.

Ferdinand Magellan's 1521 discovery of Guam and its resident population of some 50,000 Malayo-Polynesian Chamorros initiated a 150-year period of intermittent European contact. European colonization finally began in 1668, with the establishment of a Jesuit mission and an accompanying garrison of Spanish and Filipino soldiers.

The Spanish presence soon proved disastrous for the original residents: By 1700, nearly all adult Chamorro

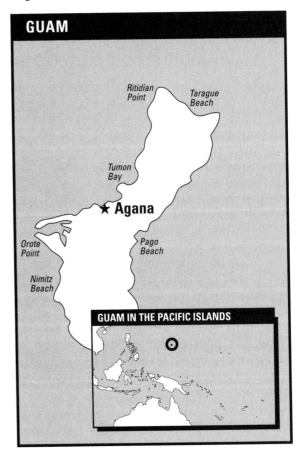

A small child becomes a citizen of the American territory of Guam during naturalization ceremonies in 1986. Into the 1990's people of Asian descent constitute a fairly sizable proportion of the population of Guam. (AP/Wide World Photos)

males had been killed, either by soldiers or by disease epidemics. The 1,500 estimated remaining Chamorros, mostly women and children, survived by marrying Spanish, Filipino, Mexican, and (later) Japanese immigrants. The native Guamanian language, Chamorro, much altered by contact with other languages (primarily Spanish) and declining in frequency of use, was nevertheless the native language of about 29 percent of Guam's population in 1990, according to U.S. census figures.

Predominantly Hispanic at the end of the nineteenth century, Guam was taken by the United States during the Spanish-American War and subsequently Americanized. Yet even at the end of the twentieth century, a broad mix of ethnic traditions prevailed: Of the four largest cultural influences on Guam, the Spanish-

Filipino has been most notable in family names and religion (mostly Catholic), the Chamorro in politics and private language, the American in education and public language, and the Asian in commerce. All four cultural groups have influenced the Guamanian culture.

Although there are obvious difficulties in precisely defining modern Guamanian ethnicity, the 1990 census identified 37.5 percent of Guam's 133,152 residents as Chamorros. The second-largest identifiable Guamanian ethnic group was Filipino (23 percent), followed by Caucasian (14 percent), mixed ancestry (10 percent), other Asian (7 percent), and other Pacific Islander (5 percent).

Despite almost 500 years of cultural evolution, Guamanians, like Americans in general, retain a strong sense of ethnic pride. The result is a vibrant and complex society, one perhaps uniquely diverse among human populations.

Guangdong: Province of southeastern China. Its population was 63.5 million in 1991; its land area is 76,100 square miles.

With its long coastline, plentiful rainfall, warm subtropical climate, and fertile river valleys (especially the PEARL RIVER DELTA surrounding the capital city of CANTON), Guangdong enjoys an abundance of grains, fruits, vegetables, and fish, as well as thriving maritime and commercial traditions. The province boasts one of the leading regional cuisines of China, famous for its breakfast delicacies (*dim sum*).

Nevertheless Guangdong has long been plagued by overpopulation. During the nineteenth century foreign invasions (the two OPIUM WARS), large-scale domestic uprisings such as the TAIPING REBELLION and the Red Turban Revolt, and chronic unrest stemming from lineage feuds and secret society activities further con-

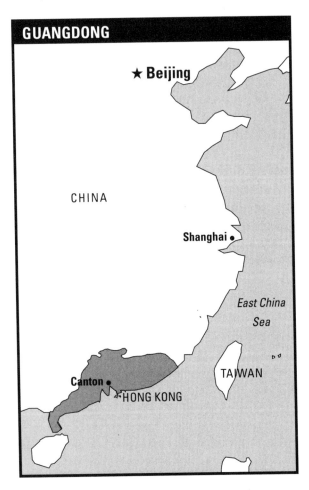

GUANGDONG

★ Beijing

CHINA

Shanghai •

East China Sea

TAIWAN

Canton •

HONG KONG

tributed to economic distress and an outflow of emigrants to Southeast Asia, North America, and other regions.

In the late nineteenth century peasants of the Pearl River Delta prospered from the expansion of sericulture and raw silk production in response to rising American and European demand. The economic benefits of export growth, however, ended with the Great Depression of the 1930's.

Guangdong suffered warlordism and political disturbances during the early twentieth century and the Japanese occupation from 1938 to 1945. Recurrent political movements under Communist rule from 1949 through the end of the Cultural Revolution in 1976 disrupted its economic development.

In 1978 the Communist government embarked on the commercialization, privatization, and internationalization of China's socialist economy. Guangdong, drawing on its links with the Cantonese population in Hong Kong, Southeast Asia, and North America, has become a leader of economic reform. In the Special Economic Zones of Shenzhen, Zhuhai, and Shantou, foreign (especially overseas Chinese) investment was attracted by various tax and economic incentives. By 1990 Guangdong had become economically integrated with nearby HONG KONG and MACAO, supplying water, agricultural products, and low-cost labor to them while receiving capital, management, and information services; Guangdong has become the first region in a socialist economy to achieve an economic takeoff comparable to the success of Taiwan and South Korea.

Guangong (Guandi): In Chinese mythology, the ancient god of war. Prior to divinization, Guangong was Guan Yu, a general under Liu Bei. Guan Yu lived from 161 until about 223, when he died fighting Chinese general Cao Cao. Deified by decree of the emperor during the sixteenth century, the god Guangong became patron to soldiers, merchants, and the Qing Dynasty (1644-1911). He is depicted as a warrior dressed in full battle armor and is known by numerous names.

Guanxi: Chinese word that refers to a special relationship two people share with each other. *Guanxi* is at the heart of the larger concept of the *guanxiwang*, or "network," which refers generally to a web of relationships weaved by the Chinese. The network is a very important phenomenon in Chinese social life.

Guanxi is best interpreted as a friendship accompanied by the implications of a continual exchange of

Among Chinese businessmen, the guanxi *network is a vital source of economic survival.* (James L. Shaffer)

favors. Two people enjoying a *guanxi* relationship can assume that they are both conscientiously committed to sustaining the relationship. They have undertaken to exchange favors in spite of official policies prohibiting such practices. *Guanxi* helps the Chinese acquire what they normally are unable to obtain through official channels.

In Chinese culture the formation of interpersonal relationships has become something of an art. The Chinese often begin to build up their network by identifying common attributes that they may share with others. The often-shared attributes are kinship, locality, common employment, common school, and teacher-student. The shared attributes are quite resilient and flexible. Locality, for example, can imply a natural village, a county, a city, a province, a regional grouping of provinces, or even the country. In the initial contact, an intermediary is often involved to facilitate the relationship.

The Chinese are also inclined to evade *guanxi* on some occasions. To develop a *guanxi* with others is a kind of social investment that incurs responsibility and obligation. Once individuals place themselves in a *guanxiwang* built either by themselves or by others, they are locked into a complicated interdependent relationship together. This means that they are socially obligated to respond to any request for help from other individuals within the *guanxiwang*. As a result a Chinese may choose to evade *guanxi* in order to maintain a certain degree of freedom from being locked in for every business decision. A compartmentalization strategy has been developed in Chinese societies to separate the functionally specific economic exchanges from the functionally diffuse social exchanges. The popular expression that "among good brothers, accounts should be kept clear-cut" lends evidence to this point.

The concept of *guanxi* has long been viewed by

many Chinese as being obstructive to the modernization of the Chinese nation. Yet the successful modernization drive in Hong Kong, Taiwan, and Singapore has not made *guanxi* a passing phenomenon. In the People's Republic of China, Deng Xiaoping's market reform has enriched the Chinese market, but *guanxi*, which in the past was used by the Chinese living in mainland China to obtain goods in short supply, is becoming increasingly active. A special term, *guanxixue* (relationology), has been developed to describe this complicated phenomenon. *Zouhoumen* (walking through the back door) has become a popular and often essential way to get things done through personal networks. *Guanxihu* (specially connected individual or social organization), an increasingly popular concept, allows preferential exchanges among specially connected people or organizations without following market rationality. Hardly any aspect of social life is not touched by *guanxi*.

In business, *guanxi* gives the Chinese a significant comparative advantage. Interlocked in various *guanxi* networks, thousands upon thousands of small Chinese family businesses give one another business opportunities. Networking has become the single most important business source for small Chinese businesses. In spite of various pitfalls involved in this business web, Chinese businesses can enjoy cheap credit, lucrative opportunities, and a business efficiency that people outside the network cannot obtain. The *guanxi* network has made Chinese businesses collectively one of the most formidable competing forces in the business world.

Guilds: Traditional associations of merchants or artisans engaged in the same business to regulate prices, market shares, product quality, and other conditions of their trade and to render mutual aid to members.

In addition to sworn brotherhoods, political parties,

Chinese toy merchants in San Francisco Chinatown, as photographed by Arnold Genthe. Numerous Chinese and Japanese artisans, merchants, and laborers living in the city belonged to assorted guilds that sprang up there. (Library of Congress)

class-action suit in 1885 against San Francisco ordinances restraining Chinese laundries.

Japanese shoemakers formed the first Japanese trade association in San Francisco in 1893. During the first two decades of the twentieth century, guilds were established by Japanese in a variety of urban trades, including art goods importers, grocers, flower shop owners, and dry cleaners. In 1915 many of these associations joined to form the Japanese Chamber of Commerce. Given the heavy concentration of Japanese employment in agriculture, however, the most significant and numerous Japanese trade associations were in farming professions: agricultural associations, producers' cooperatives, and associations of farm labor contractors.

During the twentieth century, with the decline of many of the traditional trades, the appearance of an American-born generation, and the opening up of professional careers to Asian Americans, traditional guilds have largely disappeared altogether or have been replaced by modern merchant organizations, labor unions, or recreational clubs.

Gujarat: One of India's most prosperous constitutional states. It is located along the western coast of India, north of the city of Bombay, and includes nineteen Gujarati-speaking districts. The state is 75,685 square miles in size and contained a population of about 41.2 million in 1991.

While many different dialects are spoken in the state, Gujarati is constitutionally recognized as the official language. With the spread of linguistic agitation, Prime Minister Jawaharlal NEHRU in 1960 agreed to the division of the state of Bombay into the states of Maharashtra and Gujarat.

A variety of castes in Gujarat vie for political and economic control. The two major Hindu communities are the Kshatriyas and the Patidars, although the Brahman, Bania, and Rajput upper castes are significant. A variety of other castes and tribes exist, as well as a 10 percent minority of Muslims and Jains. The upper castes have long believed in *ahisma*, or nonviolence, and are strict vegetarians. Two of the chief figures in the drive for Indian independence came from Gujarat. The revered Mahatma GANDHI based many of his pre-World War II *ashrams*, or religious retreats, in the state. After independence in 1947, Vallabhbhai Jhaverbhai Patel of the Gujarati Patels was second only to Nehru in the postwar leadership of India.

The name for the area comes from the Gujaras who ruled the region during the eighth and ninth centuries.

San Francisco photographer Arnold Genthe earned fame for his early twentieth century studies of life in the city's Chinatown district, including numerous shots of artisans, laborers, and merchants. (AP/Wide World Photos)

and associations based on regional and kinship ties, guilds and trade associations helped Asian immigrants to sink roots in North America during the nineteenth and early twentieth centuries. Such social organizations were critical to the survival of Asian immigrants who faced racial prejudice, legal discrimination, and a hostile Euro-American labor movement, often without the family support systems they had left behind in their home countries.

Guilds provided assistance and fraternizing opportunities to members and at times also engaged in political action, defending the rights of their constituents and fighting against unjust legislation. The first Chinese merchant guild in North America, established in the early 1850's in San Francisco, published an open letter rebutting the governor of California's proposal to ban Chinese immigration. Similar merchants' guilds also opened in Portland, New York, Victoria, and Vancouver in the late nineteenth century. It was in San Francisco, however, where the greatest number of Chinese guilds were founded, including those for laundrymen, shoemakers, and cigar makers in the 1860's. Tung Hing Tong, the laundrymen's guild, brought a

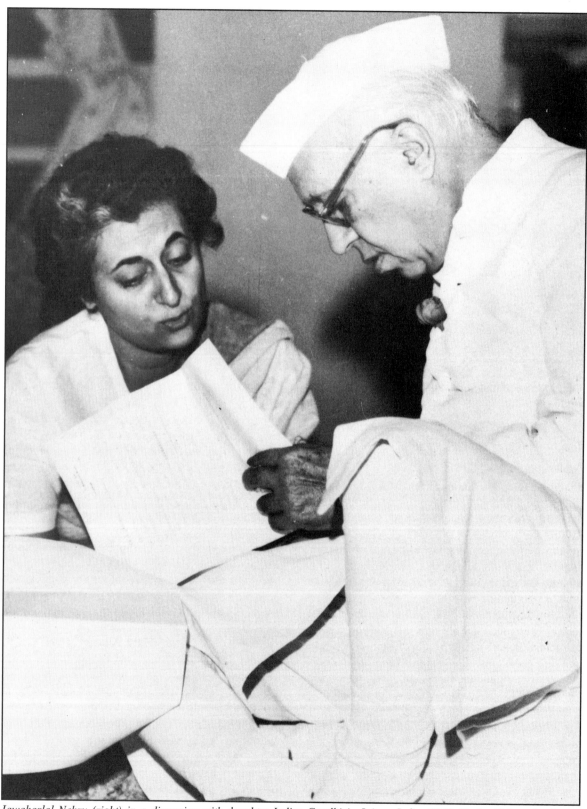

Jawaharlal Nehru (right) in a discussion with daughter Indira Gandhi in Jaipur, India, 1963. Under Nehru, the former state of Bombay was partitioned into the states of Maharashtra and Gujarat. (AP/Wide World Photos)

The state has at one time or another come under the rule of the Muslims and the Marathas; in the nineteenth century, it was an important area run by the BRITISH EAST INDIA COMPANY; and in 1857, it became a province of British India.

Geographically, Gujarat is an area of contrasts: It varies from rich, fertile agricultural areas to arid desert regions, and from rolling hill country to small plains. While it is a significant agricultural area, it is one of the chief industrialized states of India. It has a rich commercial and enterprising merchant class that is of great import to the economic development of India.

Gujarat's major cities are Ahmadabad; Gandhinagar, which became the state's capital in 1969 and is located in Gujarat's suburbs; Baroda; Bhavnagar; Broach; Jamnagar; Rajkot; and Surat. Several of these cities were capitals of princely states during the British era. Several major religious sites and monuments exist in Gujarat that are important to the Hindu worship of Vishnu and Shiva, and other sites are important to the Jains and Parsis. The magnificent architecture of the region is testimony to its varied history and wealth.

Gujarat is one of the most enterprising areas of India, famous for its economic initiative and significant political contributions to the nation as well as its international trade. As India has become more democratic, the control in Gujarat once exercised by the merchant upper castes such as the *Bania* has lessened, and the later years of the twentieth century have witnessed instances of rioting and intercommunal strife in the cities.

Gujarat is of particular significance to the Asian American communities as many Indians from that region have immigrated to Canada and the United States. Whether or not this immigration is a result of the increased level of turmoil in India, the immigrants from Gujarat have proved to be an enterprising, industrious, and significant part of their American communities.

Gulick, Sidney Lewis (1860, Micronesia—Dec. 24, 1945, Boise, Ida.): Missionary and peace activist. Son of a missionary who worked for the American Bible Society throughout the world, Gulick was educated in Oakland, California, and attended the University of California, Berkeley, before transferring to Dartmouth College. Gulick went on to get his divinity degree from Union Theological Seminary in 1886. After his marriage to Cara Fisher, Gulick was given a missionary posting in Kumamoto, Japan, in 1888. While in Japan, Gulick learned to read and speak Japanese and accepted a teaching post as an instructor in theology at Kyoto's Doshisha University. He wrote several books about Japanese history and was a vocal supporter of the Japanese peace movement in the wake of the Russo-Japanese War of 1904-1905.

Gulick returned to the United States in 1913 in order to alleviate his health problems. After his years abroad, he was horrified by the blatant racism expressed toward Japanese residents of the United States. Gulick believed that the discriminatory measures and actions proposed by members of the anti-Japanese movement were unchristian and immoral, and he tried to counteract such measures by arguing for equitable entry quotas for Japanese immigrants and nondiscriminatory naturalization processes for those Japanese wishing to become American citizens.

Gullion, Allen (Dec. 14, 1880, Carrollton, Ky.—June 19, 1946, Washington, D.C.): Military official. Provost marshal general of the U.S. Army and legal counsel for the Army during World War II, he supported the decision to intern Japanese Americans. He approved of EXECUTIVE ORDER 9066, which ordered the forced relocation of Japanese Americans, because he believed that the "military necessity" to intern outweighed adherence to constitutional law.

Gum Shan (also, Gam Saa): Cantonese for "gold mountain." The term refers to California and originated with the first Chinese miners who came to California looking for gold in 1849.

Guomindang (Chinese Nationalist Party): The political party in power in China from 1928 to 1949 and in Taiwan since 1949.

Under the leadership of SUN YAT-SEN, a charismatic Chinese nationalist, the Guomindang (GMD) emerged as a major political force in China in the early 1920's. Sun created the party, in 1923 and 1924, by reorganizing many short-lived organizations such as China's Prosperity, the Revolutionary Alliance, the National People's Party, and the Chinese Revolutionary Party. In organizing the GMD, Sun, who espoused the Three Principles of the People (nationalism, democracy, and livelihood) received financial help and policy guidance from the Soviet Union. The GMD soon became the largest and strongest party in China; its membership grew to about 200,000 in 1926.

The GMD worked closely with the Communists and accepted them as members of the GMD between 1923 and 1927. Sun's death in 1925, however, and the hostility of his successor, General CHIANG KAI-SHEK, to-

GMD and Communist Party troops were forced to band together to expel the Japanese from China during World War II. Here an endless column of Chinese troops winds toward the Burma border front to battle Japanese invasion forces in June, 1943. (AP/Wide World Photos)

ward the Communists resulted in the end of the alliance between the two parties. Chiang's forces nearly wiped out the Communists from their base in Jiangxi Province (1930-1934). Japan's invasion of China in 1937, however, necessitated a second united front between the GMD and the Communists during the Sino-Japanese War (1937-1945). The defeat of Japan was followed by a civil war between the two parties (1945-1949), won by the Communists, forcing the Nationalists to flee to TAIWAN.

Accompanied by 800,000 troops and about two million civilians, Chiang established the Republic of CHINA (ROC) on Taiwan, suppressing resistance by the native population. Seizing many of the island's most valuable assets, the GMD elite completely dominated the government of Taiwan for nearly forty years.

The United States, refusing to acknowledge the Communist-led People's Republic of China (PRC) as the legitimate Chinese government, accepted the GMD regime's claim to that role. Taiwan was given a permanent seat in the United Nations Security Council. In 1971, however, the ROC lost its seat to the PRC. On January 1, 1979, the United States formally recognized the PRC and abrogated its 1954 mutual-defense treaty with Taiwan, having severed formal diplomatic relations with the ROC on December 15, 1978. Nevertheless, the United States continues to maintain close ties, especially economic ones, with the government of Taiwan.

Taiwan had a one-party dictatorship under presidents Chiang and his successors. The GMD, however, started political reform in 1986. On July 15, 1987, President Chiang Ching-kuo terminated martial law—declared in 1949—and ended the decades-long state of emergency said to have been posed by the imminent threat of invasion by the PRC. Opposition parties were legalized in January, 1989. In the first real election for the national legislature in December 1989, the GMD maintained its control by winning 72 out of 101 seats.

A large number of Taiwanese nationals have emigrated to the United States since the 1950's. Since 1982, Taiwan has had its own annual immigration quota of 20,000, separate from that of the PRC. In addition, many students from Taiwan have entered the United States as nonquota immigrants; the overwhelming majority of these students have established permanent residence in the United States. Political divisions in Taiwan, between pro-GMD and anti-GMD factions, are mirrored in the immigrant community. (See TAIWAN INDEPENDENCE MOVEMENT.) Moreover, long before the influx of immigration from Taiwan, the GMD was a significant force in Chinese American communities, where it continues to be an influential presence even in the 1990's. (See CHINA POLITICS IN THE CHINESE AMERICAN COMMUNITY.)

Gupta, Kanta Chandra (1897, Delhi, India—Sept. 11, 1982, San Francisco, Calif.): Chiropractor. Gupta was also the first woman from India to apply for U.S. citizenship, a proponent of the women's education movement, and a Ghadr Party activist. After the death of her parents, Kanta Chandra and her four siblings left Delhi, India, to come to the United States, where an older brother had attended school. The thirteen-year-old Kanta arrived at Angel Island on July 2, 1910, with her sister and brothers and eventually settled in San Francisco. Six years later (while in high school), she became the first woman from India to begin the process of applying for citizenship in the United States. Later she interrupted her high school education to marry Sailendra Nath Gupta, a pharmacist. As the mother of three children, Kanta Gupta continued taking classes. When her husband died in 1929, she supported her family through cleaning jobs. In 1931 she completed a nursing degree through correspondence courses offered by the Chicago School of Nursing. Four years later the Los Angeles College of Chiropractic awarded her a chiropractic degree.

Gupta spoke and wrote enthusiastically about the women's education movement. She defined education broadly, recognizing the benefits of travel especially for learning about different cultures as well as one's own culture. She urged fellow Indians who had emigrated to the United States to support the movement to educate women in India and to help girls from India to travel to foreign counties in pursuit of higher education. She particularly valued scientific and practical learning for both men and women.

Gupta often spoke publicly. As an active member of the San Francisco-based Ghadr Party (see GHADR MOVEMENT), she addressed many civic groups about the need to drive the British out of India and won the sympathy of U.S. residents who otherwise would have been unfamiliar with the situation. One of her brothers, Mahesh Chandra, was a prominent leader in the movement to free India.

Making San Francisco her permanent home, Gupta established a successful chiropractic practice there.

Gurdwara. *See* **Sikh temples**

H

Haan, Kil-soo: Politician. As a spokesperson for the SINO-KOREAN PEOPLE'S LEAGUE in Hawaii (1938-1945), he warned the U.S. public of an impending Japanese attack and accused the Japanese in Hawaii of spying and conducting sabotage for the Japanese government. In 1941, the Korean Commission, the only diplomatic agency of the Korean provisional government in China, appointed him liaison officer between the United Korean Committee and the U.S. government. Conflicts with the diplomatic policies of commission chair Syngman RHEE resulted in competition between the two men to represent Korean Americans.

Hagedorn, Jessica Tarahata (b. 1949, Manila, Philippines): Novelist, poet, and short-story writer. Hagedorn moved to the United States at the age of fourteen with her mother and settled in the San Francisco Bay Area. She pursued her education at the American Conservatory Theater. Disappointed by the limited variety of roles available to ethnic actors, Hagedorn turned to a career as a writer. She published her first poetry collection in 1975. Hagedorn performed some of her poetry with accompaniment from a band known as The West Coast Gangster Choir. Her involvement in the San Francisco performance art scene and her collaborations with black female dramatists Ntozake Shange and Thulani Davis prompted Hagedorn to move to New York City in 1978. While Hagedorn continued her work as a poet, she began to write and publish short stories. She drew heavily on her experiences in the Philippines—as a child and as a visiting expatriate adult—to provide a compelling background for her 1990 debut novel, *Dogeaters*. Although the title is an ethnic slur that was once applied by white Americans to Filipino emigres, whom they disparaged as culturally backward, Hagedorn employs the term as a metaphor for the topsy-turvy condition of Filipino society during the Marcos era: the contrast between Catholic piety and the sensual indulgence that encouraged the growth of the pornography industry, between the extreme poverty of the families who lived as scavengers in Manila's garbage dumps and the fantastic wealth of the elite families who had prospered as the result of trade with the United States. *Dogeaters* was nominated for the National Book Award in 1990. As interest in her work grew, Hagedorn brought out *Danger and*

Jessica Tarahata Hagedorn portrayed the topsy-turvy condition of her native Philippines in her novel Dogeaters. (Nancy Wong)

Beauty (1993), a collection of poetry, short fiction, and prose, combining new work with material that had been previously published in small press editions. Hagedorn edited *Charlie Chan Is Dead: An Anthology of Contemporary Asian American Fiction* (1993).

Hahn, Gloria (Kim Ronyoung; March 28, 1926, Los Angeles, Calif.—Feb., 1987): Artist and novelist. Her novel *Clay Walls* (1986) was one of the first to depict the Korean American experience.

Born Kim Ronyoung, she was the daughter of Korean immigrants who had left their homeland to escape the oppressive Japanese colonial regime. She grew up in Los Angeles at a time when the Korean community

Artist and novelist Gloria Hahn promoted the cultural identity of Korean Americans. (Richard Hahn)

there was very small. Married to Richard Hahn at the age of nineteen, she went back to school after her children were grown. At San Francisco State University, where she received a bachelor's degree in 1975, Hahn studied Asian art and literature and Chinese language. In addition to her own art work—drawings, paintings, calligraphy—she helped to organize and promote cultural events within the Korean American community; she also wrote for Korean magazines and newspapers. After her death, her novel *Clay Walls* was translated into Korean and published in South Korea.

Hahn, Kimiko (b. New York, 1955): Writer. Hahn was born just outside New York City, the daughter of two artists: Maude Miyako Hamai, from Hawaii, and Walter Hahn, from Wisconsin. She is the author of two widely acclaimed books of poetry: *Air Pocket* (1989) and *Earshot* (1992). Her story "Afterbirth" was included in *Charlie Chan Is Dead: An Anthology of Contemporary Asian American Fiction* (1993), edited by Jessica HAGEDORN. In addition, Hahn is a coauthor of *We Stand Our Ground: Three Women, Their Vision, Their Poetry* (1988).

Committed to social change, Hahn was involved with protests by American writers and artists against U.S. intervention in Central America. In 1983, she interviewed black lung victims, miners and their wives, and wrote the text for Bill Brand's experimental film, *Coalfields*, which premiered at the Collective Living Cinema. From 1982 to 1984 she was an editor at *BRIDGE* magazine. In 1988, she coedited *Without Ceremony*, an anthology of writing by Asian American women. She founded and was project director of Word of Mouth: A Multicultural Arts Project (formerly the BASEMENT WORKSHOP Literature Program), where she coordinated the readings and workshops from 1985 to 1990. In 1986 and 1992 she received fellowships in poetry from the National Endowment for the Arts, and in 1987 and 1991, fellowships from the New York Foundation for the Arts.

An assistant professor of English at Queens College, City University of New York, Hahn has taught literature at Yale University, Eugene Lang College, Sarah Lawrence College, and Barnard College, and poetry workshops at Sarah Lawrence College and Goddard College. She and her husband, Ted Hannan, live in New York City with their daughters, Miyako Tess and Reiko Lily.

Hahn, Richard S. (b. April 28, 1922, Lincoln, Nebr.): Surgeon. The first Korean American cardiothoracic surgeon, Hahn developed the prototype of the coronary bypass operation in 1949.

Hahn received a B.M.D. degree from Northwestern University in 1943 and an M.D. degree from Northwestern University Medical School in 1947. Between 1947 and his retirement in 1987, Hahn enjoyed a distinguished career as a surgeon, receiving a number of research awards and prizes and introducing innovations in both surgical practice and training. He was also involved in humanitarian projects in Peru, Mexico, Central America, Thailand, China, and Bhutan.

In addition to his contributions as a surgeon and medical administrator, Hahn has played an active role in Korean American community affairs. His father, Jason Hahn (born Hahn Chang Ho), participated in the Korean independence movement (see FIRST KOREAN INDEPENDENCE AIR FORCE), while his wife, Gloria HAHN (born Kim Ronyoung), was the author of the widely acclaimed novel of Korean American life, *Clay Walls* (1987). Hahn himself has written about the Korean American experience; see "Hahn Chang Ho and the First Korean Independence Air Force," *Korean Culture* 14 (Fall, 1993): 2-15, an excerpt from Hahn's

Surgeon Richard S. Hahn worked with his wife, novelist Gloria Hahn, and played an important role in Korean American community affairs. (Richard Hahn)

work in progress, a fictionalized history of the first wave of Korean immigrants to the United States.

Haji: Japanese term for shame or disgrace. The shame not only pertains to the individual but also affects the family or community. For Japanese Americans, it is cited as a reason for individuals to control their social behavior.

Hakka: Ethnic subgroup within the Chinese (Han) nationality, different from other Han and non-Han ethnic minorities in the People's Republic of China. "Hakka" means "guest people."

Origin and Migration. The Hakka are a distinctive subgroup of the Han, even though some have tried to characterize them as non-Han. While the origin of this group remains buried in the distant past, they are known to have migrated southward from northcentral China in three or more waves from the fourth to the seventeenth centuries. The best-known migration, from Jiangxi Province in the north to Guangdong

Province in the south, came during the Southern Song Dynasty (1126-1279). Other migrations took the Hakka from Fujian Province to Taiwan (where they are called Hokkien).

Economic Conditions. Since the fertile valleys were already occupied wherever the Hakka migrated, they tended to settle in remote mountainous areas where the farming was unusually difficult. Perhaps the most distinctive Hakka characteristic, the relative equality of women within the family, derives from these special economic circumstances. Unlike other Chinese women, Hakka women farmed alongside their men in the fields giving them a more equal status within the family. Studies have found that Hakka husbands are more likely to side with their wives than their (the husband's) mothers in family disputes, an indication of the superior status of Hakka wives. At the same time Hakka women have not had the same control or responsibility for household finances as have other Chinese women.

Distinctive Customs. In a culture in which conformity is important, the Han have generally looked down upon the Hakka as poor and different. The Hakka have had different festivals, called some typical Chinese festivals by different names, and sometimes have not even observed the usual Han festivities. Most significantly the need for women to work the fields made foot-binding impractical, and throughout Chinese history Hakka women did not bind their feet as did most Han women. This big-footed characteristic of Hakka women led to false rumors that they had six toes and made nonfoot-binding Hakka women distinctly poor marriage prospects for Han men. Thus Hakka have married other Hakka and Han have married other Han, perpetuating the separation between the groups. During those periods when circumstances might vary the desirability of brides for either group, some intermarriage has occurred. In those cases Hakka daughters have commanded lower bride prices (and Hakka men have been required to pay higher bride prices).

Distinctive Architecture. While the migration was no doubt influenced by a lack of acceptance and persecution from other Han, it remains a mystery why the Hakka were not assimilated earlier and why they did not leave more traces of their culture as they migrated from north to south. They have nevertheless maintained their separate ethnic communities in southern China, where they are often the dominant local group. Especially in the mountainous border areas of Jiangxi, Fujian, and Guangdong provinces, the Hakka have evolved a distinctive form of architecture. Although using the same structural principles and materials as other Chinese, the Hakka have built three-and four-story brick-walled, pounded earth, fortresslike structures, sometimes two hundred feet high and large enough throughout to accommodate as many as thirty families. Although the *tulou* (earthen buildings) are sometimes square or rectangular-shaped, the most distinctive of them are round. Such buildings have only a few entrances on ground level and no exterior windows except on the upper floors, making them easy to defend. Community life takes place largely on the large interior courtyard of the *tulou*, reinforcing the impression that they were developed as a defense against attacks from bandits or outsiders.

Banditry and Rebellious Activities. The Hakka themselves have a reputation for banditry (although there are plenty of other Han who have turned to banditry during economic hard times). The generally poorer economic conditions of the Hakka have per-

Mao Zedong in 1949, shortly after the takeover of China. The Hakka had joined his forces in disproportionate numbers. (National Archives)

haps made this proclivity more pronounced. The Hakka have also frequently joined in many of the various rebellions in Chinese history. A Hakka led the TAIPING REBELLION in the mid-nineteenth century, and this single greatest threat to the Manchu Qing Dynasty (before its ultimate collapse in 1911) continued until the large number of Hakka troops in the Taiping ranks were depleted.

The Hakka have loomed large in the other revolutionary movements as well. One Triad (secret society) that aided SUN YAT-SEN prior to the 1911 revolution consisted solely of Hakka whose southern Chinese coastal village was the staging area for one of Sun Yat-sen's attacks. MAO ZEDONG's Communist forces appealed to poor peasants throughout China, and it is no surprise that the Hakka joined in disproportionately large numbers. Since the distinctive Hakka are regarded as outsiders by Han, their presence among the revolutionaries is not an unmixed blessing, for other Han have found it somewhat difficult to accept a revolutionary movement in which the Hakka have a large role. Still, they were credited for some of the Communist successes during the Chinese Civil War (1945-1949).

Hakka rebelliousness did not end with the Communist takeover, and the Hakka continued to show a tendency to educate their children themselves rather than to accept some elements of the Communist public education, an issue of some importance. Even with the emergence of Deng Xiaoping in 1979, the Hakka continue to resist some Dengist policies such as the "one family-one child" directive by continuing to have large numbers of children. Obviously one of the central government's standard punishments, denying educational benefits, has had little impact on the self-educated Hakka.

In modern times Hakkas have migrated to such widely scattered locales as Hong Kong, Malaysia, Singapore, Thailand, North Borneo, Sarawak, Jamaica, and North America.—*Richard L. Wilson*

SUGGESTED READINGS: • Char, Tin-Yuke. *The Hakka Chinese: Their Origin and Folk Songs.* Translated by C. H. Kwock. San Francisco: Jade Mountain Press, 1969. • Dreyer, June Teufel. *China's Forty Millions: Minority Nationalities and National Integration in the People's Republic of China.* Cambridge, Mass.: Harvard University Press, 1976. • Hsu, Immanuel C. Y. *The Rise of Modern China.* 4th ed. New York: Oxford University Press, 1990. • Kiang, Clyde. *The Hakka Odyssey and Their Taiwan Homeland.* Elgin, Pa.: Allegheny Press, 1992. • Knapp, Ronald G., ed. *Chinese Landscapes: The Village as Place*, chap-

ter 12. Honolulu: University of Hawaii Press, 1992.
• Levesque, Leonard. *Hakka Beliefs and Customs.* Translated by J. Maynard Murphy. Taichung: Kuang Chi Press, 1969. • Spence, Jonathan D. *The Search for Modern China.* New York: W. W. Norton, 1990.

Hakodate: Seaport city in Hokkaido, Japan, located on the island's southernmost tip. It was strategically important to American business in the nineteenth century and was opened to American ships and foreign trade by the Treaty of Kanagawa (1854). Hakodate's population in 1991 was 308,289.

Hakujin: Japanese word for white person or Caucasian.

Hall, Jack (Feb. 28, 1915, Ashland, Wis.—Jan. 2, 1971, San Francisco, Calif.): Union leader. Hall was regional director of the International Longshoremen's and Warehouseman's Union (ILWU) in Hawaii from 1944 until 1969. He moved to the West Coast in June, 1969, to become the union's vice president and director of organization. He was among the first twenty-four persons elected to Labor's International Hall of Fame, on December 6, 1973.

Hall graduated from high school at age sixteen. As a seaman, he first arrived in Hawaii in 1932. In 1934 he joined the Sailors Union of the Pacific and thereafter tended to engage in union activity.

Both the Hilo and Honolulu Longshoremen's Associations, for which he was organizing, were granted affiliation with the ILWU of America in November, 1936. In October, 1937, the Honolulu longshore local received an ILWU charter.

In 1938 Hall became editor of the *Voice of Labor* and did most of the writing for it and for its successor, the weekly *Kauai Herald*, which in June, 1941, became the *Herald*, published in Honolulu as a territory-wide labor paper.

The Japanese attack on Pearl Harbor, December 7, 1941, brought martial law and an end to labor organizing. In June, 1942, he married Yoshiko Ogawa. He became a labor-inspector for the Territorial government, Wages and Hours Division, and advanced to the rank of chief inspector. He left this job to become regional director for the ILWU.

Under Hall's guidance, the ILWU gained recognition as a dominant force in Hawaii, especially after the six-month longshore strike of 1949, in which the concentrated efforts of the employers failed to break the union.

Hall was among the seven arrested in Honolulu on August 28, 1951, on charges of violating the Smith Act of 1940, which makes it a criminal offense to advocate the overthrow of any government in the United States by force or violence. All seven were found guilty. The six male defendants were sentenced to five years in prison and fined $5,000. In January, 1958, the U.S. Ninth Circuit Court of Appeals reversed the Honolulu federal district court conviction and acquitted the seven.

Hall suffered a massive stroke and died in 1971.

Hamada Hikozo. *See* **Heco, Joseph**

Hampton v. Wong Mow Sun (1976): U.S. Supreme Court ruling that lawful aliens of the United States may not be denied federal employment solely on the basis of race or national origin. To do so is to deprive them of liberty without due process of law as guaranteed by the Fifth Amendment to the Constitution.

Plaintiffs Wong Mow Sun et al. were lawful U.S. citizens who applied for federal employment with the Civil Service Commission—positions for which they were qualified. The agency's hiring policy, however, stipulated that jobs in the federal sector were reserved expressly for "American citizens." Consequently, the plaintiffs were summarily turned away. They filed a class-action lawsuit in a California U.S. district court, alleging that the federal requirement of citizenship was arbitrary, discriminatory, and in violation of the due process clause. The government argued that the creation and enforcement of such a policy was within its discretionary power, that sensitive civil service positions involving policy-making and national security issues necessitate the loyalty inherent in citizenship, and that the rule encourages naturalization and therefore more active participation in American life.

The district court found for the government, but the U.S. Ninth Circuit Court of Appeals reversed in favor of the plaintiffs, and the Supreme Court upheld that ruling. The Court agreed that Congress and the president have broad authority to regulate matters pertaining to aliens, although the justices rejected any notion that such authority is plenary. Yet because these aliens were lawfully residing in the United States under provisions established by Congress and the president, an administrative decision to deprive them of their constitutional rights required the application of a legal standard that in this instance was not met. Moreover, by denying them federal employment, the commission deprived them of liberty without due process of law.

Han, Maggie (b. 1959, Providence, R.I.): Actor. American-born Han is the daughter of music professors who came to the United States from South Korea. Before acting, she was a fashion model—the first Korean American in the industry. While studying American literature at Harvard University and planning to become a journalist, she was cast in the Columbia Broadcasting Service (CBS) miniseries *Space* (1985). Dropping out of school, she left for Los Angeles, where she found theatrical work and studied acting. With *The Last Emperor* (1987), she landed her first screen role, playing the courtesan Eastern Jewel.

Hanapepe massacre (1924): Violent confrontation between striking plantation workers and police on September 9, 1924, at Hanapepe on the island of Kauai. Members of the Filipino Federation of Labor staged the strike in an unsuccessful attempt to force plantation owners to concede to their demands for better pay and improved working conditions. Sixteen strikers and four policemen were killed at Hanapepe, resulting in the arrest of union leader Pablo MANLAPIT and many other union members.

Hane, Mikiso (b. Jan. 16, 1922, Hollister, Calif.): Scholar. A professor of Japanese history at Knox College in Illinois, he went to Japan in 1933 and grew up in a peasant village in Hiroshima. He returned to the United States in 1940 and was interned in a relocation camp several years later. He is the author of *Peasants, Rebels and Outcasts: The Underside of Modern Japan* (1982) and *Japan: A Historical Survey* (1972).

Hangul (Korean letters): The script used to write the Korean language, allegedly invented five centuries ago by King Sejong of the Yi Dynasty (1392-1910). The late Edwin O. Reischauer, Harvard professor and former U.S. ambassador to Japan, has called *hangul* "perhaps the most scientific system of writing in general use in any country." This extraordinary writing system is one of the most unique in the world because it combines the best elements of alphabets and syllabaries.

The inventions of writing systems have been relatively rare in the course of human history; most scripts have been borrowed. For example the modern alphabets in the world today, including the Roman alphabet used to write English and many other Indo-European languages, have been modifications of early Near East writing from the eighteenth century B.C.E. A thousand years ago Chinese ideographs—pictorial symbols that

Basic Sounds of the Korean Alphabet (Yale romanization)	
Consonants	
ㄱ	hard g
ㄴ	n
ㄷ	d
ㄹ	l or r
ㅁ	m
ㅂ	b
ㅅ	s
ㅇ	-ng, no sound
ㅈ	j
ㅊ	ch
ㅋ	k
ㅌ	t
ㅍ	p
ㅎ	h
Vowels	
ㅏ	ah
ㅑ	yah
ㅓ	uh
ㅕ	yuh
ㅗ	oh
ㅛ	yo
ㅜ	oo
ㅠ	yu
ㅡ	no equivalent
ㅣ	ee

Korean script, or hangul, *appears on the floats and street banners in this Korean American parade in Los Angeles.* (The Korea Society/Los Angeles)

represent the meaning of words rather than their sounds—also spread all over Asia. In medieval Korea and Japan, for example, Chinese (or Chinese characters) were the only means by which people could write their native tongues. Because the Chinese and Korean languages are based upon totally different linguistic principles, however, it was difficult to modify the Chinese characters easily to write all the Korean sounds and grammatical forms. In 1446 Sejong (and most likely several other royal scholars) invented *hangul* to lessen the need for intellectuals to learn Chinese characters and to increase literacy of the masses.

The modern basic *hangul* alphabet consists of signs for fourteen consonants and ten vowels. There are also combination symbols for eleven compound vowels and five so-called double (or tense) consonants. Syllable "letters" are made in *hangul* by combining a consonant element with a vowel element, with the consonant symbol often coming above or to the left of the vowel symbol. A third consonant symbol may be added below the others, if the word being written has one. Thus individual letters get grouped into blocks of syllable units, about the size of a Chinese character, for ease of reading. This is somewhat akin to writing the English

word "cat" as ^C_TA. There are almost 3000 different syllables that could be constructed in *hangul*, though only about 350 to 400 are very common.

The most interesting property of these *hangul* symbols is the logic behind how they are written: theoretically the symbols depict, at least in some abstract way, how a particular sound is to be pronounced. Sejong and his consultants believed that the consonants in the Korean sound system fell into five classes. Bilabial sounds—sounds, such as *p* or *b*, made with the two lips—were represented by a box symbolizing the shape of the mouth. Alveolar sounds—sounds, such as *t* or *d*, made by the tongue touching the ridge of the roof of the mouth behind the teeth—were depicted with an angular *L* shape. Fricative-like sounds—such as *s* or *ch*—were written with an inverted *v*, representing the partial obstruction of air as it passes over the tongue. Velar sounds—such as *k* or *g*, which are made by the back of the tongue hitting the roof of the mouth—are drawn with a rotated *L*. Glottal sounds—such as *h*, which are made in the back of the throat—are written using a small circle depicting the larynx. All consonants with similar phonetic features have these visual cues.

The components of all *hangul* vowel symbols include either a dot, a single vertical line, or a single horizontal line. This choice of design is based on the notion of the *ying* and the *yang* (the dot representing Heaven, the horizontal line Earth, the vertical line representing Man). Though a little less transparent, the symbols for *hangul* vowels are based on linguistic principles similar to those that govern the consonants. All front vowels, for example, use the vertical straight line.

Hanihara Masanao (1876, Yamanashi Prefecture, Japan—1932, Japan): Diplomat. Born the son of prominent Japanese parents, Hanihara served as a member of the Japanese embassy staff in Washington, D.C., between 1902 and 1911. In 1922, he was appointed to serve as the Japanese ambassador to the United States. As a key diplomat during a period when anti-Japanese feeling was reaching a peak in California and elsewhere in the United States, Hanihara lobbied against proposed congressional legislation designed to prevent the entry of Japanese immigrants along with other aliens who were ineligible to become American citizens. Warning Secretary of State Charles Evans Hughes that such exclusion of Japanese immigrants would have grave consequences for the continued stability of relations between Japan and the United States, Hanihara aroused the bitter hostility of Massachusetts Senator Henry Cabot Lodge, the powerful chairman of the Senate Foreign Relations Committee. Believing that Hanihara's words posed a thinly veiled threat to U.S. security, Lodge vigorously championed the passage of the IMMIGRATION ACT OF 1924. In protest over the passage of this exclusionary legislation, Hanihara resigned his post as ambassador, as did his counterpart at the American embassy in Tokyo, Ambassador Cyrus E. Woods.

Hanka Enterprise Company: Construction company founded in the 1920's by Korean-born Hahn Si-dae in Delano, California. At the conclusion of World War I, Hahn and his family invested in agricultural land. This added space allowed them eventually to expand the company's holdings to four hundred acres. Prosperity during the 1920's led the company to expand its interests into Southern California by constructing apartments in Inglewood, a suburb of Los Angeles. The Hanka Enterprise Company provided welcome employment opportunities for many individuals in California's growing Korean community, including student immigrants who needed funds for their return to Korea. After World War II, the business was sold and Hahn returned to his homeland.

Hanmi Bank: First Korean American bank, established in Los Angeles, California, on December 15, 1982.

Hanoi: Capital of Vietnam since 1976, following the reunification of North and South Vietnam. Previously, Hanoi was the capital of North Vietnam (1954-1976) and of French Indochina (1887-1946). About 361 square miles in area, the city contained a population of almost 2.1 million people in 1992.

Hanren: Mandarin for "the Han people," the ethnic Chinese reared in China proper.

Hanyu pinyin. *See* **Chinese romanization; Pinyin**

Haole: Hawaiian word that refers to Caucasians, foreigners, and things of foreign origin.

Hapa: Hawaiian term most often used to describe a person who is half Caucasian and half Asian, or of mixed blood.

Hare Krishna. *See* **International Society for Krishna Consciousness**

Hare-Hawes-Cutting Act of 1933: Philippine independence legislation passed by the U.S. Congress. From the time of the 1907 Philippine National Assembly elections, when Manuel Quezon y Molina and Sergio Osmena won leadership of the Partido Nacionalistia (Nationalist Party), the basic question between the United States and its Asian colony was one of Philippine independence. Nine years later sympathetic Democrats in Congress, supported by President Woodrow Wilson, approved the Philippine Autonomy Act of 1916 (the JONES ACT), which pledged eventual self-rule for the Philippines as soon as a stable government could be established.

In the early 1930's circumstances prompted Congress to enact independence legislation. The Great Depression and a Democratic House of Representatives meant that legislators were more sensitive to labor and, in particular, to farm lobbies urging the exclusion of competing Filipino imports and workers from the American market. In fact West Coast Filipinos became the targets of violence and demonstration, much of it racially motivated. Moreover Japan's 1931 invasion of

Manchuria reminded the United States of the Philippines's strategic vulnerability.

In 1932 Representative Butler B. Hare and Senators Harry B. Hawes and Bronson Cutting introduced different independence measures, which after debate and compromise gained congressional adoption as the Hare-Hawes-Cutting Act. Supported by a Filipino independence mission in Washington, D.C. led by Osmena and Manuel Roxas, the proposal expressed the United States' determination to relieve itself of a colonial burden but likewise to retain some privileges. The bill provided for a ten-year commonwealth administration governed by an American-recognized charter. By its terms the U.S. president, represented by a high commissioner, would oversee constitutional changes, external affairs, and military land acquisitions. The measure permitted unlimited access to the Philippines for American exports but placed quotas on Filipino imports and immigrants.

President Herbert Hoover vetoed the Hare-Hawes-Cutting Act because of the archipelago's economic underdevelopment and military weakness. Nevertheless Congress overrode the president and the measure passed in early 1933. Under existing law the Philippine legislature was required to approve independence legislation; however, the lawmakers were influenced enough by Osmena's political rival Quezon to reject the act since provisions concerning trade, immigration, military reservations, and the high commissioner were objectionable.

Harijans (also, untouchables): Literally translated as "children of the god Hari Vishnu," an Asian Indian term popularized by nationalist leader Mahatma GANDHI during his crusade for India's freedom. "Untouchables" was the label formerly used to refer to a broad assortment of low-caste Hindu groups whose lives and work exposed them to polluting activities such as the killing of animals or the eating of meat, and the handling of bodily fluids or eliminations. Because of their plight, the untouchables were the targets of widespread discrimination and segregation: They often could not enter temples, attend schools, or draw water from wells used by higher castes. In other cases, merely to touch or see them was considered unclean.

Giving the untouchables a new name, Gandhi devoted much effort toward improving their social status and ensuring their integration into all areas of society.

Filipinos in the U.S. Navy c. 1930, shortly before passage of the 1933 independence legislation. (Filipino American National Historical Society)

The Mahatma Gandhi (center) was known for championing the cause of the poor and sick, including the "untouchables," whom he renamed the "children of Hari Vishnu" (harijans). (AP/Wide World Photos)

India adopted a new constitution in 1949 (and Pakistan in 1953) that abolished the use of the term and its accompanying social restrictions. India's modern constitution enumerates those castes that are disadvantaged and therefore eligible for special educational, vocational, and political rights administered by the government. The majority of these Scheduled Castes are Harijans.

Harris, Townsend (Oct. 3, 1804, Sandy Hill, N.Y.—Feb. 25, 1878, New York, N.Y.): Politician and diplomat. He was the first U.S. consul to reside in Japan, and his influence helped open Japan to economic penetration by Western powers. He negotiated a commercial treaty (signed July 29, 1858) between the United States and Japan, which guaranteed diplomatic and commercial privileges to the United States, such as the opening of six Japanese ports to U.S. trade. Early in his career, he persuaded the government of

Siam (now Thailand) to sign the first commercial treaty with the United States. After he resigned as consul in 1861, he became active in politics in New York City.

Harrison, Earl Grant (Apr. 27, 1899, Philadelphia, Pa.—July 28, 1955, Indian Lake, N.Y.): Government official. As director of the Alien Registration Office in Washington, D.C., he acceded to Korean American community demands that Koreans be allowed to register as Koreans, not as Japanese subjects, under the Alien Registration Act of 1940.

Harrison, Francis Burton (Dec. 18, 1873, New York, N.Y.—Nov. 21, 1957, Flemington, N.J.): Politician. Reared in New York City in a family with political connections to the Confederacy, Harrison graduated from Yale University in 1895 before studying law at New York Law School. After graduating from law

A group of Filipino Americans at a 1920's social gathering, during Harrison's heyday. (Filipinos: Forgotten Asian Americans by Fred Cordova)

school in 1897, Harrison was admitted to the New York state bar in 1898. Instead of going into private practice, he chose to teach evening classes at the law school before joining the Army to fight in the Spanish-American War. Launching his political career in 1902, Harrison was elected to Congress as a representative from New York's 13th congressional district. After running unsuccessfully to become the state's lieutenant governor in 1904 rather than seeking reelection to Congress, Harrison was again elected to a congressional seat in 1906 and was reelected for two additional terms. A member of several influential congressional committees, Harrison developed a reputation as an avowed anti-imperialist who particularly opposed American policy in the Philippines. When Woodrow Wilson took office as president in 1913, he appointed Harrison to serve as governor-general of the Philippines with specific instructions to prepare the island nation for independence by transferring decision-making power in domestic affairs into the hands of Filipinos. One of Harrison's first acts upon taking office was to appoint a majority of Filipino representatives to sit on the Philippine Commission, which served as the upper house of the Filipino legislature.

Once Congress passed the JONES ACT OF 1916, which gave the vote to all literate males and abolished the commission in favor of a mostly elected twenty-four-member Senate, Harrison transferred most of his domestic political responsibilities to the Senate and focused instead on matters of defense and foreign policy. Angry over their loss of political and economic advantages in this process of Filipinization, many American residents were overtly hostile to Harrison and were happy when he was replaced as governor-general in 1921. In 1935, he returned to the islands at the request of Manuel Quezon, president of the Philippines, to serve as an adviser to his old friend. When Quezon's government went into exile in the United States during World War II, Harrison continued to serve as an adviser. From 1946 through 1947, Harrison served as U.S. commissioner of civil claims in the Philippines and continued to serve the Filipino government in an advisory capacity. During his tenure as governor-general, Harrison earned the gratitude and respect of many Filipinos for laying the groundwork for independence; in honor of his contributions, Harrison was given a state funeral and was buried in the Philippines after his death in 1957.

Hartmann, Carl Sadakichi (Nov. 8, 1869, Deshima, Japan—Nov. 21, 1944, St. Petersburg, Fla.): Art critic, playwright, poet, and essayist. The son of Carl Herman Oscar Hartmann, a German merchant and diplomat, and his Japanese wife Osada, who died soon after her son's birth, Carl Sadakichi Hartmann was reared by wealthy relatives in Hamburg, Germany. Sent to live with a great uncle in the United States in 1882 after dropping out of a German naval academy and displeasing his father, Hartmann struck out on his own. He learned the printing trade, worked at a variety of jobs to support himself, and became an avid reader and admirer of American literature and art. After striking up a close friendship with poet Walt Whitman, Hartmann began to write critical essays on art that were published in newspapers in Boston and New York City during the 1880's and 1890's. In 1892, newspaper publisher Samuel S. McClure hired Hartmann to file stories from France as a roving correspondent. Satisfying his Bohemian impulses by traveling extensively in Europe, Hartmann became acquainted with Stéphane Mallarmé and other figures in the French Symbolist movement. Upon his return to the United States, Hartmann decided to publish his own art magazine entitled *The Art Critic* and worked diligently to gather support and a subscription base among prominent American artists, architects, and museum curators. He became a naturalized citizen in 1894. A champion of the avantgarde, he dabbled in art, dance, and Japanese poetry forms and incorporated Symbolist themes in plays such as *Christ* (1893) and *Buddha* (1897) and in the seven collected stories published as *Schopenhauer in the Air* (1899). Building on his reputation as a critic of avant-garde art, he launched the magazine *Art News* in 1896 and the periodical *The Stylus* in 1910, each of which had a brief yet influential impact on the art world. Hartmann became a close friend and disciple of noted photographer Alfred Stieglitz, who encouraged Hartmann to contribute to *Camera Notes* and later to *Camera Work*. Hartmann's passionate advocacy of photography as an art form and his distinguished criticism of photographic technique established him as a premier critic of this rapidly growing artistic discipline. In 1901, Hartmann published his two-volume magnum opus, *A History of American Art*, which soon became the standard account of the development of modern American art. In great demand as a lecturer and hailed as the "King of Greenwich Village," Hartmann drew upon his cultural heritage and published a sensitively written volume entitled *Japanese Art* in 1904. During the 1920's, Hartmann moved to Hollywood, where he tried unsuccessfully to support himself by writing film scripts. Hartmann's friendship with John Barrymore, W. C. Fields, and other harddrinking Hollywood stars aggravated his alcoholism and poor health. Settling in a shack on the Morongo Indian reservation near Banning, California, Hartmann kept in contact with a daughter who lived nearby, maintained a lively correspondence with intellectuals such as Ezra Pound and George Santayana, and avoided wartime relocation during World War II. He died while visiting his eldest daughter at her home in Florida in 1944.

Hatchet men: Particularly among the Chinese in America, enforcers or hired killers employed by the Chinese *tongs*. The *tongs* were secret fraternal organizations bound by sworn brotherhood and secrecy. Many *tongs* were involved in gambling and prostitution.

Hattori, James: Broadcast journalist. After working at local stations in Seattle and Houston, he was hired by CBS to serve as a network correspondent in Dallas. In 1993, CBS transferred him to Tokyo, where he covers Asian affairs. He also served as vice president for broadcast for the ASIAN AMERICAN JOURNALISTS ASSOCIATION.

Hawaii: The United States' fiftieth state, a chain of primarily volcanic islands in the northcentral Pacific Ocean. From East to West the main islands are Hawaii, Maui, Kahoolawe, Molokai, Lanai, Oahu, Kauai, and Niihau. Of these, only Kahoolawe is uninhabited. Of the fifty United States, Hawaii is the southernmost and forty-seventh largest in area. Its combined land area of 6,471 square miles contained a 1992 population of about 1.16 million people. The capital city is Honolulu, on Oahu.

Climate and Vegetation. The prevailing northeast trade winds traveling over cool ocean currents create a climate cooler than elsewhere in the same latitude. In the lowlands, the average yearly temperature is about 75 degrees Fahrenheit. There is more rain in winter than in summer.

The isolation of Hawaii, the barriers of deep canyons and high precipices, the wide variation in different localities of rainfall, temperature, wind, barometric pressure, and geologic age caused the evolution of a flora that is first in the world in percentage of endemic genera and species.

Isolation discouraged the introduction of fauna,

HAWAIIAN ISLANDS

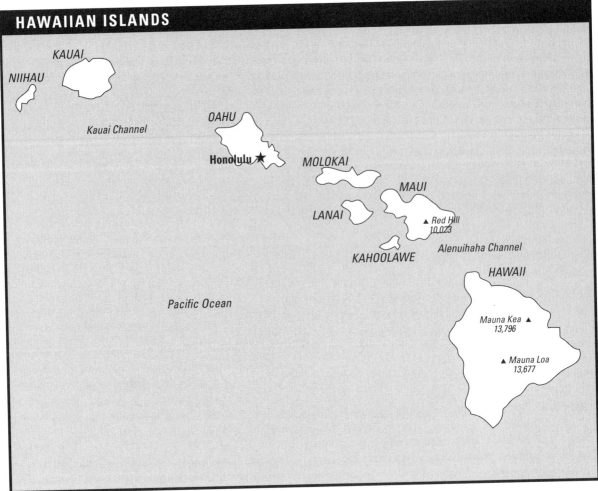

there being only one representative, a small bat, before the arrival of humans. There were about 125 species of birds, perhaps a score of which are now extinct. Nevertheless the islands form the largest and most numerous bird colony in the world. Many of the varieties of sea birds are found nowhere else.

Population. Hawaii's population in the 1990 census was 1,108,229. The state ranked forty-first among the fifty United States in total population. In 1990, Caucasians made up 33 percent of the state's population, Japanese 22 percent, Filipinos 15 percent, Native Hawaiians 12.5 percent, and Chinese 6 percent, with smaller groups making up the remainder. These figures are misleadingly precise, however, since intermarriage among ethnic groups is extremely common.

Oahu is the state's most populous island, with almost 73 percent of the total population. Close to Honolulu is the naval base of Pearl Harbor. Members of the armed forces and their local dependents made up 9.5 percent of the resident total in 1993.

Economy. In 1993 the gross state product was about $27 billion. More than six million tourists a year, many from Japan and other Asian countries, spend about $11 billion dollars annually in Hawaii; defense expenditures amount to more than $3 billion, sugar production $329 million, and pineapple production $216 million. Per capita personal income is $20,400. Cost of living exceeds that of the mainland states by about 38 percent on average.

History. The original Polynesian residents of the islands, probably from Tahiti or the Marquesas Islands, began arriving in huge sailing canoes about 400 C.E. or earlier. Voyages to and from Tahiti continued until about 1300 C.E.

There followed a long period of isolation, with only the legends of their homeland to remind the island residents that any land existed outside their archipelago. The islands were disunited, with war between rival chiefs the normal state of affairs.

The world learned of the archipelago when Captain

James Cook, the English navigator, discovered it. Cook landed at Waimea, Kauai, January 20, 1778. He named the archipelago the "Sandwich Islands" in honor of his patron, the earl of Sandwich. He identified the inhabitants, numbering perhaps 300,000, as Indians, a generic term of the period for aborigine.

Despite Cook's efforts to safeguard the natives against it, members of his crew introduced venereal disease. Ships that followed introduced more ailments. Visitors would also demoralize the residents by demonstrating that the local taboos could be violated with impunity.

One thing the newcomers introduced—which an enterprising chief, Kamehameha I of the Island of Hawaii, was quick to utilize—were firearms and sailors skilled in their use. By 1795 Kamehameha had conquered all the main islands except Kauai and Niihau. In 1804 an epidemic, probably cholera, destroyed much of the population. Kauai and Niihau fell to Kamehameha without a struggle in 1810. For the first time, the archipelago was united under a single chief.

American missionaries began arriving in 1820, making English the dominant language and introducing American concepts into the local culture. The missionaries gained the cooperation of the rulers and guided them toward governance by monarchy, with

Population of Hawaii by Ethnicity, 1853-1990

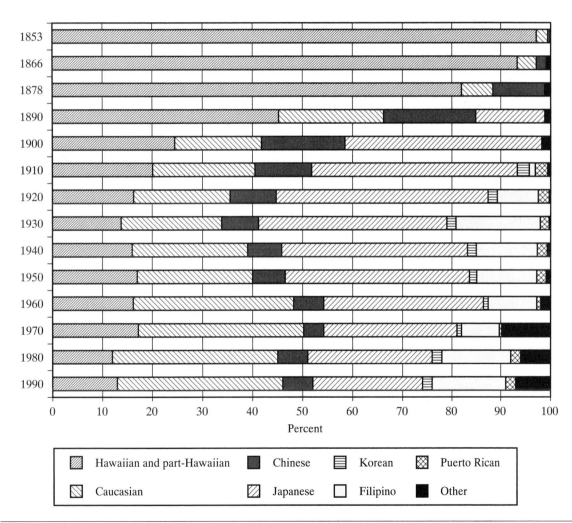

Legend:
- Hawaiian and part-Hawaiian
- Caucasian
- Chinese
- Japanese
- Korean
- Filipino
- Puerto Rican
- Other

Sources: Andrew W. Lind, *Hawaii's People.* 4th ed. Honolulu: University of Hawaii Press, 1980. U.S. Bureau of the Census, *Statistical Abstract of the United States: 1981*, 1981. U.S. Bureau of the Census, *1990 Census: General Population Characteristics, Hawaii*, 1992.

direct descendants of Kamehameha becoming the islands' first monarchs.

The archipelago became known as "Hawaii." Those aboard arriving ships (whalers, at first) found that the sandalwood of Hawaii could be sold profitably in China. As the sandalwood supply depleted, entrepreneurs cultivated sugarcane and then pineapple. To work the plantations the planters imported large numbers of laborers, first from China and then from Japan, Portugal, Puerto Rico, the Philippines, and other areas.

Dissatisfied with the monarchical government, an American business group overthrew it in a bloodless revolution in 1893 and asked the U.S. government to annex the territory. The request being rejected, the group formed the Republic of Hawaii. Hawaii became a U.S. possession in 1898 and a U.S. territory in 1900.

When Japan attacked Pearl Harbor, December 7, 1941, suspicion of collaboration with the attackers fell on the large group of residents of Japanese origin. The only substantiated case was on the isolated island of Niihau, where a Japanese alien and a Hawaii-born Nikkei couple assisted a Japanese fighter pilot who,

after the attack, had landed his disabled plane there. By contrast, the outstanding war record of the 100TH INFANTRY BATTALION, the 442ND REGIMENTAL COMBAT TEAM, and the interpreters and translators of the U.S. Military Intelligence Service (MIS) who served on the front lines in Asia and the Pacific, all primarily Nikkei, won high commendation and served to dissipate the original public distrust.

Hawaii was granted statehood on August 21, 1959.

Many Nikkei veterans went on to find high places in the civilian community. In the first election after the granting of statehood, Daniel INOUYE was elected to the U.S. House of Representatives. He would go on to become a power in the U.S. Senate. In the same election, Hiram L. FONG, son of Chinese immigrants, was elected to the U.S. Senate. In 1974 George ARIYOSHI became the first Nikkei governor.—*Allan Beekman*

SUGGESTED READINGS: • Forbes, David W. *Encounters with Paradise: Views of Hawaii and Its People, 1778-1941*. Honolulu: Honolulu Academy of Arts, 1992. • Allen, Gwenfread. *Hawaii's War Years: 1941-1945*. Edited by Aldyth V. Morris. Honolulu: Univer-

Diamond Head from Waikiki Beach and the Halekulani Hotel, Oahu: Today, tourism is one of the largest sources of income for the islands. (John Penisten, Pacific Pictures)

sity of Hawaii Press, 1952. • Hazama, Dorothy Ochiai, and Jane Okamoto Komeiji. *Okage Sama De: The Japanese in Hawaii, 1885-1985*. Honolulu: Bess Press, 1986. • Kotani, Roland. *The Japanese in Hawaii: A Century of Struggle*. Honolulu: Hawaii Hochi, 1985. • Kuykendall, R. S. *The Hawaiian Kingdom*. 3 vols. Honolulu: University of Hawaii Press, 1938-1967. • Odo, Franklin, and Kazuko Sinoto. *A Pictorial History of the Japanese in Hawaii, 1885-1924*. Edited by Bonnie Tocher Clause. Honolulu: Bishop Museum, 1985. • Ogawa, Dennis M. *Kodomo No Tame Ni: For the Sake of the Children: The Japanese American Experience in Hawaii*. Honolulu: University Press of Hawaii, 1978.

Hawaii, Annexation of (1898): On January 17, 1893, thirteen men led by sons of American missionaries, with U.S. troops standing by, proclaimed the end of the Hawaiian monarchy and set out to annex Hawaii to the United States. Queen LILIUOKALANI surrendered and appealed to President Benjamin Harrison and incoming president Grover Cleveland to restore her sovereignty. Congress, to which Cleveland referred the matter, could agree only that the United States should not intervene further in Hawaii for the time being, thus accepting the overthrow. Annexation attempts failed in 1897 and 1898, but in July, 1898, following military victory in a war against Spain, Congress voted to annex the Hawaiian Islands as a U.S. possession.

U.S. Involvement in the Overthrow. U.S. involvement, including the allegation of a conspiracy to take over Hawaii, has remained controversial. The annexationists claimed to be acting in response to the queen's stated intention to restore some of the powers taken from her predecessor in 1887 and denied any American complicity. It is generally agreed, however, that U.S. minister to Hawaii John L. Stevens' recognition of the new provisional government immediately after its proclamation, when it controlled only a single building, was not in accord with U.S. policy. He has also been widely criticized for this advance assurances of support for the coup.

Stevens' extensive collaboration with the insurrectionists prior to January, 1893, however, was consistent with U.S. policy to maintain hegemony vis-à-vis other nations and to intervene in internal political conflicts on behalf of local Americans, as it had in 1874, 1887, 1889, and 1890. During 1892 Lorrin A. Thurston, the leader of annexationists in Hawaii since 1887, communicated to the Harrison Administration his secret intention to annex Hawaii, deposing the

Lorrin A. Thurston, leader of the annexationists. (Hawaii State Archives)

queen if necessary. The administration indicated its receptivity to an annexation proposal. From late April through early November, 1892, the U.S. government paid extraordinary attention to Hawaii, stationing war vessels and reporting on every political development, apparently preparing for any contingency.

U.S. Reaction to the Overthrow. In response to the queen's appeal, Cleveland sent James H. Blount to investigate. He found that the overthrow would not have succeeded without the active intervention of U.S. representatives. Accepting his findings, the president attempted secret negotiations to restore the queen. While these were in progress, he was forced by public pressure to refer the whole matter to Congress for resolution.

Congress disposed of the matter in highly partisan fashion. The final resolution passed by the Senate on May 31, 1894, cleared both Stevens and Cleveland of charges of illegal intervention. It postponed, by ignoring, the decision over annexation for the time being. By avoiding further intervention the Senate thus relin-

Annexation ceremonies before the Iolani Palace on August 12, 1898. (Hawaii State Archives)

quished responsibility for any judgment on the overthrow.

The queen has been held responsible for the failure of the restoration attempt because of her refusal to grant amnesty to her opponents until forced to do so. This was not, however, the crucial factor that caused the president to refer the matter to Congress.

By failing to retract the recognition illegally accorded to the provisional government, Cleveland and the Congress in effect transferred effective sovereignty over the Hawaiian Islands from the monarchy to the Americans who had overthrown it. U.S. acceptance of the coup in Hawaii was thus the most important act establishing U.S. responsibility for the overthrow.

Annexation. The overthrow was not debated seriously when annexation came before Congress again in 1897-1898, the assumption apparently being that history had rendered its judgment on any questions that had previously being raised. Senator John T. Morgan, chair of the Senate Foreign Relations Committee and the man most responsible for annexation, argued that annexation was incidental to a long-standing policy of advancing exclusive U.S. interest in Hawaii. Arguments for annexation were explicitly embedded in an imperialist ideology. Opposition to annexation, as in 1894, was based upon the claims that admission of such an offshore territory would depart from U.S. anticolonial tradition and/or set a precedent for additional acquisitions. Such arguments stalled annexation until July of 1898.

The Newlands Resolution annexing Hawaii passed before a decision had been made to retain the Philippines, and when the Philippine insurgency was only beginning. It probably passed because of Hawaii's unique position on world trade routes, together with a felt need for American expansion into the vast market of Asia, coming at the end of a long and severe depression in which domestic unrest had reached unprecedented levels.

Racist attitudes in Congress provided a rationale for imperialism and prevented serious consideration of the rights of indigenous Hawaiians. In several votes, both houses of Congress decided that requiring a vote on annexation by the people of Hawaii was not required by the federal or Hawaii state constitutions.

Significance. As a result of the overthrow and annexation, indigenous Hawaiians lost their nationality, polity, lands, and other resources and became a people without any recognized right to self-determination or a land base. Lands belonging to the Hawaiian government at the time of the overthrow were taken over by the provisional government and ceded to the U.S. government upon annexation. They have subsequently been used for general public purposes without compensation to Hawaiians until 1992. Indigenous Hawaiians, who as a whole condemn the overthrow, maintain that it was the result of an armed invasion by U.S. forces, planned as part of a conspiracy between Minister Stevens and the American insurrectionists. This belief has long been a source of feelings of loss and betrayal and has led an increasing number of Hawaiians in the 1990's to demand restitution and to reassert their inherent sovereignty in some form.

The increasing attention being given internationally to the claim of indigenous peoples to be treated as subjects equal to nation-states under international law gives this demand a broader significance.—*Stephen T. Boggs*

SUGGESTED READINGS: • Liliuokalani, Queen of Hawaii. *Hawaii's Story by Hawaii's Queen.* Boston: Lothrop, Lee and Shepard Co., 1898. • Osborne, Thomas J. *"Empire Can Wait": American Opposition to Hawaiian Annexation, 1893-98.* Kent, Ohio: Kent State University Press, 1981. • Russ, William A., Jr. *The Hawaiian Revolution, 1893-94.* Selinsgrove, Pa.: Susquehanna University Press, 1959. • U.S. Congress. House. *President's Message Relating to the Hawaiian Islands.* 53rd Congress, 2d Session, 1893. Executive Document 47. • U.S. Congress. Senate. *Senate Report 227 ("Morgan Report").* 53rd Congress, 2d session, 1894.

Hawaii, Martial law in: On December 7, 1941, during World War II (1939-1945), Japan launched a surprise air attack against the U.S. Navy stationed at PEARL HARBOR, Oahu, Hawaii. Following the bombardment, the Hawaiian Islands, as well as the Midway Islands, an atoll that today forms part of Honolulu County, became a war zone under constant threat of assault. From June 6, 1942, when U.S. forces were victorious in the Battle of MIDWAY, the external threat dissipated, but among the military high command the belief persisted that if Japanese aliens or Japanese American traitors were responsible for intelligence leading to the attack, acts of sabotage would occur during the war. As a result martial law was imposed throughout Hawaii; civilian efforts to chip away at martial law excesses failed until the war ended.

Scope of Military Control. A few hours after the attack, Lieutenant General Walter Short, commander-in-chief of Pacific forces at Pearl Harbor, called upon Joseph Poindexter, the civilian governor, to declare martial law, to suspend the writ of habeas corpus, and to hand over authority to the military. Poindexter then acceded to the request, and Short declared himself military governor. Instead of relying on the civilian government, as is customary in a situation of martial law, military authorities took over nearly all functions of civilian government. All citizens were subject to peremptory arrest at the discretion of military authorities, with subsequent trials in military rather than civilian courts. Hawaii thereby began the war under military rule, not martial law. All civilian law was superseded by military orders. General Delos EMMONS, who replaced Short on December 17, refused to restore civilian rule after the Battle of Midway.

The military assumed powers unprecedented in American history, exceeding even those enforced against Southern states during and after the Civil War. The press, subject to censorship, could not report on court proceedings. The vast majority of defendants were found guilty, without the possibility of appeal, and sentences for even mild misdemeanors were severe. All residents were fingerprinted, and both mail and telephone calls were censored. A blackout was imposed; heavy blankets had to block all light emanating from within private homes, even during the heat and humidity of the summer. Dogs and humans had to be indoors during the nightly curfew. Sugar workers were forbidden to change jobs, all holidays were suspended, and those people out of work were assigned jobs by the U.S. Employment Service. Everyone carried gas masks, and every house had to build a bomb shelter. The military regulated garbage disposal, public health facilities, prices and rent, taxicabs, and traffic, and even collected court and liquor permit fees. At the same time, the military supplied enough food and other provisions to civilians so that there was no cause for complaint over material conditions.

Political Effects. During the war the Federal Bureau of Investigation (FBI) gathered information on individual Japanese who were suspected of conspiring with Tokyo. Although the president of Hawaiian Telephone urged the removal of all Japanese from Hawaii to the mainland, half the population of the islands was Japanese, who in turn ran businesses vital to the war

On December 7, 1941, the Japanese bombed Pearl Harbor. Martial law in Hawaii followed in June, 1942. (National Archives)

effort, so the suggestion was impractical. Although staff at the Japanese consulate engaged in spying, no evidence ever emerged about any disloyal acts on the part of Japanese residents or Japanese Americans in Hawaii. Nevertheless some 540 aliens were interned in small camps on Oahu, 930 were transferred to mainland camps, and families who lived near military bases continued farming their land but were not allowed to live in their homes. Although Japanese Americans were dismissed from the territory's National Guard, they soon formed the VARSITY VICTORY VOLUNTEERS (VVV), were accepted as laborers for the Army Corps of Engineers, and ultimately formed the core of the 100TH INFANTRY BATTALION and the 442ND REGIMENTAL COMBAT TEAM, which fought in Europe. Many Japanese residents, including their U.S.-born children, were harassed by persons of other races during the war.

Efforts to Restore Civilian Authority. When Poin-

dexter's term expired in 1942, U.S. President Franklin D. Roosevelt appointed Federal District Court Judge Ingram Stainback as the new civilian governor. Hawaii's civilian government was under the jurisdiction of the Department of the Interior, so Stainback soon flew to Washington, D.C. to urge Interior Secretary Harold Ickes to effect a restoration of civilian government, which occurred by early 1943. Military rule ended, Emmons was replaced by General Robert Richardson, but martial law (including the nightly blackout and curfew) continued until October, 1944, when it was rescinded by the president. Among persons detained by the military for political reasons, some 413 Hawaii internees were then allowed to go home, 50 aliens remained in internment camps, and 67 Japanese were shipped to relocation camps on the mainland to await the end of the war.

Federal courts were called upon to decide whether military rule in Hawaii was constitutional. In *Zimmer-*

man v. Walker (1942) a naturalized German claimed that he was illegally interned in 1942 because of his national origin; the matter was finessed when the military shipped the plaintiff to the mainland, where he was released from custody, rendering the case moot. Two other naturalized Germans, also detained without charges, pressed similar claims successfully; in mid-1943, when the court ordered their release, Richardson refused to do so, whereupon he was ruled to be in contempt of court in *United States v. Richardson* (1943). Richardson then banned the issuance of writs of habeas corpus, refused to pay even a reduced fine of $100, and shipped the two to the mainland to be released. In 1944 a civilian who had quarrelled with two marine sentries was sentenced to jail by a military court for six months. After a petition for a writ of *habeas corpus* was then filed in federal court, thereby challenging the legality of martial law, the district court ruled in favor of the petition a few months later. The military appealed the case, Roosevelt rescinded martial law by executive order, and in 1946 the Supreme Court retroactively ruled martial law unconstitutional in *Duncan v. Kahanamoku.—Michael Haas*

SUGGESTED READINGS: • Anthony, J. Garner. *Hawaii Under Army Rule*. Stanford, Calif.: Stanford University Press, 1955. • Daws, Gavan. *Shoal of Time: A History of the Hawaiian Islands*. New York: Macmillan, 1968. • Lind, Andrew. *Hawaii's Japanese: An Ex-*

Although many Japanese Americans in Hawaii were interned in camps on Oahu and elsewhere, there were others who served in the armed forces for the United States. (National Archives)

periment in Democracy. Princeton, N.J.: Princeton University Press, 1946. • Ogawa, Dennis, and Evarts C. Fox, Jr. "Japanese Internment and Relocation: The Hawaii Experience." Paper presented at the International Conference on Relocation and Redress: The Japanese-American Experience, 1983.

Hawaii, Republic of: The Hawaiian Islands following the 1893 deposing of the last reigning monarch, Queen LILIUOKALANI, who was replaced by a provisional government, until the 1898 annexation of Hawaii as a U.S. possession. The Republic of Hawaii was founded on July 4, 1894, with the adoption of a new constitution and the naming of Sanford B. Dole as president. The republic ended on July 7, 1898, when U.S. president William McKinley signed the annexation bill. Formal annexation ceremonies followed in Hawaii on August 12, 1898.

Hawaii's brief history as a republic is best seen as a transitional stage between independent monarchy and U.S. possession. In early 1893 a group calling itself the "COMMITTEE OF SAFETY," with the cooperation of the U.S. minister to Hawaii, John L. Stevens, orchestrated the landing of a small contingent of American troops, ostensibly to protect American lives and property. In the ensuing confusion the committee announced the establishment of a provisional government. Liliuokalani, wishing to avoid bloodshed and believing that the U.S. government would return her to power, abdicated under protest.

The provisional government, run largely by sugar-business interests whose immediate goals included American annexation, was frustrated by newly elected U.S. president Grover Cleveland, who recognized that the queen had been unlawfully deposed and who therefore refused to annex Hawaii. Yet Cleveland also refused to send the American troops needed to restore Liliuokalani to power. Subsequently the provisional government soon created the temporary Republic of Hawaii.

Counterrevolution was attempted only once, in 1895, and served only to strengthen the hold of the new

The short-lived Republic, with Sanford B. Dole as its president, can be seen as a transitional stage between independent monarchy (to 1894) and U.S. annexation (1898). Its legacy—the incursion of wealthy white agricultural interests—can be seen to this day. (John Penisten, Pacific Pictures)

government. An American trade agreement in 1894 aided the thriving sugar industry, and many Japanese laborers were brought in to work the sugar plantations.

Under the laws of the republic, only wealthy male property owners could vote and participate in the highly centralized government, comprising two legislative houses of fifteen members each. Finally, with the inauguration of a proannexation U.S. president and the strategic importance of Hawaii underscored by the 1898 Spanish-American War, the Republic of Hawaii realized its goal of becoming a U.S. possession. It became a U.S. territory, the Territory of Hawaii, in 1900.

Hawaii Herald: Semimonthly, English-language newspaper, published in Honolulu and directed at Hawaiians of Japanese ancestry. The approximately twenty-page tabloid has a circulation of about ten thousand and is published on the first and third Friday of each month, in the same building as the bilingual (Japanese/English) daily *Hawaii Hochi*.

The Hawaii Herald was officially established in March, 1969, as a weekly, eight-page tabloid. It had been, however, briefly published earlier, in connection with the *Hawaii Hochi*. The *Hawaii Hochi* was established in 1912 by Fred Kinzaburo MAKINO, who was born in Yokohama, Japan, of a British father and a Japanese mother; his parents had immigrated to Hawaii in 1899.

Following the Japanese attack on PEARL HARBOR on December 7, 1941, the military closed the *Hawaii Hochi*, but it was published the following month as *The Hawaii Herald*. In 1952, it began publishing again under the name *Hawaii Hochi*.

In 1962, Konosuke Oishi, of the *Shizuoka Shimbun*, in Japan, purchased the *Hawaii Hochi*. He decided that the community needed an English-language publication directed at the growing number of those of Japanese descent (Nikkei) who are unable to read Japanese. With *Hawaii Hochi* president and publisher Paul Yempuku, Oishi created *The Hawaii Herald* in 1969.

In the 1970's, however, a national shortage of newsprint caused *The Hawaii Herald* to suspend its publication. It began republishing in May, 1980, and continued to appear as a semimonthly.

The majority of subscribers to *The Hawaii Herald* are Nikkei. The newspaper focuses primarily on the Nikkei of Hawaii, and it seeks to dissipate stereotypes of the Nikkei and to present them as a diverse socioeconomic group with diverse livelihoods, skills, talents, and interests.

It publishes historical articles about the plantations, World War II, the postwar period, and Japanese cultural observances such as New Year's. It also includes articles about Japanese immigrants and their descendants in Hawaii, interviews with Nikkei who have made a significant contribution to Hawaii, book reviews, short stories with a Nikkei motif, and interviews with Nikkei authors. The newspaper also publishes articles from the *Japan Times* and short articles gleaned from the mainland Nikkei press.

Other features include special issues commemorating events such as the Nikkei internment, the anniversary of the formation of the 100th Infantry Battalion, and the ninetieth anniversary of Okinawan immigration to Hawaii. Among its sections are those devoted to art, local events, business and money, Japanese-language lessons, sports, and cartoons.

Hawaii Hochi: Japanese-language newspaper founded in Hawaii by Fred Kinzaburo MAKINO, a Japanese-born merchant turned publisher, in 1912. Unhappy over the alleged connections between the HAWAII SUGAR PLANTERS ASSOCIATION and *Nippu Jiji*, Hawaii's leading Japanese-language newspaper, Makino began publishing his own newspaper. Under his editorial leadership, the *Hawaii Hochi* took a strong pro-labor stance in supporting the 1920 Plantation Strike and increased its circulation despite its criticism of the role played by the Japanese Federation of Labor in the dispute. The *Hawaii Hochi* pledged its support to the campaign against restrictions placed on Hawaii's burgeoning Japanese-language schools. Arguing for the rights of Japanese Americans to full citizenship, the paper's editorials also spoke out against the caste system in Hawaii and argued for Nisei to break their ties with Japan in order to convince the U.S. government of their serious intent to become citizens. In 1942, the name of the paper was changed to the *Hawaii Herald*, but it resumed publication under its original title in 1952. After Makino died in 1953, the paper continued under Hawaiian ownership until 1962, when it was purchased by Japanese newspaper owner Konosuke Oishi. In 1969, the paper began to publish an English-language edition under the name *Hawaii Herald*.

Hawaii International Film Festival (HIFF): Internationally acclaimed annual film event, created in 1981 to promote films from Asia, the Pacific region, and the United States. It was founded at Honolulu's East-West Center.

A major film festival that charges no admission fees, the HIFF is a popular event featuring workshops, seminars, awards, and film screenings. The winner of the HIFF's Best Documentary Award is automatically considered for an Academy Award (Oscar) nomination. Other awards include the East-West Center Award to the film that best promotes understanding among the peoples of Asia, the Pacific, and North America; the Hawaii Filmmakers Award; the Vision in Film Award to an organization; and the Eastman Kodak Cinematography Award.

In 1990 the HIFF began the Children and Family Film Series, a program that utilizes film study guides to help Hawaii's high schoolers analyze films from other countries in an effort to promote cross-cultural literacy.

In 1991 one of the highlights of the festival was the introduction of films from what used to be Soviet Central Asia: children's films such as *Summer Heat* (1988), *A Wolf Cub Among Men* (1989), and *To Bring up a Man* (1982); *Spotted Dog Running Along the Seashore* (1990), which describes the lives of the people living on Sakhalin Island, north of Japan; and *The Running Target* (1991), which includes documentary footage of the brutal suppression of a 1986 student demonstration in Alma-Ata.

In 1992 the twelfth annual HIFF, employing forty-seven screens on six Hawaiian Islands, showed 125 films from twenty countries to fifty thousand people in two weeks. Activities included The Eastman Kodak Seminar on the Art of Cinematography, with three-time Academy Award winner Haskell Wexler; First-Time Directors of Feature Films; A Tribute to Satyajit Ray; The Independent Spirit of Japan; How the West Looks at Asia; Environmental Films; and Chinese Films in 1992. There was also the announcement of the formal inauguration of the Network for the Promotion of Asian Cinema (NETPAC), a group of twenty member countries dedicated to expanding the distribution of Asian films worldwide and encouraging the inclusion of Asian cinema in educational curricula.

Hawaii Seven: Seven island residents, "alleged Communist leaders," tried in the early 1950's for violating the Alien Registration Act of 1940 (Smith Act). The act made it a crime to teach or advocate the forceful overthrow of the U.S. government or to form or join groups devoted to that purpose. Arrested in 1951, the seven defendants were convicted of conspiracy in 1953. Years later, in 1958, an appeals court reversed their convictions.

Beginning in the mid-1940's, the International Longshoremen's and Warehousemen's Union (ILWU) had launched a series of successful industry-wide labor strikes on the sugar and pineapple plantations of Hawaii. The ILWU then proceeded to unionize the well-established BIG FIVE island companies. Such activities provided the union with an expanding base of political clout. The ILWU united workers regardless of race and won important concessions for them. Yet conservative factions backed by Republican business interests fought the spread of union influence by accusing the ILWU of being sympathetic to the Communist Party and therefore a threat to national security. Soon, as former ILWU members as well as the media turned against the organization, so did the tide of public opinion.

Meanwhile, in Washington, D.C., the House Select Committee to Investigate Un-American Activities had been convened for the purpose of exposing Communist infiltration in the country. In 1951, based on the testimony of Jack KAWANO, formerly a key ILWU figure who had recently lost a power struggle for union control to Jack HALL, the committee authorized the arrests of Hall and six others, at least several of whom had known Communist Party ties.

Five of the seven had been among the Reluctant 39, so called because they had refused to answer leading questions put to them by the committee during hearings in Honolulu in 1950. The thirty-nine were eventually cleared of all charges.

Hawaii Times: Japanese-English newspaper founded in Hawaii in 1892. The islands' first Japanese newspaper, it appeared first as the *Nippon Shuho*. After undergoing half a dozen name changes, it was published as the *Nippu Jiji* from 1906 until 1942, the year it became the *Hawaii Times*. Through the 1910's and early 1920's, the publication remained the Territory's most popular Japanese newspaper; its influence continued to be widely felt in the several decades that followed. The newspaper is no longer published.

Hawaiian Creole English. *See* **Pidgin**

Hawaiian dance. *See* **Hawaiian music and dance**

Hawaiian Homes Commission Act of 1920: U.S. legislation that, with regard to the Territory of Hawaii, mandated the return of specified U.S. public lands to Native Hawaiians under a program of so-called rehabilitation. When the U.S. government annexed Hawaii in 1898, about 1.7 million acres of government and crown lands were ceded to the former by the Republic of Hawaii, which had been created by a group of Americans who had seized power in 1893 with the assistance of U.S. government minister John L. Stevens and the U.S. Navy. It was these lands and the way in which they had come into American possession that figured in the passage of the act. In passing the act the U.S. Congress recognized an obligation to Native Hawaiians and sought to fulfill it by returning them to their native lands. Congress was, however, persuaded to exempt the most useful of the ceded lands from the act. Underfunded from the start and with lands not suited for agriculture, the Hawaiian Homes program was doomed in carrying out its announced intent of returning Hawaiians to the land. The resulting disappointment has caused continued protest by Hawaiians.

Congressional Intent of the Hawaiian Homes Commission Act. In passing the act, Congress clearly recognized that the Native Hawaiians had a moral, if not a legal, right to some of the public lands of Hawaii as a matter of fairness in the light of the fact that the lands had been taken from the Hawaiians without any payment to them, and that Hawaiians, like Indians, had been deprived of their lands without their consent.

Yet despite this recognition of Native Hawaiian rights by Congress, the actual political motive for passage of the act was to prevent some 26,000 acres of public land then being leased by the Territory for sugar production from becoming available for homesteading

Ola'a Sugar Company in Keaau, on the Island of Hawaii, c. 1920. (Lyman House Memorial Museum)

by Hawaiians and the public. Leases on these lands, part of the crown and government lands ceded to the United States, were about to run out, threatening to deprive the Territorial government of a major source of its income. Accordingly, when Territorial senator John Wise in 1920 presented to Congress a plan for offering public lands to Hawaiians, it was opposed by the remainder of the Territorial delegation. Wise, however, captured the sympathy of the House Committee on the Territories by describing the plight of the Native Hawaiians, whose numbers had been greatly reduced by disease and the destruction of their traditional way of life. The Territorial representatives therefore decided to compromise by proposing to continue leasing public lands for sugar so that a portion of the revenues from these leases could be used to finance the rehabilitation program. As a result, only about 10 percent of the approximately 200,000 acres made available to Hawaiians for homesteading were useful for agriculture.

The History of Rehabilitation. The idea of rehabilitating Native Hawaiians by returning them to the land originated in the writings of the Reverend Akaiko Akana and the experience of the Ahahui Puuhonua O Na Hawaii (Hawaiian Refuge Association), which had largely failed in its attempt to "uplift" Hawaiians living in the tenements of Honolulu. The homesteading plan that resulted also grew out of the frustration of Prince Johan Kuhio, Hawaii's Territorial delegate to Congress, over failure of the Republican Party in Hawaii to provide public lands to Hawaiians.

No serious consideration was given, however, as to how 20,000 pure-blooded Hawaiians, much less thousands of part-Hawaiians, were to be returned productively to less than 200,000 acres of the least productive lands of the Territory. There were also concerns in Congress over the constitutionality of using public lands for the sole benefit of Hawaiians. Ostensibly in order to meet these concerns of Congress, Wise and Kuhio accepted a proposal to limit the program to those with 50 percent or more Hawaiian blood quantum. Yet even with such limitations, the amount of money needed for major development projects, such as supplying water to arid lands, was never seriously studied; the maximum loan available to the individual homesteader initially was only $3,000.

Significance. Despite these limitations, the Hawaiian Homes program aroused great expectations among the Native Hawaiian people. The program was seriously underfunded throughout its first seventy years, however, and was administered in ways that contradicted its intent. According to official reports issued in

1983 and 1991, for example, it was found that lands were illegally transferred to federal, state, and local governments without any lease payment or were leased to non-Hawaiians, often at extremely low rents, for purposes of generating program revenue. This history has led to continued efforts to sue the state and federal governments to compel proper administration of the act. The courts have, however, not accepted jurisdiction. As a consequence of this history, several Native Hawaiian organizations have demanded that ownership of the Hawaiian homelands be returned to a sovereign Hawaiian government.—*Stephen T. Boggs*

SUGGESTED READINGS: • Hawaii Advisory Committee to the U.S. Commission on Civil Rights. *A Broken Trust: The Hawaiian Homelands Program—Seventy Years of Failure of the Federal and State Governments to Protect the Civil Rights of Native Hawaiians*. Author, 1991. • McGregor, Davianna P. "Kupa'a I ka 'Aina: Persistence on the Land." Ph.D. diss., University of Hawaii, Manoa, 1989. • U.S. Congress. House. Committee on the Territories. *Proposed Amendments to the Organic Act of the Territory of Hawaii*. 66th Congress, 2d session, 1920. • U.S. Congress. House. Committee on the Territories. *Proposed Amendments to the Organic Act of the Territory of Hawaii*. 67th Congress, 1st session, 1921. House Report 7257. • Vause, Marylyn M. "The Hawaiian Homes Commission Act, 1920: History and Analysis." Master's thesis, University of Hawaii, Manoa, 1962.

Hawaiian language. *See* **Austronesian languages; Hawaiian Renaissance; Southeast Asian languages; Southeast Asian languages—prehistory of**

Hawaiian music and dance: Hawaiian music may be divided into four stylistic/historical categories: ancient Hawaiian; post-European contact, c. 1820-1900; traditional Hawaiian c. 1900-1970; and contemporary Hawaiian, c. 1970-present. The basic stylistic/historical framework provides a flexible model with which to understand Hawaiian music.

Ancient Hawaiian. In ancient Hawaii, *mele* were created to commemorate an event, place, or person. Hawaiian *mele* is often described as chanted poetry decorated by melody, rhythm, movement, and various instruments. The pleasure of hearing chant lies in the beauty of the poetry as well as the manner of performing it. Musical features of chant are enjoyed for their ability to carry the poetry forward. The chanter uses a small number of pitches (2 to 4), usually one as a primary reciting tone (usually the highest tone) and

Much of the dance performed in Hawaii shows a Polynesian influence. (Unicorn Stock Photos)

The Kahunokus family band demonstrates the soft, melodious style of slack key music.

another as a secondary reciting tone. Verses follow a strophic form (the same melody with different text for each verse).

The two main forms of pre-European contact music and dance are *mele oli* and *mele hula*. *Mele oli* are unaccompanied chants that are usually performed by one individual. *Mele hula* are chants accompanied by either dance movements alone or dance movements together with musical instruments. In pre-European contact Hawaii, *mele* and *hula* were taught at the *heiau* (temple) and in the *halau* (school). Each *halau* had its own interpretation for a given chanting style, vocal quality, and movement, a practice that continues in contemporary *halau*.

HULA is the traditional dance form of Hawaiians. There are two kinds of *hula*, *kahiko* and *auwana*. The *kahiko* style refers to older dances accompanied by traditional percussion instruments, including the *pahu* (sharkskin drum) and *ipu* (double gourd). Texts are exclusively in the Hawaiian language and generally concern serious themes. *Hula kui* formed a transition to the *auwana* style, which included newer dances accompanied by Western instruments. Texts are in Ha-

waiian or English or both and generally concern lighter subjects.

Post-Contact. The coming of seafarers, traders, and missionaries beginning in the late eighteenth century permanently altered civilization on the Hawaiian Islands. Westerners brought new music and dance forms, new instruments, new melodies, and music based on harmony. Missionaries from the United States brought American Christianity and its style of hymn singing, which became known in Hawaii as *himeni*. *Himeni* refers to the repertoire of hymn singing and the style of singing, also used in secular music, in which the vocal parts are harmonically based. *Himeni* from early missionary hymnals, including those found in *Na Himeni Hawaii* (1823), are widely sung in Hawaiian-language churches.

European brass bands aboard ships stopping in Honolulu brought popular music and dance from around the world. In 1872, King Kamehameha V invited the Prussian Heinrich Berger to become band director of "The Royal Hawaiian Band." The band was especially active during the last quarter of the nineteenth century under the patronage of King David

Kalakaua, the "Merry Monarch," who was a renowned lyricist and composer. The band's repertoire included Hawaiian tunes, waltzes, polkas, and *schottisches* as well as Western orchestral pieces. The Royal Hawaiian Band is the oldest municipal band in the United States.

Instruments including the guitar and *ukulele* were introduced by Westerners. The exact arrival date of the guitar in Hawaii is not known, but most likely it was introduced around 1832. Hawaiian music played on guitars having an open tuning is called *ki ho alu*, or "slack key." Portuguese immigrants introduced the *branguinha* in 1879, which was later to become the *ukulele*. An instrument made famous in Hawaii is the steel (or Hawaiian steel) guitar, which by local accounts was invented by Joseph Kekuku around the beginning of the twentieth century. Numerous technical innovations were introduced later, including a raised bridge, pedals, and electrification. The new instrument later became a standard feature of country-and-western music on the mainland United States.

Traditional Hawaiian. Acculturated forms of music reflect the adaptation of Western-derived forms and the development of distinctive Hawaiian genres and styles. "Traditional Hawaiian" music refers to primarily vocal music, usually sung in parts and accompanied by guitar, *ukulele*, and bass. The musical sound, which crystallized during the early twentieth century, was influenced by mainland American musical genres including ragtime, Tin Pan Alley, and jazz. *Hapa-haole* (literally "half-white" or "half-American") refers to song lyrics composed primarily in English that include some Hawaiian words or reference to Hawaii (for example, Sonny Cunha's "My Honolulu Tomboy," 1905). Hawaiian music during the period 1910 to 1940 influenced American popular music composers through recordings, films, touring troupes, and sheet music. During the 1930's to 1960's, mainland composers, including Harry Owens, Don McDiarmid, Sr., and Alex Anderson, used Hawaiian themes that helped to construct an exotic image of Hawaii. During the 1950's and 1960's, tourism in the islands accelerated, and performers including Alfred Apaka and Don Ho gained fame playing nightly shows in hotel venues for largely tourist audiences. By the 1960's, interest in

Hawaiian dancers performing at the Polynesian Cultural Center in Oahu, Hawaii. (Marshall Prescott, Unicorn Stock Photos)

traditional Hawaiian music had waned, and a younger generation seemed to prefer mainland U.S. folk and rock genres rather than traditional Hawaiian ones.

During the 1970's, a Hawaiian music renaissance was sparked by a renewed awareness and definition of ethnic heritage in Hawaii. Expressive culture, including music and dance, became a key ingredient in the definition of Hawaiian identity. KCCN, a radio station that broadcast exclusively Hawaiian music, and other organizations sponsored concerts, publications, and public programs aimed at reviving older musical styles and promoting local music composition. The renaissance sparked a renewed interest in styles uniquely associated with Hawaii, such as steel guitar and slack key, and in individual performers including Gabby Pahinui and Genoa Keawe.

Contemporary Hawaiian. Encouraged by renewed interest in Hawaiian music and sparked by small local recording companies, the "contemporary Hawaiian" sound emerged during the late 1960's. The sound of contemporary Hawaiian music is characterized by the synthesis of "traditional Hawaiian" styles with contemporary musical styles including folk-rock, jazz, pop, rock, country and western, and reggae. The typical string band instrumentation of "traditional Hawaiian" is often augmented by a drum set, electric guitars, and synthesizers. Songs are sung in the Hawaiian language as well as English and concern themes of local importance.

The influential album "Guava Jam" (1969) by the Sunday Manoa combined the talents of guitarist Peter Moon and the vocal duo Robert and Roland Cazimero (the Brothers Cazimero). The tune "Kawika" (1969) is an interpretation of a traditional *mele*, which combines a rock sensibility with indigenous musical instruments. Significant contributions were made in the folk-rock style of Olomana and the rich harmonic vocal texture of Makaha Sons of Niihau. "Honolulu City Lights" by Keola and Kapono Beamer (1977) and "Waimanalo Blues," which was first recorded by Country Comfort during the mid-1970's, were two hits that dealt with love of the land (*aloha aina*) in contemporary Hawaiian musical idioms. Local manifestations of global music include the late 1980's success of *Jawaiian*, a fusion of reggae and contemporary Hawaiian music, best represented by the bands Kapena and Hoaikane.—*Andrew Weintraub*

SUGGESTED READINGS: • Emerson, Nathaniel B. *The Unwritten Literature of Hawaii: The Sacred Songs of the Hula.* Rutland, Vt.: Charles E. Tuttle, 1965. • Kanahele, George S., ed. *Hawaiian Music and Musicians: An Illustrated History.* Honolulu: University Press of Hawaii, 1979. • Roberts, Helen Heffron. *Ancient Hawaiian Music.* New York: Dover Publications, 1967. • Stoneburner, Bryan C., comp. *Hawaiian Music: An Annotated Bibliography.* New York: Greenwood Press, 1986. • Tatar, Elizabeth. *Nineteenth Century Hawaiian Chant.* Honolulu: Department of Anthropology, Bernice P. Bishop Museum, 1982.

Hawaiian Native Claims Settlement Bill: Legislative proposal presented to a U.S. congressional subcommittee in 1975. The Subcommittee on Indian Affairs had been conducting hearings on each of the Hawaiian islands in an effort to compensate Native Hawaiians for losses stemming from the U.S.-backed overthrow of Queen Liliuokalani in 1893. Earlier American attempts at compensation had produced the HAWAIIAN HOMES COMMISSION ACT OF 1920 (Hawaii Rehabilitation Act). Under that law, individuals who were at least half Hawaiian could claim land earmarked for homesteading. By contrast, the proposed Hawaiian Native Claims Settlement Bill, sponsored by Hawaii congressional representatives Spark MATSUNAGA and Patsy MINK, offered monetary compensation to anyone of Hawaiian blood.

The terms of the act included a $1 billion appropriation from the U.S. Treasury, doled out in amounts of $100 million annually for ten years. A specially created corporation would be responsible for distributing the payments to all Native Hawaiians. The bill never became law, however, and through the early 1990's has neither been revived nor reintroduced in modified form.

Hawaiian religion: The indigenous belief system of the Polynesian chiefdoms of the Hawaiian Islands. The polytheistic religion was grounded in a basic belief that inanimate objects such as unusual stones, certain places, chiefly possession, and human bones could contain sacred power, or *mana*. Categories of sacred and profane formed a continuum, and *mana* was a manifestation of this diffuse and often dangerous divine power of the gods (*akua*).

Within Society. Elaborate *kapu* (taboos) associated with items possessing *mana* formed a classification system, assessing and regulating the relative sacredness of people, places, and objects. *Kapa* ordered both the biological and the social world, reflecting the creation of the cosmos. In Hawaiian mythology, categories of male and female, light and darkness, gods and humans, and water and sea grew from an undifferentiated dark-

A heiau *(Hawaiian temple) at Napoopoo. Captain James Cook saw this temple during a visit to the islands in the late 1700's.* (Lyman House Memorial Museum)

ness (Po) at the beginning of creation. The *kapu* system, with its elaborate sumptuary restrictions, kept work activities, sleeping areas, food items, meal preparation, and eating (*aikapu*) strictly segregated according to gender. The female nature was considered especially defiling toward males. Similarly, the commoners (*maka ainana*) were prohibited from either direct or indirect contact with high chiefs (*alii nui*), possessing certain *kapu* as repositories of godly *mana*. Should even the shadow of a commoner fall upon the body of a high *kapu chief or chiefess, the transgressor could be put to death. The alii*, as a class, served as intermediaries between commoners and the "destructo-reproductive" gods. In order to be considered a righteous (*pono*) chief, the *alii* especially had to uphold the *aikapu*.

Hawaiian religion centered around four anthropomorphic gods, each regulating a specific human activity: Ku, the god of war and fishing, was the antithesis of Lono, the god of fertility and nonirrigated horticulture; Kane regulated irrigated cultivation and fresh water, while Kanaloa was identified with death, seawater, and the subterranean world. Each of the ma-

jor gods had myriad forms, such as Kamapuaa, a pig-man who was an emanation of Lono. Other divine forms could be found in natural phenomenon, such as lightning, thunder, and vulcanism (for example, the goddess Pele).

The great gods were available to all through prayer and sacrifice, either directly or hierarchically mediated through priests (*kahuna*) of the state cult. Tutelary gods (*aumakua*), by contrast, were identified with specific human genealogical lineages and were the guardians of individuals or families. *Aumakua* were often deified ancestors who assumed the form of some biological species. These creatures were often those that posed physical danger to humans or were competitors for natural resources. The shark *aumakua*, for example, protected their human descendants from attack by other sharks and provided good fishing in their territory for their "family." The *aumakua moo*, a giant reptile, almost always female, guarded freshwater ponds and rivers and provided resources from these environments to their specific families. Kihawahine, for example, protected the royal family of Maui. She

A Chinese pastor and his school in Hilo c. 1900. (Lyman House Memorial Museum)

found her home in the royal fishpond of Mokuhinia in Lahaina, once the capital of that chiefdom.

End of the Established Order. One of the most dramatic ends to an indigenous belief system anywhere occurred in Hawaii in 1819, one year prior to Western missionary contact. Ever since the arrival of English captain James COOK in 1778, Hawaiian chiefs had been questioning their own religious system, having noted that the foreigners did not suffer divine retribution for their continual breaking of the *kapu*. With the death of Kamehameha the Great in 1819, the entire edifice of state religion would be overthrown in short order. The mourning period for a dead king was a traditional time when the *aikapu* would be temporarily suspended. These rites of reversal, which included free eating and cohabitation of the sexes, ended with the installation of a new king proclaiming the reestablishment of the *kapu*. On the night of Kamehameha's death, one of his daughters, Kekauluohi, ate forbidden pork that had been sacrificed to the gods at the temple (*heiau*). Normally, this act would be considered blasphemous—but it was perfectly acceptable within the context of freed *kapu* in observance of the king's death. After the new king was proclaimed, however, the widows of the dead king, including the powerful Kaahumanu, her sister Kaheiheimalie, and the sacred Keopuolani, encouraged the young King Liholiho Kamehameha II to eat with them. When he sat with them at a great feast, and ate with histrionic voracity, the *kapu* of segregated eating ended. This act ultimately led to the abandonment of other *kapu* that had provided religious definition to the relations between men and women, commoners and chiefs, people and their gods—it led to the destruction of the traditional order.

Christian Influence. Into the morass Calvinist missionaries from Boston arrived preaching a new, Christian system of prohibitions. Kaahumanu, Keopuolani, and Kaheiheimalie were quickly converted. Kaahumanu, emboldened by her success at ending the *kapu* system and backed by the ministers of the foreign religion, ordered the destruction of the hundreds of *heiau* throughout the islands. Not content with the destruction of the images of the gods and the elimination of an entire class of traditional religious practitioners, Kaahumanu broke into Hale o Keawe, sepulchre of the ancient chiefs of Hawaii, a place of pilgrimage for centuries. She had the remains secretly reburied and burned down the building.

While the Native Hawaiian state religion had been replaced by Christianity, certain aspects of Hawaiian religion survived in secret. The religion of the commoners, with its emphasis on *aumakua* worship, continued to be practiced in a domestic setting. Sorcery, which was traditionally esoteric, also continued after the abolition of the state religion. In Hawaii the belief in inherited protector spirits and the sacredness of locales was still evident at the end of the twentieth century.—*P. Christiaan Klieger*

SUGGESTED READINGS: • Ellis, William. *Journal of William Ellis*. Honolulu: Advertiser Publishing, 1963. • Kamakau, Samuel. *Ruling Chiefs of Hawaii*. Rev. ed. Honolulu: Kamehameha Schools Press, 1992. • Kameeleihiwa, Lilikala. *Native Land and Foreign Desires*. Honolulu: Bishop Museum Press, 1992. • Valeri, Valerio. *Kingship and Sacrifice*. Chicago: University of Chicago Press, 1985.

Hawaiian Renaissance: The revival or rebirth of interest in the past, the renewed pursuit of knowledge and learning, the redirecting and reshaping of the future of the Hawaiian people, and the revitalization of the human spirit in all aspects of Hawaiian life. The Hawaiian Renaissance, which began in the 1960's and 1970's, is also associated with psychological renewal, a purging of feelings of alienation and inferiority, a reassertion of self-dignity and self-importance. Some take exception of the use of the term "renaissance" as meaning "rebirth," arguing that since the culture had never died, there was no need for a rebirth. Others believe that the term Hawaiian Renaissance is overused, and that it can distract attention from the issues of real concern to Native Hawaiians—foremost the issue of HAWAIIAN SOVEREIGNTY. Nevertheless most Hawaiians agree that the Hawaiian Renaissance represents one of the most important phases of Hawaiian history.

Causes. Following the arrival of Captain James COOK in 1778, Hawaiian culture, language, arts, and population rapidly declined. From a pre-Cook contact population of between 800,000 to one million inhabitants in 1778, the Native Hawaiian population fell to barely 40,000 by the early 1890's. King David KALAKAUA (1874-1891), Hawaii's "Merry Monarch," revived Hawaiian HULA (dance) and Hawaiian music,

and renewed interest among the Hawaiian people in legends and oral histories of old Hawaii. Seeds of the Hawaiian Renaissance were planted by King Kalakaua and nurtured by his sister, Queen LILIUOKALANI, an accomplished musician and composer of many Hawaiian songs, one of the most famous of which is "Aloha oe." The Hawaiian Renaissance survived the overthrow of Queen Liliuokalani and the Hawaiian Kingdom.

Since the arrival of the *haole* (foreigners) in Hawaii, the islands and their people have undergone a process known as "acculturation." It is a process that works both ways, affecting Native Hawaiians and non-ethnic Hawaiians alike. In fact, the acculturation of foreigners in Hawaii helped to create the conditions which made the Hawaiian Renaissance possible. Consciously or unconsciously, all those who claimed Hawaii as their home wanted to share in Hawaii's "Hawaiianness." The wearing of an "aloha shirt," the giving of a "flower lei," the greeting of "Aloha," the surfing competitions—these everyday traditions are in the spirit of the Hawaiian Renaissance.

The development of tourism in Hawaii has also played a part in the Hawaiian Renaissance. Some Native Hawaiians see tourism solely as a form of exploitation, another indignity imposed upon the Hawaiian people. Others have seen the same problems as a challenge to do better in preserving the cultural integrity of exhibits, dances, songs, crafts, arts, and language of the Hawaiian people. Places such as Waimea Falls Park (Oahu), the City of Refuge (Hawaii), and the POLYNESIAN CULTURAL CENTER (Oahu) are some examples of tourist-oriented sites which do a good job in preserving the cultural integrity of much of what they present to their visitors.

The Hawaiian Renaissance is also a product of the "Age of Ethnicity." At one time, Hawaii was known as the "melting pot" of the Pacific. However, beginning in the 1960's, Hawaii benefited from the ethnic revolution among African Americans, Native Americans, and other ethnic minorities in the United States, as well as similar ethnic and cultural activism in the Pacific among the Maoris (New Zealand), the FIJIANS (Fijii), the Tahitians (Tahiti), and the CHAMORROS (Guam). Wherever there are people who feel strongly about their identities and their legacies, there are strong efforts to preserve and strengthen them. The Hawaiian people feel the same urgency.

Things revived. Hawaiian music, hula, language, education, scholarship, politics, voyaging, and Hawaiian values are some areas of culture being revived by the Hawaiian Renaissance.

The resurgence of Hawaiian music is one of the strongest areas of the Hawaiian Renaissance. Musicians and vocalists such as Gabby Pahinui, The Brothers Cazimero, Olomana, Sons of Hawaii, Willie "K," and Makaha Sons of Niihau are familiar to all who live in Hawaii. In 1971 the Hawaii Music Foundation was organized; in 1972 it held its first Hawaiian "slack key" (Hawaiian-style guitar playing) concert. In 1973, the first Hawaiian "falsetto" and steel guitar concerts were held. The Hawaii Music Foundation publishes a monthly newsletter, *Hai lono mele*, which features Hawaiian music, Hawaiian lyrics, Hawaiian themes, and Hawaiian composers. More musicians are playing Hawaiian music, learning to play Hawaiian slack key guitar, and composing Hawaiian songs.

After the arrival of Christian missionaries in Hawaii in 1820, many forms of HULA were forbidden to be performed in public. However, from the time of King KALAKAUA onward, Hawaiian hula gained great popularity among Hawaiian and non-Hawaiian alike. Beginning in the 1970's, more young people in Hawaii became interested in hula, with the *hula kahiko* (ancient Hawaiian dances) and *hula kane* (dances of men)

being the most exciting parts of the hula revival. In addition, hula schools (*halau hula*) have grown from a handful of strictly regulated family-run operations in the mid-1950's to more than one hundred schools, some of which are owned and operated by corporations and non-Hawaiians. Hula events such as the Merry Monarch Hula Festival, the King Kamehameha Hula Festival, the Prince Lot Hula Festival, and the Keiki Hula Festival, which attract hula groups from Nevada, California, Washington, Canada, the South Pacific, Germany, and Japan, show that the hula is thriving.

In ancient Hawaiian society, the scholar was not only a teacher but also the keeper and transmitter of all accumulated knowledge and tradition of the culture. The Hawaiians had no written language. Everything had to be recorded and stored in the memory of the scholar. Hawaiians always had great respect for the power of the mind and its ability to retain, preserve, and transmit knowledge. Hawaiian language, education, and scholarship are critical elements of the Hawaiian Renaissance. Hawaiians say, we must not only *nana i ke kumu* (look to the source) but also *hoi ana i*

Dancers perform a version of modern hula (hula auana) *at the Merry Monarch festival in Hilo, c. 1990.*

ke kumu (return to the source). The source for Hawaiians is their language. Because the Hawaiian language is an official language of the State of Hawaii, Immersion Schools, grades K-7, have been implemented on Oahu, Maui, Hawaii, Molokai, and Kauai. The goal is to have designated Immersion Schools from grades K-12 implemented by 1995. This great interest in language, education, and scholarship has led to the founding of Hawaiian Studies programs at the University of Hawaii-Manoa, the University of Hawaii-Hilo, and many of the state community colleges scattered throughout Hawaii. Brigham Young University-Hawaii offers a B.A. degree in Pacific Islands Studies and is developing a Hawaiian language program.

Involvement. The Hawaiian Renaissance does not belong only to Native Hawaiians, though they are the primary originators and sustainers of the movement; it also belongs to non-ethnic Hawaiians. People such as Donald Mitchell, Sir Peter Buck, Lorenzo Lyons, Kenneth Emory, Y. H. Sinoto, Thor Heyerdahl, and Paul Spickard are but a few of the non-ethnic Hawaiians who have contributed to the Hawaiian Renaissance. Because of this joint effort, the Renaissance offers Hawaiians the greatest opportunity since the reign of Kamehameha I to unify the people of Hawaii, not by the power of war but by the influence of values such as *lokahi* (unity and harmony in all things), *kokua* (helping each other), *laulima* (collective effort to complete a task), and *aloha* (unconditional love-charity for all people).

Future. The Hawaiian Renaissance will endure. It is not a passing fancy but is rather a permanent commitment. Like the Hawaiian voyaging canoe, Hawaiians have taken to the sea again. They are on a journey of rediscovery. This journey, which will continue to include non-ethnic Hawaiians and will never be a purely Native Hawaiian venture, is the most important journey in modern Hawaiian history: a cultural rebirth bringing about new political awareness which will be transformed into a purposeful, articulate, and organized movement. Hawaiians celebrate the Renaissance because it proves that their culture is still alive, is not merely surviving, but is in fact thriving. It has been a remarkable comeback for a people who were close to extinction in the 1890's and who in fact lost their sovereignty in 1893.—*William R. Wallace III*

SUGGESTED READINGS: • Kanahele, George S. *Hawaiian Renaissance*. Honolulu: Project Waiaha, 1982. • Kanahele, George S. *Ku Kanaka, Stand Tall: A Search for Hawaiian Values*. Honolulu: University of Hawaii Press, 1986. • Stagner, Ishmael W. *Hula!*.

Laie, Haw.: Institute for Polynesian Studies, Brigham Young University-Hawaii, 1985. • Stannard, David E. *Before the Horror: The Population of Hawaii on the Eve of Western Contact*. Honolulu: Social Science Research Institute, University of Hawaii, 1989. • Uemoto, Shuzo. *Nana Iho Loea Hula*. Honolulu: Kalihi-Palama Culture and Arts Society, 1984.

Hawaiian reparations: Reparations is usually associated with settlement of a claim for monetary compensation. Native Hawaiian claims for reparations are associated not only with settlement of claims for monetary compensation but also with claims over loss of crown (lands belonging to the king) and government lands plus loss of HAWAIIAN SOVEREIGNTY. Many organizations were active in the reparations movement of the 1970's including the Council of Hawaiian Organizations, the Congress of the Hawaiian People, the Hawaiians, the Friends of Kamehameha, and the Hawaiian Civic Clubs. The ALOHA (Aboriginal Lands of Hawaiian Ancestry) Association is generally acknowledged as being the organization that first focused congressional attention on Hawaiian claims for reparations.

The ALOHA Association was founded in 1972 by Louisa K. Rice. The mission of ALOHA was to ensure that the U.S. Congress passed legislation that would fairly compensate Native Hawaiian people, through monetary reparations, for losses resulting from the overthrow of Queen LILIUOKALANI and for the illegal and unlawful taking of Native Hawaiian lands in 1893. A series of reparations bills modeled after the Alaska Native Claims Settlement Act of 1971 was introduced in Congress in 1974. Congress did not resolve claims asserted by ALOHA and other groups in 1974. In the mid-1970's, Hawaii's congressional delegation proposed a HAWAIIAN NATIVE CLAIMS SETTLEMENT BILL, but it failed to win congressional approval. Early attempts for reparations, though unsuccessful, brought attention to Native Hawaiian claims on a national and state level and encouraged more inquiry surrounding the overthrow of the Hawaiian Kingdom in 1893.

In 1980 Congress created the NATIVE HAWAIIANS STUDY COMMISSION (NHSC) to study the culture, needs, and concerns of Native Hawaiians. This commission was appointed by the president of the United States. Three of the nine commission members had to be Hawaii residents. In 1983 the commission submitted two separate reports, one by the majority and one by the minority (the three Hawaii committee members). The majority report stated that no reparations were due the Hawaiian people. Though an obstacle to congressional action on Native Hawaiian claims, the NHSC provided needed statistical and background information on the education, health, and social welfare needs of Native Hawaiians. It also revealed that Native Hawaiians had turned their focus from monetary settlement of claims to restoration of their land and their sovereignty.

Hawaiian society, traditional: At the time of earliest contact with the West, Hawaiian society consisted of two classes: the *alii* (chiefs) and the *makaainana* (commoners; literally "people who attend the land"). The *alii* ruled, and the *makaainana* produced the food and all other goods. In fact and concept these classes were greatly interdependent. The welfare of all was conceived to depend upon the ritual sacrifices made by and on behalf of the *moi* (ruling chief) by a class of *kahuna* (ritual specialists). The actual power possessed by the *alii* was reinforced by strong values of loyalty and obedience on the part of the *makaainana*. The *alii*, by contrast, had an obligation to provide for the people or be deserted by them. Rank among the *alii* was based upon genealogy and success in endemic warfare.

This society was mythically legitimized by a system of *kapu* (prohibition, sanctity). When this system was abrogated in 1819, the spiritual basis of the class structure was eliminated. In subsequent decades the *alii* were involved through indebtedness in the capitalist world economy and were deprived of the labor of the *makaainana* through conversion of the land tenure system to freehold. Despite this, people retained strong sentiments of loyalty to the *alii*, manifested particularly in reverence for the last *moi wahine* (ruling chiefess), Queen Liliuokalani, who was overthrown by Americans in 1893.

Introduction of diseases, alcohol, and other practices, together with changes in diet and lifestyle urged by missionaries and necessitated by the capitalist economy, resulted in a population decrease of 90 to 95 percent by the end of the nineteenth century. This, in essence, constituted cultural genocide.

Today traditional values continue to be manifested within the *ohana* and in relations with other groups, although these values may be weakening. Despite heterogeneity, indigenous Hawaiians are united by resentment of the overthrow and by a refusal to assimilate completely, even when that is possible. A number of traditional institutions are being reemphasized and reinterpreted. The resurgence includes efforts for redress under the symbol of "sovereignty," directed at both state and federal governments. Some degree of autonomy seems certain in the future.

Hawaiian sovereignty: Sovereignty is the ability of a nation to govern itself, to provide for its people and to maintain the integrity of its lands and revenues. Prior to January 17, 1893, the Kingdom of Hawaii was a sovereign nation. In order to understand the loss of Hawaiian sovereignty and the struggle to regain it, the following questions should be considered: Why was the Kingdom of Hawaii overthrown? What role did the United States play in the loss of Hawaiian sovereignty? What have Native Hawaiians done since the overthrow in 1893 to regain their sovereignty?

Why Was the Kingdom of Hawaii Overthrown? Shortly after Christian missionaries arrived in Hawaii in 1820, it became apparent that Hawaii would soon become an important commercial center for many American and other foreign businesses. The sandalwood trade (1811-1830), the whaling industry (1854-1880), the rise of mercantilism (1823 onward), and the growth of the sugar industry (1835 onward) swiftly made Hawaii part of American expansion in the Pacific. In 1842 the Tyler Doctrine was issued by the United States, giving notice to European powers that Hawaii was part of the American "sphere of influence" and off-limits to European nations for purposes of colonization. Americans in Hawaii as well as outside Hawaii were encouraged to acknowledge their own interests in these islands as a virtual "right of conquest" over the heart and mind of the Hawaiian people. Commercial development and control of economic growth by foreigners in Hawaii was one of the first steps taken to disenfranchise Native Hawaiians.

Acquisition of land and changing of the traditional land tenure system by Westerners further disenfranchised Native Hawaiians and contributed greatly to the loss of Hawaiian sovereignty. Beginning on January 27, 1848, all lands of Hawaii were divided between the king and chiefs and recorded in the *Mahele Book*. Historians refer to this act as "the GREAT MAHELE." Many Native Hawaiians say that the only "great" thing resulting from the *Mahele* was the loss of their native lands. The word *mahele* as used by Westerners at the time of the act was interpreted to mean "division," referring to the division of lands among the King, the chiefs, and the common people. To Native Hawaiians, however, *mahele* also meant to share. Initially, many commoners felt that the *Mahele* would allow them to share in land ownership. The reality was that fewer than 1 percent of the Native Hawaiian popu-

The overthrow of Queen Liliuokalani in 1893 and the transition to a white-dominated government represents, for many Native Hawaiians, the demise of the traditional society of alii *(chiefs) and* Makaainana *(commoners). (Hawaii State Archives)*

lation would share in the acquisition of land resulting from the Great *Mahele*.

On August 6, 1850, the *Kuleana* Act was passed, authorizing the Land Commission to award fee simple title to native tenants for their plots of land. In order to secure title to these lands, the native tenants had to prove that they actually cultivated the land, pay for the survey, and provide two witnesses to testify as to the tenants' right to the land. It is estimated that of the 8,205 awards given by the Land Commission, 7,500 awards involved *kuleana* land. However, only 28,600 acres of land, much less than 1 percent of the total available land, went to the *makaainana* (commoners). As the rights of the Native Hawaiians in land decreased, the rights of Westerners increased. By 1890, 76 lessees controlled 752,431 acres of crown and government land. Of a total population in 1890 of about 90,000, fewer than 5,000 actually owned land. Of every four acres belonging to private owners, three were held by Westerners. Westerners owned more than a million acres of Hawaiian lands.

In addition to being disenfranchised economically and in land ownership, Native Hawaiians also lost their political power. When Kamehameha IV ascended the throne in 1855, he felt that the Constitution of 1852 placed harsh limitations on his powers. When Kamehameha V came to the throne in 1863, he refused to take an oath to maintain the constitution. A constitutional convention was convened, but it could not decide the question of universal suffrage, which the king opposed. The convention was dissolved and the constitution was abolished. For a week, Hawaii was without a constitution, until Kamehameha V signed the Constitution of 1864, which reasserted his powers.

In 1887, King KALAKAUA yielded to the demands of Western interests to appoint a new cabinet whose foremost task was to write a new constitution. The result was the Constitution of 1887, also called the "Bayonet Constitution," which greatly diminished the power of the king, reducing his status to that of a ceremonial figurehead. His power over the military became subject to legislative control; executive powers were placed in the hands of the cabinet, who were appointed by the king but were responsible to the legislature; and membership in the house of nobles became an elective office. Under this "Bayonet Constitution" the privilege of voting was extended to American and European males regardless of citizenship. This new provision shifted political power in favor of Westerners living in Hawaii at that time.

What Role Did the United States Play in the Loss of Hawaiian Sovereignty? In 1892, when Queen LILIUOKALANI ascended the throne, she, like her brother, King KALAKAUA, felt that the 1887 Constitution not only put excessive limits on the power of the monarch but also put too much power in the hands of Westerners. On January 14, 1893, Liliuokalani was about to declare a new constitution, which included provisions to limit the right to vote in Hawaii to Hawaiian-born or naturalized citizens and to make cabinet ministers subject to removal by the legislature. Although Liliuokalani was persuaded to postpone her actions, members of the ANNEXATION CLUB, which advocated the annexation of Hawaii by the United States, met and plotted the overthrow of the Hawaiian kingdom. A group of these annexationists, the Committee of Thirteen, sought and received help from U.S. minister to Hawaii, John L. Stevens, who ordered the landing of U.S. marines in Honolulu to protect American lives and property. With American troops for support, the Committee of Thirteen took control of the government building, declared the monarchy abolished, and proclaimed the existence of a provisional government until annexation with the United States could be negotiated. Minister Stevens unhesitatingly and immediately recognized the provisional government, even before Queen Liliuokalani yielded to the superior forces of the United States. On February 1, 1893, Stevens placed the provisional government under the protection of the United States, pending annexation negotiations, and hoisted the American flag over Hawaii. The Kingdom of Hawaii had ceased to exist. Hawaii had lost its privileges and its recognition as a sovereign nation.

On December 18, 1893, President Grover Cleveland sent a message to the U.S. Congress which stressed the following points concerning the overthrow of the Kingdom of Hawaii. First, possession of Hawaii was tendered to the United States by a provisional government set up to succeed the constitutional ruler of the islands, who had been dethroned without the sanction of either popular revolution or popular vote. Second, the landing of military troops upon the soil of Honolulu was done without the consent of the government of the Hawaiian queen and was itself an act of war. Third, by this act of war, a substantial wrong was done to the national character of the United States as well as to the rights of the injured people of Hawaii, which must be redressed by the United States. Fourth and finally, restoration of the Hawaiian queen's government to her and to her people was a matter of honor, integrity, and morality for the United States. Cleve-

U.S. Minister to Hawaii John L. Stevens ordered the landing of U.S. Marines in Honolulu in 1893, leading to the overthrow of Queen Liliuokalani's government. (Hawaii State Archives)

land's views, however, did not prevail. In 1898, five years after the overthrow of the Hawaiian kingdom, Hawaii was annexed and became a U.S. territory. In 1959, Hawaii became the 50th state in the United States.

What Have Native Hawaiians Done Since the Overthrow of the Hawaiian Kingdom to Restore Their Sovereign Powers? In January of 1895, two years after the overthrow of the monarchy, supporters loyal to Queen LILIUOKALANI attempted to regain control of the government. By this time, in the interim before annexation, Hawaii had become a republic. Martial law was declared, and some of those loyal to the queen were killed. Within two weeks the conflict between those loyal to the queen and those loyal to the republic had been suppressed, and more than two hundred people were arrested. Among those arrested were Queen Liliuokalani and the young princes, David Kawananakoa and Jonah Kuhio Kalanianaole. While confined under house arrest, Liliuokalani signed a document in which she formally abdicated and renounced all claims to the throne. Fearing that those loyal to her would be put to death and seeking to avoid further bloodshed, Liliuokalani also signed an oath of allegiance to the republic.

While never entirely extinguished, the spirit of resistance among Native Hawaiians was not strongly rekindled until the 1960's, when, after many years during which the Hawaiian cultural heritage was scorned and devalued, there began a revival of interest in traditional Hawaiian music, arts, crafts, language, and culture. The HAWAIIAN RENAISSANCE, which gained momentum in the 1970's, reaffirmed Native Hawaiians' sense of identity. This renaissance had a political dimension as well. The Kalama Valley protest of 1970 on Oahu, where Hawaiians banded together against the development of high-priced homes by Henry J. Kaiser on their farm lands, played an important role in creating a movement for self-determination among Native Hawaiians. It caused people to begin questioning and investigating the actions of big business and government, and it empowered Native Hawaiians. Hawaiian rights became a central part of the Hawaiian movement in the 1970's. In 1972, an organization called Aboriginal Lands of Hawaiian Ancestry (ALOHA) was founded by Luisa K. Rice. This group focused on reparations from the United States to the Hawaiian people arising from claims of the unlawful and illegal overthrow of the Hawaiian kingdom in 1893.

From 1974 onward, groups specifically dedicated

not only to reparations but more specifically to Hawaiian sovereignty were formed. Within the movement, different approaches, strategies, and proposed solutions to the sovereignty question have evolved. In 1974, Ohana O Hawaii (The Extensive Family of Hawaii) was founded by Peggy Hao Ross, who believed that while Queen Liliuokalani had agreed, under duress, to abdicate her claim to the throne, the Hawaiian people (the *Kanaka maoli*) had never surrendered their sovereignty. In 1975, members of ALOHA and *Hui Ala Loa*, led by George Helm, Walter Ritte (both from Molokai), and Dr. Emmett Aluli, formed the Protect Kahoolawe Ohana, which protested the military bombing of the island of Kahoolawe and took court action which resulted in agreements restricting bombing, forcing the cleanup of the area, and allowing Hawaiians access to the island again. Kahoolawe is in the process of being returned to the Hawaiian people, and the Protect Kahoolawe Ohana has been given stewardship over that island.

At the 1987 Constitutional Convention for the State of Hawaii, the Office of Hawaiian Affairs (OHA) was organized to receive and to spend for the benefit of Native Hawaiians a portion of the income from the leases of the Ceded Lands. OHA is also charged with holding the State of Hawaii accountable for its administration of both the Hawaiian Home Lands and the Ceded Lands. OHA is a state agency, established by the state's constitution and funded by its legislature. In addition to OHA, there are other sovereignty groups in Hawaii which are not state agencies but are independent initiatives. Ka Lahui Hawaii, Ka Pakaukau, Hui Naauao, and the Ohana Council are examples of such groups.

Ka Lahui Hawaii (literally "The Hawaiian Nation") held its first Constitutional Convention in 1987. Delegates from each island met and drafted a tentative constitution, which, like the American Constitution, provides for three branches of government. Members of this group believe that the three elements of nationhood are sovereignty, self-determination, and self-sufficiency. They define sovereignty as the ability of a people who share a common culture, religion, language, value system, and land base to exercise control over their lands and lives, independent of other nations. In order to do this, they must be self-determining. Ka Lahui Hawaii contends that self-determination will be realized when the native people organize a mechanism for self governance. Only when the Native Hawaiian people create a governmental structure which provides for democratic representation of their members and begin to interrelate with the state and federal trustees who control their lands will they be able to gain control over their assets and their future. Ka Lahui Hawaii further maintains that self-sufficiency is the goal of nationhood, that the people should be able to be self-supporting, capable of feeding, clothing and sheltering themselves. There are approximately 30,000 citizens of Ka Lahui Hawaii. Their approach to achieving sovereignty is to seek inclusion of Hawaiian people in the federal policy of the United States that affords all native Americans the right to be self-governing. Once this is achieved it is believed that the sovereign nation will then be able to explore the government's resolution of claims to the Native Hawaiian trusts and other entitlements.

On October 8, 1989, Ka Pakaukau, a coalition of Native Hawaiians, joined to commit themselves to "the exercise of our inherent sovereignty." The coalition declared that Native Hawaiians "accept no higher human authority over our lives, our lands, our ocean resources, and our future than ourselves." There are three primary objectives of this coalition: To occupy the lands of Hawaii and to take possession of resources that rightfully and historically belong to the Native Hawaiian people and to use and nurture these in revitalizing the culture and providing for the livelihood of the Native Hawaiian people; to oppose measures, such as legislation proposed by state and federal officials, which are not initiated by Native Hawaiians, which lack their input, and which violate their inherent sovereignty (including acts that continue to subjugate Native Hawaiians as dependent wards of a foreign government); and to resist the ongoing takeover and destruction of Hawaiian forests, farmlands, fishing grounds, coastal submerged lands, other natural resources, and archaeological sites; and the desecration of religious sites, Kahoolawe, Makua Valley, Heiau Kukui-o-Kane, Halawa Valley, and the iwi (bones) of Native Hawaiian ancestors.

In March, 1991, Hui Naauao, another coalition of Hawaiian organizations, was formed. The purpose of Hui Naauao is to increase knowledge of, and promote informed decision-making regarding, Native Hawaiian sovereignty and self-determination. This group's emphasis is on education. Its three fundamental objectives are hoala—to awaken and enlighten, to educate

On a street corner in Hawaii, Hawaiians demonstrate for sovereignty.

through cultural, spiritual, and historical knowledge; hookahua—to lay a foundation and to educate through examining elements and models of sovereignty; and hoolokahi—to bring about unity, to build consensus culminating in a final report setting out a Hawaiian perspective on self-determination and governance.

On November 23, 1993, President Bill Clinton signed into law Senate Joint Resolution 19, which acknowledged the illegal overthrow of the Kingdom of Hawaii on January 17, 1893, and apologized to Native Hawaiians on behalf of the people of the United States. Hawaii senator Daniel K. AKAKA, the author of the proposal, said, "This is indeed one of the most satisfying days of my life. We began the year in grim remembrance of the darkest episode in our history, and we end it having established a firm foundation for reconciliation and hooponopono." Senator Akaka went on to say, "one need only look at the eruption in the strength of the Native Hawaiian rights movement itself to find undeniable proof of what happens when the truth is set free."

On January 16, 1994, another coalition, the Ohana Council, issued a proclamation asserting the independence of the sovereign nation of Hawaii. This coalition, by virtue of the right of self-determination, claims the right freely to determine Native Hawaiians' political status and freely to pursue their economic, social, and cultural development pursuant to the United Nations Charter. They will continue to seek the guidance of their Kupuna (elders) on decisions that affect their lives, to restore customs and teachings of their culture, language, and knowledge. They foresee a council of elders serving as a provisional government until such time as the Native Hawaiian people convene a constitutional convention. This proclamation, however, like similar statements by other groups in the sovereignty movement, has not been accepted by the U.S. government.

The question of Hawaiian sovereignty is complicated by the fact that Native Hawaiians make up only a small minority of Hawaii's population—12.5 percent, according to the 1990 census. Other Asian Pacific Islander groups in Hawaii include Japanese (22 percent), Filipino (15 percent), Chinese (6 percent), Korean (2 percent) and Samoan (1 percent). Whites make up 33 percent of Hawaii's population. Many of these people have deep roots in Hawaii, extending back for several generations, and they will play a significant part in determining Hawaii's future.—*William R. Wallace III*

SUGGESTED READINGS: • Dudley, Michael Kioni. *A Call For Hawaiian Sovereignty*. Honolulu: Na Kane O Ka Malo Press, 1990. • Dudley, Michael Kioni. *Man, Gods, and Nature*. Honolulu: Na Kane O Ka Malo Press, 1990. • Kent, Noel J. *Hawaii: Islands Under the Influence*. New York: Monthly Review Press, 1983. • MacKenzie, Melody Kapilialoha. *Native Hawaiian Rights Handbook*. Honolulu: Native Hawaiian Legal Corporation, 1991. • Trask, Haunani-Kay. *From a Native Daughter: Colonialism and Sovereignty in Hawaii*. Monroe, Maine: Common Courage Press, 1993.

Hawaiian statehood: On August 21, 1959, U.S. president Dwight D. Eisenhower signed the document proclaiming Hawaii the fiftieth state.

For most Hawaiians statehood had little appeal until the 1930's; American interest in Hawaiian statehood, however, began as early as the 1890's. Particularly interested were Hawaiian-American sugar plantation owners and businesses, because statehood would eliminate all quotas and tariffs on Hawaiian sugar imported by the United States. Domestic American sugar producers naturally opposed statehood for the same reason, though they sometimes fueled their arguments with the unfounded charge that the majority population of ethnically non-Caucasian Hawaiians held un-American attitudes.

Other arguments against Hawaiian statehood included distance (mitigated by the advent of air travel in the 1930's) and the desire of many Native Hawaiians to preserve their traditional lifestyles. By 1940, however, the advantages of statehood for most Hawaiians had become clear: Territorial citizens had no vote in national elections, no vote in Congress, little say in who was appointed governor, and small reward in terms of federal government spending—yet paid federal income taxes.

Across the continental United States, interest in Hawaii grew greatly following the attack on Pearl Harbor and during World War II. By 1948 both major American political parties agreed that Hawaii was ready for statehood. The Korean War (1950-1953) temporarily halted the movement, but finally, on March 12, 1959, Congress voted to grant Hawaii statehood.

A statehood vote was then held in Hawaii on June 27, followed on July 28 by a general election for its newly created state and national offices. Fully 95 percent of Hawaii's 138,000 voters supported statehood. William F. Quinn was elected governor, with a Native Hawaiian, James Kealoha, as lieutenant governor. Oren E. Long took one U.S. Senate seat, with the other going to Hiram L. FONG, the first American of

Dignitaries at the Hawaiian statehood celebration included Duke Kahanamoku and his wife (center and left of center). (Hawaii State Archives)

Chinese ancestry to win such office. Similarly honored as the first American of Japanese ancestry elected to the U.S. House of Representatives (and later as the first elected to the U.S. Senate) was the World War II combat veteran Daniel K. INOUYE.

Hawaiian Sugar Planters' Association (HSPA): Organization of Hawaiian plantation owners, originally founded as the Royal Hawaiian Agricultural Society in 1850. The society arose during a time of intense labor shortage throughout the islands. By arrangement of the society, about two hundred Chinese immigrant laborers arrived in Hawaii from Xiamen in early 1852, and more of them followed later in the year. They were put to work on the sugar plantations. Soon, securing foreign labor became one of the society's chief activities. The organization merged with the Planters' Society in 1865, becoming known as the latter designation.

Following the signing of the Reciprocity Treaty of 1875, sugar production in Hawaii soared to new levels. As the sugar boom continued, planters again saw the value of forming a unified association geared to protecing their intersts. In 1882 the Planters' Labor and Supply Company was formed. In 1894 it became the HSPA.

The HSPA represented the interests of the sugar plantations organized by the BIG FIVE. Its powerful lobby in Washington, D.C., sought to influence the U.S. Congress to enact laws favorable to the Hawaiian sugar industry. It aggressivley recruited workers from Japan, Korea, and the Philippines and brought them to Hawaii to work on the sugar planatations. Yet while the association helped to unify planters throughout the islands, providing them with a voice with which to address labor and agricultural issues, resolving labor shortages, and confronting strikers, over time its chief objective was to see that wages were kept at minimal levels.

To this end, various schemes were adopted. Wage-fixing tactics kept wages uniformly low, meaning that unhappy workers had little chance of increasing their pay by jumping to another plantation. The HSPA even created maximum wage schedules in 1901 to ensure uniformity. The association also monitored the status of the many laborers and their wages and told managers to offer new job applicants nothing more than what they had received at other plantations. Other strategies included contract conditions that kept workers at a disadvantage for a prolonged period of time and tough strike-breaking tactics.

Hawaiians: Indigenous Polynesian people of the Pacific Ocean islands of Hawaii. The date of the earliest settlement in Hawaii cannot be established with certainty, but it is likely that by 300 C.E., Polynesians had migrated from the Marquesas Islands to Hawaii. Hawaiians lived in isolation, self-sufficiency, and pros-

perity until the late eighteenth century, when the first Westerners arrived in the islands. Since then Hawaiians have experienced massive social and cultural decline. In 1959, Hawaii became the fiftieth state of the United States. As American citizens Hawaiians continued to experience cultural change. In the later years of the twentieth century, Hawaiians entered a period of "cultural renaissance" (see HAWAIIAN RENAISSANCE) in which they actively began to reestablish their cultural traditions and values and reassert their rights as a native people.

This article examines the circumstances of Hawaiians through a discussion of five major areas: population characteristics, historical background, contemporary problems and issues, cultural values, and cultural survival and perpetuation. Specifically the discussion will trace the evolution of Hawaiian society from the time of postcontact and will address trends that concern the perpetuation of Hawaiian culture in the United States.

Population Characteristics. According to the 1990

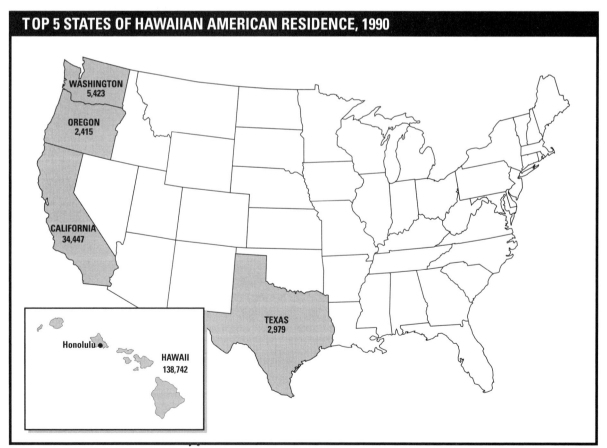

TOP 5 STATES OF HAWAIIAN AMERICAN RESIDENCE, 1990

WASHINGTON 5,423

OREGON 2,415

CALIFORNIA 34,447

TEXAS 2,979

Honolulu

HAWAII 138,742

Source: Susan B. Gall and Timothy L. Gall, eds., *Statistical Record of Asian Americans.* Detroit: Gale Research, 1993.

Asian Americans in Hawaii, Selected Characteristics, 1990

Percent of State Population

Total State Population: 1,108,229

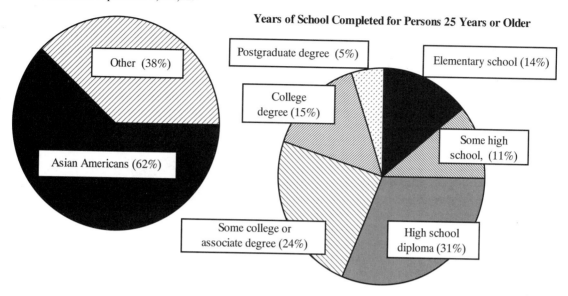

Years of School Completed for Persons 25 Years or Older

Other (38%)

Asian Americans (62%)

Postgraduate degree (5%)

Elementary school (14%)

College degree (15%)

Some high school, (11%)

Some college or associate degree (24%)

High school diploma (31%)

Asian Language Spoken and English Proficiency	
Speak Asian language	22%
Do not speak English "very well"	11%
Linguistically isolated	5%

Labor Status of Persons 16 Years or Older	
In labor force	68%
(Unemployed	3%)
Not in labor force	32%
Income, 1989	
Mean household income	$48,682
Per capita	$14,616

Source: U.S. Bureau of the Census, *Population and Housing Characteristics of Congressional Districts of the 103d Congress, Hawaii,* 1992.

census, Hawaiians constitute the largest Pacific Islander population in the United States, with approximately 211,000 persons. Most Hawaiians reside in two states, Hawaii (139,000) and California (34,000).

Native Hawaiians constitute only 12.5 percent of the total state population of more than 1 million. Other large Asian and Pacific Islander populations in Hawaii include Japanese (22 percent), Filipinos (15 percent), Chinese (6 percent), Koreans (2 percent), and Samoans (1 percent). The majority of Hawaii residents are of Asian and Pacific Islander descent (62 percent), with Caucasians (33 percent), African Americans (3 percent), and American Indians and Eskimo Natives (.5 percent) constituting minority groups.

Gender distribution for Hawaiians has been about equal since 1950. In addition Hawaiians are a young population, with 76 percent below the age of thirty-five. As a result many Hawaiians are in the public school system, although only a small number of students at the state's university are of Hawaiian ancestry. Educational attainment affects family income, and statistics show that Hawaiians are disproportionately represented in the lower-income brackets, with 19 percent of Hawaiian families making less than $15,000 per year, as compared to 13 percent of families in other ethnic groups in Hawaii.

An important population characteristic for Hawaiians concerns those Hawaiians who are of mixed an-

Hawaiian American Statistical Profile, 1990

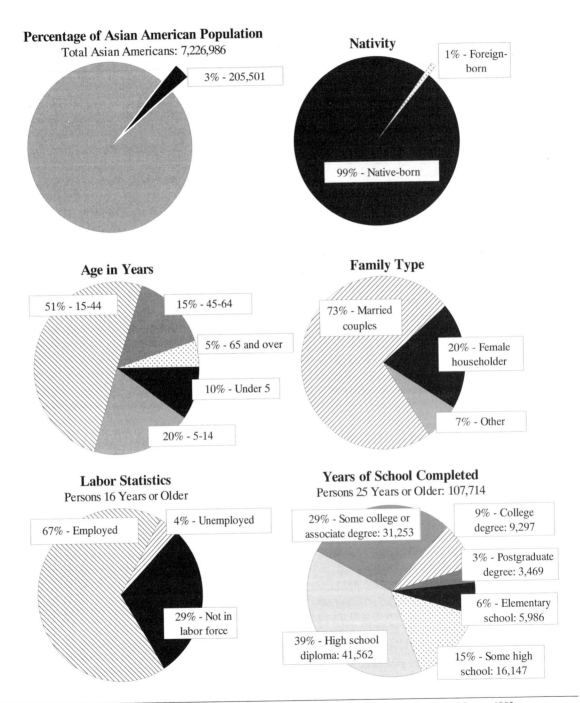

Percentage of Asian American Population
Total Asian Americans: 7,226,986

3% - 205,501

Nativity

1% - Foreign-born

99% - Native-born

Age in Years

51% - 15-44

15% - 45-64

5% - 65 and over

10% - Under 5

20% - 5-14

Family Type

73% - Married couples

20% - Female householder

7% - Other

Labor Statistics
Persons 16 Years or Older

67% - Employed

4% - Unemployed

29% - Not in labor force

Years of School Completed
Persons 25 Years or Older: 107,714

29% - Some college or associate degree: 31,253

9% - College degree: 9,297

3% - Postgraduate degree: 3,469

6% - Elementary school: 5,986

39% - High school diploma: 41,562

15% - Some high school: 16,147

Source: U.S. Bureau of the Census, *1990 Census of Population: Asians and Pacific Islanders in the United States,* 1993.

cestry and those who are pureblood. Those of mixed ancestry account for 96 percent of the Native Hawaiian population. The blood of most Native Hawaiians is less than 50 percent pure Hawaiian. Because of a variety of factors such as interracial marriages and high rates of death, there has been a tremendous decline in the number of pure-blooded Hawaiians. The major concern generated from this fact relates to the depopulation of Hawaiians as an indigenous people.

Historical Background. David E. Stannard estimates that 800,000 to 1 million Hawaiians were residing in Hawaii when the first Westerner, Captain James COOK, arrived in the islands in 1778. These Hawaiians were healthy and robust as a result of a healthful diet, exercise, and a philosophical worldview of coopera-

Occupation	
Employed Persons 16 Years or Older	Percentage
Managerial and professional specialty	20%
Technical, sales, and administrative support	32%
Service	19%
Farming, forestry, and fishing	2%
Precision production, craft, and repair	12%
Operators, fabricators, and laborers	15%

Income, 1989	
Median household income	$34,830
Per capita	$11,447
Percent of families in poverty	13%

Household Size	
Number of People	Percentage
1	14.9%
2	23.6%
3	17.7%
4	18.6%
5	12.0%
6	6.6%
7 or more	6.6%

Source: U.S. Bureau of the Census, *1990 Census of Population: Asians and Pacific Islanders in the United States,* 1993.

tion and harmony. Contact with the Western world unleashed significant social and cultural changes, resulting in the decimation of the indigenous Hawaiian population and the dislocation of Hawaiian norms and practices.

Disease and Death. In the years that followed Cook's arrival, sailors and merchants introduced diseases which devastated a population that had developed no immunities during its centuries of relative isolation. Sexually transmitted diseases such as syphilis and gonorrhea as well as epidemics of tuberculosis, cholera, smallpox, measles, influenza, and the bubonic plague led to depopulation. Traditional Hawaiian systems of healing were ineffective against these diseases, and limited efforts were made to provide Western medical care to Hawaiians. By 1893, slightly more than one hundred years from the time of Cook's arrival, the Hawaiian population had been reduced to 40,000—a decline of as much as 95 percent.

Land Division: The Great Mahele. In 1848 traditional land tenure in Hawaii was altered in a reform known as the "GREAT *MAHELE*." Lilikala Kameeleihiwa has extensively studied the reform, which called for a conversion of communal land to private, individual ownership. The result of such land reform was that the majority of Hawaiians became dispossessed of land and resources while rates of foreign land ownership quickly escalated. The loss of control of the land led to a loss of *pono*, or equilibrium, among Hawaiians and paved the way for a loss of sovereignty. By the end of the nineteenth century, white persons owned four acres of land for every acre owned by a native. This land was then used for capitalist enterprises focusing on the sugarcane and pineapple industries.

Overthrow of the Hawaiian Monarchy. In 1893 American businesspeople supported by the American military dethroned and imprisoned the Hawaiian monarch, Queen LILIUOKALANI. A provisional government was established, and the government officials and their business associates purchased large quantities of land. This provisional government also took actions to have Hawaii annexed to the United States. In 1898 Liliuokalani wrote about how Hawaiians opposed annexation and favored a return to self-rule. Their desires were not to be heard, however, as the provisional government developed a constitution that prevented Hawaiians from voting on the issue of annexation. Without the support or legal vote of the native people, Hawaii in 1898 became a territory of the United States.

Statehood and Tourism. In 1959 Hawaii became the fiftieth state. In the period between annexation and statehood, Hawaii's economy revolved around the agricultural industries of sugarcane and pineapple. From the mid-1900's onward, however, skyrocketing land values and the prospects of greater profits in tourism motivated major landowners to shift their interests from agribusiness to resorts. Premier hotels, golf courses, and luxury housing have been developed in Hawaii in an effort to attract tourists to the islands. Major consequences of such development include pollution and the depletion or loss of access to natural resources. Hawaii's economy in the 1990's is overly dependent on tourism and is increasingly characterized by low-paying service jobs.

(3) Contemporary Problems and Issues. Hawaiians have experienced an array of health and social problems. While there are multiple causes for these problems, circumstances of culture loss and decline noted above emerge as important contributory factors. Cultural change has led to stresses that serve as the precursors of health and socioeconomic problems in contemporary times. Hawaiians are overrepresented in major health disorders and social problem indicators and occupy the lowest socioeconomic levels among peoples in Hawaii.

Health and Wellness. Hawaiians fare poorly on major indices of health and wellness. These indices include life expectancy and mortality rates from cardiovascular disease and cancer. A 1989 report edited by Eldon L. Wegner focuses on the range of health problems experienced by Hawaiians. Research in the 1980's showed that Hawaiians live five to ten years less than other populations in Hawaii.

The leading causes of death among the total U.S. population are also the major causes of death for Hawaiians. The mortality rates for Hawaiians, however, are higher. According to U.S. government statistics

It is believed that the earliest humans to migrate to the Hawaiian Islands were Polynesians who migrated from the Marquesas Islands c. 300 C.E. Their ethnicity survives in modern Hawaiians. (Brigham Young University, Hawaii)

Native Hawaiian Population Decline and Growth, Hawaii, 1853-1990

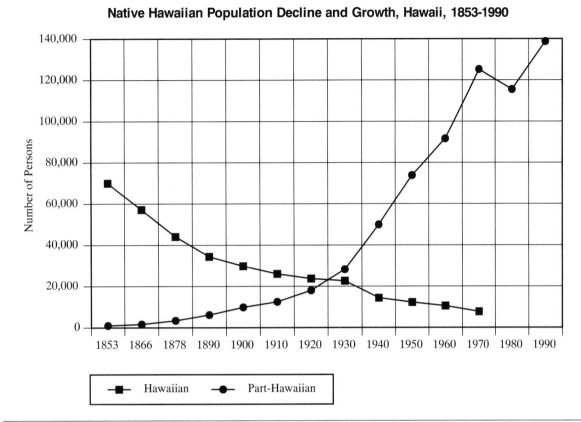

Sources: Clarence E. Glick, *Sojourners and Settlers: Chinese Migrants in Hawaii.* Honolulu: University of Hawaii Press, 1980. Andrew W. Lind, *Hawaii's People.* 4th ed. Honolulu: University of Hawaii Press, 1980. U.S. Bureau of the Census, *1990 Census: General Population Characteristics, Hawaii,* 1992.
Note: With the census of 1980, all those of Hawaiian ancestry are designated "Hawaiian."

published in 1987, the death rate for Hawaiians from diseases of the heart is 44 percent higher when compared with the total U.S. population. The death rate for Hawaiians from cancer is 39 percent higher.

Problems in health status among Hawaiians are exacerbated by a health care system that historically has not been responsive to the unique needs of this population. Health care services have not been accessible to Hawaiians because such services were either too costly or too far away from high-density Hawaiian communities. In addition, health care services have been predicated on mainstream or Western models, and so the design and delivery of services may not be culturally acceptable to many Hawaiians.

Social Problems and Issues. Social problem indicators portray a population that has not fared well under a Western-based system. In addition to low income and poor educational achievement, Hawaiians experience an array of social and psychological difficulties. For example, Hawaiians rank highest in comparison with

other ethnic/racial populations in Hawaii in social problem categories, including cases of child abuse and neglect, teenage pregnancies, and placements in correctional facilities.

Although child abuse is at variance with traditional Hawaiian practices of child-rearing, Hawaiians have experienced escalating rates of child abuse and neglect. Associated risk factors include low socioeconomic status and the young age of mothers. The high rate of teenage pregnancies among Hawaiians correlates with the fact that Hawaiians also have the highest rate of illegitimacy in Hawaii.

Hawaiians have high rates of residence in correctional facilities at both the juvenile and the adult levels. Adults have high rates for felon conviction and imprisonment, and juveniles have high rates of arrest for larceny, theft, burglary, assault, and vandalism. Associated risk factors include low socioeconomic status and substance abuse.

These social problems would appear to indicate an

inability among Hawaiians to adjust to modernization and cultural change. Alternatively they could suggest a lack of willingness to conform to Western norms that are different from Hawaiian norms. Furthermore, like the health care system, the social service system is still largely neglectful in providing services that are culturally relevant for Hawaiians.

Despite the preponderance of health and social problems that exist for Hawaiians, there has been a core set of cultural values that has endured. These values represent the strengths and positive aspects of Hawaiian culture.

(4) Cultural Values. There are many values that form the foundation of Hawaiian culture. These values emphasize the importance of relationships among people. George H. S. Kanahele identified several key values such as humility, spirituality, generosity, graciousness, trustworthiness, intelligence, cleanliness, and helpfulness. While cultural values evolve and function in different ways at different times, a core set of values continues to exist. Three values that are interwoven and have special meaning to Hawaiian people are love and caring (*aloha*), caring for the land (*malama aina*), and family (*ohana*).

While the word *aloha* has multiple meanings for Hawaiians, including "hello" and "good-bye," it generally refers to love and caring for people. *Aloha* refers to the common bond of humanity and to the interrelatedness of the individual with the family, community, nature, and spiritual world. It connotes an attitude of respect and mutuality.

The meaning of *aloha* is reflected in the way Hawaiians view their evolution. According to tradition, all Hawaiians were descended from the same ancestors, Wakea and Papa, and thus are all related. The importance of *aloha* reflects Hawaiians' emphasis on the unity of people and a willingness to give and share with others.

Malama aina is another strong value in Hawaiian culture. In the same way that Hawaiians believe in the importance of relationships among people, they also believe that it is vital to maintain a respectful relationship with the land and with nature. Hawaiians are people whose lives and culture center around the land and a caring for the land.

This value is predicated on two important beliefs. One belief is that ancestral spirits dwell in nature in various forms. Common forms include the shark, the lizard, and various birds and plant life. To a certain extent caring for the land can be broadly interpreted as caring for ancestral family and other spiritual beings. A second belief is that there is a reciprocity or mutuality between people and the land. If people care for the land, it will in turn provide necessary resources for propagation of the people.

Ohana is a structural concept of the Hawaiian family as well as a value based on the interpersonal relationships of family members. As a structural concept, *ohana* refers to those persons related by blood or marriage in the nuclear and extended family systems. In addition to referring to persons bonded by blood ties, *ohana* has taken on additional meaning for groups that are not genetically related but share a common purpose and common responsibilities.

The value of the *ohana* is in having a support group in which there is love, guidance, and sharing. The roles of family members are clear, with the elders serving as respected teachers and the children as cherished learners. The family is a primary transmitter of other values, and so from childhood the values of relationships are learned and reinforced.

One specific illustration of the strength of family relates to a traditional Hawaiian practice of "giving" a child away (*hanai*) to other family members such as the grandparents. Historically the purposes of *hanai* were multiple and emphasized the transmission of knowledge through oral traditions; grandparents taught their grandchildren specific knowledge and skills. The practice of *hanai* was always done in the spirit of sharing a very precious treasure. The child gained a broader network of family members who loved and cared for him or her.

(5) Cultural Survival and Perpetuation. The cultural values and practices that have endured among Hawaiians establish a basis for cultural survival and perpetuation. *Aloha, malama aina* and *ohana* are values that aim toward cultural resurgence. There are also organized activities that are part of the resurgence of Hawaiian culture, such as the sovereign nation movement, community-based health care, and community-based economic development.

Sovereign Nation Movement. For many Hawaiians a key to cultural survival is the reclaiming of an indigenous land base. These efforts are based on the premise that an indigenous land base would serve as a foundation for HAWAIIAN SOVEREIGNTY. Sovereignty would provide for opportunities for Hawaiians to participate in their own decision-making processes regarding all major institutions of society, including government, religion, education, and health care. Undergirding such a movement for self-governance and self-determination are values that address the importance of the land, the family, and caring for others.

Hawaiian activists involved in the sovereign nation movement do not all necessarily subscribe to the same model of sovereignty. Michael K. Dudley and Keoni K. Agard identify three models for sovereignty. One model that promotes a "nation-within-a-nation" concept would have the Hawaiian nation operate within the system of American government. A second model that advances a "nation-to-nation" concept would have the Hawaiian nation exist within the boundaries of the United States but assume a separate and egalitarian status. A third model calls for total separation from the United States. The sovereignty movement gained momentum in 1993—the year that marked the centennial of the overthrow of the Hawaiian monarchy. While there may be no consensus on the model for sovereignty, many Hawaiians are convinced that the way to address contemporary problems and issues among Hawaiians is through self-governance.

Community-Based Health Care. In order to deal with the multiple and complex health problems confronting Hawaiians, efforts have been made to develop a community-based health care system. These efforts derive from the belief that health services that are within the community would enhance accessibility and cultural responsiveness. For example, for the many Hawaiians who reside in rural areas, community-based health care services would facilitate their utilization of such services. Increased utilization leads to prevention and early detection and treatment of diseases. Community-based models promote a perspective of caring for family and community members in ways that are personalized.

A major impetus for community-based health care is the Native Hawaiian Health Care Act of 1988, which mandates the development and implementation of health care centers in high-density Hawaiian communities in Hawaii. A key aspect of planning and implementation is the participation of Hawaiians from these high-density communities. Hawaiian health care providers who are Western-trained, as well as indigenous healers, participate in the planning and imple-

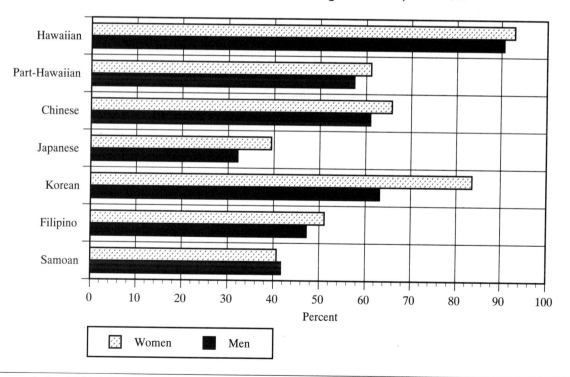

Asian American Outmarriage in Hawaii, 1970-1977

Sources: Andrew W. Lind, *Hawaii's People.* 4th ed. Honolulu: University of Hawaii Press, 1980. Harry H. L. Kitano and Roger Daniels, *Asian Americans: Emerging Minorities.* Englewood Cliffs, N.J.: Prentice Hall, 1988.
Note: From 1970-1980, 17%-34% of Asian American outmarriages in Hawaii were to members of other Asian groups.

mentation of the centers. Efforts include the assessment of priority health concerns in major communities, increasing community awareness, and networking and establishing linkages with mainstream health care providers.

Community-Based Economic Development. Economic development based in the community is also considered a key to cultural and economic survival. Projects that are community-based are viewed as an alternative to an economy that is reliant on tourism and consequently depletes natural resources. Community-based economic development is a strategy to promote the collective interests of residents of high-density Hawaiian communities. The emphasis is on traditional Hawaiian economic activities such as fishing (including aquaculture and ocean harvesting) and farming (such as cultivating taro).

Exemplary projects are family-run or community projects staffed by various community members sharing a common goal of reestablishing a traditional Hawaiian economic system. In addition to an economic product, these projects provide cultural education and cultural enrichment to Hawaiian participants. For example, some projects offer employment to "high-risk" Hawaiian youth and adults and attempt, through work, to reconnect individuals with the land and reshape their identity around being Hawaiian. Participants learn to respect the power of the land and to care for it so that food products can be replenished. Funding is received from various public and private donors as well as from the sale of project products.—*Noreen Mokuau*

SUGGESTED READINGS:

• Blaisdell, Kekuni, and Noreen Mokuau. "Kanaka Maoli: Indigenous Hawaiians" In *Handbook of Social Services for Asian and Pacific Islanders*, edited by Noreen Mokuau. New York: Greenwood Press, 1991. Provides an overview of the social and psychological problems confronting Hawaiians in contemporary times and describes the evolution of culturally sensitive social services for Hawaiians. There is value in the specification of intervention/treatment principles, theories, and skills that are useful in practice with Hawaiian people.

• Dudley, Michael Kioni, and Keoni Kealoha Agard. *A Call for Hawaiian Sovereignty*. Honolulu: Na Kane O Ka Malo Press, 1990. The sovereign nation movement is an important part of contemporary Hawaiian life, and the authors recount the dispossession of Hawaiian lands and the native people's efforts to reclaim their homelands. The book is useful in its provision of a context from which to understand Hawaiian activism and in its description of sovereign nation activities.

• Kameeleihiwa, Lilikala. *Native Land and Foreign Desires: Pehea La E Pono Ai?* Honolulu: Bishop Museum Press, 1992. Describes the 1848 *Mahele*, the land reform that converted communal properties to private ownership. Unlike many books on Hawaiian history, this study provides an account of historical events from the perspective of a Hawaiian. Noteworthy is the use of the concept of *pono* to explain how land conversion reflects changes in Hawaiian worldviews.

• Kanahele, George H. S. *Ku Kanaka, Stand Tall: A Search for Hawaiian Values*. Honolulu: University of Hawaii Press and Waiaha Foundation, 1986. An analytic discussion of Hawaiian values viewed within a cultural context. Such a discussion is intended to restore Hawaiian ethnic identity and pride. Useful in helping to answer the question, Who and what is a Hawaiian?

• Liliuokalani, Queen of Hawaii. *Hawaii's Story*. Reprint. Rutland, Vt.: Charles E. Tuttle, 1962. Written by Hawaii's last monarch in 1898, this account depicts events occurring during her lifetime and provides the reader with a sense of traditional Hawaiian customs and practices. Circumstances surrounding the overthrow of the monarchy are highlighted. This book is unique because it describes the overthrow from the perspective of the queen.

• *Social Process in Hawaii* 32 (1989). Special journal issue focusing on the health of Native Hawaiians. Examines historical and cultural aspects of Hawaiian health, frameworks for assessing health needs, and specific health problems such as diabetes, heart disease, and cancer. Dual emphasis on describing the incidence and prevalence of health disorders as well as looking at health care services. Useful volume edited by Eldon L. Wegner.

• Stannard, David E. *Before the Horror: The Population of Hawaii on the Eve of Western Contact*. Honolulu: Social Science Research Institute, University of Hawaii, 1989. Stannard is a noted historian who writes on oppressed peoples. Challenges conventional estimates of the Hawaiian population at the time of the arrival of James Cook in 1778. Stannard's population estimate is based on a reexamination of historical documents.

• U.S. Congress, Office of Technology Assessment. *Current Health Status and Population Projections of Native Hawaiians Living in Hawaii*. Washington, D.C.: Government Printing Office, 1987. Provides statistics on Hawaiian mortality rates and further specifies population projections. Describes the number of deaths of Hawaiians as a result of diseases such as heart disease, cancer, and diabetes and indicates that there will be no pureblooded Hawaiians in the mid-twenty-first century. Good summary of health statistics on Hawaiians.

Hayakawa, Sessue (Kintaro Hayakawa; June 10, 1890, Honshu, Japan — Nov. 23, 1973, Tokyo, Japan): Actor, director, and producer.

Possibly the best-known actor of Japanese ancestry in twentieth century American films, Hayakawa was raised in Japan by aristocratic parents in the strict samurai warrior tradition. He graduated from Tokyo Naval Preparatory School in 1908, but a ruptured eardrum shortly before he was to enter the Naval Academy disqualified him from military service. Believing himself dishonored, he attempted hara-kiri. While recovering he began to study Zen.

Entering the United States in 1909, Hayakawa graduated from the University of Chicago in 1913 with a degree in political science. On his way home to Japan, he stopped in the Little Tokyo section of Los Angeles, where he began acting and directing for a Japanese American theater company. He adopted the stage name "Sessue Hayakawa." In 1914 he married an actress, Tsuru Aoki. They reared two girls and a boy, Hayakawa's son by another American actress.

Hayakawa was soon discovered by Thomas Ince and cast as the lead in the 1914 movie *The Typhoon*. A year later his dynamic screen presence made him famous as Tori, the wealthy villain in Cecil B. DeMille's 1915 movie *The Cheat*. In 1918 Hayakawa formed his own studio company, producing many films and entertaining extravagantly during the silent film era.

Living abroad for much of the 1920's and 1930's, acting and directing, he found himself stranded in France when World War II began. Not until after the war was he able to return to the United States, to star in *Tokyo Joe* (1949) with Humphrey Bogart.

A Zen Buddhist priest by the early 1950's, Hayakawa continued to act. In 1957 he had his most memorable role, as the Japanese prisoner of war camp commandant, Colonel Saito, opposite Sir Alec Guinness in *The Bridge on the River Kwai* (1957). For that performance he received an Academy Award nomination as best supporting actor.

Hayakawa accepted additional movie roles until 1966 and made occasional appearances on American television before returning to Japan, where he lived quietly until his death, studying Zen philosophy and teaching acting.

Hayakawa, S. I. [Samuel Ichiye] (July 18, 1906, Vancouver, British Columbia—Feb. 27, 1992, Greenbrae, Calif.): Scholar, college president, and politician. The Canadian-born Hayakawa, after receiving a bachelor's degree from the University of Manitoba and a master's degree from McGill University in Montreal, earned a doctorate in 1935 from the University of Wisconsin, where he remained as a member of the English department. In 1941, he published *Language in Action*, which became a standard textbook and made Hayakawa's reputation in the field of semantics, and in 1949 he published *Language in Thought and Action*. Hayakawa taught at the Illinois Institute of Technology and the University of Chicago before he joined the faculty of San Francisco State College in 1955, becoming the institution's first Japanese American faculty member. In 1968, during a period of unrest during which many students demanded that the college's curriculum be more representative of its culturally diverse student population, Hayakawa was elected president of San Francisco State College. Hayakawa

Senator S. I. Hayakawa was known for his conservatism in an era of student unrest and social upheaval. (AP/Wide World Photos)

condemned the protesters and refused to negotiate with them, stating that their actions constituted an "infringement on academic freedom." His conservative stance made him a hero to those who disapproved of the student activism of the late 1960's. He called in the police to quell campus demonstrations, and on one occasion, he pulled out the wires of the loudspeakers that were being used by student protesters. Hayakawa retired as college president in 1972. In 1976, Hayakawa, who had changed his party affiliation in 1973 from Democrat to Republican, ran for the U.S. Senate and won. He became best known during his tenure in office for speaking his mind unhesitatingly and bluntly, sometimes to the detriment of his political career, and for his habit of falling asleep while the Senate was in session. In 1982, Hayakawa headed a subcommittee on Far Eastern and Pacific Affairs, and in 1983 he served as a special adviser to the U.S. Secretary of State. Always a political conservative, Hayakawa opposed the movement to redress the grievances suffered by Japanese Americans during World War II and introduced legislation that would have made English the official and exclusive language of government and education.

Hayashi, Dennis: Attorney. Appointed in 1993 as head of the Office of Civil Rights in the U.S. Department of Health and Human Services, he was formerly executive director of the national JAPANESE AMERICAN CITIZENS LEAGUE (JACL). As an attorney at the ASIAN LAW CAUCUS (1979 to 1991), he specialized in employment and discrimination cases and served as cocounsel in the *coram nobis* case *Korematsu v. United States* (1984).

A third-generation Japanese American—both of his parents were interned during World War II—Hayashi grew up in a predominantly African American neighborhood in Los Angeles. In 1974, he was graduated cum laude from Occidental College with a bachelor's degree in philosophy. He received his law degree in 1978 from the University of California Hastings College of Law, in San Francisco. Strongly committed to civil rights issues throughout his career, Hayashi is a cofounder of the National Network Against Anti-Asian Violence.

Hayashi, Eric (b. Dec. 28, 1952, San Francisco, Calif.): Theatrical producer. A founding member of San Francisco's Asian-American Theatre Workshop (which became the ASIAN-AMERICAN THEATRE COMPANY in 1977), he served as that organization's execu-

tive director from 1986 until 1989, when he became artistic director. Under his leadership the company produced works by leading Asian American dramatists Frank CHIN, David Henry HWANG, Philip Kan GOTANDA, Momoko Iko, R. A. SHIOMI, Genny LIM, and Warren Kubota. As president of Sansei Productions, Records, and Tapes, Hayashi produced Lane Nishikawa's *Life in the Fast Lane* (pr. 1981), Charlie Chin's *ABC (American Born Chinese)* (pr. 1983), and the Asian American rock group Noh Buddies (1983-1984).

Hayashi, Harvey Saburo (Hayashi Saburo; 1866, Aizuwakamatsu, Japan—June 1, 1943, Holualoa, Kona, Territory of Hawaii): Physician and newspaper publisher. Hayashi was the son of a samurai who was exiled for staging an unsuccessful rebellion against the Meiji emperor. After being graduated from medical school in 1884, he went to Tokyo and then to the United States for more medical training. He landed in San Francisco, where he joined the GOSPEL SOCIETY and began attending Hahnemann Hospital and College, from which he was graduated in 1892. He was also given the English name of "Harvey," after English physician William Harvey, by one of his professors.

Hayashi eventually moved to Holualoa in Kona, Hawaii, and there opened a medical practice treating Issei plantation laborers. Despite the stress of a busy practice and having to rear twelve children with his wife, Matsu Kawarada, he also began publishing a newspaper for the rural community's Japanese American residents. The *Kona Hankyo* (Kona echo) remained in circulation for more than forty years.

Hayslip, Le Ly (Phung Thi Le Ly; b. Dec. 19, 1949, Ky La, Vietnam): Writer and humanitarian. Her first autobiographical book, *When Heaven and Earth Changed Places: A Vietnamese Woman's Journey from War to Peace* (1989), written with Jay Wurts, presented to a wide American audience the Vietnam War (1965-1975) from the viewpoint of a young Buddhist peasant girl from a Vietnamese village, caught between Viet Cong and republican forces. *Child of War, Woman of Peace* (1993), written with her son, James Hayslip, discusses her subsequent adjustment to life in the United States. Both books are notable for their honesty and nonjudgmental outlook and emphasis on compassion and reconciliation between two former enemies.

Born in a village near Da Nang in central Vietnam, Hayslip was a lookout and courier for the Viet Cong as a young girl. After being captured, tortured, and released by South Vietnamese soldiers, she was sentenced to death by the Viet Cong. Her life was spared, but she was raped by her two appointed executioners. Leaving her village in disgrace, Hayslip's subsequent life in Saigon and later in Da Nang is a story of survival and hardship. Accompanied by her mother, she first was a servant in a well-to-do Saigon household. After becoming pregnant by her employer, however, she was thrown out of the house by his wife and went to Da Nang. There, her relationships with American military men introduced her to the marketing of black-market American goods in order to support herself, her mother, and her young son. Marriage in 1970 to an American civilian much older than herself brought her to Southern California at the age of twenty. Adapting to a new culture and way of life was often painful and difficult. Widowed twice, and with three sons to raise, Hayslip became an American citizen and attained success as a businesswoman in California. Her two books are the basis for the 1993 film *Heaven and Earth*, directed by Oliver Stone.

After a visit to Vietnam in 1986 to see her family (related in her first book), Hayslip established the East Meets West Foundation in 1988 to counteract the aftereffects of the Vietnam War on the people of Vietnam and further peaceful relations between Vietnam and the United States. The foundation, headquartered in San Diego, provides medical assistance, educational facilities, and other rehabilitation programs for Quang Nam-Da Nang Province in central Vietnam.

Hearst, William Randolph (Apr. 29, 1863, San Francisco, Calif.—Aug. 14, 1951, Beverly Hills, Calif.): Publisher. A strong advocate of the internment of Japanese Americans, he was a prominent figure in the anti-Japanese movement in the United States, preceding and during World War II (1939-1945). His newspapers participated in a determined and systematic campaign to foment anti-Japanese sentiment and activities, while publishing pro-German articles.

Heart Mountain: One of ten U.S. government camps under the administration of the WAR RELOCATION AUTHORITY (WRA) used to house Japanese American evacuees during World War II. Officially the camps were designated as "RELOCATION CENTERS."

General Information. The concentration camp at Heart Mountain was located near the cities of Cody and Powell in the northwestern part of Wyoming on federal reclamation-project land. It opened in August,

1942, and held more than ten thousand internees at its peak. Initially the citizens of Powell and Cody did not welcome the internees. Despite their prejudices, however, the residents soon saw the benefit of having cheap, exploitable labor nearby. Powell, an agricultural town with a severe labor shortage, benefited from Nisei labor, while Cody benefited from the sale of construction materials and other items to the camp.

As in the other concentration camps administered by the WRA, the internees lived in standard barracks that measured from 20 by 100 to 120 feet. Each barrack was divided into four to six rooms, each 20 by 16, 20, or 25 feet. In general, families received the larger rooms while couples and singles were assigned the smaller facilities. Since the barracks were built to accommodate army personnel, privacy was difficult for the internees. Many, for example, were forced to create their own sleeping facilities by hanging bedsheets across the room. The barracks were also hastily constructed. According to a former construction worker at Heart Mountain, cracks were found in the barracks, which led his foreman to comment: "Well, I guess those Japs will be stuffing their underwear in there to keep the wind out."

The foreman knew exactly what was in store for the internees. Heart Mountain had a reputation for harsh winters and dust storms. Former internee Frank Emi, for example, arrived at the camp in the middle of a dust storm where "you could not see further than ten or fifteen feet." Emi, who had arrived from Los Angeles with his family in early September of 1942, had not seen the worst yet. By the end of the month, snow had begun to fall, and the area experienced the coldest and harshest winter in Wyoming history. As temperatures dipped to under 30 degrees below zero, most of the internees were forced to fight the elements with inadequate clothing.

The harsh winter and the poor living conditions only intensified other inadequacies within the camp. During the first few months, the food supply was both unhealthy and inadequate. Rations, which in general cost from 31 cents to 45 cents per internee per day, were often limited to one ladle of the cook's concoction per meal. Very often, the poor diet left the internees either sick or hungry. The meals at Heart Mountain did not reach minimum Army standards until late January of 1943.

The medical facilities at Heart Mountain were also inadequate. When they needed medical attention during the first winter, the internees often faced a small staff of overworked doctors, nurses, and aides who

Intern survivor stands before a quilt commemorating the camps, including (top) Heart Mountain. (National Japanese American Historical Society)

were unprepared to handle the hundreds of cases per day. During the winter months, all 150 hospital beds were filled with patients waiting to be treated.

In general, Heart Mountain's problems concerning food, shelter, and medical facilities declined as the first winter passed. The project director addressed the problem of food shortages by firing the head steward. Larger clothing allowances and additional coal were allotted to help the internees battle the snow. Also, preventive care was stressed so that epidemics could be avoided.

Resistance. In February of 1943, the U.S. Selective Service began registering all eligible Nisei in the WRA camps for the draft and also began accepting volunteers for military service. To some people in camp, including members of the JAPANESE AMERICAN CITIZENS LEAGUE (JACL), military service was an opportunity for the Nisei to prove their loyalty to America. To many others, it was an insult to be asked to serve in the military while they were still imprisoned behind barbed wire. One group that protested the "loyalty questionnaire" that was administered by the Selective Service and the WRA was the Heart Mountain Congress of American Citizens. This group challenged the JACL's leadership and urged the Nisei to reject the

segregated ("Jap Crow") unit proposed by the military.(That unit eventually became the much-heralded 442ND REGIMENTAL COMBAT TEAM.) Their tactics were successful. One out of seven Nisei at Heart Mountain refused to cooperate with the registration program.

Later in the year, Nisei Kiyoshi Okamoto began lecturing other Nisei at Heart Mountain about their constitutional rights as American citizens. Calling himself the "Fair Play Committee of One," he was soon joined by Paul Nakadate, Frank Seishi Emi, Isamu Sam Horino, Minoru Tamesa, Tsutomu Ben Wakaye, and Guntaro Kubota. Together, they became known as the FAIR PLAY COMMITTEE (FPC). In February of 1944, one year after the Selective Service registration, the FPC organized around the drafting of Nisei for military service while they were still imprisoned in concentration camps. They drafted three bulletins, held several open meetings that attracted a few hundred other Nisei, and engaged in an editorial battle with the WRA camp newspaper, the *Heart Mountain Sentinel.* Eventually, eighty-five Nisei refused to be inducted for military service and were sentenced to three years in prison. The leaders of the FPC were tried and sentenced to Leavenworth Federal Penitentiary.

Later, their convictions were overturned, and the draft resisters were pardoned by President Harry S Truman in 1947.

Microcosm. Heart Mountain eventually closed in November of 1945, three months after the end of World War II. The events at Heart Mountain were a microcosm of the turbulence at the WRA concentration camps. While Heart Mountain was the site of the only organized resistance to the draft, similar episodes occurred at the other camps as well. For example, incidents at Poston and Manzanar (labeled by some as "riots") underscored the tensions at the camps over food supplies and suspected *inu* (informers). In addition, because resistance to the loyalty questionnaire was so enormous, the camp at TULE LAKE had to be converted into a segregation center for so-called disloyals. In the end, many lives were tragically altered because of the government's treatment of its own citizens. Heart Mountain was a prime example of the government's failure.—*Glen Kitayama*

SUGGESTED READINGS: • Drinnon, Richard. *Keeper of Concentration Camps: Dillon S. Myer and American Racism.* Berkeley: University of California Press, 1987. • Emi, Frank. "Draft Resistance at the Heart Mountain Concentration Camp and the Fair Play Committee." In *Frontiers of Asian American Studies: Writing, Research and Commentary*, edited by Gail M. Nomura, Russell Endo, Stephen H. Sumida, and Russell C. Leong. Pullman: Washington State University Press, 1989. • Hansen, Asael T. "My Two Years at Heart Mountain: The Difficult Role of an Applied Anthropologist." In *Japanese Americans: From Relocation to Redress*, edited by Roger Daniels, Sandra C. Taylor, and Harry H. L. Kitano. Rev. ed. Seattle: University of Washington Press, 1991. • Nelson, Douglas W. *Heart Mountain: The History of an American Concentration Camp.* Madison: The State Historical Society of Wisconsin, 1976. • U.S. Commission on Wartime Relocation and Internment of Civilians. *Personal Justice Denied: Report of the Commission on Wartime Relocation and the Internment of Civilians.* Washington, D.C.: Government Printing Office, 1983.

Heart Mountain Fair Play Committee: Group organized at the HEART MOUNTAIN concentration camp that protested the drafting of Nisei for U.S. military service while Japanese Americans were still being denied their basic constitutional rights.

Kiyoshi Okamoto, Paul Nakadate, Frank Emi, Sam Horino, Min Tamesa, Ben Wakaye, Ken Yanagi, Guntaro Kubota—the average Japanese American would not recognize these names. Yet together they spearheaded the only organized draft resistance in the World War II concentration camps.

In late 1943 Okamoto formed the Fair Play Committee of One (with himself as the only member) and had the audacity to challenge the U.S. government's unconstitutional policy of jailing Japanese Americans without due process of law. Soon Okamoto's words drew an audience at Heart Mountain, and he was later joined by the others. At first the newly named Fair Play Committee (FPC) involved itself in issues related to camp conditions. Its focus, however, quickly changed when Nisei were subjected to the draft in January of 1944.

In February of 1944 the FPC issued the first of three newsletters that called on the government to restore to the internees their rights as U.S. citizens. The FPC held public meetings in mess halls, waged an editorial war with the camp newspaper over the draft issue, and attracted a few hundred Nisei members. By the time it issued a third newsletter on March 4, 1944, the committee members' minds were set: The leaders of the FPC would refuse entry into the military until their constitutional rights were restored.

Later in March, when the draft notices were issued, fifty-three men followed their conscience and refused to be inducted. By the end of May ten more followed suit. These sixty-three men were arrested, tried, and sentenced to three years in prison for draft evasion. By August of 1944 they had been joined by another twenty-two resisters. As for the leaders of the FPC (with the exception of Yanagi), they were tried for sedition and sentenced to Leavenworth Federal Penitentiary. After the war their convictions were overturned on appeal. Later, on December 24, 1947, President Harry S Truman issued a pardon to all the draft resisters.

Heco, Joseph (Hamada Hikozo; 1837, Harima Province, Japan—1897): First U.S. citizen of Japanese descent. Orphaned at an early age, Hamada became a sailor on the coastal trade routes between Edo and Hyogo. In 1850 his ship encountered a storm, became disabled, and drifted for fifty-two days far into the Pacific Ocean. He and the other surviving sailors were rescued by a passing American ship and taken to San Francisco, where they arrived in 1851. After a year there, they were ordered to be sent to Hong Kong along with other Japanese castaways to be repatriated by Commodore Matthew C. Perry on his historic voyage to Japan. Angered by the way he and other Japanese were being treated aboard ship and weary of waiting for Perry's arrival, Hamada chose to return to the United States. There a San Francisco customs officer, C. B. Sanders, offered to take him to Baltimore, where he received a Western education and became a Christian as well as a U.S. citizen. Also during this time he changed his name to "Joseph Heco."

With all the excitement surrounding the opening of trade with Japan, the bilingual Heco found himself in great demand. In 1858 he returned to Japanese waters aboard a survey ship and eventually was hired as an interpreter by Townsend Harris, the first American consul to Japan. Heco accompanied Harris to Yokohama in 1859. Later he left the consulate to pursue private business interests and became a leading figure in the establishment of foreign trading communities at Yokohama and Kobe. He also had business connections with Thomas B. Glover in Nagasaki during these turbulent years.

Throughout his career in government service and business, he used his unique position and language skills in a variety of ways. In 1864 he began publishing in Japanese a newspaper, the *Kaigai Shimbun*, which specialized in covering news of foreign affairs translated from foreign newspapers into Japanese. He also published a Japanese translation of the Book of Genesis and served as a consultant to the Japanese Finance Ministry. He wrote several accounts of his colorful career: *Hyoryuki*, published in Japanese in 1868, describes his experiences as a castaway in the United States; *The Narrative of a Japanese* appeared in English in 1895.

Hemet Valley incident (1913): In Hemet, California (south of Riverside), eleven Korean agricultural workers were sent to the fields to pick apricots. The Koreans, mistaken for the more hated Japanese agricultural workers, were driven away by a mob of angry whites.

Following the incident, the consul-general for the Japanese consulate in Los Angeles arrived in Hemet to issue a public protest and to seek monetary compensation for the mob's actions. The nationalistic Koreans refused any Japanese assistance, however, and turned to the KOREAN NATIONAL ASSOCIATION (KNA) for recourse. The president of the association, the Reverend David Lee, wired U.S. Secretary of State William Jennings Bryan, explaining that he (Lee) was in control of the situation, which had already begun to abate. He requested that Bryan regard the workers as Koreans, not Japanese, since the former had immigrated to America before the Japanese formally annexed Korea;

as such, while in the United States, Koreans were under American, not Japanese, jurisdiction. This incident created a dilemma for the American government over whether to recognize Japan's control of Korea.

Bryan's reply to Lee supported Korean independence from Japanese jurisdiction while the Koreans remained in the United States. Bryan stated further that any future assistance the Koreans should need while in America would be a matter for the KNA and not a Japanese association. This strengthened the KNA's status while indirectly denouncing Japan's control of Korea.

Heney, Francis J. (Mar. 17, 1859, Lima, N.Y.—Oct. 31, 1937, Santa Monica, Calif.): California State Senator. Heney was a cosponsor of the Webb-Heney Bill. (See ALIEN LAND LAW OF 1913.) White owners of small farms had pressured the California legislature to enact anti-Asian laws in order to drive Asian immigrants out of agriculture; the 1913 act was the first in a series of Alien Land Laws enacted in California and many other states.

Herbal medicine: Medicine derived from plants, including both herbaceous and woody plants.

Herbal medicine has been used by the Chinese for thousands of years and is nowhere as extensive or as widely accepted as in Chinese society. In the 1970's about 85 percent of all medicines used in rural areas of the People's Republic of China consisted of herbal drugs. For example, ginseng has been widely used in the treatment of hypotension and as a tonic for cardiac conditions.

Herbal medicine may be collected from the roots, stem, leaves, flowers, fruits, or the whole plant. Special attention must be given to collect the plants in a specific location and at a given time.

Herbal medicine is based on encyclopedic accumulations of empirical knowledge. Shen Nong (divine peasant) was revered as the pharmacist sage. The great catalog of remedies traditionally ascribed to him, *Shen Nong Bencaojing* (Shen Nong materia medica classics), is the earliest work of its kind in Chinese literature. Fragments of the lost original were published in the sixth century. Other important classical texts include *Huang Ti nei Ching* (the Yellow Emperor's esoteric classic), thought to have been written in the third century B.C.E., and *Bencao Gangmu* (compendium of materia medica) by Li Shizhen, published in 1578. Li describes 1,892 different remedies and more than 1,000 standard medical prescriptions, many of which

The herbal college at Emperor's College, Santa Monica, California, archives a large collection of herbal medicines. (Alon Reininger, Unicorn Stock Photos)

are still in use. *Zhongguo Bencao Tulu* (pictorial handbook of China's materia medica), a ten-volume encyclopedia edited by Xiao Peigen, was published in 1993. It records about 5,000 species of medicinal herbs.

Herbal medicine is a major branch of traditional Chinese medicine, a well-organized system of medical knowledge based on observations, experiments, and clinical trials. Though not all theories of herbal medicine are grounded on scientific principles, old remedies increasingly have been verified by modern science. In China traditional Chinese medicine has been integrated with Western medicine to develop the "New Chinese Medicine." In the United States herbal medicine has always been used among many Asian Americans and is available in Chinese pharmacies. As a natural product herbal medicine is especially attractive.

Hermit Kingdom: Name attributed to Korea during its self-imposed period of isolation, which began in 1636 and lasted for two and a half centuries.

Herzig, John A. "Jack" (b. July 30, 1922, Newark, N.J.): Researcher. As a consultant to the U.S. Commis-

sion on Wartime Relocation and Internment of Civilians (CWRIC), Herzig testified before Congress on the passage of Japanese American redress legislation then under consideration. That movement culminated in the enactment of the Civil Liberties Act of 1988. He also served as the principal consultant for the Justice Department's Office of Redress Administration (ORA) as it executed the terms of the act. He and his wife, Aiko, testified during the Gordon K. Hirabayashi *coram nobis* case of 1988, which overturned the latter's World War II conviction for violating the curfew and exclusion orders. Their testimony during that appeal helped refute allegations of subversive activities by Japanese Americans, evidence disclosed by the so-called magic cables introduced by the government. Herzig and his wife also undertook the job of preparing for publication the transcripts of the 1981 CWRIC hearings.

Hibakusha: Surviving victims of the atomic bombings of Hiroshima and Nagasaki during World War II (1939-1945). The term is derived from the Japanese phrase *genbaku hibakusha*, which translated means

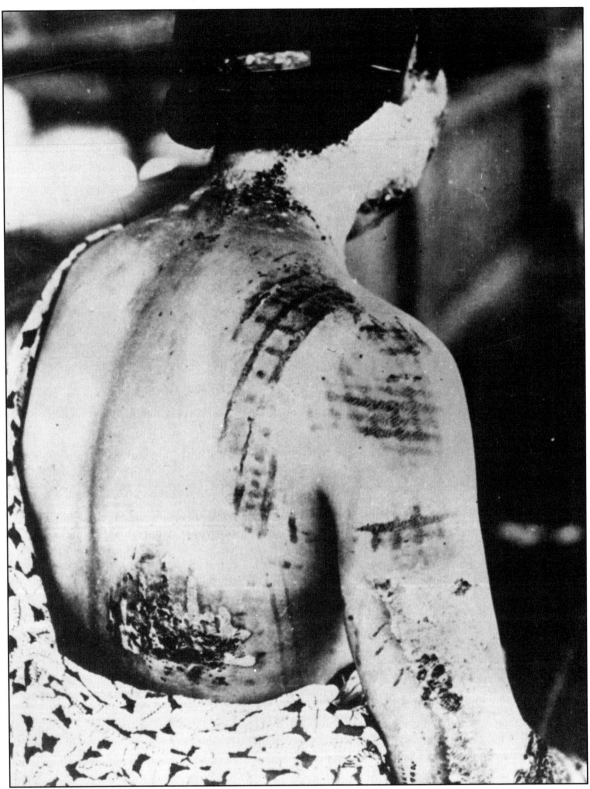

Radiation burns suffered by a victim of the atomic bombing of Hiroshima on August 6, 1945. Although the bomb brought an end to World War II, in which countless lives were lost, it also killed and permanently maimed many Japanese civilians. (National Archives)

"atomic bombing victims."

The number of surviving atomic bomb victims counted by Japanese prefectural and national registration in 1979 was more than 370,000. Many *hibakusha* have moved away from Hiroshima and Nagasaki. Almost one-quarter live in other parts of Japan, and a few thousand have migrated as far away as the western United States. About half of all registered *hibakusha* continue to live in the city and surrounding prefecture of Hiroshima. A little more than one-quarter live in the city and surrounding prefecture of Nagasaki.

Non-Japanese *hibakusha* are included among seventy thousand Koreans who were doing forced labor in the two cities when the atomic bombings took place. Twenty thousand returned to Korea after the war. Several hundred Okinawan *hibakusha* returned to the Ryukyu Islands.

Some *hibakusha* were not present at the atomic bombings. Japanese law defines as *hibakusha* those who came to live in Hiroshima and Nagasaki within fourteen days after the bombing and those in the womb when their mothers suffered radiation from the blast. Second generation *hibakusha* are called *hibaku nisei*. They live in fear of genetic abnormality, birth defects, and higher incidence of a wide range of normal illnesses, despite research that apparently shows no appreciable hereditary transmission.

During the Allied occupation of Japan, any mention of the *hibakusha* in the mass media was censored. Even after the occupation, the *hibakusha* struggled for recognition of their particular problems. Organizations of *hibakusha* in Japan continue to fight for a more comprehensive government program to provide medical and social aid. *Hibakusha* claim that they face discrimination in employment, in marriage, and in the purchase of life insurance.

The *hibakusha* are a living symbol of the horror of nuclear war. For this reason their plight is tied to the antinuclear movement in Japan and around the world.

highbinders: Particularly among the Chinese in America, enforcers or hired killers employed by the Chinese *tongs*. The term "highbinders" was originally applied to Irish thugs early in the nineteenth century.

High-caste Hindus: Hindus of the Brahmin caste. The phrase was adopted by Bhagat Singh Thind when he went before the U.S. Supreme Court to secure for himself and other Asian Indians the right of American citizenship. In the case of *United States v. Bhagat Singh*

Thind (1922), he characterized Indians of a high caste as descendants of the Aryan race who were therefore Caucasian—the prerequisite for naturalization. The Court, however, found that he was not Caucasian and declined to grant his petition.

Higher Wage Association: Hawaii labor organization established in 1908 by a group of Japanese intellectuals to seek better pay and lodgings for Japanese sugar plantation laborers. The association argued that the Japanese workers, of which there were about thirty thousand, were being treated less fairly than the Portuguese and Puerto Rican employees.

Spreading the Message. The wages of a Japanese laborer working twenty-six days a month did not exceed $18. Describing the housing furnished by the Waianae Plantation, one writer asserted that though the plantation "was doing a profitable business the dwellings of the [Japanese] laborers were filthy and unsanitary. . . . It would be more proper to refer to these dwellings as pig sties than to refer to them as human habitations."

Instead of the $18 a month and substandard quarters allotted the Japanese, the Portuguese and Puerto Ricans were each given $22.50 a month and, if married, a house and an acre of land.

In an article in the August 25, 1908, issue of *Nichi Nichi*, Gunkichi Shimada wrote that "prices had recently increased more than 20 percent" and that the Japanese laborers' wages accordingly should be increased by more than 20 percent. Yokichi Tasaka of the rival *Nippu Jiji* read Shimada's article and took up the cause.

Thirty-five-year-old Motoyuki Negoro read Tasaka's articles and wrote a long treatise on the subject of higher wages. Negoro had personally felt the pain of discrimination. He had come to America at age seventeen, worked his way through high school in California, matriculated at the University of California, Berkeley, in 1896, and received a bachelor of letters degree in 1901 and a bachelor of laws in 1903. After spending time in Hawaii, he returned to Berkeley and received a juris doctor degree in 1908.

Yet despite this impressive background, as an alien Negoro was barred from practicing law. Under the law of that time he was also ineligible for naturalization.

After the treatise was rejected elsewhere, Negoro took it to Yasutaro Soga, owner and editor of the *Nippu Jiji*. Soga published the treatise serially and gave it his full support. The newspaper asserted that the Japanese laborers, "when compared with the laborers of other countries, were competent laborers, and not one whit less efficient, and that persons of equal labor capacity should be given equal wages and equal treatment."

Prelude to a Strike. Interest in the movement for better pay and working conditions grew. On December 1, 1908, at a meeting at the Japanese Young Men's Christian Association (YMCA) attended by forty-two persons, the Higher Wage Association was formed. Yukichi Ishii, a druggist, was elected president, Fred Kinzaburo Makino vice president, Negoro secretary, and Matsutaro Yamashiro treasurer. Ishii soon withdrew, and Makino moved up to fill the office of president while the other offices remained unchanged.

Though he had no official connection with the organization, Soga met almost daily with Makino, Tasaka and Negoro—the movement's four core members. From their hub at the Yamashiro Hotel, the unofficial headquarters of the organization, lines of communication radiated to the farthest perimeter of the islands and reached all plantations. On the plantations autonomous higher wage associations sprang up and these associations turned to the "Big Four" for guidance.

Makino and Negoro, kept busy with speaking engagements, hired an automobile and roared about the countryside to plantation after plantation, where they harangued the laborers who gathered by the thousands to hear them. The *Nippu Jiji's* circulation soared.

The association made representations to the planters. Though some among the planters thought the requests reasonable and favored granting them in whole or in part, the majority opposed them. The majority ruled; with a facade of unanimity that was never to crack, the planters peremptorily denied the requests.

The association then decided that their objectives could be obtained only through a strike. The group formed a strike fund and ordered provisions for the anticipated siege. The plan was to have the laborers on the island of Oahu, site of the capital city of Honolulu, bear the brunt of the conflict by striking, with those on the other islands continuing to work while donating money to support the strikers. The 1909 strike would eventually last four months.

The Work Stops. As the Japanese struck each Oahu plantation, management evicted them and their families from the plantation. The thousands of strikers moved to the places assigned them, most traveling on foot, those from faraway Kahuku spending a night on the road. The largest contingent of strikers straggled into Honolulu, where they were quartered in several places around town.

The largest concentration was in the Aala district,

Japanese female sugarcane laborers, c. 1910. (Lyman House Memorial Museum)

where huge tents had been erected and where volunteers fed and cared for the evicted. There were small children among the evicted. Some families were burdened with sick members.

The leaders of the strike constantly counseled against violence toward their opponents. The police, however, based on trumped-up charges lodged against the strikers, made wholesale arrests. Beginning on the afternoon of June 10, 1909, and continuing into the night, the police, without warrants, went about arresting the leaders of the strike, including some staff members of the *Nippu Jiji*.

Finally, the Big Four were brought to trial on the charge of conspiracy to boycott plantation business. On August 5th, the Higher Wage Association convention passed a resolution urging the strikers to return to work.

Though the delegates to the convention recognized defeat, they did not permit it to degenerate into a rout. They set up an employment office at association headquarters and agreed to seek work for those wishing to transfer to other islands. The association would attempt to help with traveling expenses through other anticipated donations.

The conspiracy trial dragged on for three weeks. The defendants were found guilty and sentenced to ten months in jail and $300 fine each. They appealed, but the Territorial Supreme Court ruled against them.

Meanwhile the planters had begun replacing the Japanese quarters with better dwellings. Within three months of the end of the strike, the owners proclaimed that, thereafter, pay would be proportionate to individual ability without regard to nationality. This promise was never fully carried out.—*Allan Beekman*

Suggested Readings: • Beekman, Take, and Allan Beekman. "Hawaii's Great Japanese Strike." In *Kodomo No Tame Ni: For the Sake of the Children*, by Dennis Ogawa. Honolulu: University of Hawaii Press, 1978. • Negoro, Motoyuki. *Meiji Yonjuichi, ni-nen Hawaii Hojin Katsuyakushi*. Honolulu: Taisho 4, 1915. • Soga, Keiho. *Gojunenkan No Hawai Kaiko*. Honolulu: Kankokai, 1953. • Wakukawa, Ernest Katsumi. *A History of the Japanese People in Hawaii*. Honolulu: The Toyo Shoin, 1938.

Hill, Amy (b. Seattle, Wash.): Performance artist. She achieved critical and box-office success with her one-woman show "Tokyo Bound." Her work explores her experience as a multiracial Asian American of Japanese and Finnish extraction. She has also worked with the Cold Tofu and Great Leap performance groups, appeared in television shows and films, including *Dim Sum: A Little Bit of Heart* (1984) and *Singles* (1993), and recorded voice-overs for commercials.

Hilo massacre (1938): Clash between public officials and prounion demonstrators protesting the use of nonunion workers at Hilo Harbor, Hawaii. In 1935 Congress legalized collective bargaining in the Wagner Act. Although the law encouraged labor organizations to seek recognition, employers in Hawaii refused to deal with such organizations as the Inland Boatmen's Union, which went on strike on February 4, 1938. The union sought wage parity with the West Coast and preferential hiring for union members, a concession that had been granted to West Coast dockworkers three years earlier. When negotiations failed interisland shipping ground to a halt, though automobile, mail, and passenger cargo continued.

On August 1 some two hundred demonstrators, representing several ethnic groups and labor organizations, as well as sympathizers and family members, marched to Hilo Harbor to protest the unloading of the *Waialeale* by nonunion workers. When the *Waialeale* had docked at Hilo ten days earlier, eight members of the police force, on hand to assure the safety of the nonunion crew, were greatly outnumbered by peaceful if boisterous demonstrators. For the August 1 protest, therefore, the Hilo police assigned seventy-four officers and special deputies for an expected confrontation. Singing, the crowd did not hear orders of the sheriff to stop; when they reached the pier, the police threw about a dozen tear gas grenades into their midst. The fire department then hosed the demonstrators off the pier, but it soon ran out of water, whereupon the demonstrators regrouped. The ship's captain, meanwhile, told the police chief that the ship was heavily armed and that the crew was ready to fire upon order. Fearing that the townspeople would be slaughtered, the chief ordered his men to load their rifles with birdshot pellets and then to fire to disperse the crowd. After an altercation provoked by a police officer, in which one demonstrator was bayoneted and another's jaw was rifle-butted, the officer opened fire, followed by his comrades. Fifty persons were shot. None died.

Responding to a public outcry, an official investigation was undertaken. The report blamed the union and absolved the police of charges of criminal misconduct. No one was found guilty of any wrongdoing, and the public appeared mollified, as the authorities had hoped.

Hindi: A modern Indo-Aryan language spoken in South Asian countries (India, Pakistan, Nepal) and in countries outside Asia (Mauritius, Trinidad, Fiji, Surinam, Guyana, South Africa, and others). Approximately six hundred million people speak Hindi, as either a first or second language. It is ranked among the five most widely spoken languages of the world. Along with English, it is the official language of India. In addition, it is the state language of Bihar, Haryana, Himachal Pradesh, Madhya Pradesh, Uttar Pradesh, and Rajasthan.

Hindi, which is a descendant of the Sanskrit language, is not strictly the name of any chief dialect of the area but is an adjective, Persian in origin, meaning "Indian." Historically, it was synonymous with Hindui, Hindawi, Rexta, and Rexti. All these labels denote a mixed speech spoken around the area of Delhi, north

India, which gained currency during the twelfth and thirteenth centuries as a contact language between native residents and the Arabs, Afghans, Persians, and Turks.

Hindi is written in the Devanagari script, which is ranked as the most scientific writing system in the world. The Devanagari script is written from left to right and is descendant of the Brahmi script, which was well established in India before 500 B.C.E. The script is phonetic in nature, and there is a fairly regular correspondence between the letters and their pronunciation.

The literary history of Hindi goes back to the twelfth century. Some notable literary figures of Hindi are Kabir, Surdas, and Tulsidas. The two notable linguistic features of the language are as follows: Hindi still retains the original Indo-European distinction between aspirated and unaspirated consonants, which results in a four-way contrast as shown by the following examples: *kaal* for "time," *khaal* for "skin," *gaal* for "cheek," and *ghaal* for "to put into." It has the feature of retroflexion in its consonant inventory. A good comparison is *Taal* for "to put off" and *taal* for "pond." The retroflex consonant is transcribed as the capital *T*.

Hindi has an approximately three-centuries-old, well-attested, and rich grammatical tradition of its own. It is a by-product of the colonial era and was born shortly after the arrival of Europeans in India.

Hindu Association of the Pacific Coast: Asian Indian independence group formed to advance the dissemination of revolutionary literature calling for a free India, founded in the early 1900's. The association was composed of Hindu intellectuals, Sikh farmers, peasants, and laborers and was open to anyone from the Indian subcontinent. The coalition motivated Asian Indians in America to add their voices to the cry for liberation from the British Empire. It also led to the founding of the Ghadr Revolutionary Party. (See GHADR MOVEMENT.)

Hinduism: Major world religion. It is the source of three other religions: Buddhism and Jainism in the sixth century B.C.E. and Sikhism in the fifteenth century C.E. Hinduism, a nonevangelizing, tolerant, and accommodative religion, developed in the Indian subcontinent over three millennia but did not spread to other parts of the world. Most Hindus live in India, where they constitute 83 percent of the population. Nepal, a small Himalayan kingdom, has a Hindu population of about 90 percent. Hinduism is also found in Sri Lanka, where Hindus form 15 percent of the population, and in Bali, Indonesia.

Hinduism is different from other major world religions. Unlike Christianity and Islam, Hinduism is not a "revealed" religion; it does not have a founder or a single religious text. It is a non-creedal religion. It is a religious system, a social system, and a way of life. Since Hinduism lacks any central authority, hierarchy, or organization, it appears to be incoherent and disorganized. Though Hindus have three main deities—Brahma (the creator of the universe), Vishnu (its preserver), and Shiva (its destroyer)—there is a bewildering diversity within Hinduism. All Hindus do not believe in the same things: Some worship one god, others worship many gods; some go to temples to worship, others worship in small shrines at home; some revere holy men and saints (yogis and gurus), others worship particular trees, animals, and stones. It is, in fact, possible for a good Hindu to be an atheist. Beneath this diversity, however, there is a common basis for its various beliefs.

Hindu Doctrines. The doctrinal and spiritual bases of Hinduism are found in the ancient scriptures or sacred writings: They are the four Vedas (Rigveda, Samaveda, Yajurveda, and Arthavaveda), the *Upanishads* (dialogues between the teachers and the taught), and the two great epics, *Ramayana* and *Mahabharata.*

Hindus believe in the doctrine of birth, rebirth, and reincarnation or transmigration of souls (samsara). The Upanishads talk about the unity of individual soul (atman) with the ultimate reality (Brahman). The goal of Hindus is to escape from the bondage of individual existence (*moksa*), which is temporary and painful, and be one with Brahman. The law of *Karma* (action), the moral law of causation, determines the sequence of rebirth. Thus, the existence of one's life and position in society is determined by one's action in previous births, and one's action in this life will determine whether one will be reborn as a human being, an animal, or a plant. Since Hindus aim at liberation from rebirth, and since liberation does not depend on any intervention from the gods, Hindus follow the provisions of a rule called *dharma* (duty or conduct). The *dharma* of a person is related to caste, a social group that is determined by birth. According to the Bhagavadgita, it is "better to do one's own duty though void of merit than do another's duty, however well performed."

Hindu Social Order. Hindu society is hierarchical and is divided into four *varnas*, or castes, that conform

A Hindu temple in Agoura, California. (Martin A. Hutner)

A Hindu funeral service being conducted in Sacramento. (California State Library)

to the law of spiritual progression and structural social relations. They are, in descending order of importance, the Brahmana class (priests), the kshatriya class (warriors and administrators), the Vaishya class (cultivators and merchants), and the Sudra class (artisans and laborers). The first three *varnas* are "twice-born"; they are initiated into full Aryan status, and their lives consist of four consecutive stages: student, householder, anchorite, and ascetic. The Sudras, by contrast, are the serving caste who are not allowed to hear or repeat the Vedas. These four *varnas* are further divided into more than three thousand *jatis*, or occupational groups, to which every Hindu belongs. Hindus marry within their own *jati*, and *jatis* set their elaborate code of conduct and rules, which govern the behavior of most Indians.

Outside the fourfold caste system are the untouchables, or outcastes, who do not have a *varna* status. Though not mentioned in the ancient scripture, they rank below Sudras because of the defiling tasks that they have traditionally performed. These untouchables are also known as Harijans (children of God—the name given by Mahatma GANDHI), or "schedule castes" (the category used in the constitution of India). Although in independent India it is illegal to discriminate against the Harijans, who number more than 135 million, and although many of them have improved their occupational and economic status by taking ad-

vantage of "protective discrimination," discrimination against them continues, especially at the village level.

Popular Hinduism. The religious practices of the Hindu masses in everyday life are not uniform; they are usually in the tradition of their localities, which may vary from village to village. Hindus worship different gods and goddesses, which are limited portrayals of the unlimited—one Ultimate Reality that is formless, is nameless, and has no personality. This makes Hinduism a highly philosophical religion. Since ordinary people cannot grasp the concept of Atman-Brahman in total abstraction, the religion of the masses is a work-a-day religion, unlike the high religion of the Brahmins, which is aimed at meeting the requirements of everyday existence. The Hindu masses therefore worship the village godlings to whom they look for rain, good harvests, and escape from epidemics. At the same time, they may worship the vedic deities. Because of this variety of religious practices, the Hindus are accustomed to saying that their deities number 330 million.

After India came in contact with Western religion and science, there were liberal reform movements within Hinduism in the nineteenth and twentieth centuries, such as the Brahmo Samaj, the Arya Samaj, the Ramakrishna Mission, and the movement of Mahatma Gandhi against the outcastes. In the first three decades of independent India, the congressional government passed laws—giving the right of inheritance to daughters and widows, enforcing monogamy, and outlawing dowries, for example—that undermined traditional Hinduism and offended orthodox Hindus. In the 1980's and 1990's, however, rapid growth occurred in the activities of militant fundamentalist Hindu organizations such as the Rashtriya Swayamsevak Sangh and the Vishwa Hindu Parishad. The Hindu nationalist party, which became the largest opposition party in 1991, has successfully exploited the insecurity of the Hindu majority. It has championed the Ayodhya temple movement, which culminated in the destruction of the Babri Masjid in Ayodhya by a mob of two hundred thousand Hindu militants on December 6, 1992, followed by a wave of communal violence against Muslims in Bombay and other places in India. Hindu nationalism is an important force in Indian politics in the 1990's.

Hindus are a majority among Asian Indian immigrants in the United States, where they have built more than forty Hindu temples. The temples in Chicago, New York, Houston, Flint (Michigan), and Pittsburgh are the most important among them.—*Sunil K. Sahu*

SUGGESTED READINGS: • Basham, A. L. *The Origins and Development of Classical Hinduism*. Boston: Beacon Press, 1989. • Embree, Ainslie T., ed. *The Hindu Tradition*. New York: Random House, 1966. • Hopkins, Thomas J. *The Hindu Religious Tradition*. Encino, Calif.: Dickenson, 1971. • Kinsley, David R. *Hinduism: A Cultural Perspective*. Englewood Cliffs, N.J.: Prentice-Hall, 1982. • Sarma, D. S. *Studies in the Renaissance of Hinduism in the Nineteenth and Twentieth Centuries*. Benares: Benares Hindu University, 1944. • Singer, Milton. *Traditional India: Structure and Change*. Philadelphia: American Folklore Society, 1959. • Weber, Max. *The Religion of India*. Glencoe, Ill.: Free Press, 1958. • Williams, Raymond Brady.

Devout chanting at a Hindu temple in Chatsworth, California. (Martin A. Hutner)

Religions of Immigrants from India and Pakistan: New Trends in the American Tapestry. New York: Cambridge University Press, 1988. • Zaehner, R. C. *Hinduism*. New York: Oxford University Press, 1971.

Hindustan Gadar: Weekly newspaper published in San Francisco from 1913 until 1917 and occasionally in the 1930's. It was owned by the Ghadr Party, which had been promoting the cause of India's independence since the beginning of the twentieth century. Printed in a variety of native Indian dialects, the publication documented the efforts of the GHADR MOVEMENT in the United States and advocated support for the nationalists back in India. The newspaper first appeared as the *Gadar*; it acquired its new name in 1914 when Ram Chandra succeeded Har DAYAL as editor.

Hindustani: Hybrid language spoken in modern India before independence in 1947. After India's invasion by the Muslims, Persian, an Iranian language and the official tongue of the Mughal Empire, became the most widely used tongue in northern India from the thirteenth century onward. The Muslim influence gave rise to Hindustani, a dialect based on Khari Boli (itself a dialect based on the language spoken in Delhi). English educator John Borthwick Gilchrist studied the dialect in the late eighteenth and early nineteenth centuries and authored a Hindustani grammar and dictionary. It was Gilchrist who coined the term "Hindustani." In time, two literary languages emerged from colloquial Hindustani: HINDI, with its strong Sanskrit influence, and URDU, with its Persianized vocabulary. Today Hindustani is a dialect that avoids both Sanskrit and Persian elements; it can still be heard in various parts of India outside the north, although Hindi and English are the country's official languages. Urdu is the official language of Pakistan.

Hing, Alex: Labor and community activist. Hing has been a community and labor organizer in San Francisco and New York for more than twenty-five years. He was minister of information for the Red Guards, a radical Chinese American group, founded in 1969, which merged with I WOR KUEN in 1971. As a hotel cook, he is a member of the Hotel Employees and Restaurant Employees union (HERE), Local 6, and he served on the interim steering committee of the ASIAN PACIFIC AMERICAN LABOR ALLIANCE (APALA) of the American Federation of Labor-Congress of Industrial Organizations (AFL-CIO). Hing has published articles in *East Wind* and *Amerasia Journal*; see his article

"Organizing Asian Pacific American Workers in the AFL-CIO: New Opportunities," *Amerasia Journal* 18, no. 1 (1992): 141-148.

Hinode Company: Founded in New York in 1876 by two members of the Oceanic Group. The latter had arrived in the United States earlier that year aboard the *Oceanic*. In New York, group member Soto Momotara started several businesses. One of these was a store opened in collaboration with Morimura Toyo, another member of the group. It sold goods imported from Japan such as china, silk, scrolls, fans, and teas. Later the various establishments begun by the two men were merged into the Hinode Company. It represents the commencement of the Japanese American trade effort.

Hirabayashi, Gordon Kiyoshi (b. Apr. 23, 1918, Seattle, Wash.): Conscientious objector to Japanese American internment. Hirabayashi, a twenty-four-year-old University of Washington student, fit the pattern of the type of person likely to challenge the exclusion order that applied to both Japanese immigrants and Japanese American citizens living on the West Coast. His training as a Quaker had instilled in him a high sense of moral values that encouraged him to correct a law he knew was unjust. On May 16, 1942, he went to the local Federal Bureau of Investigation

Gordon Hirabayashi testifies before the Commission on Wartime Relocation and Internment of Civilians on Capitol Hill in 1981. (AP/Wide World Photos)

(FBI) office and handed them a statement titled, "Why I Refused to Register for Evacuation." With that action he joined Minoru YASUI and became the second conscientious objector to the government's policy.

Hirabayashi was given a chance to rethink his actions and obey the exclusion order. He refused and was then charged with violating the order. On May 20, 1942, he was granted bail for $5,000 on the condition that he join his family and other Japanese Americans interned at the Puyallup fairgrounds near Tacoma, Washington. On principle he refused to go and remained in jail. Eight days later, on evidence confiscated by the FBI, the charges against him were amended to include his violation of the curfew order.

On October 20, 1942, Hirabayashi stood trial for violating the curfew and exclusion orders. He and his attorney, Frank Walters of the American Civil Liberties Union (ACLU), argued that his Fifth Amendment right to due process was violated by the exclusion order. The judge disagreed and ordered the jury to find Hirabayashi guilty on both counts. After deliberating for ten minutes they came back with the requested verdict: guilty. On the next day Hirabayashi was sentenced to 90 days each for both counts, to be run concurrently. He appealed the verdict.

On February 19, 1943, the one-year anniversary of EXECUTIVE ORDER 9066, Hirabayashi joined fellow resisters Fred T. KOREMATSU and Minoru Yasui before the court of appeals. At this level, the court used an obscure procedure called "certification," which allows it to ask the Supreme Court questions on constitutional issues. In Hirabayashi's case the Supreme Court was asked to rule on the legality of the exclusion order, the curfew order, and Public Law 503.

On June 21, 1943, the Supreme Court upheld the curfew order conviction but declined to rule on the exclusion order. Officially the reasoning was that since the sentences ran concurrently there was no reason to rule on the second count. More than forty years later, on January 12, 1988, Hirabayashi's conviction was vacated through a petition for a writ of *coram nobis*.

Hirabayashi, James (b. Oct. 30, 1926, Meredith, Wash.): Scholar. Going on strike from his faculty position at San Francisco State University, he played a key role in the school's 1969 strike by supporting the Third World Liberation Front. After the strike succeeded, he became dean of ethnic studies for six years. A Nisei, he was interned at Tule Lake during World War II. An anthropologist by training with a Ph.D. from Harvard (1962), he has conducted research in the United States,

Japan, and Nigeria. After working at San Francisco State from 1959 to 1989, he became the chief curator of the JAPANESE AMERICAN NATIONAL MUSEUM. He has also worked as a professional actor with the ASIAN AMERICAN THEATRE COMPANY since 1977.

Hirabayashi, Lane Ryo (b. Oct. 17, 1952, Seattle, Wash.): Scholar. An active proponent of ethnic studies, he has taught at the University of California, Los Angeles; California State University, Long Beach; the University of California, Santa Barbara; San Francisco State University; and the University of Colorado, Boulder. An anthropologist like his father, James Hirabayashi, he received his Ph.D. degree from the University of California, Berkeley, in 1981, conducting his dissertation research on the Zapotec Indians of Mexico. He has since researched Japanese American internment, education, and communities, particularly that of Gardena, California. He is also a professional blues and folk guitar player and has appeared in a variety of bands.

Hiragana. *See* **Japanese language; Kana**

Hirano, Irene Ann Yasutake (b. Oct. 7, 1948, Los Angeles, Calif.): Administrator. Among the many offices she has held are executive director and president of the Japanese American National Museum, cofounder and president of Leadership Education for Asian Pacifics, chair of the National Network of Asian and Pacific Women, president of the Asian Pacific Legal Defense and Education Fund, chair of the California State Superintendent's Council on Asian Pacific Affairs, and vice president of the Southern Christian Leadership Conference.

Hirano grew up in Gardena, a multiethnic suburb in Southern California, in a closely knit extended family that had endured the trials and triumphs of World War II. While her grandfather and father's family were interned at the relocation camp in Rohwer, Arkansas, her father served in the Military Intelligence Service of the U.S. Army. Strong family ties forged from living in the same household with her grandfather, aunts, and uncles provided Hirano with a great appreciation of her ethnic identity and cultural heritage, a lasting support network for her later endeavors, and a resolute determination to improve societal conditions.

Graduating from the University of Southern California with bachelor's and master's degrees in public administration, Hirano became involved in community affairs. She served on committees and held a variety of leadership positions in educational, political, and social service organizations. Early in her career, she boldly dealt with public health and minority issues, expanding the To Help Everyone (T.H.E.) Clinic for Women into an institution of national renown. Hirano has championed multiethnic causes and broadened the perspectives of the women's movement.

Irene Hirano has championed multiethnic causes and has broadened the perspectives of the women's movement. (Japanese American National Museum)

Hirano's numerous contributions to the Asian Pacific American community have been concurrent with her involvement in mainstream public interest groups. She has held leadership positions in a variety of organizations and served on local, state, and national boards and commissions while gaining extensive experience in nonprofit management of multicultural institutions. In 1988, Hirano accepted the challenge of developing a new ethnic museum, the JAPANESE AMERICAN NATIONAL MUSEUM, into a national educational institution. Throughout her career, Hirano has empowered people of diverse backgrounds and interests to work together to achieve strategic results.

Hirasaki, Kiyoshi "Jimmy" (1900, Kumamoto Prefecture, Japan—1963): Garlic grower. Arriving in Milpitas, California, as an adolescent, Hirasaki attended school for awhile before leaving to take a job with a farmer in Gilroy, who taught him how to produce onion and carrot seeds. Sometime after the early 1920's Hirasaki began to plant garlic. By 1941, with fifteen hundred acres of garlic crops, he had become the most successful garlic grower in California. During World War II, he and his family accepted voluntary relocation to Grand Junction, Colorado. They returned to Gilroy after the war, however, and resurrected the business. Hirasaki later belonged to the group of investors who helped launch the *HOKUBEI MAINICHI* newspaper.

Hiroshima: Coastal city in Hiroshima Prefecture, in the southwestern part of the island of Honshu, Japan. The city's population exceeded one million in 1991. On August 6, 1945, the U.S. military detonated the world's first atomic bomb over Hiroshima, immediately killing as many as one hundred thousand residents. (A second and final bomb was detonated over Nagasaki three days later, on August 9.) Many *HIBAKUSHA* (atom bomb survivors) continue to suffer from the effects of the radiation. More Japanese immigrants came to the United States from Hiroshima Prefecture than from any other.

The former Industry Promotion Hall in Hiroshima, now called the A-Bomb Dome. (Japan Air Lines)

Hiroshima: Contemporary popular music group founded in Los Angeles in the early 1970's. The band's original nine members, most of whom are Sansei, include cofounders Dan and June Okida Kuramoto. The group released its first album, *Hiroshima*, in 1979 on the Arista Records label and became known for blending traditional Japanese instruments (koto and taiko drums, for example) with jazz and other Western musical rhythms. The album brought the band good critical notices, a Grammy Award nomination, and *Performance* magazine's Breakout Artist of the Year award in 1980. Recognition as Best Live Jazz Group by *Cashbox* magazine also followed. Hiroshima's fifth album, *Go*, released in 1987, spent eight weeks at the top of *Billboard* magazine's Contemporary Jazz Album chart. Other releases include *Odori* (1981), *Third Generation* (1983), *Another Place* (1985), *East* (1989), and *Providence* (1992).

Hiura, Barbara (b. Mar. 24, 1950, Chicago, Ill.): Journalist. A reporter for *Hokubei Mainichi* in San Francisco, she was president and board member of the National Association for Ethnic Studies. She earned an M.A. degree at the University of California, Berkeley.

HMCS Rainbow: Canadian army ship that escorted the *Komagata Maru*, a Japanese ship carrying Asian Indian emigrants destined for Canada, out of Vancouver Bay in July, 1914. The Japanese vessel sailed into the harbor in May. The Canadian government, however, steadfastly refused for two months to allow the passengers to disembark: A new law had been enacted expressly to curb the flow of immigration from India. The *Rainbow*, previously out of service and docked near Victoria, was quickly restored and rushed to Vancouver with orders to expel the recently arrived Sikh emigrants. (See KOMAGATA MARU INCIDENT.)

Hmong: The Hmong are a highland tribal people found in southern and western regions of the People's Republic of China and in the northern tier of Southeast Asia. Numbering a total world population of six million people, the Hmong are a mountain-dwelling group, farming the highest ridges, upland valleys, and steep mountain slopes of remote districts in Southeast Asia. The Hmong are thought to have originated in prehistoric times in central Asia or northern China. They are known to have migrated into Burma (now Myanmar), Vietnam, Thailand, and Laos beginning in the early nineteenth century. The Hmong have vigorously preserved and defended their unique language,

religion, and cultural heritage in the face of assimilationist threats by majority governments. The Hmong maintain a proud warrior tradition. In recent centuries they have taken up arms to protect themselves and in the service of regional powers.

Hmong Traditional Communities. Highland slash-and-burn farmers, Hmong villagers moved their villages every seven or eight years as the fertility of their highland fields declined. The migratory agriculture of the Hmong, along with their strong desire to preserve their independence and cultural integrity, have facilitated their broad dispersion. Yet Hmong language and culture remain remarkably constant despite the fact that traditional communities residing in five Asian countries across thousands of miles of difficult terrain have oftentimes lost contact with one another. Hmong kinship is patrilineal. Descent is traced from a common male ancestor who is recognized as founder of the clan. There are twenty-three Hmong clans. So strong is the identification of clan members as belonging to one family that marriage within a clan is forbidden. In such traditional kinship systems, marriage between members of the same clan (people with the same last name) is thought to be equivalent to marriage between brothers and sisters.

Traditional Culture. Remotely situated astride the highest mountains, Hmong villages typically were far from government administrative, educational, and health services. For centuries Hmong villages have governed themselves, organizing common agricultural activities, planning village ceremonial events, and defending villages against external threats. Hmong child-rearing practices are both emotionally nurturing and nutritionally sound. Infant mortality in Hmong villages is lower than that of other highland communities because of dietary and work restrictions that are placed on mothers of newborn infants. Hmong women are oftentimes accomplished textile artists. The Hmong excel in the arts of appliqué (meticulously cutting and sewing cloth into symbolic designs). Hmong also are skilled in weaving and in the art of *batik* decoration, applying hot wax to a white cloth and repeatedly dipping the waxed textile into indigo dye. Hmong men produce silver jewelry, which in traditional times was the principal measure of wealth and status in the village community.

As is true for most of the mountain people of Southeast Asia, the Hmong embrace a small-scale, primal or ethnic religion. That is to say, Hmong religion is not a world faith (such as Buddhism or Christianity, for example) but a special religion and belief system devel-

Hmong dancers in traditional garb. (Eric Crystal)

oped over centuries within the Hmong community it-self. Hmong ceremony and ritual are organized in each community by a specialist, the *tse neng*, or shaman. The work of a shaman in this and some other Asian societies is to help the ill, the weak, and the disturbed to regain their mental balance and physical well-being. The shaman communicates with the spirit world on behalf of people in need, oftentimes curing the physically ill and alleviating the concerns of the mentally unsettled.

The traditional Hmong world is one of small family farms and isolated village communities. The traditional Hmong living environment is adjacent to the highland tropical or cloud forest, where mornings are oftentimes shrouded in low clouds and where occasional frosts are encountered in December and January. Hmong textiles reflect the changing of the seasons, the importance of wild and domesticated animals in the local economy, and the strength of kinship and generational ties within the village.

Hmong in Laos, 1960-1975. A substantial minority in Laos, the Hmong are thought to have numbered 350,000 individuals out of a total Laotian population of nearly 4 million in 1970. Because of their warrior heritage, considerable numbers of Hmong were enlisted by French colonial forces in their war (1945-1954) against the nationalist/Communist forces of Vietnam headed by Ho Chi Minh. After Laotian independence was confirmed in 1954, a civil conflict slowly gathered momentum in Laos. Communist Laotian forces, under Vietnamese patronage, established a secure base area in Sam Neua Province in northeastern Laos. Between 1954 and 1960 Communist forces advanced across the whole of northern Laos. American secret agents contacted Hmong veterans of the French army at this time. VANG PAO, a former sergeant in colonial times, was cultivated by the Americans as leader of a "secret army" of Hmong irregulars. In the space of a few years Vang Pao, elevated to the rank of general by the Royal Lao government, came to command an army of some 20,000 largely Hmong soldiers. A secret command headquarters and air base were established in northern Laos at Long Chieng. From there aircraft supplied isolated Hmong positions on the high ridges and mountaintops across northern Laos. Oftentimes Hmong soldiers held their positions for years, surrounded by Communist forces on the ground yet supplied and supported by both cargo and combat aircraft based at Long Chieng, at Vientiane, and in northern Thailand. Hmong soldiers readily perfected the skills imparted by their American mentors. Hmong units continually harassed Vietnamese supply lines moving down the Ho Chi Minh Trail, challenged Communist advances in the north, and assisted in the rescue of scores of downed American pilots. Despite the valor of the Hmong secret army, Vang Pao and the Royal Lao Government that he supported continually lost ground to the Communists. By 1973 the Americans had withdrawn combat air cover from Laos. By 1975 the last Central Intelligence Agency (CIA) advisors were pulled out of Long Chieng.

During the course of the conflict in Laos the contributions of the Hmong to the American cause were little known in the United States. Because the U.S. government had signed a treaty acknowledging Lao neutrality, disclosure of U.S. direct involvement in the conflict there would have constituted admission of the violation of international law. No American journalists were ever allowed to visit Long Chieng, even at the apogee of Hmong strength, when an all-Hmong air force piloted a fleet of T-28 jets on daily missions across the north.

Nearly all the Hmong pilots were killed in action in Laos. So many Hmong soldiers were lost during the conflict that toward the end Vang Pao resorted to drafting thirteen- and fourteen-year-old boys. Hmong villages in the north were oftentimes abandoned during the course of the conflict, generating tens of thousands of internal highland refugees. American-supported governments in Vietnam, Cambodia, and Laos fell to victorious revolutionary Communist forces in 1975. The Americans withdrew all support for their erstwhile allies, abandoning to their fates many who had thrown in their lot with the apparently invincible great power from the West.

Hmong in Laos, 1975-1981. Vang Pao and the Hmong military leaders fled by plane from Long Chieng to Thailand in May, 1975. Thousands of other Hmong residing relatively close to the Mekong River border also fled shortly after the demise of the Royal

Agriculture is a common occupation of the Hmong, both in the United States and in their native China. (James L. Shaffer)

Lao government. Most Hmong soldiers returned to their natal villages, which were sometimes far from the border. Yet the Hmong were wary of future developments and in the event of renewed conflict hid large caches of arms in remote jungle locales. The worst fears of the Hmong came to pass. Many veterans were rounded up to be sent to reeducation "seminars" (prisons from which few returned). Other villages soon found themselves occupied by Lao and sometimes Vietnamese troops. A bitter armed struggle soon broke out, pitting the new Laotian government, supported by its Vietnamese and Russian allies, against the Hmong, who had been abandoned by the Americans. The result was continued loss of life on the Hmong side, the persistence of a bitter conflict by armed Hmong bands pressed further and further into remote jungle regions,

and an increased flow of refugees to Thailand. Hmong survivors allege that chemical and biological weapons were used against them during this time. These allegations have never been conclusively proven or disproven.

Hmong in the United States. The first Hmong refugees from Laos were admitted to the United States in 1975. Initial resettlement locales were in San Diego, Los Angeles, Minneapolis/St. Paul, and Montana, where Vang Pao had purchased a large ranch. By 1992 more than 100,000 Hmong lived throughout the United States. The largest Hmong community outside Asia is in Fresno, California, where approximately 30,000 Hmong resided in 1993. Fully half of the Hmong population of the United States resides in California.

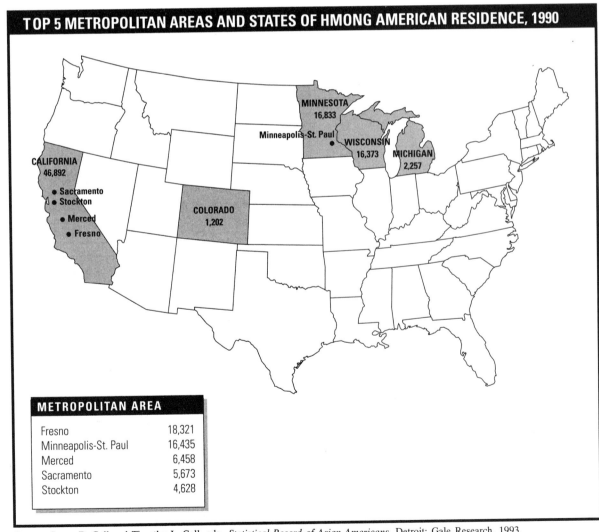

TOP 5 METROPOLITAN AREAS AND STATES OF HMONG AMERICAN RESIDENCE, 1990

MINNESOTA
16,833

Minneapolis-St. Paul

WISCONSIN
16,373

MICHIGAN
2,257

CALIFORNIA
46,892

Sacramento
Stockton

Merced

Fresno

COLORADO
1,202

METROPOLITAN AREA	
Fresno	18,321
Minneapolis-St. Paul	16,435
Merced	6,458
Sacramento	5,673
Stockton	4,628

Source: Susan B. Gall and Timothy L. Gall, eds., *Statistical Record of Asian Americans.* Detroit: Gale Research, 1993.

A Hmong musician holds the bamboo mouth organ known as the gaeng. (Eric Crystal)

Older Hmong have not adapted well to the United States. Most of those who arrived in this country at age fifty or older were preliterate, unable to write the national language of Laos, much less English. By contrast younger Hmong refugees and their siblings born here have demonstrated remarkable diligence, dedication, and performance in school. The energy, group vitality, and determination to overcome all obstacles—hallmarks of Hmong culture—have served Hmong American students well in U.S. schools. Encouraged by parents who oftentimes had no opportunity to attend school in their own country, young Hmong Americans are already making an impact. The first Hmong doctors and lawyers are entering the professional work force in the 1990's. Many more are certain to follow in the coming years. In California the Hmong desire to return to the land is demonstrated by the ongoing secondary migration from large cities to small, central valley farming communities. With each passing year more Hmong buy or lease farmland and produce specialty crops such as snow peas, lemon grass, and long beans for Asian food stores and farmers' markets.

Considerable tension is expressed within the Hmong community between adherents of traditional values and advocates of rapid assimilation to American life. Oftentimes this tension is experienced by young Hmong women whose parents wish to see them married at an early age but whose teachers hope they will enter college. Hmong Americans clearly appear determined to adapt successfully to their new homelands. Typically they are also committed to maintaining their unique language and cultural identity.—*Eric Crystal*

SUGGESTED READINGS: • Bliatout, Bruce T. *Hmong Sudden, Unexpected Nocturnal Death Syndrome: A Cultural Study*. Portland, Oreg.: Sparkle Publications, 1982. • Geddes, William. *Migrants of the Mountains*. Oxford, England: Clarendon Press, 1976. • Hamilton-Merritt, Jane. *Tragic Mountains: The Hmong, the Americans, and the Secret Wars for Laos, 1942-1992*. Bloomington: Indiana University Press, 1993. • Hendricks, Glenn, Bruce Downing, and Amos Deinard, eds. *The Hmong in Transition*. Staten Island, N.Y.: Center for Migration Studies of New York, 1986.

Hmong Americans: After the end of the war in Laos in 1975, many Hmong fled the country for refuge in camps on the Thai border. The Hmong feared reprisals from the Communist regime against which perhaps one-third of the Lao Hmong population had fought, both as guerrilla insurgents and as part of the United States military's so-called "Secret Army," led by the Hmong general VANG PAO. In 1992, there were still fifty thousand Hmong refugees remaining in Thai refugee camps, awaiting resettlement or repatriation. The United States, in keeping with its promise to Hmong troops, hosted the bulk of the Hmong resettled abroad (there were ninety-seven thousand Hmong Americans by 1992), with smaller numbers going to France (eight thousand in 1992), French Guyana (twelve hundred in 1992), and even fewer to Argentina and Australia.

Refugee Sponsorship and Resettlement. Within the United States, sponsorship of Hmong refugees was largely provided by religious and philanthropic organizations in urban areas, supervised by the federal Office of Refugee Resettlement (ORR). Sometimes, individual families sponsored a refugee family or individual. Special resettlement agencies were set up in cities receiving the largest numbers of refugees, to provide social services such as health, education, and job training and placement. By a process called "secondary migration," many Hmong left their first place of settle-

Hmong American Statistical Profile, 1990

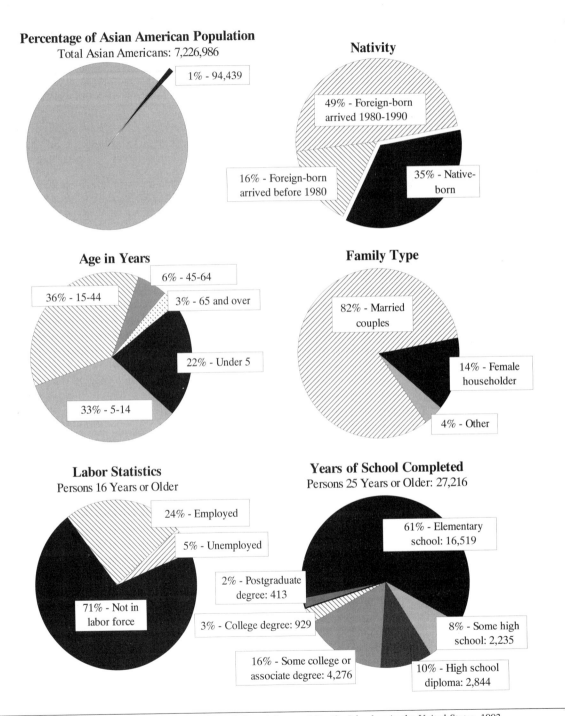

Percentage of Asian American Population
Total Asian Americans: 7,226,986

1% - 94,439

Nativity

49% - Foreign-born arrived 1980-1990

16% - Foreign-born arrived before 1980

35% - Native-born

Age in Years

6% - 45-64

3% - 65 and over

36% - 15-44

22% - Under 5

33% - 5-14

Family Type

82% - Married couples

14% - Female householder

4% - Other

Labor Statistics
Persons 16 Years or Older

24% - Employed

5% - Unemployed

71% - Not in labor force

Years of School Completed
Persons 25 Years or Older: 27,216

61% - Elementary school: 16,519

2% - Postgraduate degree: 413

3% - College degree: 929

16% - Some college or associate degree: 4,276

8% - Some high school: 2,235

10% - High school diploma: 2,844

Source: U.S. Bureau of the Census, *1990 Census of Population: Asians and Pacific Islanders in the United States,* 1993.

ment to join other relatives or clan members, or to seek better economic, educational, or climatic conditions. (The ORR has a program for assisting in secondary migration from overly impacted areas to other areas.) By 1988, nearly sixty thousand Hmong resided in California, chiefly in the Central Valley, where agriculture and warm weather were major attractions; more than sixteen thousand remained in Wisconsin and nearly fourteen thousand in Minnesota. Smaller groups of one thousand to three thousand resided in Michigan, Rhode Island, Colorado, Washington, and Oregon, while twenty-two other states had fewer than one thousand. Most Hmong live in urban areas, although some have succeeded in re-creating their rural past in such places as the mountains of North Carolina.

Occupation

Employed Persons 16 Years or Older	Percentage
Managerial and professional specialty	13%
Technical, sales, and administrative support	19%
Service	20%
Farming, forestry, and fishing	2%
Precision production, craft, and repair	14%
Operators, fabricators, and laborers	32%

Income, 1989

Median household income	$14,276
Per capita	$2,692
Percent of families in poverty	62%

Household Size

Number of People	Percentage
1	2.5%
2	4.9%
3	7.3%
4	9.6%
5	12.1%
6	13.6%
7 or more	50.0%

Source: U.S. Bureau of the Census, *1990 Census of Population: Asians and Pacific Islanders in the United States,* 1993.

A Hmong schoolchild in Sacramento. Many Hmong have immigrated to the Central Valley of California. (Eric Crystal)

Hmong Leadership in the United States. General VANG PAO was among the earliest to be resettled in the United States in 1975. He remained a major political leader for many years as head of Lao Family Community, which he founded in 1977 and which has had branches in virtually every Hmong community in the United States. Many other military officers from the war continued to serve in their relatively recently acquired leadership roles upon arriving, while traditional clan and kin-based leaders functioned as a second type of leader; these two types often supported the goals of returning to Laos and funding anticommunist guerrilla forces there. A third type of leader was newly formed to meet the need for spokespersons to represent the Hmong to the American people. More than ninety-five Hmong community organizations and more than one hundred Hmong educational associations have been established throughout the United States.

Hmong Adaptation. Since most Hmong coming to the United States were illiterate, they faced a disadvantage in adapting to the American work environment. Learning English was a major obstacle for adult

Hmong, which many conquered nevertheless. Younger Hmong had less trouble adapting, and were found in at least one community (San Diego) to rank third in scholastic achievement among all Indochinese students, after Vietnamese and Chinese Vietnamese. In the Yang clan alone, 135 college degrees, 22 masters degrees, and 7 doctorates and J.D. degrees were granted between 1968 and 1991 in the United States. Hmong women are especially hindered by cultural patterns that see the supporting of an unmarried girl's education as furthering her future in-laws' prosperity rather than that of her own family, since brides always go to live with their new husbands, who are always of a different clan. Leadership in each community plays a major role in setting standards for adaptation and employment, as do economic factors such as local economies.

Hmong Society, Language, and Religion. The Lao Hmong differ somewhat from their counterparts in Thailand and Vietnam (where perhaps five hundred thousand remain as swidden agriculturists in the mountainous regions) and even more markedly from their forebears in southern China, a diverse population of more than two million. Most Lao Hmong Americans belong to either Blue (for the use of indigo in their textiles; although they prefer to call themselves "Hmong Leng") or White (for the color of some women's garments) subgroups, although other subgroups do occur, such as Striped Hmong and Flowery Hmong. Whatever the subgroup, each Hmong belongs to an exogamous patrilineal clan, of which more than twenty exist, including Chang, Chue, Fang, Hang, Her, Khang, Kue, Ly, Lor, Moua, Thao, Vang, and Yang. Clans believe themselves to be descendants of a common ancestor, and hence marriage is not permitted within the clan. This belief, along with many other traditions and regulations, is being challenged by some younger Hmong Americans.

The Hmong language is monosyllabic and tonal, with seven standard tones. Dialectic differences exist as well as regional distinctions, between Blue Hmong and White Hmong. White and Blue Hmong can be written using the Roman popular alphabet of twenty-

A Hmong American family in Minnesota. (James L. Shaffer)

A Hmong girl plays with the family's fishing rod during a fishing expedition in Madison, Wisconsin. (Mary Langenfeld)

six letters as in English, although six consonants are also used as unpronounced tone markers at the ends of words. Another less widely used script consists of original characters devised by a Hmong messianic leader. Newspapers and newsletters circulate in both scripts.

Hmong religion is a unique blend of animism and Chinese and Lao Buddhist elements. Many Hmong Americans continue their traditional religion, especially for healing rituals performed by shamans, marriages performed by expert singers and musicians, and funeral rituals performed by priests and musicians. Most ritualists are male, while women dominate the realm of visual expression in their elaborate and highly symbolic textile arts. Both men and women participate in annual courtship song festivals at the New Year, usually held in December; nearly twenty thousand may attend the largest festivals in Fresno and Wisconsin. Alongside these traditional expressive forms, young Hmong have formed musical bands blending Hmong lyrics with Western and Asian popular musical styles, just as Hmong medicine and religion are fos-

tered side by side with Western medicine and Christianity.—*Amy Catlin*

SUGGESTED READINGS: • Geddes, William R. *Migrants of the Mountains: The Cultural Ecology of the Blue Miao (Hmong Njua) of Thailand.* Oxford, England: Clarendon Press, 1976. • Hendricks, Glenn, Bruce Downing, and Amos Deinard, eds. *The Hmong in Transition.* Staten Island, New York: Center for Migration Studies, 1986. • Quincey, Keith. *Hmong: History of a People.* Cheney: Eastern Washington University Press, 1988. • Smalley, William A. *Mother of Writing: The Origin and Development of a Hmong Messianic Script.* Chicago: University of Chicago Press, 1990.

Hmong-Mien languages (also Miao-Yao): Small family of languages spoken mainly in southern China and other parts of Southeast Asia, particularly Vietnam, Thailand, and Laos. Hmong-Mien languages are not especially well documented, and their speakers number probably between four million and eight million. In the United States, some Hmong-Mien languages have become well known because of the Hmong refugees who have resettled in America since the end of the Vietnam War (1965-1975). More than one hundred thousand Hmong immigrants have resettled overseas, mostly in the United States.

The linguistic affiliations of the various Hmong-Mien languages and dialects are rather complicated and still in dispute. Some scholars place them as independent lines of the Sino-Tibetan family, while others postulate relationships between Hmong-Mien and the Tai or Mon-Khmer languages. There appear to be four subdivisions of the Hmong-Mien group. The most numerous includes the Hmong or Mong dialects (called "Meo" in Thai or Lao, and "Miao" in Chinese). The second group consists of the Mien languages (called "Yao" in Thai or Chinese, and "Zao" in Vietnamese; the word "Mien" itself simply means "people"). The third branch, Punu, is closely related to the Hmong languages (and some even argue that Punu languages are dialects of the Hmong languages). The fourth branch, Laka, is most distantly related to the others, showing many similarities in vocabulary with the Tai languages.

The Hmong are the most widespread of the southern Chinese minority ethnic groups to emigrate into Southeast Asia. They have often settled in pockets of isolated village groups, usually in marginal or mountainous lands. Different dialects are sometimes known by colors (Green Miao, Black Miao, Striped Miao, and so on), referring to the colors of clothing worn by the different groups (especially the female attire).

Mien languages have been greatly influenced by China, and maybe half of the current Mien vocabulary has come from Chinese. The cultural implications of this, however, are difficult to determine (recall, for example, that about 40 percent of everyday English vocabulary has a French origin). Mien speakers have been in a unique position to write their languages using up to three orthographies (some Chinese characters borrowed hundreds of years ago, Thai script, and the roman alphabet introduced by Western missionaries).

Hmong-Mien languages are tonal, where a difference in pitch when pronouncing a word makes a difference in meaning. Most Hmong-Mien languages have around half a dozen tones. Word order is the same as in English: subject-verb-object. As with many Asian languages, Hmong-Mien languages use so-called numeral classifiers when counting things (similar to a "head of cattle" or a "pair of jeans" in English). For example, saying "one dog" in Hmong would be *ib tug dlev* (literally, "one animal dog," *tug* being a classifier used to count animals and people).

Hmong religion: The Hmong are a highland minority people residing in southern China and along the northern tier of Southeast Asia. In Southeast Asia cultural distinctions often follow ecological adaptations and environmental conditions. Lowland peoples in Southeast Asia have for centuries planted the most fertile and productive rice fields on the plains. Great civilizations have grown up around these fertile alluvial farmlands, civilizations influenced by world religions such as Hinduism, Buddhism, and Islam over the past two thousand years. In the far mountain hinterlands small tribal migrant groups were historically forced to farm the least favorable land. Little contact was sustained between the civilizations of the lowlands and the small-scale societies in the hills. Peoples such as the Hmong developed their own religious systems to remain in touch with their ancestors, assure a successful harvest, and cure the ill of ailments unresponsive to herbal medicine.

The primal, ethnic, small-scale religions of people such as the Hmong address the same questions and serve the same human needs as world religions such as Christianity, Islam, Judaism, Hinduism, and Buddhism. The traditional Hmong religion, then, marks important life crisis rites such as birth, adulthood, marriage, and death. Traditional Hmong religion is nurtured by a group of learned specialists who function much as priests and pastors do in other societies. Hmong beliefs have traveled with the Hmong people as in the last few years many of them established new homes in Europe, Canada, South America, and the United States.

Shamanism. The term "shamanism" is sometimes incorrectly utilized to describe any small-scale, non-Western ritual tradition. Shamanism refers to religious traditions that rely upon ceremonial specialists who have the unique ability to communicate directly with the spirit world, usually falling into a state of altered consciousness or trance during the spirit journey. In fact the Hmong religious tradition is an expression of true shamanism. Shamanic traditions are normally lodged in preliterate cultures, that is, in societies that traditionally do not have access to reading and writing. The shaman, the religious specialist, is an especially gifted individual with the unique ability to communicate with the spirit world. This ability is sometimes inherited. Yet even if the father of five sons is a recognized shaman, normally only one of his sons will assume such a role upon his death. Shamans normally experience a personal near-death experience before assuming their role in the society. Hmong shamans often acquire their special spirit guide when critically ill, establishing a pact with this spirit to work together to help others recover from illness.

Hmong Shamanism in Practice. Central to the work of the Hmong shaman is the concept of the *neng*. The *neng* is the special helping spirit of the shaman, the spirit that the shaman can dispatch on a special mission in search of the missing souls of living persons. The shaman is called the *Tse neng*, the master of the spirit. This spirit may be summoned in the vicinity of a special altar that is constructed in the house of the shaman; this altar is termed the *taa neng*. Hmong shamans usually construct elaborate altars in their homes that are normally decorated with gold and silver paper and sometimes with cutout figures symbolizing ancestral generations many years in the past.

Each human being on earth has a life soul. The Hmong term this life soul the *tchu plee*. When a person is both physically and mentally well the life soul remains secure within the body. Sometimes people become ill, sometimes babies become sick, sometimes members of the community develop mental as well as physical maladies that must be corrected. The Hmong in their traditional village communities are well aware of a range of useful medicines rendered from forest plants or garden crops. When, however, an illness responds to neither folk herbal nor Western medicine

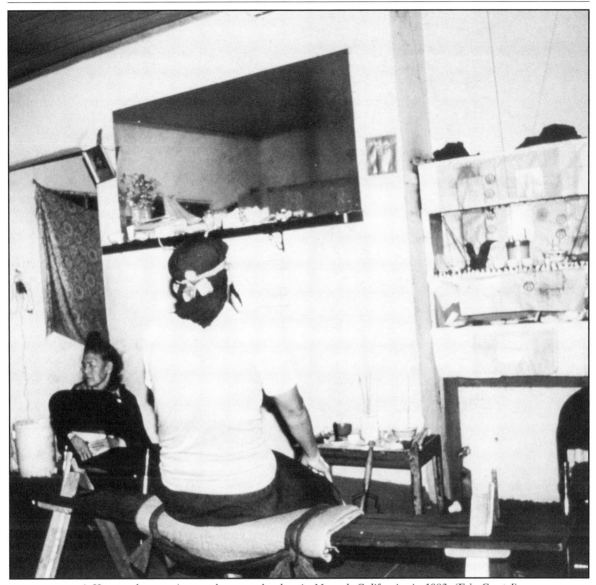

A Hmong shaman sits at a home-made altar in Merced, California, in 1983. (Eric Crystal)

then the suspicion is that the illness is caused by a temporary loss of the soul.

The life souls of humans from time to time escape the safety and security of the physical body. In the case of adults such loss of life soul might occur as the result of a sudden shock, a fall, or a minor accident. The life souls of young babies and children are somewhat more prone to fly from the small bodies they normally inhabit than are the souls of adults. The souls of the very young are especially attracted to the sound of a babbling brook, to the music of jungle songbirds, or to the bright colors of blossoming tropical flowers. Indeed, the Hmong are so determined to prevent babies from

losing their life souls that the cloth baby carriers that Hmong mothers typically strap on their backs sometimes employ magical designs that function as traps and mazes for the souls, thus preventing easy exit.

The Work of the Shaman. When an illness is determined to have been caused by the loss of a life soul, the shaman must be summoned. The shaman is always assisted by two or more associates who see that all ceremonial preparations are in order and who ensure that the shaman in trance does not injure himself or others. Some of the important implements used by the shaman are a large gong, a set of wrist and finger cymbals, and a simple black cloth. The shaman always

A Hmong shaman. (Eric Crystal)

sits on a long, flexible wooden bench. Assistants alert the *neng* of the shaman with rhythmic beating of the gong. The shaman preparing to enter a trance state covers his or her face with the black cloth. Now the shaman can symbolically leave this world and establish contact with the spirit world. The *neng* must be dispatched with precision. As the shaman chants his or her body rocks back and forth. The shaman's feet stamp the ground with ever more force as if propelling himself or herself into the spirit world. As the ceremony reaches its climax the shaman jumps on top of the bench, ready for the return of the *neng*, which will have recaptured the errant life soul of the patient.

Hmong Religion in the United States. The traditional Hmong religion, Daa Kwaah, is in 1993 adhered to by approximately half of the Hmong in the United States. Some Hmong embraced Christianity in Laos as early as the mid-1950's. Many more converted during long sojourns in refugee camps in Thailand prior to coming to the United States. Evangelical churches have made a significant effort to convert Hmong refugees in the United States over the past fifteen years, with considerable success. Some Hmong Christians

have totally forsaken ancestral beliefs and ceremonies. Others maintain syncretic or mixed religious beliefs, attending church services on Sundays but also summoning the shaman to their homes as the need arises.

Many obstacles have been placed in the way of Hmong traditionalists who wish to maintain their ancient religion in the United States. The extended and noisy rituals managed by the shaman sometimes cause problems with non-Hmong neighbors. Hmong religion frequently calls for the community members to offer an important meal to their ancestors. To do this a chicken or a pig must be killed, butchered, and cooked, ideally all in the house of the family concerned. Sometimes such practices violate local codes or customs. Often there is no one to mediate between Hmong religious needs and the concerns of the host community.

The Future of Hmong Religion in the United States. The heart of Hmong culture is embodied in the traditional shamanic religious practices and beliefs of this unique highland culture. Links with past generations are maintained by Hmong ritual specialists, who summon ancestors to partake in ritual feasts at new year time. Much of Hmong belief and practice recalls American Indian concepts of harmony with nature and reciprocal responsibility within the village community. Hmong religion is as valid and true for those who believe in it as any of the many other faiths practiced by Americans. The long-term future of Hmong traditional religion in the United States is uncertain. Few if any schools or public education programs have recognized the important leadership role of Hmong shamans or have encouraged Hmong refugees to become aware of their religious rights as guaranteed by the U.S. constitution. Hmong religion will continue only if the younger generation of Hmong Americans remains conscious of its cultural importance and determined to preserve Hmong ceremonial traditions.—*Eric Crystal*

SUGGESTED READINGS: • *Between Two Worlds: The Hmong Shaman in America.* Video. Northwestern University Performance Studies Department, 1985. • Lemoine, Jacques. "The Bridge, an Essential Implement of Hmong and Yao Shamanism." In *Shaman's Path: Healing, Personal Growth and Empowerment*, edited and compiled by Gary Doore, pp. 63-72. Boston: Shambhala Press, 1988. • Symonds, Patricia. "Blessing Among the White Hmong." Unpublished paper delivered at the 1993 Association for Asian Studies Meetings in Los Angeles. • Tapp, Nicholas. *Sovereignty and Rebellion: The White Hmong of Northern Thailand.* Singapore: Oxford University Press, 1989.